Crushing the Categories
(*Vaidalyaprakaraṇa*)

The *Treasury of the Buddhist Sciences* series is copublished by the American Institute of Buddhist Studies and Wisdom Publications in association with the Columbia University Center for Buddhist Studies and Tibet House US.

The American Institute of Buddhist Studies (AIBS) established the *Treasury of the Buddhist Sciences* series to provide authoritative translations, studies, and editions of the texts of the Tibetan Tengyur (*bstan 'gyur*) and its associated literature. The Tibetan Tengyur is a vast collection of over 4,000 classical Indian Buddhist scientific treatises (*śāstra*) written in Sanskrit by over 700 authors from the first millennium CE, now preserved mainly in systematic 7th–12th century Tibetan translation. Its topics span all of India's "outer" arts and sciences, including linguistics, medicine, astronomy, socio-political theory, ethics, art, and so on, as well as all of her "inner" arts and sciences such as philosophy, psychology ("mind science"), meditation, and yoga.

Volumes in this series are numbered with catalogue numbers corresponding to both the "Comparative" (*dpe bsdur ma*) Kangyur and Tengyur ("CK" and "CT," respectively) and Derge (Tōhoku number) recensions of the Tibetan Tripiṭaka.

THE DALAI LAMA

Message

The foremost scholars of the holy land of India were based for many centuries at Nālandā Monastic University. Their deep and vast study and practice explored the creative potential of the human mind with the aim of eliminating suffering and making life truly joyful and worthwhile. They composed numerous excellent and meaningful texts. I regularly recollect the kindness of these immaculate scholars and aspire to follow them with unflinching faith. At the present time, when there is great emphasis on scientific and technological progress, it is extremely important that those of us who follow the Buddha should rely on a sound understanding of his teaching, for which the great works of the renowned Nālandā scholars provide an indispensable basis.

In their outward conduct the great scholars of Nālandā observed ethical discipline that followed the Pāli tradition, in their internal practice they emphasized the awakening mind of *bodhichitta*, enlightened altruism, and in secret they practised tantra. The Buddhist culture that flourished in Tibet can rightly be seen to derive from the pure tradition of Nālandā, which comprises the most complete presentation of the Buddhist teachings. As for me personally, I consider myself a practitioner of the Nālandā tradition of wisdom. Masters of Nālandā such as Nāgārjuna, Āryadeva, Āryāsaṅga, Dharmakīrti, Candrakīrti, and Śāntideva wrote the scriptures that we Tibetan Buddhists study and practice. They are all my gurus. When I read their books and reflect upon their names, I feel a connection with them.

The works of these Nālandā masters are presently preserved in the collection of their writings that in Tibetan translation we call the Tengyur (*bstan 'gyur*). It took teams of Indian masters and great Tibetan translators over four centuries to accomplish the historic task of translating them into Tibetan. Most of these books were later lost in their Sanskrit originals, and relatively few were translated into Chinese. Therefore, the Tengyur is truly one of Tibet's most precious treasures, a mine of understanding that we have preserved in Tibet for the benefit of the whole world.

Keeping all this in mind I am very happy to encourage a long-term project of the American Institute of Buddhist Studies, originally established by the late Venerable Mongolian Geshe Wangyal and now at the Columbia University Center for Buddhist Studies, and Tibet House US, in collaboration with Wisdom Publications, to translate the Tengyur into English and other modern languages, and to publish the many works in a collection called *The Treasury of the Buddhist Sciences*. When I recently visited Columbia University, I joked that it would take those currently working at the Institute at least three "reincarnations" to complete the task; it surely will require the intelligent and creative efforts of generations of translators from every tradition of Tibetan Buddhism, in the spirit of the scholars of Nālandā, although we may hope that using computers may help complete the work more quickly. As it grows, the *Treasury* series will serve as an invaluable reference library of the Buddhist Sciences and Arts. This collection of literature has been of immeasurable benefit to us Tibetans over the centuries, so we are very happy to share it with all the people of the world. As someone who has been personally inspired by the works it contains, I firmly believe that the methods for cultivating wisdom and compassion originally developed in India and described in these books preserved in Tibetan translation will be of great benefit to many scholars, philosophers, and scientists, as well as ordinary people.

I wish the American Institute of Buddhist Studies at the Columbia Center for Buddhist Studies, Tibet House US, and Wisdom Publications every success and pray that this ambitious and far-reaching project to create *The Treasury of the Buddhist Sciences* will be accomplished according to plan. I also request others, who may be interested, to extend whatever assistance they can, financial or otherwise, to help ensure the success of this historic project.

May 15, 2007

Crushing the Categories

(*Vaidalyaprakaraṇa*)

By Nāgārjuna

Introduction, Translation, and Commentary
by Jan Westerhoff

TREASURY OF THE BUDDHIST SCIENCES SERIES
TENGYUR TRANSLATION INITIATIVE

CT 3053, 3057 (TŌH. 3826, 3830)

COPUBLISHED BY
THE AMERICAN INSTITUTE OF BUDDHIST STUDIES AND WISDOM PUBLICATIONS
IN ASSOCIATION WITH THE COLUMBIA UNIVERSITY CENTER FOR BUDDHIST STUDIES
AND TIBET HOUSE US

Wisdom

Treasury of the Buddhist Sciences series
Tengyur Translation Initiative
A refereed series published by:

American Institute of Buddhist Studies
Columbia University
80 Claremont Avenue, Room 303
New York, NY 10027

www.aibs.columbia.edu

Wisdom Publications
199 Elm Street
Somerville, MA 02144 USA

www.wisdompubs.org

In association with Columbia University's Center for Buddhist Studies and Tibet House US.
Distributed by Wisdom Publications.

Library of Congress Cataloging-in-Publication Data

Names: Nagarjuna, active 2nd century, author. | Westerhoff, Jan, translator, writer of commentary. | Nagarjuna, active 2nd century. Vaidalyasutra. Tibetan. | Nagarjuna, active 2nd century. Vaidalyasutra. English.
Title: Crushing the categories (Vaidalyaprakarana) / by Nagarjuna ; introduction, translation, and commentary by Jan Westerhoff.
Other titles: Crushing the categories | Vaidalyaprakarana
Description: New York : American Institute Of Buddhist Studies, 2018. | Series: Treasury of the Buddhist sciences series. Tengyur translation initiative ; CT 3053, 3057 (TOH. 3826, 3830) | Includes bibliographical references and index. |
Identifiers: LCCN 2018024996 (print) | LCCN 2018031393 (ebook) | ISBN 9781949163018 (eBook) | ISBN 9781949163001 (cloth : alk. paper)
Subjects: LCSH: Nagarjuna, active 2nd century. Vaidalyasutra. | Madhyamika (Buddhism)--Early works to 1800.
Classification: LCC BQ2910.V342 (ebook) | LCC BQ2910.V342 W47 2018 (print) | DDC 181/.043--dc23
LC record available at https://lccn.loc.gov/2018024996

ISBN 978-1-949163-00-1 (cloth) ebook ISBN 978-1-949163-01-8

22 21 20 19 18 1 2 3 4 5

Cover and interior design by Gopa&Ted2. Set in Diacritical Garamond Pro 11/13.9.

Printed on acid-free paper and meets the guidelines for permanence and durability of the Production Guidelines for Book Longevity of the Council on Library Resources.

♻ This book was produced with environmental mindfulness. For more information, please visit wisdompubs.org/wisdom-environment.

Printed in the United States of America.

For Yuka & Ayami

Contents

Publisher's/Series Editor's Preface

WE ARE EXTREMELY PLEASED to present Jan Westerhoff's outstanding work on the difficult *Crushing the Categories*, among the most important though stubbornly neglected of Nāgārjuna's critical philosophical works. It is also clearly one of the most difficult: it had already caused confusion among ancient scholars in India and Tibet, and has been continuing to do so among modern scholars. Some have even considered it to be falsely ascribed to Nāgārjuna. Jan Westerhoff skillfully avoids the two main reasons for this: (1) the general misunderstanding of the Centrists (*Mādhyamika*) as nihilistic skeptics; and (2) the historical supposition that, as for the formal Logicians' School (*Naiyāyika-darśana*), though its founding sūtra is quite old, its commentarial tradition doesn't really get under way until some time after Nāgārjuna's supposed date of the 2nd century CE. As to the first, quite a few scholars, ancient as well as modern, tend to think that Nāgārjuna had already shown in the *Wisdom Root Centrist Verses* (*Prajñā-nāma-mūlamadhyamakakārikā*) that all things are empty of intrinsic reality, and, in the process—they mistakenly think—that logic is inherently self-contradictory and its results illusory. Surely, they conclude, he wouldn't have bothered to reject in detail the categorical instruments of logicians. As to the second, while Nāgārjuna may have been mainly focused on his colleagues in the early centuries of Nālandā monastic university, certainly those learned mendicant panditas would have been well versed in the machinery of Indian reasoning that was codified as early as the 4th century BCE by another Gautama, the author of the *Nyāyasūtra*.

I am also personally very grateful for Jan Westerhoff's re-calling my attention to this work and opening it up for me with his careful and thorough translation and analysis. I too had long neglected it, even though my mentors in the study of Nāgārjuna had alerted me to its importance. Westerhoff makes clear—for the first time among contemporary students of the work—how the *Crushing the Categories* fits in with Nāgārjuna's main critical philosophy works; indeed, how it is the natural complement of the *Wisdom Root* and logically precedes the *Dispeller of Disputes* (*Vigrahavyāvartanī*). Westerhoff's interpretation is supported by no less a scholarly authority than the great Tsong Khapa (1357–1419), dean of Tibetan Centrist scholars, who wrote:

> [Nāgārjuna,] in order to demonstrate mainly the truth of the relativity free of the extremes of existence and nonexistence, first [wrote] the *Wisdom Root* to negate the probandum—the intrinsic reality of persons and things presumed by the advocates of the [intrinsic] objectivity of phenomena—and [he then wrote] the *Crushing the Categories* to negate the means of proving it, the sixteen categorical instruments of [Indian] logicians, such as [that of intrinsically real] validating cognition.[1]

Thus, Tsong Khapa ranks this work as the close partner of Nāgārjuna's most famous critiques that make up the *Wisdom Root*, on the same level and with the same importance. And yet I never gave it the attention it deserved, turning to it now and then, and then turning away due to its many technicalities.

It is significant that Dr. Westerhoff came to wrestle with this work from his deep study of the *Dispeller of Disputes*, which fits very closely with the *Wisdom* and the *Crushing*. Again, Tsong Khapa writes:

> To summarize these points: [Nāgārjuna, in] the *Wisdom Root* and the *Crushing the Categories*, teaches the manifest truth of relativity by refuting in detail the [intrinsically real] probandum and the probans of the opponents. [Again] to counter what one might think in regard to his system of such refutation—since [the critique shows that] the objective and the activity of [intrinsically real] refutation and proof are invalid, it follows

1. *dang po (yod med kyi mtha' spangs pa'i rten 'byung gi de kho na nyid gtso bor ston pa) la gnyis las dngos po'i ngo bo nyid smra ba rnams kyis gang zag dang chos la sgro btags pa'i rang bzhin bsgrub bya 'gog pa ni rtsa ba shes rab yin la / de'i sgrub byed tshad ma la sogs pa rtog ge'i tshig gi don bcu drug 'gog pa ni zhib mo rnam 'thag go / /* (From Tsong Khapa's *rigs pa'i rgya mtsho*, Kumbum Jampa Ling woodblock, 5a.5–6.)

> that one cannot [absolutely] refute another's position and cannot prove one's own position—[he] taught in the *Dispeller of Disputes* the [conventional] validity in his own [system] of all objectives and activities of those [rational refutations and proofs] and so forth.[2]

It was a pleasure to read carefully as secondary editor Westerhoff's great effort with the many textual and philosophical difficulties in the work, pushing the understanding of Nāgārjuna's task in applying his trenchant critical relativist analysis to the causal zone of logic and reasoning. Westerhoff in this way is emerging as a leader in the movement of contemporary philosophical scholars to take Nāgārjuna seriously *as a philosopher*, releasing him from the false branding as an anti-rationalist skeptic imposed on him by most scholars of previous generations in the West and Western-scholarship-influenced Japan, where philosophical studies (*tetsugaku*) is still all Western and is largely segregated away from Buddhist Studies (*bukkyogaku*).

If, as Tibetan authors have maintained, Nāgārjuna is mainly critiquing intra-Buddhist realist trends in the Nālandā of his day, and if the *Dispeller of Disputes* serves as a rebuttal of the objections of logic-inclined substantialist mendicant scholars (perhaps having come to the Saṅgha from Brahmin families and so previously educated about the *Nyāyasūtra*), the *Crushing the Categories* makes a more aggressive final effort to extirpate the influence of proto-Naiyāyika-style logical substantialism from the intellectual circles in and around Nālandā, by going through the root categories of the Naiyāyika school explicitly to show definitively how it cannot work on an assumed intrinsically real, non-empty, objective basis.

The fact that Nāgārjuna accords these logical categorical instruments such a laborious and exacting treatment also brings more clearly into focus how he and his Mādhyamika-style school is not at all an anti-logic, anti-reason school of purely negativist skepticism, but how it took logic seriously

2. *de dag gi don mdor bsdu na rtsa she dang zhib mo rnam 'thag gis phas rgol gi bsgrub bya dang sgrub byed rgyas par bkag nas rten 'byung gi de kho na nyid bstan pa na / de ltar 'gog pa de'i lugs la yang dgag sgrub kyi bya byed mi 'thad pas gzhan phyogs 'gog pa dang rang phyogs sgrub pa med par 'gyur ro snyam pa la rang la de dag la sogs pa'i bya byed thams cad 'thad par rtsod zlog gis bstan no / /* (From Tsong Khapa's *rigs pa'i rgya mtsho*, Kumbum Jampa Ling woodblock, 7b.4–6.)

as part of the universal causality *on the conventional level.* Nāgārjuna thus aims to show how reasoning works precisely and compellingly as an important *conventional* practice, without being a substantialist method of capturing ultimate reality as a realist or substantialist would have it.

The modern scholars who have questioned Nāgārjuna's authorship of the *Crushing* may have done so because they imagined the nihilistic skeptic they took him to be would not have bothered to go beyond the twenty-seven critiques given in the *Wisdom Root* and the further elaboration of specific points in the *Dispeller of Disputes*, the *Emptiness Seventy* (*Śūnyatā-saptati*), and the *Reason Sixty* (*Yuktiṣaṣṭikā*), to give such a detailed critical treatment to the logicians' system. He is not dealing with the later elaborated full-fledged Naiyāyika school system, but with his substantialist Buddhist colleagues in the Individual Vehicle (*Hīnayāna*) using the long-developed categories from the ancient *Nyāyasūtra*.

We warmly welcome Jan Westerhoff's hard work of unpacking the enigmas of the *Crushing the Categories*, building on the momentum of his previous study of the *Dispeller of Disputes*, following what seems to be the very path of the noble Nāgārjuna, and we are honored to bring out this edition of his illuminating achievement.

Robert A.F. Thurman (Ari Genyen Tenzin Choetrak)
Jey Tsong Khapa Professor of Indo-Tibetan Buddhist Studies,
Columbia University
Director, Columbia Center for Buddhist Studies
President, American Institute of Buddhist Studies
President, Tibet House US

Ganden Dechen Ling
Woodstock, New York
January 13, 2017 CE
Tibetan Royal Year 2143, Year of the Fire Monkey

Author's Acknowledgments

MY UNDERSTANDING of the *Vaidalyaprakaraṇa* owes much to the help and kindness of other scholars. In the first place I must mention Fernando Tola and Carmen Dragonetti, whose fine study and translation contributed greatly to making the contents of the *Vaidalyaprakaraṇa* accessible to Western scholars. Even though my own interpretation sometimes differs on small (and some not so small) points from theirs, the great importance of their work for making sense of the *Vaidalyaprakaraṇa* should be apparent to any reader of this book. Other scholars whose help was greatly appreciated while writing the translation and commentary include Sung Yong Kang, Dan Lusthaus, Mattia Salvini, Kazuko Yokoi, and Stefano Zacchetti.

The *Vaidalyaprakaraṇa* is a difficult text, not least because the Sanskrit original is not available. Any reader of the text will quickly realize that the most puzzling passages are those where it is either not clear how to understand the Tibetan (accordingly we find examples of vastly different renderings in different contemporary translations, some of which will be discussed in the commentary) or, even if the language is clear, it is not evident what kind of philosophical point is made or what argument is expressed.

I cannot claim that I have managed to clarify all the obscure passages in the *Vaidalyaprakaraṇa* even to my own satisfaction. But I believe that I have elucidated a sufficient number to demonstrate the great philosophical interest of the text. As for the remaining ones I hope that the remarks made in these pages will help future scholars of Madhyamaka to shine the light of understanding on the sections of the *Vaidalyaprakaraṇa* currently still veiled by the mists of ignorance.

J.C.W.

Abbreviations

ABBREVIATIONS for the titles of Sanskrit works are given in the first list below. References throughout the book citing such abbreviations are often followed by numbers; in such cases the numbers refer either to the verse of that work or, for works divided into chapters, to chapter and verse.

References citing modern sources (e.g., in the footnotes) are given in author-date format (Author Year, page#). When such references contain two numbers separated by a colon (Author Year, ##:##), the numbers denote either *page:line*, *volume:page*, or *chapter:verse*, as appropriate to the work in question. Full citations for all modern sources (including modern editions and studies of classical Sanskrit texts) may be found in the bibliography (p. 291ff).

Abbreviations for Tibetan canonical collections are given in the second list below. Full citations for these sources also may be found in the bibliography.

Sanskrit Works

AK	*Akutobhayā* (Huntington 1986)
MĀ, MĀBh	*Madhyamakāvatāra*, *Madhyamakāvatārabhāṣya* (Poussin 1912)
MMK	*Mūlamadhyamakakārikā* (Ye 2011)
NS, NSBh	*Nyāyasūtra*, *Nyāyasūtrabhāṣya* (Śāstrī 1998) The numbering of the *sūtras* follows Ruben 1928
PP	*Prasannapadā* (Poussin 1903–13); (de Jong 1978)
RĀ	*Ratnāvalī* (Hahn 1982)

ŚS	*Śūnyatāsaptati* (Lindtner 1982, 31–69)
VP	*Vaidalyaprakaraṇa* (Tola and Dragonetti 1995a)
VS	*Vaidalyasūtra* (D 3826 dbu ma, tsa 22b6–24a6; P 5226 dbu ma, tsa 25a7–27a4; N 3999 dbu ma, tsa 22b4–24a4)
VV	*Vigrahavyāvartanī* (Yonezawa, 2008)
YṢ	*Yuktiṣaṣtikā* (Loizzo 2007)

Tibetan Canonical Collections

C	Choney (*co ne*)
D	Derge (*sde dge*)
N	Narthang (*snar thang*)
P	Peking
T	Taisho

Typographical Conventions

To facilitate pronunciation for the non-specialist, we have strived to present Sanskrit and Tibetan names (and some terms) in a phonetic form. Toward this end, while we generally have kept conventional diacritics for Sanskrit names, we have added an *h* to convey certain sounds (so *ś*, *ṣ*, and *c* are often rendered as *sh*, *ṣh*, and *ch* respectively). For Sanskrit terms that have entered the English lexicon (such as "nirvana" or "mandala"), we use no diacritical marks. For Tibetan names, a complete list of phonetic-transliterated (Wylie) equivalents may be found in the Appendix.

In more technical contexts—italic Sanskrit or Tibetan terms in parentheses; the names of Sanskrit texts (which are treated as if technical terms); Sanskrit or Tibetan passages cited in footnotes; bibliographical citations; and so on—we use standard diacritical conventions for Sanskrit, and Wylie transliterations for Tibetan.

Translation and Commentary (Part Two)

⌘ Marks the beginning of a passage of Nāgārjuna's VP text, including prologue (if any), root verse (**set in bold type**), and commentary.

⌘ ⌘ Marks the end of Nāgārjuna's VP passage (prologue, verse, and commentary) and the beginning of the translator's commentary.

Translator's citation of Nāgārjuna's text is indented as a block quote and set in italic type.

Throughout the translation, text in square brackets has been added by the translator for clarity.

Part One

Introduction

Introduction

The *Vaidalyasūtra* and the *Vaidalyaprakaraṇa*

WHEN CONSIDERING the *Vaidalyaprakaraṇa* we are in fact looking at two texts. The Tibetan collection of translations of Indian commentarial works, the Tengyur (*bstan 'gyur*), contains the shorter *Vaidalyasūtranāma* (VS, *zhib mo rnam par 'thag pa zhes bya ba'i mdo*), as well as the longer *Vaidalyanāmaprakaraṇa* (VP, *zhib mo rnam par 'thag pa zhes bya ba'i rab tu byed pa*) that embeds the VS in a commentary.[3] Unfortunately the relation between these two texts cannot be captured by the simple formula VP = VS + commentary.

First of all, the VS and the VP were translated into Tibetan by different teams of translators. The VS was translated by the Kashmiri pandit Ānanda (*kha che'i pandi ta ā na nta*) and the Buddhist monk and translator Drakjor Sherab, while the VP was translated by the Kashmiri pandit Jayānanda and the monk Kudo Dewar.[4] Kajiyama[5] notes that the texts of the VS and its version embedded in the longer VP "often deviates in verbal form, though not in the sense, from the text of the separately extant Vaidalya-sūtra" (which is just what we would expect of two separate translations of the same text).

Secondly, even though the VP is structured according to the familiar model of a concise root text that is elaborated and commented upon in a

3. VP has been translated into English by Tola and Dragonetti (1995) and into Japanese by Yamaguchi (1944) and Kajiyama (1974). Sempa Dorje (1974) offers a reconstruction of the Sanskrit text of the VS. At least three further English translations of VP have been announced (an "annotated English translation" by Yūichi Kajiyama [1965, 131]; one by Christian Lindtner [1986, 358n110]; and one by Ole Pind), though none of these have been published so far.

4. See p. 286.

5. Kajiyama 1965, 131.

commentary, distinguishing root text and commentary in a precise way is often difficult since the VP does not follow the convention of contrasting a metrically structured root text with a prose commentary. Rather, both the root text and the commentary are written in prose.

It is tempting to speculate on what motivated this unusual form, since the usual reason, that the metrical root text can be more easily memorized, does not apply in this case. According to the colophons of the two texts, the VS was received orally from Nāgārjuna[6] while the VP is said to be composed by him.[7] This suggests the possibility that the VS is effectively a set of notes based on a lecture by Nāgārjuna (which would explain its lack of metrical structure) and the VP was then subsequently composed by him in order to elucidate and explain this abbreviated summary of his lecture.[8]

While it is frequently the case that (despite their extremely compressed form) root texts can be understood without referring to a commentary, several passages in the VS would be incomprehensible without the commentary.

For a particularly clear example consider VS 04 and 05. Reading them without a commentary one would understand VS 05 as contradicting VS 04. Yet this is not the case, as Nāgārjuna's "This is not so" (*ma yin te*) at the beginning of VS 05 is not directed at the position put forward in VS 04, but rather against a suggestion made by the opponent before VS 05, which is only found in the commentary. Without the commentary no amount of guesswork would allow us to infer what position VS 05 is reacting against.

For this reason it seems somewhat unlikely that Nāgārjuna first composed the VS as a concise treatment of the topic, and subsequently explained and elaborated it in the autocommentary we now find in the VP. If the combination of root text and commentary expresses what Nāgārjuna wanted to say, examples like the one just mentioned suggest that the VS could not have been conceived as a concise "stand-alone" exposition of the same meaning.[9] Root text and commentary rather seem to form an integral unit and give

6. *slob dpon 'phags pa klu sgrub kyi zhal snga nas mdzad pa.*

7. *slob dpon 'phags pa klu sgrub kyis mdzad pa.*

8. Venkata Ramanan's (1966, 37) list of Nāgārjuna's works classifies the VP under "Commentaries or/and Records of Oral Instruction (*upadeśa*)."

9. See Pind 2001, 155. He points out that the *sūtras* of the VS "could not have been conceived independently of the prose in which they are embedded" and appear more like "truncated arguments or brief topic markers buttressed by the corresponding prose."

the impression of having been composed in dependence on one another. The commentary obviously depends on the root text (because that is what it is explaining), but as we have just seen, the root text also depends on the commentary for preventing the reader from misunderstanding the way the different parts of the root text relate to one another.

The distinction between the VS and the VP is therefore somewhat artificial. Not all sections of the VS are able to stand on their own as an independent text; moreover, it would not be too difficult to conceive of the VP as a continuous prose text with no root text/commentary distinction at all.

In addition, the boundary between the root text and the commentary is often somewhat blurred. The term *gzhan yang* (*api ca*, "moreover") is usually regarded as part of the prose commentary, introducing a new section of the root text. In some cases (e.g., VS 30 and VS 40), however, this constitutes part of the root text without there being an obvious distinction in meaning between these instances of *gzhan yang* and all the other instances that did not get included in the root text. It is not very implausible to argue that these instances of *gzhan yang* were included by mistake and should not be considered part of the root text, even though they are included in the VS.

The not entirely perspicuous relation between root text and commentary also makes it difficult to number the parts of the root text and associated commentarial sections.[10] As the root text is in prose, we cannot just count metrical units to individuate the items. In some cases VP and VS are only distinguished by the fact that the VP contains some additional short phrase in the middle of a passage that is missing in the VS. Are we then to count these as two distinct sections of the root text, separated by the short phrase, or as one continuous section interrupted by a piece of commentary?

For example, *sūtra* 68 from the VS reads as follows:

> *khyod kyi thams cad tshig don du brjod pa yin gyi | don dam pa ni ma yin no zhe na | ma yin te | lan thams cad la thal bar 'gyur ba'i phyir ro*

10. Such numbering is not included in the Tibetan translation, nor is it likely that it was part of the original Sanskrit. Yet all modern editions use some system of numbering of the elements of the root text as a means of structuring the work.

The version we find in the VP is very similar, but it adds the phrases set in boldface:

> ***smras pa*** | *khyod kyi thams cad tshig don du brjod pa yin gyi don dam par ma yin no zhe na* | ***brjod par bya ste*** | *ma yin te* | *lan thams cad la thal bar 'gyur ba'i phyir ro*

As this makes clear, we are dealing here with an objection by the opponent (introduced by the phrase *smras pa* ["Objection"]), followed by Nāgārjuna's reply (following the phrase *brjod par bya ste* ["it is to be replied"]).

We appear to be equally justified in saying that "*sūtra* 68" from the VS is actually not one *sūtra*, but two, an objection and a reply, or that it is one *sūtra*, and that the VP interpolates its commentary into the *sūtra*.

While not much hangs on the way of numbering we choose for understanding the contents of the text, problems arise if different authors group different units together in different ways and thereby end up referring to different passages when they talk about "verse x." Kajiyama includes what Tola and Dragonetti regard as the second *sūtra* as part of the first.[11] Thus, according to Kajiyama, the root texts consist of 72 *sūtra*s, whereas for Tola and Dragonetti there are 73. Pema Dorje's Sanskrit reconstruction also counts only 72 *sūtra*s, but he does not fuse what Tola and Dragonetti count as *sūtra*s 1 and 2 into *sūtra* 1, but what they count as *sūtra*s 2 and 3 into *sūtra* 3. In the present discussion we will follow the numbering of the *sūtra*s adopted by Tola and Dragonetti, although we regard what they count as *sūtra* 73 as being two separate *sūtra*s. According to our counting, the VP thus contains 74 *sūtra*s.

11. Kajiyama VP 1 thus includes Tola and Dragonetti VP 1 and 2; Kajiyama VP 2 is Tola and Dragonetti VP 3; and in general Kajiyama VP x is Tola and Dragonetti VP x+1. Whether Kajiyama's counting is right, and whether that of Tola and Dragonetti is wrong, as claimed by Pind (2001, 149n2), is a moot point. The two *sūtra*s do not obviously form a whole, and since the numbering of the *sūtra*s is not part of the text, how one way of counting can be established as the right one is far from clear.

The Question of Authenticity

With the exception of the MMK, which is regarded as a work of Nāgārjuna by definition, the authenticity of all other works traditionally ascribed to him has been questioned. The VP is no exception.

The VP belongs to a set of six texts, sometimes referred to as the Yukti corpus, which the Tibetan tradition has canonized as Nāgārjuna's "six works on reasoning" (*rigs pa'i tshogs drug*).[12]

The VP differs from other works traditionally included in the Yukti corpus, the *Mūlamadhyamakakārikā*, *Śūnyatāsaptati*, *Yuktiṣaṣṭikā*, and *Ratnāvalī*, in not having any Indian or Tibetan commentaries associated with it.[13] It shares this trait with the *Vigrahavyāvartanī* (the only extant commentary on both texts is what is assumed to be Nāgārjuna's autocommentary). As opposed to the *Vigrahavyāvartanī*, which is quoted relatively often in the Buddhist commentarial literature[14] however, the VP appears not to have been quoted much by later authors.[15]

The Sanskrit originals of both the VS and the VP are lost; both texts are preserved in Tibetan translation. The colophons of both texts identify Nāgārjuna as the text's author. Among Indian Madhyamaka authors, Bhavya[16] and Chandrakīrti[17] mention the VP as a work of Nāgārjuna's.

12. See Butön 2013, 230; Chimpa and Chattopadhyaya 1970, 108; Tsong Khapa 1975, 23 (4b.1–2); Ruegg 1981, 81.

13. One reason for the absence of any Tibetan commentarial tradition on the VP is likely to be its close conceptual connection with the NS, a text that was never translated into Tibetan. Understanding the point of many of the discussions in the VP without frequent reference to the NS is extremely difficult.

14. Westerhoff 2010, 63.

15. Lindtner (1982, 87) remarks that he has "never noticed any quotation from the VP." (There are some quotations, though. The 12th-century Tibetan scholar Maja Changchub Tsöndru quotes VP 01 in his commentary on the MMK.) Whether this scarcity of quotations results from the fact that Nāgārjuna's "disciples and followers" regarded the VP as not authentic, as Tola and Dragonetti (1995, 8) seem to suggest, or whether it is a result of this text's specific engagement with Nyāya, which was not a focus of the Tibetan scholastic tradition, remains debatable.

16. *dbu ma'i rtsa ba rtsod pa bzlog | stong nyid bdun chu rigs drug chu | rnam par 'thag pa la sogs pas | dngos rnams skye med shes par bya* (*Madhyamakaratnapradīpa*, D 3854:264b). There is, however, some debate about whether the author of this text is indeed the Madhyamaka author or a later writer of the same name (Ruegg 1981, 66–67).

17. *dṛṣṭvā sūtrasamuccayaṁ parikathāṁ ratnāvalīṁ saṁstutī abhyasyāticiraṁ sa śāstragaditās tāḥ kārikā yatnataḥ | yuktyākhyām atha ṣaṣṭikāṁ sa vidalāṁ tāṁ śūnyatāsaptatiṁ yā cāsāv*

Modern scholarship is divided over the question whether the VS and VP are indeed the work of Nāgārjuna. Yūichi Kajiyama and Christian Lindtner explicitly argue in favor of this attribution,[18] while Fernando Tola and Carmen Dragonetti, as well as Ole Pind, raise arguments against it.[19]

Kajiyama bases his positive verdict on its ascription to Nāgārjuna in the colophon, together with the authority of later Tibetan historians such as Butön. Moreover, he argues that "its contents nowhere suggest any other author to whom the work might be better ascribed."[20]

Lindtner considers the VS and VP as genuine because they agree with the MMK in style, scope, and doctrine, and are additionally ascribed to Nāgārjuna by trustworthy witnesses such as Bhavya and Chandrakīrti:

> Judging solely from the text itself, the style and tenets would indicate the same author as for VV, the work where the parallels are closest out of all those ascribed to Nāgārjuna.[21]

Tola and Dragonetti[22] mention various reasons that might raise doubts regarding Nāgārjuna as the author of the VP, even though they admit that none "by themselves alone, discard in an absolute sense the authenticity of the work."[23] The most interesting of these refer to specific topics or assumptions Tola and Dragonetti identify in the VP, arguing that insofar as these topics or assumptions can be found in other texts, such texts are too late to allow Nāgārjuna to be the author of the VP.[24] Yet this approach has too many methodological problems to allow us to form any reliable view of

---

atha vigrahasya racitā vyāvartanī tām api. Madhyamakaśāstrastuti (de Jong 1962, 51). See also Pind 2001, 150.

18. Other scholars who ascribe the VP to Nāgārjuna include David Ruegg (1981, 19, 21), Susumu Yamaguchi (1944, 113), and Paul Williams (1978, 280).

19. When Kang (2008, 75) claims that the VP is "no longer ascribed to Nāgārjuna by serious scholars," he seems to have these last three authors in mind.

20. Kajiyama 1965, 130.

21. Lindtner 1982, 87.

22. Tola and Dragonetti 1995a, 7–15.

23. Tola and Dragonetti 1995a, 15.

24. E.g., Tola and Dragonetti 1995a, 12: "If it is accepted that the Idealistic school inspired the arguments of VP, then we would have to locate it after the appearance of the Yogāchāra school more or less in 350 A.D."

whether or not Nāgārjuna can be regarded as the author of the VP. First of all it is often not clear whether the respective topics or assumptions are indeed the ones the VP talks about (regarding the parallels with Bhartṛhari and Yogāchāra that Tola and Dragonetti identify, I believe this is in fact somewhat doubtful). But even if we accept that the very same idea is expressed in the VP and in a text that probably was not around until some centuries after the generally accepted date of Nāgārjuna in the first or second century CE, what does this show? In order to draw any firm conclusion regarding the VP's authorship from this we would have to exclude the possibilities that (a) the later text borrowed the idea from the VP, (b) both texts derive the idea from a common predecessor, and (c) that two texts can discuss identical or similar ideas without one drawing on the other. As it is impossible to exclude any of these possibilities, the parallels mentioned cannot provide evidence that allows us to decide the question of the authenticity of the VP.

Pind's argument focuses on the idea that some passages of the VP are incompatible with Madhyamaka views, a fact he considers "to settle, once and for all, the debate about the authenticity of the VP."[25] He remarks with respect to VP 58 that:

> In any case, it seems certain that the paragraph of the VP is not consistent with basic Madhyamaka assumptions. It is therefore highly unlikely that the VP was written by a Mādhyamika in the original sense of the word.... VP cannot under any circumstances be attributed to Nāgārjuna.[26]

Pind's argument presupposes an emendation of the text; neither this emendation nor the conclusions he draws from it appear wholly cogent to me.[27] Pind's conclusion that they refute Nāgārjuna's authorship "once and for all" and that "we can now safely exclude the VP from the corpus of Nāgārjunian writings"[28] thus appears somewhat premature.

25. Pind 2001, 152.

26. Pind 2001, 169.

27. I discuss this in more detail in my commentary on VP 58 below.

28. Pind 2001, 172.

It seems to me that in the absence of more decisive considerations than those that have at present been brought forward against the authenticity of the VP, ascriptions from the Indian and Tibetan tradition (such as those found in the colophons and the works of later Indian and Tibetan authors) should be taken very seriously. There is no denying that the VP occupies a unique position in the Yukti corpus, differing from the other members of that set with respect to its formal features, and with respect to the degree of its embedding in the scholastic tradition via commentaries and quotations. But unless some harder evidence emerges that would allow us to exclude the VP from the collection of Nāgārjuna's key Madhyamaka works I suggest that it should be considered as authentic.

The Aim of the *Vaidalyaprakaraṇa*

Nāgārjuna's aim in the VP seems very clear: it is to refute the sixteen Nyāya categories.[29] Yet we need some more explanation in order to understand what precisely this refutation amounts to,[30] and what its role is in the larger Madhyamaka enterprise.

29. For a discussion of the sixteen Nyāya categories, see below, p. 30ff. Trying to determine the historical relationship between the VP and the NS is a difficult undertaking, as both texts appear to quote each other (Williams 1978, 287). The most we seem to be able to say is that there must have been a version of the NS extant at Nāgārjuna's time that closely resembled the key terms and definition of the first two books of the NS as we know it today (Williams 1978, 290). Kang (2006, 165n78) wants to go further than this; he argues that it is "extremely likely" that the VS has been composed on the basis of thorough knowledge of both the NS and Vātsyāyana's *Bhāṣya*, though it appears that this thesis would need a rather more detailed defense than Kang himself provides.

30. There appears to be an agreement among at least some of the contemporary commentators on the VP that Nāgārjuna's arguments in the text are fallacious. E.g., Lindtner (1986, 358n110) states: "[The VP] is without compare the most lively and amusing of all texts ascribed to Nāgārjuna, full of sophistries as it is"; and Pind (2001, 157) speaks of "the author's relentless sophistry"; see also Kajiyama 1974, 393–94n45, and 1991, 109. This evaluation raises a number of problems. In the case of a concise text like the VP that is also not preserved in its original language the precise spelling out of many of the arguments requires a considerable amount of interpretation. The principle of charity would require that in order for an argument to qualify as fallacious we should be able to show that on any interpretation the interpreter could think of the argument is invalid—a task that neither Lindtner nor Pind have undertaken. Secondly, in the case of scholars like Lindtner who argue for the authenticity of the VP, it is unclear how they would explain why the author of the MMK (a text not generally regarded as filled with sophisms) suddenly dropped his

A first question to ask is whether Nāgārjuna wants to refute the Nyāya categories from an ultimate or from a conventional perspective. Tola and Dragonetti[31] suggest that we distinguish two different aims Nāgārjuna might want to accomplish in the VP:

1. "[To] examine and analyze the *padārtha*s from this metaphysical point of view [of emptiness], in the metaphysical level, in order to reach the conclusion that they are *śūnya*, that they do not exist *paramārthataḥ*...."
2. To show "that the *padārtha*s are affected by manifold logical defects," to criticize "logic from the point of view of empirical reality, although not from a metaphysical point of view."

Even though I am not quite sure what is meant by criticizing logic "from the point of view of empirical reality," this is the underlying idea suggested by Tola and Dragonetti: One criticism Nāgārjuna can bring forward against the Naiyāyika's set of logical categories (and against several other parts of the Nyāya system) is that it conflicts with the Mādhyamika's anti-substantialist metaphysics.

There can be little doubt that according to the Naiyāyika's own view the sixteen categories exist at the level of ultimate truth. Not only do they belong to the ultimate furniture of the world, knowledge of them is also instrumental for obtaining liberation (*niḥśreyasa*).[32] It is evident that the anti-foundationalist standpoint of Nāgārjuna's Madhyamaka does not cohere well with this understanding of the categories as ultimately real.[33]

A second line of criticism is purely internal. Here the problem is not that the Nyāya theory fails to measure up to the demands of another metaphysical system, but that it encounters problems on its own terms. Its

---

argumentative standards in the VP. Our interpretation is based upon the assumption that Nāgārjuna's arguments in the VP can be interpreted in a way that renders them sound.

31. Tola and Dragonetti 1995a, 179n1.

32. Bernard 1981, 21–22.

33. Tola and Dragonetti (1995, 14) argue that in his remarks in VP 68 Nāgārjuna holds that "in his refutation of the *padārthas* he has not considered the *padārthas* as entities devoid of an own being...his intention has not been to demonstrate the *śūnyatā* or *niḥsvabhāvatā* of the *padārthas*." Since this would contradict familiar Madhyamaka positions they mention this as an argument against the authenticity of the VP. As will become clear in my commentary on this verse, I read the passage in a somewhat different way.

contradictions are internal, not just external and arising when confronted with the theory of emptiness.

It is not entirely clear, however, that we can really draw a sharp distinction between these two aims.

Consider, for example, VP 47, which criticizes the idea that something can be a reason for something else. The argument is that either the reason requires another reason, in which case we have an infinite regress, or it does not, in which case we have to justify why we are comfortable with letting this reason stand without a reason, but not the conclusion of the original argument. We might wonder whether this actually is a *logical* defect of the notion of a reason. If it were then the opponent could not bite the bullet and remain a rational agent. But there is nothing irrational in asserting that there is no principled way of deciding which statements need reasons and which do not. All we can appeal to is the fact that we feel a need for certain things to be justified but not for others. The point is not that such a position would be logically deficient, but that it would be incompatible with a foundationalist understanding of reasons such as the one the Naiyāyika is supposed to espouse. The problematic consequence that the notion of a reason either leads to a regress or begs the question (as Nāgārjuna argues) only follows if we assume that there is a way of deciding which statements need reasons and which do not that is somehow objectively grounded in the nature of things—that is, if we make substantialist assumptions about reasons.

In order to do justice to such passages, it is essential to be aware of two points when trying to make sense of Nāgārjuna's aims in the VP:

1. In keeping with the overall Madhyamaka outlook Nāgārjuna wants to refute the ultimate existence of all of the sixteen categories.
2. He does not want to refute the conventional reality of the categories, since if they were taken to be lacking any functional role even at the transactional level, there would be no possibility for a Mādhyamika (or indeed for anybody else) to employ any of them in an argument.

Tola and Dragonetti are right when they point out that Nāgārjuna wants to show "that the *padārthas* are affected by manifold logical defects," but this statement might easily be misunderstood. Nāgārjuna does not want to say that because all of the Nyāya categories lead to contradictions they should all be rejected at the conventional level. Rather, he wants to point out that they lead to contradictions if *understood against the background of the Nyāya framework*. Nāgārjuna's main aim is to show that the way the categories are interpreted by the opponent makes certain substantialist assumptions about ultimately existent entities, and that these assumptions have to be rejected, without, however, giving up the conception of the categories *tout court*. For each category we therefore have to investigate how (a) following the Nyāya understanding it brings with it such substantialist assumptions, and (b) how these assumptions can be removed and the conception of the category be reinterpreted without losing its functionality. As a result, we will then be able to show that we can still formulate a Madhyamaka-compatible form of these categories that does not connect them with the problematic metaphysical assumptions that the Naiyāyika wants to make. A suitably desubstantialized variant of the Nyāya categories, Nāgārjuna argues, may still be retained.

It is useful at this point to consider what the Tibetan tradition understood the purpose of the VP to be.

In his commentary on the MMK, Maja Changchub Tsöndru points out that:

> Some may object that if things have no intrinsic nature, it would contradict the establishment of such natures by intrinsically qualified means of knowledge [*rang bzhin tshad ma*]. [However,] to establish that things exist intrinsically, using epistemic means, it is necessary that when the epistemic means are investigated, there is no contradiction, yet this is not the case. In this way, the epistemic means and objects, etc., the sixteen categories of the Naiyāyikas are contrary to reason [*mi 'thad pa*]:
>
> So that those intent on dispute,
> Priding themselves in their expertise in logic,
> May give up this pride,
> I shall explain this detailed examination.

> It is pointed out that, having investigated the epistemic means and objects, etc., establishing the intrinsic nature of things in detail, they are rejected.[34]

Tsong Khapa is a bit more concise but makes essentially the same point:

> These treatises [i.e., the Yukti corpus] are of two primary kinds: those which demonstrate the way things really are—free from two extremes of existence and nonexistence—and those which demonstrate that the path free from these extreme views leads to liberation. The former is demonstrated in two ways: *Mūlamadhyamakakārikā* refutes the thesis concocted by the reificationists, viz., that persons and phenomena have essences; the *Vaidalya* refutes the Naiyāyika's use of their sixteen categories,[35] such as epistemic instruments, to prove that they do.[36]

Maja Changchub Tsöndru and Tsong Khapa therefore understand the VP as a reply to an opponent who claims that if things are established by reliable epistemic instruments, they have intrinsic nature or *svabhāva*.[37]

34. *dngos po rnams rang bzhin med na rang bzhin tshad mas grub pa dang 'gal lo zhes rgol ba la | dngos po rnams rang bzhin yod par tshad mas grub pa la tshad ma nyid brtags na mi 'gal ba zhig dgos pa las de nyid ma grub ste | 'di ltar rigs pa can gyi brtags pa'i tshad ma dang gzhal bya la sogs pa rtogs ge'i tshig gi don bcu drug mi 'thad pa'i phyir ro zhes ston pa | rtog ge shes pa'i na rgyal gyis | | gang zhig rtsod par mngon 'dod pa | | de yi nga rgyal spang ba'i phyir | | zhib mo rnam 'thag bzhad par bya | | zhes dngos po'i rang bzhin gyi grub byed tshad ma dang gzhal bya la sogs pa zhib mor brtags nas 'gog pa gsungs pa yin no.* rMa bya 1975, 8b:4–6.

35. Cf. Butön: "The purpose of the VP is to show the manner of debating with logicians (*rtog ge ba, tārkika*)." *gzhan rtog ge ba dang rtsod pa'i tshul ston pa zhib mo rnam 'thag.* Chandra 1965–71, 24 (ya: 670:3–5).

36. *gzhung de dag kyang yod med kyi mtha' spangs pa'i rten 'byung gi de kho na nyid gtso bor ston pa dang yod med kyi mthar mi lta ba'i lam gyis 'khor ba las grol ba gtso bor ston pa gnyis su 'du'o | | dang po la gyis las dngos po'i ngo bo nyid smra ba rnams kyis gang zag dang chos la sgro btags pa'i rang bzhin bsgrub bya 'gog pa ni rtsa ba shes rab yin la | de'i sgrub byed tshad ma la sogs pa rtog ge'i tshig gi don bcu drug 'gog pa ni zhib mo rnam 'thag go.* Tsong Khapa 1975, 23 (4b.3–5).

37. To exist by *svabhāva* means not borrowing its nature from other things, in the way that a chariot, for example, borrows its nature from its parts, none of which is a chariot itself. In Buddhist commentarial literature the absence of *svabhāva* is sometimes spelled out as existence that is logically, causally, or conceptually dependent. For further discussion of the notion of *svabhāva*, see Westerhoff 2009, 19–52.

Why would one think this? It is perhaps easier to look at the reason for the contrapositive: if things have no intrinsic nature then they are not established by reliable epistemic instruments. The reason for this is that if the Mādhyamika's thesis of universal emptiness is accepted, all epistemic instruments are empty too. They are thus not knowledge-producers by their intrinsic nature; in fact, ultimately speaking there are no epistemic instruments. How could the theory of emptiness then be established as the kind of view of the world required for attaining liberation?[38] The opponent thus argues that because we have access to the world by means of epistemic instruments, the Madhyamaka thesis of universal emptiness cannot be correct. One way for Nāgārjuna to reply to this charge is to point out that the epistemic instruments (together with the remainder of the Nyāya categories) are in fact not reliably established themselves. If they are rejected (*'gog pa*) as unreasonable (*mi 'thad pa*) the opponent's argument based on their authoritative role loses much of its force.

It therefore appears clear that both Tibetan authors understand Nāgārjuna as not simply rejecting the ultimate establishment of the Nyāya categories. According to them, Nāgārjuna's aim is not just to point out that the sixteen categories, together with everything else, are empty, but to refute their probative force (*sgrub byed...'gog pa*) by showing that they are not "without contradiction" (*mi 'gal ba*). At the same time it seems unsatisfactory to assume that these contradictions rule out any employment of the categories at the conventional level, for in this case any talk of epistemic instruments or objects, inferences, examples, and so forth, would have to be given up, thereby effectively robbing oneself of the ability to put forward any structured philosophical arguments. When "refuting the Naiyāyika's use of their sixteen categories" the aim is not to refute any use of the categories whatsoever, but to reject those kinds of usage that make unacceptable substantialist presuppositions, such as that behind the discussion in VP 47, namely that each justification has to be traceable to an unjustified justifier. The Nyāya categories are not contradictory as such, but only when coupled with certain *svabhāva*-entailing assumptions. It is the refutation of these assumptions, not of the categories themselves, that is the aim of Nāgārjuna's criticism in the VP.

38. See Westerhoff 2010, 66–67.

When Nāgārjuna begins his discussion of the epistemic instruments and objects he spends a considerable amount of time refuting the idea that they are self-established, that is, that their ability to act as sources of knowledge or as objects known flows from their intrinsic nature, from being the very kind of things they are. Nāgārjuna rejects this idea, but this does not mean that he denies the existence of epistemic instruments or objects *tout court*. If this were the case, the Mādhyamika would have no way of accounting for the fact that we know things, and that some ways of getting knowledge are better than others. His aim is rather to underline the necessity of developing an understanding of these two crucial epistemological notions that does not presuppose their existing by intrinsic nature. Such an understanding is achieved, for example, by conceptualizing the epistemic instruments and objects as mutually existentially dependent. If each could not exist if the other did not, the existence and properties of either could not flow solely from itself.

Similarly, when examining the notion of examples, Nāgārjuna's arguments in verses 28–31 set out to refute the notion of a similarity relation that exists "out there" in the objects, a relation that depends on nothing else but the intrinsic properties so related—in other words, a similarity relation existing by *svabhāva*. Again, Nāgārjuna rejects this idea, but not in order to make the point that no object is similar to any other one, but in order to justify the introduction of another, *svabhāva*-free similarity relation, one that depends crucially on the conceptualizing mind that regards objects as similar or dissimilar.

I would want to propose that understanding the purpose of the VP as a justification for a desubstantialized understanding of the logical categories discussed by the Naiyāyika is one that allows us to make sense of the aim of the text in the context of Nāgārjuna's other philosophical works. It is certainly superior to considering it as a mere display of sophistical fireworks (which would set it apart from other texts by the same author), an attempt to show that the Nyāya categories are as empty as everything else (failing to explain why Nāgārjuna devoted an entire book to the topic, given that this follows simply from the thesis of universal emptiness he defends elsewhere), or as aiming at demonstrating the inner inconsistency, and thus conventional deficiency of the sixteen categories (making it impossible for the Mādhyamika ever to engage in a philosophical debate using these categories).

At this place it is useful to point out the relation of the VP with the methodology usually associated with Prāsaṅgika Madhyamaka. The Prāsaṅgika, it is argued, does not endorse any philosophical conclusions of his own, but simply deduces deficiencies from the theses put forward by his opponent.

> Instead of formal probative proof statements, Mādhyamikas should restrict themselves to arguments that proceed from the opponent's own premises, either through a consequence (*prasaṅga, thal 'gyur*) or through an inference whose elements are accepted by the opponent alone (*gzhan grags kyi rjes dpag, *paraprasiddhānumāna*).[39]

In the Mādhyamika's deductions, some logical concepts and techniques have to be used. Is the Prāsaṅgika approach now not vitiated if these logical techniques presuppose philosophical propositions that the Mādhyamika is implicitly taking on board by employing them in his refutation? Put more simply, if these concepts and techniques themselves presuppose the existence of *svabhāva* somewhere, is the Prāsaṅgika not committed to accepting these, thereby contradicting the theory of universal emptiness?

One potential reply would be to say that these concepts and techniques are simply *paraprasiddhānumāna*, that is, something that the Prāsaṅgika uses because *his opponent* accepts them, not because he is himself committed to them. But this understanding does not cohere well with the arguments we find in the VP. If Nāgārjuna had argued that the entire logical machinery of the sixteen Nyāya categories is to be used on the understanding that it is accepted by the opponent alone, once again there would have been no reason to critique the categories one by one, and therefore no reason to compose the VP. It would have been sufficient to bracket them all collectively, in the same way in which other assumptions made by other opponents are bracketed.

It is therefore plausible to assume that Nāgārjuna was aiming to show something about the categories that necessitated the examination of each category individually. This, I have argued, is that each of the categories as understood by the Naiyāyika presupposes the existence of *svabhāva* in

39. Dreyfus and McClintock 2003, 7.

some form, that these presuppositions lead to contradictions and that it is possible to develop versions of these logical concepts and techniques that do not make such problematic presuppositions. Nāgārjuna's aim in the VP is to show that the Naiyāyika's understanding of the sixteen categories is not *svabhāva*-free, but that it can be made to be, and that the Nyāya categories can then be employed by Mādhyamikas in their reasoning.

Synopsis of the Text

The purpose of this synopsis is to make navigating the VP easier by providing brief summaries of the key points and arguments expressed in the individual *sūtras*. The compressed nature of this survey necessitates some simplification. The individual summaries are therefore not to be understood as expressing the entire meaning of each passage in a comprehensive manner, but merely serve as pointers to facilitate following the flow of the argument.

Introduction

01 Rejection of the sixteen Nyāya categories for the proponent of emptiness.

Pramāṇa

02 Mutual dependence of epistemic instruments and epistemic objects.
03 Epistemic instruments and objects are not self-established.
04 Dependent existence rules out existence by *svabhāva*.

05 Assuming epistemic instruments and objects leads to an infinite regress.
06 Opponent: There is no regress, since the epistemic instruments are self-illuminating.
07 The light does not illuminate whether or not it is connected with darkness.
08 Contactless illumination is unsatisfactory.
09 Darkness is a mere absence, so light cannot be cleared away.
10 Self-illumination fails, since there is no darkness in the light.

11 Self-illumination fails, as otherwise darkness would be self-concealing.

12 Epistemic instruments and objects cannot have temporal relations.
13 Opponent: In this case the epistemic instruments and objects and their negation cannot have temporal relations either.
14 It is not the case that the negation of the epistemic instruments and objects establishes their existence, as the Nyāya understanding of negation would presuppose.
15 Once the rejection of epistemic instruments and objects has been established in VP 12 there is no room for any further moves such as those described in VP 13 and VP 14.

16 The negation of epistemic instruments and objects is possible because objects that are erroneously assumed to exist can be negated too.

17 Opponent: Epistemic instruments and objects exist because there is correct knowledge.
18 Even if there are epistemic instruments, there might be no epistemic objects.
19 A pot is not an epistemic object.
20 Mental cognitions are no epistemic instruments.

Saṁśaya

21 There is no doubt, since it can neither be directed at conceived nor at non-conceived objects.
22 Opponent: There is doubt because there are indistinct perceptions.
23 There is no doubt because every perception is determinate.

Prayojana

24 There is no purpose, because it can be neither existent nor non-existent.

Dṛṣṭānta

25 Opponent: Examples and purposes exist, because there are examples of things with purposes.

26 Distinguishing between actions with purpose and those without does not avoid the difficulty mentioned in VP 24.
27 The end (*anta*) is not seen (*dṛṣṭa*), because beginning and middle are not seen.

28 There are no concordant examples.
29 There are no discordant examples.
30 There is no slight similarity between example and exemplified.
31 There is no major similarity either.

Siddhānta

32 The end (*anta*) is not established (*siddha*) because beginning and middle are not established.

Avayava

33 There are no parts of a syllogism because no whole exists in the parts taken together.
34 There is also no whole in the parts taken individually.
35 The whole is not the same as its parts because the parts could have inconsistent properties, and because the whole would exist in addition to the parts.

36 The whole does not exist in the three times.

37 Opponent: The whole exists in the aggregate of the parts.
38 The whole cannot be taken to be an aggregative effect of the parts because this would require a separate argument.
39 The whole cannot be taken to be an aggregative effect of the parts because they are not simultaneously present.

40 The parts cannot be established by something else, nor can they be self-established.

41 Thesis and reason are neither identical nor different.
42 Reasons generate an infinite regress.
43 If the first three members of a syllogism cannot exist, the last two cannot exist either.

44 The relation between example, application, and reason is unclear.
45 All other parts apart from the reason are meaningless, as it has exclusive probative force.
46 If another part had such force, the other members would be meaningless.
47 Successful inferences are not sufficient to establish the individual members of a syllogism.

48 Only one part of a syllogism can exist at a given time.
49 Inferences can be successful at the conventional level despite momentariness, as the case of polysyllabic words shows.

Tarka

50 *Tarka* is like doubt, which exists neither for known nor for unknown things.

Nirṇaya

51 There is no determination since neither a thesis nor its negation can be regarded as ultimately true.

Vāda

52 There is no debate, because there are no expressions and referents.
53 Claiming that expressions and their referents are linked by convention does not help.
54 One thing can be denoted by many words.
55 There is no essential connection between a word and what it denotes.
56 Expressions and referents are neither identical nor distinct.

Jalpa and Vitaṇḍā

57 Both are refuted in the same way as *vāda*.

Hetvābhāsa

58 A pseudo-reason is neither similar nor dissimilar to a reason.
59 A pseudo-reason cannot be what is a reason by nature nor what is not a reason by nature.
60 Opponent: Yet there are examples of pseudo-reasons.

61 The examples indicated are not pseudo-reasons.

62 There are no pseudo-reasons because of momentariness.

Viruddha

63 Opponent: There are contradictions because of the disagreement about the existence of pseudo-reasons.
64 The contradictory items do not exist at the same time, so there is no contradiction.

Kālātīta

65 Opponent: Momentariness entails the existence of mistimed reasons, so there are pseudo-reasons.
66 Opponent: Mistimed reasons exist because language commonly refers to time.
67 Past reasons cannot exist in the present.

Chala

68 Opponent: There is an equivocation, because Nāgārjuna only has ultimate existence in mind.

Jāti

69 Because there is no production there is no production of false rejoinders.

Nigrahastāna

70 There is no repetition, because it is neither identical with nor distinct from the original.
71 Grounds of defeat cannot be produced from what is the same or different.
72 There is no defeat in grounds of defeat, as there is no binding in a place of binding.

Conclusion

73 Rejecting the categories does not make it impossible to assert negations.
74 Expressions and referents do not exist.

Part Two

Translation and Commentary

Translation and Commentary

Veneration to Mañjuśrī Kumārabhūta![40]

VP 01 **To dispel the pride of those intent on debate, stemming from their arrogance of skill in reasoning, I shall teach the *Vaidalyaprakaraṇa*.**

All others discussing this have asserted the following as unquestionable:

1. epistemic instruments (*pramāṇa, tshad ma*)
2. epistemic objects (*prameya, gzhal bya*)
3. doubt (*saṁśaya, the tshom*)
4. motive (*prayojana, dgos pa*)
5. example (*dṛṣṭānta, dpe*)
6. established conclusion (*siddhānta, grub pa'i mtha'*)
7. constituent of an argument (*avayava, yan lag*)
8. hypothetical reasoning (*tarka, rtog ge*)
9. determination (*nirṇaya, gtan la phab pa*)
10. debate (*vāda, rtsod pa*)
11. devious debate (*jalpa, brjod pa*)
12. mere refutation (*vitaṇḍā, sun ci phyin du brgal ba*)
13. pseudo-reason (*hetvābhāsa, gtan tshigs ltar snang ba*)
14. equivocation (*chala, tshig dor*)
15. irrelevant rejoinder (*jāti, ltag chod*)
16. grounds of defeat (*nigrahastāna, tshar gcad pa'i gnas rnams*)

Because those asserting emptiness never cling, entities such as 1. epistemic instruments, etc., are not acknowledged.

40. The VS opens with a salutation to Ācārya Ārya Nāgārjuna.

The Title of the Text

The term *vaidalya* is commonly regarded[41] as derived from *vi-√dal*, which Böhtlingk's *Sanskrit-Wörterbuch*[42] translates as "*auseinander bersten, auseinander sprengen; zersprengen, zerreissen, aufreissen,*" indicating that this treatise is concerned with something being blown apart or with blowing or tearing something apart.[43]

The Tibetan translation renders this as *zhib mo rnam par 'thag pa*, where *rnam par* corresponds to the Sanskrit *upasargaḥ* "*vi*" ("apart," "asunder"),[44] the expression *rnam par 'thag pa* thereby mirroring closely the Sanskrit *vi-√dal*.[45] *Zhib mo* usually translates the Sanskrit *sūkṣma* ("fine," "subtle"), adding extra semantic information on the end-product of the destructive process referred to.[46]

The most obvious candidate for what is being blown apart in this context is the list of the sixteen Nyāya categories.[47] Yet it is possible that the term *vaidalya* is here used in a wider meaning.[48] The last member of the Theravāda nine-fold classification of the Buddha's teaching[49] is referred to by the Pali term *vedalla* (corresponding to the Sanskrit *vaidalya*). This is in

41. Kajiyama 1974, 425; Tola and Dragonetti 1995a, 4; Pind 2001, 150.

42. Böhtlingk 1879–89, 3, 73.

43. Chandrakīrti refers to the text as *Vidala* (de Jong 1962, 51; Pind 2001, 150).

44. *Aṣṭādhyāyī* 1.4.58–59 (Jäschke 1998, 314 s.v.).

45. The Tibetan title is sometimes translated into English as "The Treatise Called 'The Finely Woven'" (see, e.g., Cozort 1998, 159). This is a mistake. While the Tibetan *'thag pa* can indeed mean "to weave" or "to knit" (Negi 2005, vol. 5, 2141), it is here used to render an expression derived from the Sanskrit root *√dal*.

46. It might be worthwhile to point out that the object of the critique in the VP is described as *rigs pa phra ba* = *Nyāyasūkṣma* (which can be rendered as "subtle Nyāya" or "little Nyāya" [see Lindtner 1982, 250n194; Pind 2001, 157–60]) in verse 53. So perhaps the phrase *zhib mo rnam par 'thag pa* was not just intended to refer to the "tearing apart into fine pieces" of the system of sixteen categories, but as indicating the "tearing apart of the fine or subtle (Nyāya)." Bhavya (*Madhyamakaratnapradīpa* [D 3854:264b]) refers to the text simply as *rnam par 'thag pa*.

47. Pind 2001, 150.

48. For further etymological remarks, see Kajiyama 1965, 131–33. A detailed discussion is in Skilling 2013.

49. *navaṇga-satthu-sāsana*. See Dhammajoti 2007, 4.

turn equated with the term *vaipulya*, and Saṁghabhadra comments on this as follows:

> Vaipulya refers to the extensive analytical clarification of *dharma*s by means of logical reasoning (正理, **yukti*, **Nyāya*); for, all *dharma*s have numerous natures and characteristics that cannot be analytically clarified without extensive discussion. It is also known as extensive bursting (廣破, *vaidalya* < *vi* + √*dal*), for this extensive discussion is capable of bursting the extremely strong darkness of nescience (*ajñāna*).[50]

In this wider sense, what is being torn to pieces in this treatise is not just the specific philosophical system of an opponent, but ignorance, one of the three poisons (*triviṣa*) more generally.

It is interesting to note that Asaṅga in the *Abhidharmasamuccaya* considers the *vaidalya/vaipulya* heading to comprise the Bodhisattvapiṭaka.[51] A key teaching of the texts subsumed under this heading is the emptiness of all phenomena;[52] he notes that these texts are referred to by the former term because they crush all obstacles.[53] In his *Bhāṣya*

50. T 29, 595a–b. The translation follows Dhammajoti 2007, 5.

51. Rahula and Boin-Webb (2000, 180): "What is a development (*vaipulya*)? It consists of accounts contained in the Canon of the Bodhisattvas (*bodhisattvapiṭaka*). Whatever is called *vaipulya* is also called *vaidalya* or *vaitulya*. Why is it called *vaipulya*? Because it is the basis of the welfare and happiness of all beings, and because it is the supreme and profound teaching. Why is it called *vaidalya*? Because it shatters (*vidalana*) all impediments (*sarvāvaraṇa*)." *shin tu rgyas pa'i sde (*vaipulya) gang zhe na | gang byang chub sems dpa'i sde snod dang ldan pa'o (*bodhisattvapiṭakapratisaṁyukta) | shin tu rgyas pa ji lta ba de bzhin du rnam par 'thag pa (*vaidalya) dang mtshungs bral (*vaitulya) yang de bzhin no | ci'i phyir shin tu rgyas pa (*vaipulya) zhes bya zhe na | sems can thams cad la phan pa dang bde ba'i gnas yin pa dang | rgyas pa dang | rgya che ba dang | zab pa'i rnam par chos bstan pa'i phyir ro | ci'i phyir rnam par 'thag pa (*vaidalya) zhes bya zhe na | sgrib pa (*āvaraṇa) thams cad rnam par 'thag pa'i (*vi-dal) phyir ro* (D 101b1–3; P 120b2–4).

52. Rahula and Boin-Webb 2000, 192.

53. *sarvāvaraṇavidalanataḥ*. See Pradhan 1975, 79; Rahula and Boin-Webb 2000, 180. The same point is made in Vasubandhu's *Vyākhyāyukti*: "According to another school of thought, [the Mahāyāna is called] *rnam par 'joms pa'i gtsug phud kyi sde* and *rnam par 'joms pa chen po'i sde*, because it destroys (**vi-dal*) defilements (**kleśa*) with its impression (**vāsanā*)." *sde pa gzhan dag las ni rnam par 'joms pa'i gtsug phud kyi sde dang | rnam par 'joms pa chen po'i sde ste | de ni bag chags dang bcas pa'i nyon mongs pa rnam par 'joms pa'i phyir ro* (D 83a3–83b3; P 97b4–98a5).

Sthiramati notes that the term *vaidalya* is in fact a synonym for the Mahāyāna.[54]

It is therefore evident that the destruction referred to by the title of this "Treatise on Vaidalya" can be understood on a variety of levels: as the destruction of the Nyāya system of epistemology and logic as described in the set of sixteen categories, as the destruction of the darkness of ignorance, and specifically also as its destruction by the realization of both the emptiness of persons as well as the emptiness of phenomena, which is a specific characteristic of the Bodhisattva vehicle.[55]

The Nyāya Opponent

It is interesting that in a text so obviously concerned with Nyāya as the VP the Naiyāyikas are not addressed by name: the term *rigs pa can pa* is not used in the VP. Instead, Nāgārjuna refers to his opponents by the term "those intent on debate" (*rtsod par mngon 'dod pa*, **tarkajñānābhimāna*), a much wider expression that does not just subsume the Naiyāyikas but refers to a group of "the others" (*gzhan dag*) that is put in opposition to "those asserting emptiness" (*stong pa nyid du smra ba*, **śūnyatāvādin*).

The system of Nyāya familiar to Nāgārjuna is its earliest phase of development and should be distinguished from the system emerging as Nyāya developed as a philosophical school.[56] The early system was very much a debate manual (*vāda-śāstra*), a set of logical categories, rules of debate and classification of debate situations. Such manuals were widespread, and those associated with different philosophical schools were likely to have shown considerable overlap.[57] Nāgārjuna's criticism is directed against the

54. Tatia (1976, 96:3): *vaipulyaṁ vaidalyaṁ vaitulyam ity ete mahāyānasya paryāyāḥ*. Skilling (2013, 84) uses the term "Vaidalya movement" "for an early period of Indian Buddhism, for the Mahāyāna *avant la lettre*."

55. Asaṅga notes that there is a specific penetration (*prativedha-viśeṣa*) had by the Bodhisattvas, glossed as the realization of not just the emptiness of persons (*pudgalanairātmya*) but also of the emptiness of phenomena (*dharmanairātmya*) (Rahula and Boin-Webb 2000, 220n82).

56. Matilal (1977, 77): "From the Vāda rules they eventually developed a full-fledged philosophic system by adding the doctrine of the soul, of final release, as well as a doctrine of *pramāṇas* (means of knowledge)."

57. Matilal (1977, 76): "Several *vāda*-categories were probably the common property of almost all philosophical schools of ancient India." Tucci (1981, xxvi): "We cannot in fact,

larger group of thinkers who adopt the Nyāya framework (or something very much like it) in their philosophical discussions, not simply against members of a specific school of Classical Indian philosophy. It is therefore useful to regard the VP not simply as a document of an attack of one ancient Indian system of thought by another one, but as concerned with a much wider philosophical agenda, namely that of refuting specific philosophical assumptions that are clearly present in the thoughts of the Naiyāyikas as well as in the thoughts of those who operate in the Nyāya conceptual framework.

Nāgārjuna's Motivation for Composing the VP

Nāgārjuna specifically mentions as his motivation in composing the text the desire to dispel the pride (*nga rgyal*, **ahaṁkāra*, **adhimāna*) of his opponents. While not as fundamental as the three poisons (*triviṣa*, *dug gsum*), pride is one of the six root afflictions (*rtsa nyon*, *mūlakleṣa*).[58] In the *Ratnāvalī* Nāgārjuna lists seven different kinds of pride:[59] the pride of selfhood (*māna*, *bdag nyid nga rgyal*), exceeding pride (*atimāna*, *lhag pa'i nga rgyal*), pride beyond pride (*mānātimāna*, *nga rgyal las kyang nga rgyal*), pride of thinking I (*asmimāna*, *nga'o snyam pa'i nga rgyal*), blatant pride (*abhimāna*, *mngon pa'i nga rgyal*), erroneous pride (*mithyāmāna*, *log pa'i nga rgyal*), and the pride of inferiority (*ūnamāna*, *dman pa'i nga rgyal*).[60] It is now tempting to speculate which of these, if any, Nāgārjuna is referring to in this stanza. The second pride, "exceeding pride," comes closest to our everyday understanding, and Nāgārjuna spells it out as:

---

deny that when any new development took place in the elaboration of the *vāda*-rules the change must have worked almost contemporaneously in all schools, because no discussion is possible without a fundamental agreement as regards the chief elements of the discussion itself. The same *vāda*-rules must have been accepted and followed by the two disputants."

58. Together with desire (*rāga*, *'dod chags*), anger (*pratigha*, *khong khro*), ignorance (*avidyā*, *ma rig pa*), doubt (*vicikitsa*, *the tshom*), and wrong views (*kliṣṭadṛṣṭi*, *lta ba nyon mongs can*).

59. The same types are distinguished in Vasubandhu's *bhāṣya* on *Abhidharmakośa* 5.10 (Poussin and Pruden 1988–90, 784–85).

60. RĀ 5:7–12; Hahn 1982, 134–37.

> Boasting that one is equal to those
> Who by some good quality are superior to oneself
> Is called exceeding pride.[61]

The fourth pride, the "pride of thinking I," certainly stands out, insofar as it is not a perspective on the direct comparison of one's own and others' achievements, but rather a wrong view regarded by Buddhists to lie at the very core of cyclic existence. Nāgārjuna explains it as follows:

> Conceiving an I through obscuration
> In the five empty [aggregates],
> Which are called the appropriation,
> Is said to be the pride of thinking I.[62]

Depending on the kind of pride we take Nāgārjuna to be referring to here, we can understand his aim of dispelling the pride of his opponents on different levels. On the ethical level pointing out their mistake in regarding the Nyāya categories as "unquestionable" (*gdon mi za ba*) removes their harmful tendency of regarding themselves as equal to their superiors and is thereby ultimately conducive to removing their suffering. On the metaphysical level the pride to be dispelled by the VP can be regarded as the wrong view in a substantial self of persons (and, by extension, in a substantial self of phenomena) that is the fundamental mistake underlying their wrong understanding of the Nyāya categories.

The Structure of the Sixteen Categories

The sixteen categories mentioned in the commentary on VP 01 are of course the sixteen categories listed in the first verse of the *Nyāyasūtra* (NS). A question that arises immediately is whether we can make out any underlying structure in this list. On the face of it the list seems to contain a

61. *yo 'dhamas tulyam ātmānaṁ viśiṣṭād abhimanyate | so 'timāno, chos gang bdag nyid khyad 'phags dang | mnyam par rlom pa gang yin de | lhag pa'i nga rgyal khyad* (RĀ 5.8; Hahn 1982, 134–35).

62. *yad upādānasaṁjñeṣu skandheṣv eteṣu pañcasu | mohād aham iti grāhaḥ so 'smimāna udāhṛtaḥ, nye bar len pa zhes bya ba | lnga po stong pa de dag la | rmongs bas nga snyam 'dzin pa gang | de ni nga'o snyam par bshad* (RĀ 5.10; Hahn 1982, 134–35).

variety of diverse items, belonging to the theory of knowledge (1. epistemic instruments), logic (7. constituents of an argument), and rhetoric (10. debate). It is therefore not immediately clear what the list of the sixteen categories is a list of, and whether it is anything more than the table of contents of the NS.[63]

However, if we look at the list of categories in a bit more detail, it becomes apparent that there is a noticeable division between an earlier part, consisting of categories (1) epistemic instruments to (9) determination, which deals with concepts necessary in constructing an argument, while the later part, from (10) onward, deals primarily with the notions that become relevant in the debate with an opponent.[64]

This division can be explained by the fact that we first have to have established a conclusion by some kind of argumentative process before we can begin pitching our conclusion against that of an opponent in the course of the debate. The list of the sixteen categories can therefore be understood as following the temporal structure of the successive steps in a philosophical discussion from its very beginning to the end.[65]

A discussion of any matter begins with our epistemic access to the world by means of some epistemic instruments (1).

63. See, e.g., Randle (1930, 47n2), who believes that the Nyāya categories "are in no sense 'categories', but rather a list of contents of the *śāstra*."

64. See Bernard (1981, 24): "The first nine [categories] deal more strictly with logic, while the last seven [from *vāda* onward] have the function of preventing and destroying error." See also Chatterjee (2011, 116): "All fourteen categories starting with doubt [which is the third category] relate to the process of effective argumentation and rules of debate; the first seven constitute the 'prior stage,' and the last seven, beginning with debate, constitute the 'posterior stage' of the Nyāya method. That is, an argument, according to Nyāya, starts with an initial doubt and ends with the establishment of a hypothesis by evidence, having demolished all the objections raised by the opponents." This bipartite division, consisting of an analysis of debate terms followed by a discussion of objections and grounds of defeat, is familiar from a variety of other ancient Indian debate manuals. See Oberhammer 1963–64, 70–71; and Frauwallner 1957, 106–7. An alternative division makes the cut after (2) epistemic objects, dividing the list into an epistemological part of two categories and a logical part of fourteen categories. Vātsyāyana notes that in this case an opponent could regard the second part as strictly redundant, given that it is wholly included under (2) epistemic objects (Śāstrī 1998, 5:4–8). The Naiyāyika could reply that such an enumeration allows us to specify which particular ones among the many objects of knowledge the NS is concerned with.

65. See Vidyabhusana 1971, 52.

These instruments then supply us with some items of knowledge, namely the epistemic objects (2).

More specifically they supply the proponent with knowledge of the thesis he sets out to establish. With the third category the second participant in the debate, the opponent, enters the picture; he raises a doubt about the thesis the proponent has just put forward (3). This doubt is a basic condition for the employment of reasoning. We do not reason about objects that are wholly unknown (since we would not know what to reason about) nor about those that are known for certain (for there would be nothing to reason about). Only in cases where an object is known and there are two distinct opinions about it, those of the proponent and of the opponent, is there room for a debate.

In order to bring about a discussion, the mere doubt that something may or may not be so is not sufficient; the opponent must have the clear motive of refuting the proponent by raising this doubt, and the proponent's subsequent replies must be motivated by a desire to defend his claim against the opponent's challenge (4).

The proponent then mentions an example, a parallel case that is going to support his thesis (5).[66] The examples that the proponent (as well as the opponent) raise in order to support their conflicting claims are illustrations of more general established conclusions (6) that represent their respective views.[67] The proponent now sets out to demonstrate this established conclusion or thesis by means of the syllogism comprising five constituents (7).

Hypothetical reasoning (8) can now be employed to draw out the implications of the proponent's thesis (just established by a syllogism) and the opponent's denial of this.[68]

66. Vātsyāyana notes in his commentary on NS 1.1.1 that the example "is the basis of the application of reasoning (*nyāya*). Rejecting the opponent's position is through contradiction with the example, one's own position is to be established through corroboration by the example." *tadāśrayā ca nyāyapravṛttiḥ | dṛṣṭāntavirodhena ca parapakṣapratiṣedho vacanīyo bhavati dṛṣṭāntasamādhinā ca svapakṣaḥ sādhanīyo bhavati* (Śāstrī 1998, 8:3–4).

67. See Vātsyāyana's comment on NS 1.1.1: "debate (*vāda*), tricky debate (*jalpa*), and destructive debate (*vitaṇḍā*) are only employed when there is a difference between positions, not otherwise," *siddhāntabhedeṣu vādajalpavitaṇḍāḥ pravartante nāto 'nyatheti*, (Śāstrī 1998, 9:2).

68. See Uddyotakara's *Vārttika* on NS 1.1.40: "How again does it [*tarka*] bring about true cognition [even though it is itself devoid of true cognition]? Through the nondistinction

Vātsyāyana[69] mentions as an example a case where it is unclear whether the cause of some effect is permanent, impermanent, or whether its production is accidental. *Tarka* can then be used to draw out implications of each possibility with respect to specific issues. If, for example, we examine the three possibilities with respect to the possibility of the effect itself going out of existence, it becomes clear that this is possible if the cause is impermanent, but not if it is permanent or if there is no cause at all (in the first case the cause will keep producing the effect, and in the second case the effect will keep being produced, because the cause was not necessary for its production in the first place). Having thus drawn out the consequences of the different possibilities by means of hypothetical reasoning, we still don't know which of the three is right, but assuming the presence of some other information (e.g., if we have independent reason to believe that each effect will pass out of existence at some time), we may be able to select one possibility as the best one.

As a result of this deliberation of the proponent's thesis and its denial, it—hopefully—becomes clear that the proponent's theory is better supported and should be accepted as the correct conclusion (9).[70]

The opponent can now respond by asserting the negation of the proponent's thesis, thereby starting a debate. The list of sixteen categories distinguishes three different kinds of exchanges of argument: debate (*vāda*) (10), which is not undertaken with the desire for victory, but only to determine the truth about some disputed matter; devious debate (*jalpa*) (11), where

---

of the subject of an epistemic instrument. By this [*tarka*] one differentiates the subject of an epistemic instrument saying 'this is the right meaning.' The epistemic instruments brought forward understand the object investigated by *tarka* in the way it is." Dvivedin 1986, 144:1–4: *kathaṁ punar ayaṁ tattvajñānārthaṁ bhavati pramāṇa-viṣaya-avivecanāt pramāṇaviṣayam anena vivinakti ayamartho yukta iti pramāṇāni pravartamānāni tarka-viviktamarthaṁ tathābhūtamavagacchantīti.*

69. Śāstrī 1998, 10.

70. See Vātsyāyana's comment on NS 1.1.41: "The two, *sādhana* ['establishing (one's own position)'] and *upālambha* ['refuting (the opponent's position)'] are based upon thesis and counter-thesis, and because of the connection this interlinked pair is called 'thesis and counter-thesis.' Of these, one is necessarily to be rejected, and one is necessarily to be accepted. The ascertainment of the meaning of the accepted one is the determination." *sthāpanā sādhanam pratiṣedha upālambhaḥ | tau sādhanopālambhau pakṣapratipakṣāśrayau vyatiṣaktāv anubandhena pravartamānau pakṣapratipakṣāv ity ucyete | tayor anyatarasya nivṛttir ekatarasyāvasthānam avaśyambhāvi, yasyāvasthānaṁ tasyārthāvadhāraṇaṁ nirṇayaḥ.* (Śāstrī 1998, 65:9–66:1)

desire for victory is the main incentive for both parties; and mere refutation (*vitaṇḍā*) (12), where the aim is only to prove the opponent wrong, without attempting to prove one's own position. Only a debate ends with the determination (*nirṇaya*) (9) of a true conclusion; devious debates and mere refutations are over as soon as the opponent has nothing left to say.[71]

Primarily in the course of devious debates and mere refutations, a variety of rhetorico-logical means (11–15) are likely to be employed. Given that these two latter types of debate exclusively aim at defeating the opponent rather than at a determination of the truth, such sophistical maneuvers can lead to the desired goal. Yet it is important that even those only interested in debate (*vāda*) are aware of them, to prevent them from unwittingly committing such fallacies themselves.

If the defeat of the opponent is the aim, it is of course necessary to have some set of criteria when the opponent has been defeated. These are subsumed under the last of the sixteen categories, grounds of defeat (*nigrahastānāni*).

The Focus of the Commentary

We can get a good first idea of which categories among the sixteen Nāgārjuna considered to be particularly interesting by having a look at how many verses of the VP comment on each category. The distribution looks like this:

01/02: *******************

03: ***

04: *

05: *******

06: *

07: *****************

71. We may compare this situation to an architecture competition where the participants can have one or both of two motives: producing the best building and winning the competition. The debate corresponds to a competition where each participant genuinely wants to produce the best building for the empty space. In the second case (corresponding to the devious debate), one might not even be convinced oneself of the merits of the design proposed, but might think that the judges will like it, and so it will allow one to win the competition. In the last case (corresponding to mere refutation), one does not want to build anything oneself at all; one's only purpose is to keep the other participants from winning.

08: *
09: *
10: *****
11/12: *
13: **********
14: *
15: *
16: ***

It is evident that Nāgārjuna puts particular emphasis on the theory of knowledge; categories 1 (epistemic objects) and 2 (epistemic instruments) receive the greatest number of individual verses discussing them. Leaving aside these two categories, a further focus of interest is the earlier part of the list (up to and including category 10, debate), which discusses the various notions employed in constructing an argument. Categories 5 (example), 7 (constituents of an argument), and 10 (debate) receive particular attention. By comparison, the latter half of the list (from category 11 onward) dealing with the defense of a thesis in a debate with an opponent, is discussed in less detail; not more than a quarter of the verses in the VP deal with this portion of the list of the sixteen categories.

Epistemic instruments and epistemic objects are also discussed in considerable detail in Nāgārjuna's VV. In fact there is some overlap between the discussions in the two texts, especially in the treatment of the example of the self-illumination of light presented in VP 6–11 and VV 34–39. Given the amount of discussion this epistemological topic receives in two treatises of the Yukti corpus, it was evidently of great theoretical interest to Nāgārjuna. It is tempting to speculate what motivated the comparatively greater emphasis put by the commentary on the earlier logic part of the list of Nyāya categories, as opposed to the later debate part.

Nāgārjuna notes that those asserting emptiness do not acknowledge the sixteen Nyāya categories, let alone accept them as "unquestionable" (*gdon mi za ba*). The reason for this is that, unlike the opponent, the adherents of emptiness are free from clinging (*zhen pa*, *sneha*). Tola and Dragonetti[72] read this as referring to clinging to a specific thesis or view, which the

72. Tola and Dragonetti 1995a, 179n5.

Mādhyamika rejects.[73] This is very reasonable, especially if we regard this absence of a thesis or view as a description of the Prāsaṅgika methodology of only deriving a contradiction from the opponent's assertions, without putting forward a positive thesis oneself.[74] For it appears that if one did defend such a thesis of one's own, then one would have to take the epistemological and logical preconditions described in the list of the sixteen categories that are employed in the proof of this thesis as "unquestionable." For if our epistemological and logical standards are not secure, how could we put trust in philosophical results we arrive at by basing ourselves on such standards? Yet according to the Prāsaṅgika methodology, all that is required is that the opponent accepts these epistemological and logical tools, so that a contradiction can be derived from the assumptions the opponent himself accepts. There is no need for the Prāsaṅgika to make these assumptions his own.

Nevertheless, there is also some justification for taking the freedom from clinging in a somewhat wider sense, since the clinging to specific views is just one manifestation of the clinging to a substance or *svabhāva* mistakenly projected onto objects.[75] Thus the idea would be that the proponents of emptiness do not acknowledge the Nyāya categories because of their specific substantialist presuppositions. By adopting the epistemological and logical framework embedded in the sixteen categories, the Naiyāyika, as well as those who accept this framework as a satisfactory theory of cognition, reasoning, and debate, commit themselves to the existence of *svabhāva*, an assumption that, as Nāgārjuna sets out to show in the remainder of this work, leads to a variety of contradictions.

⌘ In this respect it has to be remarked:

VP 02 **The epistemic instrument and epistemic object are both interlinked.**

73. See, e.g., YṢ 50; VP 29; PP on MMK 1:3 (Poussin 1903–13, 23, line 3); MĀ 6:119. Compare also *Samādhirājasūtra* 19:33 (Régamey 1990, 48, 81). In connection with the reference to pride in VP 01, it is interesting to note that this passage links attachment to views (whether they are true or false) with the defilement of arrogant pride (*mada-māna*).

74. See Poussin 1903–13, 23n3; Huntington 2003, 79.

75. See Chandrakīrti's commentary on YṢ 50 (Loizzo 2007, 201, 350).

Here the epistemic instrument and epistemic object are both seen as interlinked. Because if the epistemic object exists, the epistemic instrument becomes that very epistemic instrument, and also, if the epistemic instrument exists, the epistemic object becomes that very epistemic object. The epistemic instrument is established from the epistemic object, and the epistemic object is also established from the epistemic instrument. Therefore, the epistemic instrument becomes the epistemic object's epistemic object, and the epistemic object also becomes the epistemic instrument's epistemic instrument. Because of this, they obtain their own nature (*bdag nyid, ātma-bhāva*) in dependence on one another. Therefore, the epistemic instrument also becomes both, the epistemic object also becomes both, and because of this both are interlinked.

In this respect, it has to be remarked:

VP 02 The epistemic instrument and epistemic object are both interlinked.

Nāgārjuna begins his discussion of the first two Nyāya categories, epistemic instruments and epistemic objects, by pointing out their mutual dependence.[76]

Such dependence is far from obvious, since at least *prima facie* these two categories involve very different kinds of things. One contains the means by which we gain knowledge of the world, the instruments by which objects are represented in our mind, and the other the objects themselves, the furniture of the world that is the subject-matter about which information is conveyed to us via the instruments. Drawing an analogy from the case of carpentry, if we put all the instruments (saw, hammer, screwdriver, etc.) into one group, and all the objects operated

76. Tola and Dragonetti (1995, 180n1) gloss the term *'dres*—here translated as "interlinked"—as "being the same thing," reading Nāgārjuna's argument here as an early form of the *sahopalambha-niyama* argument. This argument, which sets out to show that cognition and cognized object are one because they always occur together, was regarded by the Buddhist's Brahmanical opponents as one of the key arguments used by Yogāchārins to establish the nonexistence of external objects (Taber 2010). On this argument, see Chatterjee 1975; Iwata 1991; Arnold 2010; and Chakrabarti 1990. I am not convinced, however, that in this passage Nāgārjuna is trying to make the point that everything is mental in nature.

upon (wood, nails, screws, etc.) into another, we do not end up with two groups depending on each other. Both the tools of the trade as well as the raw materials seem to exist quite separately from each other.

> *Here the epistemic instrument and epistemic object are both seen as interlinked. Because if the epistemic object exists, the epistemic instrument becomes that very epistemic instrument; and also, if the epistemic instrument exists, the epistemic object becomes that very epistemic object.*

Yet as the instruments of carpentry only become instruments by there being some raw materials they can operate on, and as the raw materials only become raw materials fit for a certain kind of assembly (rather than random chunks of matter), if there are instruments that can so assemble them, the epistemic instruments and objects bring each other into existence. Only if there is something we can have epistemic access to does it make sense to speak of epistemic instruments that make such access possible, and only if there are ways of epistemically connecting with the world could we have objects of knowledge (rather than, e.g., noumenal objects entirely beyond our cognitive powers).

> *The epistemic instrument is established from the epistemic object, and the epistemic object is also established from the epistemic instrument. Therefore, the epistemic instrument becomes the epistemic object's epistemic object, and the epistemic object also becomes the epistemic instrument's epistemic instrument.*

In our usual understanding the epistemic instruments function as a means that establishes the knowledge of epistemic objects, which are the things established. But given that Nāgārjuna has just argued that each requires the other for being what it is, the established-establisher relationship also runs the other way round: not only do we need the instrument to bring about the object, we also need the object to bring about the instrument.[77] The second sentence of this passage becomes clearer if we keep the synonymy of "epistemic object" and "established," as well as of

77. This "transposition" (*vyatyaya*) of the roles of epistemic instruments and epistemic objects is also discussed by Nāgārjuna in VV 45 (see Westerhoff 2010, 84).

"epistemic instrument" and "establisher" in mind and make some substitutions accordingly. The result then reads as follows: "Therefore the epistemic instrument becomes the epistemic object's established, and the epistemic object also becomes the epistemic instrument's establisher."

> *Because of this, they obtain their own nature (bdag nyid, ātma-bhāva) in dependence on one another. Therefore, the epistemic instrument also becomes both, the epistemic object also becomes both, and because of this both are interlinked.*

It is quite clear that up to this passage Nāgārjuna has argued for the notional mutual dependence of epistemic instruments and epistemic objects, that is, for the idea that each depends on the other for *being described* in the way they are. In his *Bhāṣya* on NS 2.1.16 Vātsyāyana points out that in the case of any one entity, such as a piece of gold, its description as either epistemic object or epistemic instrument is dependent on our interests and concerns. If we use a pair of scales to determine the weight of a piece of gold, the piece of gold is to be described as an epistemic object, but if we use it in order to determine the weight of something else the piece of gold becomes part of the balance and is now an epistemic instrument.[78]

An object might even occupy roles that merit descriptions in these different terms at the same time. The light of the lamp is an epistemic instrument if it allows us to see something else, but it is also an epistemic object since it makes itself visible in the process of illumination.[79]

78. "The measuring instrument is an epistemic instrument when it gives knowledge of correct weight. The objects of knowledge, in this case, are gold and so forth which have weight. If, however, the accuracy of another measuring instrument is determined by gold and so forth then for the knowledge of the other measuring instrument, gold and so forth are the epistemic instruments and the other measuring instrument is the epistemic object." *gurutvaparimāṇjñānasādhanaṁ tulā pramāṇaṁ | jñānaviṣayo gurudravyaṁ suvarṇādi prameyam | yadā ca suvarṇādinā tulāntaraṁ vyavasthāpyate tadā tulāntarapratipattau suvarṇādi pramāṇaṁ tulāntaraṁ prameyamiti* (Śāstrī 1998, 105:3–5).

79. "Just as the light of the light, after being itself perceived, becomes instrumental to the perception of other visible objects and attains the status of both the object as well as the cause of visual perception, so also something, in spite of being an object of knowledge, acquires the status of both an epistemic instrument as well as that of an epistemic object by virtue of its producing knowledge." *yathā eva dṛśyaḥ san pradīpaprakāśo dṛśyāntarāṇāṁ*

Interpreting the claim Nāgārjuna makes now leaves us with two interpretative options, depending on how the phrase *phan tshun ltos nas bdag nyid thob par 'gyur* is construed. The stronger reading is suggested by Tola and Dragonetti,[80] who translate this passage as:

> thereby (only) through (this) mutual relation of dependence they come into existence,

construing *bdag nyid thob pa* as *ātma-lābha*, "obtaining existence."[81]

Read in this way this claim asserts that epistemic instruments and objects are *existentially* dependent on one another, and that if one did not exist the other would not exist either.[82]

We can certainly make a case for this stronger existential dependence of the epistemic instruments on the epistemic objects. These epistemic raw materials, the objects of knowledge, comprise everything that can be known, and since we can know the epistemic instruments, they also include the epistemic instruments.[83] This implies that the epistemic instruments depend for their existence on the epistemic objects, since they, as a subset, could not exist without the superset of epistemic objects existing. A different way of arguing for the same conclusion is to point out that if we understand an epistemic instrument as being directed at something that it makes known (namely the epistemic object), it is hard to see how it could exist without being directed at anything. An aboutness without something it is about appears to be a genuine impossibility.

The reverse dependence of epistemic objects on epistemic instruments is somewhat more difficult to make sense of. Certainly, if there were no

---

darśanaheturiti dṛśyadarśanavyavasthāṁ labhate evaṁ prameyaṁ sat kiṁcidarthajātam-upalabdhihetutvāt pramāṇaprameyavyavasthāṁ labhate (Śāstrī 1998, 108:6–8).

80. Tola and Dragonetti 1995a, 58.

81. Tola and Dragonetti 1995a, 180n3.

82. It is instructive to compare verse 45 and the following ones of the VV. In verse 45 Nāgārjuna mentions exactly the transposition of epistemic instruments and objects that we have just encountered in the gold/balance example. But he then continues (in verses 46–50) by arguing that this entails not just a conclusion about how we can describe epistemic instruments and objects, but results in the stronger ontological claim that neither can be established by their own nature. For some comments on this passage see Westerhoff 2010, 84–90.

83. As well as all of the fifteen remaining categories (Śāstrī 1998, 5:4–8).

epistemic instruments, and thereby no epistemic agents who would have any knowledge of the world, the objects of knowledge would not be called "epistemic objects."[84] But the epistemic objects that are not also epistemic instruments would still be there, and so the dependence in this case would be mere notional dependence, dependence for description, rather than existential dependence.

Yet it appears as if Nāgārjuna wants to say that epistemic instruments and objects come into existence in dependence on one another. In fact, he makes the same point in verse 10 of the *Lokātītastava*:

> There is no object of knowledge unless it is being known. Consciousness does not exist without it. Therefore, you have said that knowledge and its object do not exist substantially.[85]

There is thus no consciousness without an object but, more importantly for present purposes, also no object of knowledge without some epistemic instrument accessing it. What can be the argument for this stronger claim about the dependence of the existence of the epistemic objects on that of the epistemic instruments?

To regard epistemic objects as existentially independent from epistemic instruments would imply that there is a way to make sense of a world existing independently of our epistemic access to it, that there is a way "things are anyway" whether or not minds try to form representations of these. Yet this view of the world is precisely what is denied by the Mādhyamika.

Nāgārjuna points out in the *Acintyastava*:

84. As Jha (1984, vol. 2, 609) remarks on NS 2.1.10: "Though the existence of a thing, by itself, does not depend upon *pramāṇa*s, yet its existence *as object of cognition*, as *prameya*, depends entirely upon the operation of the *pramāṇa*s; a thing cannot be the *object of cognition* until that cognition has come about, and the cognition can come about only by the *Instruments of Cognition*." Compare also Chatthopadyaya and Gangopadyaya (1967–76, vol. 2, 23): "It may be argued that an object as object may exist even before it becomes an object of valid knowledge. To this Vācaspati answers that the real point of the objection (in NS 2.1.10) is that though the existence of an object as object may be independent of the *pramāṇa*, its status as an object of valid knowledge is determined by a *pramāṇa*, and, therefore, *pramāṇa* cannot be posterior to an object as an object of valid knowledge."

85. *ajñāyamānaṁ na jñeyaṁ vijñānaṁ tad vinā na ca | tasmāt svabhāvato na sto jñānajñeye tvam ūcivān* (Lindtner 1982, 132).

> You have said clearly that the entire world is a mere name. Nothing expressible is to be found apart from the expressed. Therefore you have said that all things are merely conceptual constructions.[86]

Since conceptual construction involves epistemic access to whatever is constructed, if there is no such access, there is no conceptual construction. But if everything is conceptually constructed,[87] everything epistemically inaccessible must be nonexistent, so that there cannot be a noumenal world lying wholly out of reach of our epistemic powers.

However, a second, weaker reading, following the translation we have adopted here ("*Because of this, they obtain their own nature in dependence on one another*") may also be able to deliver all we want. Understood in this way, Nāgārjuna continues to stress the notional dependence of epistemic instruments and objects, pointing out that their respective own natures (*bdag nyid*, *ātma-bhāva*), rather than their existence, depend on one another. What this means is that neither the property of being an epistemic instrument nor that of being an epistemic object could exist intrinsically, by *svabhāva*. For if something bears a nature all on its own, it could potentially do so without there being anything else around. But it is hard to conceive how something could be an epistemic instrument if there were not anything it could reveal to us, or how something could be an epistemic object without there being means of epistemic access to it. The properties of being an epistemic instrument and being an epistemic object are dispositions: something is such an instrument if, given the right circumstances, it can reveal an object, and something is such an object if, given the right circumstances, it can be so revealed. As such dispositional properties essentially involve something outside of the object, they therefore cannot be intrinsic properties that the object possesses all on its own. For this reason even the weaker reading is sufficient to make the point

86. 35–36a: *nāmamātraṁ jagat sarvam ity uccair bhāṣitaṁ tvayā | abhidānāt pṛthag-bhūtam abhidheyaṁ na vidyate || kalpanāmātraṁ ity asmāt sarvadharmāḥ prakāśitāḥ* (Lindtner 1982, 152–53).

87. What is the Mādhyamika's argument for this? One consideration that can be brought in as support at this point is the idea that being causally produced excludes being intrinsically existent, because causal relations involve essential reference to conceptualization. See Siderits 2004 for further discussion.

Nāgārjuna wants to make here, namely that neither epistemic instruments nor epistemic objects exist by *svabhāva*.

⌘ Therefore:

VP 03 **They are not self-established.**

If the epistemic instrument and epistemic object were established by their own nature, they would become epistemic instrument and epistemic object. However, because they are established as dependent, they are mutually produced—this is the meaning. Therefore they are not self-established. ⌘ ⌘

If epistemic instruments and epistemic objects are what they are because of their own nature, then each would be what it is independently of what is going on around it. Yet, as VP 02 sets out to argue, an epistemic instrument can only exist if there is an object it can cognize, and an epistemic object can only exist if there are instruments to cognize it, so it is not the case that each is what it is independent of what is going on around it, as each is the ground of the other's existence. For this reason, neither of them is established by its own nature.

This matter is discussed in greater detail by Nāgārjuna in verses 42–51 of the VV.[88] The point at issue here is whether it makes sense to speak of an objective division of the world into a set of things to be known and a set of things knowing them. This combined epistemological and ontological issue is closely connected with the Madhyamaka rejection of substantially existent entities, i.e., entities existing by *svabhāva*. The Madhyamaka arguments for emptiness that set out to refute the existence of such entities are completely general, that is, if they are successful they also apply to the central concepts of epistemology, such as epistemic instruments and epistemic objects. One important consequence of this is that the Madhyamaka epistemology is best construed as coherentist, rather than foundationalist

88. Westerhoff 2010, 82–94.

in nature.[89] On Madhyamaka premises, it is hard to make sense of the idea that some epistemic instruments are intrinsically knowledge-producing and could function as a foundation on which our entire knowledge of the world could be based. It is more satisfactory to conceive of the epistemic instruments as knowledge-producing because they are mutually supportive, in the same way as the reason that a ship stays afloat is not because it rests on any individual plank or set of planks, but because the planks are fastened together in a certain way.[90]

⌘ Moreover,

VP 04 **Objects that are existent, nonexistent, or both are not dependent.**

Also, if something is established as dependent, is it something that is existent, nonexistent, or both? Concerning that, first of all, because of its very existence the existent is not dependent. An existent pot does not depend on something other, such as clay, and so forth. Precisely because it does not exist, the nonexistent is also not dependent, because this would have the absurd consequence that a hare's horn, etc., is also dependent. Because both faults exist, something that is both is also not dependent. ⌘ ⌘

Continuing with the observation in VP 03 that epistemic instruments and epistemic objects are not self-established (and are therefore established by others and hence dependent), Nāgārjuna argues that as a consequence

89. Note that my use of terms here is somewhat non-standard. "Foundationalism" usually refers to a position according to which justification flows from some privileged set of propositions to the rest of the known propositions. The notion I am concentrating on here is not justification but the property of being knowledge-producing. By "foundationalism" I therefore mean the position that some things are intrinsically knowledge-producing, and by "coherentism" the claim that whatever has that property could never have it in the lonely state, that is, without other objects being around.

90. For more discussion, see Westerhoff 2010, 86–87.

epistemic instruments and objects neither exist, fail to exist, nor both exist and fail to exist.

The notion of existence in play here is existence with *svabhāva* or substantial existence. When Nāgārjuna denies that the epistemic instruments and objects lack existence, nonexistence, or a combination of the two in this way he therefore negates that they have any ontic status, where such status involves any existence with *svabhāva*.

The example Nāgārjuna uses to establish the failure of existent objects to depend on anything is a clay pot "that does not depend on something other, such as clay, and so forth." In this example, clay can be understood to refer either to the pieces of clay that form the constituents of the pot, or to the clay that is, together with the potter, his wheel, and so on, the cause of the pot.

The former reading is suggested by Tola and Dragonetti,[91] who note that "for the Naiyāyika (whom the author of this treatise is refuting) everything has an existence independent and apart from its constituent parts (for instance: the clay). From the Naiyāyika's point of view, it can be affirmed that the pot, as having an existence independent and apart from its constituent parts, does not depend on anything."

They are referring to the well-known Nyāya mereological theory that postulates the existence of a whole over and above the mere conglomeration of its parts (*samudayamātra*).[92] The arguments for this view are mainly epistemological and not of crucial importance in the present context, in particular as it seems to me doubtful that the Nyāya view of whole and parts really constitutes the background of the present passage.

First of all, it is difficult to make sense of the structure of the debate at this point if we think that the Nyāya conception of wholes is appealed to here. As Nāgārjuna is speaking in VP 04, we would not want to think that his thesis that "objects that are existent, nonexistent, or both are not dependent" is backed up by a claim only the Naiyāyika, but not the Buddhist, is going to endorse.

Second, it is not even clear that the Nyāya claim could be used to back up the claim that existent objects are not dependent. Note that for the Naiyāyika, the whole and its constituent parts are related by the relation

91. Tola and Dragonetti 1995a, 101.

92. For a detailed discussion see Bhadhuri 1947, 229–70.

of inherence (*samavāya*),[93] a relation that for the Naiyāyika also forms the connection between generalities and particulars. Unlike the relation of conjunction (*saṁyoga*), the relation of inherence can only be destroyed if at least one of its relata is destroyed.[94] But then it cannot be the case that part and whole exist in an independent manner, since the existence of both depends on the fact that the inherence relation holds between them; if this failed to hold, at least one of the two would have to go out of existence.

And even if we somehow could argue for the independent existence of the whole on Nyāya grounds, the argument would still not go through, for the independent existence of the whole from its parts does not mean that therefore the whole is independent of anything whatsoever. The pot is still dependent on the clay the potter used to make it, i.e., the clay as one of the causes that brought it about.[95]

An alternative and, in my view, preferable way of reading this passage[96] is to understand Nāgārjuna as saying that if some object existed substantially, i.e., with *svabhāva*, then it could not be dependent in the way a clay pot is dependent on the clay, that is, it could neither be dependent on its constituent parts nor on its causes and conditions, since it is the mark of the substantial that it does not require other objects for its existence. If something failed to exist by its very nature, by *svabhāva*, it could also not be dependent, because the "depends on" relation needs two relata, and in this case the first relatum would not exist.[97]

If there could be something that both existed by *svabhāva* and failed to exist by *svabhāva*, it could not be dependent, since either property excludes dependence. If such a thing could not exist (because we may think that nothing can have contradictory properties) it could not be dependent either, for it has just been argued that substantially nonexistent things cannot be dependent.

93. Bhaduri 1947, 238; Hiriyanna 1993, 236.

94. Hiriyanna 1993, 235.

95. Note that this is the way the reference to clay is understood in VP 24.

96. This appears to be also the interpretation Lindtner (1986, 273) suggests.

97. Compare the comment of the twelfth century Tibetan scholar Maja Changchub Tsöndru on MMK 10:11: "Any form of dependence must always involve two things, that which is dependent and that which is depended upon. Unless there is something that depends, it does not make sense to speak of something being depended on." *ltos pa la ltos sa ltos chos gnyis kyis khyab pas ltos pa po med pa'i ltos sa mi 'thad par dgong pa'o* (rMa bya 2011, 285).

If the pot existed by *svabhāva*, it would be independent; if, by *svabhāva*, the hare's horn failed to exist, it would also be independent. Of course for the Mādhyamika, nothing exists by *svabhāva*, and so both are dependent. This is obvious in the case of the pot that depends on its constituents and its causes to exist, but perhaps slightly less obvious in the case of a non-existent object such as a hare's horn. But if we take the hare's horn to be an empty name or property under which nothing falls, it becomes clear that *qua* name or *qua* property it is dependent, since for the Mādhyamika all names and properties are dependent.

On this interpretation the point made in VP 04 is very close to that made in MMK 10:11, where Nāgārjuna also notes the incompatibility of (substantial) existence and dependence:

> That entity that is established in dependence,
> How does that, before being established, depend?
> But if it is something established that is dependent,
> Its being called dependent is incorrect.[98]

Chandrakīrti's PP comments:

> If it is the case that something called "fire" is established dependent on something called "fuel," is what depends on fuel established or not established? If it is not established, because of its non-establishment, like a donkey's horn, it would not be dependent on fire. But if it is established, because of its establishment, what is the point of its dependence on fuel? For what is established is not established again later, because that is pointless.[99]

Chandrakīrti's exposition here essentially makes the same point Nāgārjuna makes in his commentary on VP 04, including the use of the example of the nonexistent horn. Of course, Chandrakīrti follows the specific discussion

98. *yo 'pekṣya sidhyate bhāvaḥ | so 'siddho 'pekṣate katham || athāpy apekṣate siddhas | tv apekṣāsya na yujyate.*

99. *yo hyagnyākhyo bhāvaḥ indhanākhyaṁ bhāvamapekṣya sidhyati so 'siddho vendhanam-apekṣate siddho vā | yady asiddhas tadā asiddhatvāt kharaviṣāṇavannendhanamapekṣeta | atha siddhaḥ | siddhatvātkimasyendhanāpekṣayā | na hi siddhaṁ punarapi sādhyate vaiyarthyāt* (Poussin 1903–13, 209:3–5).

of the relation between fire and fuel set out in chapter 10 of the MMK, but the core of the philosophical issue (that neither substantial existence nor substantial nonexistence is compatible with dependence) is identical in both passages.

Nāgārjuna now applies this general point to the specific subject matter of epistemic instruments and objects. As we have just seen in VP 02–03, epistemic instruments and epistemic objects are dependent, and because of this they cannot exist by *svabhāva*, fail to exist by *svabhāva*, both or neither. For this reason, they are empty. This same point is also raised in the epistemological discussion in VV 42:

> Since there is no dependence for an unestablished object, an unestablished Devadatta does not depend on any object. The establishment of the already established is not sensible; there is no making of what one has already made.[100]

Nāgārjuna is here responding to an opponent who suggests that epistemic instruments and objects could both be established (*siddha*), by which he means substantially existent, and at the same time dependent on other objects. Yet this suggestion leads to problems, since the unestablished and nonexistent does not require anything for its existence (since it has none), whereas the substantially existent will, by its very nature as *substantially* existent, as existent by *svabhāva*, not require any other objects to depend on either. For this reason, the dependence of the epistemic instruments and objects rules out their having any substantial ontological status such as substantial existence and substantial nonexistence.

100. *nahyasiddhasyārthasyāpekṣaṇaṁ bhavati | na hyasiddho devadattaḥ kaṁcidarthamapekṣate | na ca siddhasya sādhanamiṣṭaṁ kṛtasya karaṇānupapatteriti* (Yonezawa 2008, 288:5–7). See also Westerhoff 2010, 82–83.

⁜ It is objected: "Just as if there are no scales, etc., the object to be measured is not grasped, similarly also if there is no epistemic instrument the epistemic object is not grasped." If this is objected, it is to be replied:

VP 05 **This is not so, because there would be the contradictory consequence of an infinite regress.**

If it is said that because there is no epistemic instrument there is no epistemic object, by what are the epistemic instruments said to be established in the absence of epistemic instruments? In particular, it is necessary to state the reason or the specific difference. If it is also that all things are established by the epistemic instruments, this implies the contradictory consequence of being established by epistemic instruments that are other than those epistemic instruments, because the epistemic instruments are subsumed among all things. If epistemic instruments are not established by epistemic instruments, the thesis "all things will be established by epistemic instruments" is refuted. ⁜ ⁜

It is objected: "Just as if there are no scales, etc., the object to be measured is not grasped, similarly also if there is no epistemic instrument the epistemic object is not grasped." If this is objected, it is to be replied:

In this objection the opponent compares the epistemic instruments (*pramāṇa*) to a pair of scales (*tulā*), and the epistemic objects to the object weighed, an analogy suggested by the etymology of the terms themselves, as the first derives from the root *pra* √*mā*, meaning both "to measure" and "to know," while the second derives from √*tul*, meaning "to weigh" and "to examine."[101]

101. The equation of the pair of scales with epistemic instruments (and, by implication, of the object to be weighed with the epistemic objects) can also be found in NS 2.1.16. Vātsyāyana comments: "The pair of scales is called 'epistemic instrument' when it is the means of bringing about the cognition of the exact weight, in which case the object of cognition is the weighty substance, gold, etc., which is therefore called 'epistemic object.'" *gurutvaparimāṇajñānasādhanaṁ tulā pramāṇam | jñānaviṣayo gurudravyaṁ suvarṇādi prameyam* (Śāstrī 1998, 105:3).

But now epistemic objects are grasped, that is, we are acquainted with a variety of objects of knowledge. The opponent thus wants to reason by *modus tollens* that for this reason there must be epistemic instruments. Our knowledge of the world out there must be produced by something, and whatever this something is, it is an epistemic instrument. Its existence is guaranteed by our knowledge of the world.[102]

VP05 This is not so, because there would be the contradictory consequence of an infinite regress.

If it is said that because there is no epistemic instrument there is no epistemic object, by what are the epistemic instruments said to be established in the absence of epistemic instruments?

If we follow the opponent's suggestion, our epistemology does not start with epistemic instruments to explain knowledge of objects. Nevertheless, we cannot have a satisfactory theory of knowledge without some account of epistemic instruments. We therefore have to ask how, in an epistemology from which the epistemic instruments are initially absent, epistemic instruments are going to be accounted for. As we have just seen, the opponent wants to derive the epistemic instruments from the epistemic objects.

In particular, it is necessary to state the specific reason or difference.

It is then important to explain what the reason is that epistemic objects do not need an establisher, yet they can establish other things, while epistemic instruments need an establisher. In other words, the opponent has to indicate the difference (*mi 'dra ba, *visadṛśtva*) that makes it possible to establish the specific reason (*khyad par gyi gtan tshigs, *viśeṣahetu*) showing that the objects, but not the instruments, function as a foundation on which the other constituents of the epistemological theory rest.[103]

102. This suggestion of establishing epistemic instruments via the epistemic objects is also discussed (and criticized) in VV 43–48.

103. Compare NS 2.1.18, which makes the point that if certain elements of our ontology do not need an establisher, it becomes difficult to see without further explanation why this should not apply to all elements.

If it is also that all things are established by the epistemic instruments this implies the contradictory consequence of being established by epistemic instruments that are other than those epistemic instruments, because the epistemic instruments are subsumed among all things.

Yet it is difficult to see how there could be such a difference, since for the Naiyāyika all objects are known by epistemic instruments.[104] Therefore epistemic objects too are known by epistemic instruments and are therefore unable to constitute an epistemic foundation. Of course if *everything* is known by epistemic instruments, so are the epistemic instruments. This has the peculiar consequence that the universe, understood as the collection of all things, could never be known. For example, assume you collect together everything there is, including all the epistemic instruments. In order to know this collection, we would need some further things, some additional epistemic instruments. But this implies that the original collection cannot have been the collection of absolutely everything there is. Even if we include the additional epistemic instruments, this move can be repeated. But the more substantial worry (the "contradictory consequence" Nāgārjuna refers to) is that no epistemic object could ever be known, since the epistemic instrument required for knowing it would itself require another epistemic instrument to be itself known, and so on, down the abyss of an infinite regress (*anavasthā, thag pa med pa*).

The opponent might suggest that both worries could be avoided if we accepted the self-establishment (*svayaṁsiddhatva*) of the epistemic instruments discussed in NS 2.1.17–20.[105] If the epistemic instruments can know

104. NS 4.2.29: *pramāṇataścā 'rtha pratipatteḥ*. See also Vātsyāyana's *Bhāṣya* on NS 1.1.1: "Without epistemic instruments there is no cognition of objects." *pramāṇaṁ antareṇa nārthapratipattiḥ* (Śāstrī 1998, 1:7). Compare also the thesis of Nāgārjuna's Nyāya opponent that "the objects are established through the epistemic instruments" (*pramāṇato 'rthānāṁ prasiddhiḥ*) quoted by Nāgārjuna in the commentary on VV 31. It is clear from the context that "objects" here includes the epistemic instruments. See Oberhammer 1963–64, 64, 72; Westerhoff 2010, 69.

105. On the relation of this section to Nāgārjuna's discussion in the VV, see Oberhammer 1963–64, 64–70; and Meuthrath 1999, 3–29. NS 5.1.10 mentions the example of the light as well, to argue that an example requires another example for its establishment. There is a discussion of the question whether the example of the self-illumination of light that is usually understood as supporting the self-establishment of the epistemic instruments is used in this way in the NS. The version quoted by Nāgārjuna (and representing the view of his opponent) in 33 certainly supports the self-establishment of the epistemic instruments,

themselves, we could know the collection of all things without having to rely on additional epistemic instruments, since those instruments already in the collection would be able to produce knowledge both of the epistemic objects contained in it, as well as of themselves.

Yet Nāgārjuna is unlikely to be impressed by this move, given his conviction that the idea of the self-establishment of the epistemic instruments is fundamentally mistaken. He presents his arguments for this in the immediately following verses, VP 06–11, and the same topic is also discussed in detail in VP 33–39.[106] Note that a modified version of the self-establishment view, suggesting a circular establishment of epistemic instruments, does not help much either. Such an account would argue that an object can be known by an epistemic instrument, this instrument is then known by another epistemic instrument, and this second instrument is in turn known by the first instrument. The infinite regress is therefore stopped in a loop (the loops themselves can be of arbitrary size). Yet this model still implies that the second epistemic instrument knows itself, although mediated by the first epistemic instrument. Even in this indirect case, we therefore continue to face the main difficulties of the self-establishment of epistemic instruments that arise in the direct self-illumination model.[107]

> *If epistemic instruments are not established by epistemic instruments the thesis "all things will be established by epistemic instruments" is refuted.*

Nāgārjuna concludes that the Naiyāyika cannot have it all: if he wants to argue that epistemic instruments are established by epistemic objects, and that these objects then constitute an epistemic foundation, he cannot *also* hold on to the thesis that all things are established by epistemic

---

but there is disagreement whether NS 2.1.19 (the most relevant mention of the self-illumination example) is to be understood in the same way. See Oberhammer (1963–64, 67), who claims that it is not, and Bhattacharya (1977, 265–73) who claims that it is.

106. See Westerhoff 2010, 72–80.

107. See Westerhoff 2010, 81–82. It is interesting to note that infinitism, i.e., the view that epistemic justification stretches infinitely backward, which is rejected both by Nāgārjuna and the Naiyāyikas, has found some supporters in the contemporary philosophical literature. See Klein 2011, 245–56; and Aikin 2011.

instruments, since that would contradict the epistemic objects' fundamentality. In fact, Nāgārjuna also holds that the Naiyāyika cannot have either. As he notes here and elsewhere, the thesis of the universal scope of epistemic instruments, though an important Nyāya tenet, is problematic to the extent that it sends us on the way to an ever-receding regress of justification, given that the concepts of self-establishment or circular establishment appear to have their own internal difficulties. And the foundation of epistemology in epistemic objects faces a variety of difficulties on its own, independent of its conflict with the self-illumination thesis.[108]

Perhaps, however, there is a way around the infinite-regress objection that does not involve the potentially problematic notion of self-illumination. After all, regress considerations only become truly problematic if we make the internalist assumption that, to know anything, we also have to have second-order knowledge of our source of knowledge. In short, in order to know we have to know that we know (this is occasionally referred to as the "KK thesis"). An externalist, on the other hand, would not make this assumption. For him, epistemic instruments can deliver knowledge of the world even if we have no knowledge of how they do so, and if we do not know whether they do so correctly. The Naiyāyika is an externalist, and it has sometimes been argued that Nāgārjuna's criticism of Nyāya epistemology fails because it mistakenly attributes the KK thesis to him.[109] According to this view, the Naiyāyika could simply say that we can avoid the regress charge because the epistemic instrument required for knowing some object *x* would not itself require another epistemic instrument to be known in turn. It is sufficient that the epistemic instrument delivers the object; we do not in addition need to *know* that it does. So at best Nāgārjuna's arguments might show that there are certain things we cannot know about epistemic instruments and objects. We might have false beliefs about some instruments, and we might not know what we think we know about them. But this is hardly a devastating critique of Nyāya epistemology.

The difficulty with this defense is that, in order to ensure that the epistemic instruments can deliver knowledge of the epistemic objects, the Naiyāyika has to put a considerable amount of weight on the causal relation. As an externalist, he will have to regard causation as a guarantor that

108. See VV 43–48.

109. See Siderits 1988, 315.

conveys features of the object to perception in a reliable manner, arguing that the nature of the causing object will determine the nature of the perception that is the effect. But Madhyamaka points out that causation is itself conceptually constructed.[110] A reliable epistemic instrument that incorporates causation as a central element, therefore, has to be conceptually constructed as well. Causation cannot be made to bear the epistemological weight the Naiyāyika wants it to bear, because causal connections are so much bound up with conceptualization that we cannot rely on them as objective transmitters of information from a mind-independent world. For this reason, there is no way in which we can regard epistemic instruments as providing us with accurate knowledge of an objectively existent set of epistemic objects, existent, as it were, *svabhāvatas*, independent of human conceptual practices.

⌘ It is objected:

VP 06 **There is no epistemic instrument for epistemic instruments. In this respect, epistemic instruments are like a light that establishes both itself and others.**

In the same way in which a light is seen to illuminate itself as well as others, similarly, epistemic instruments also establish themselves and others. Therefore, there is no infinite regress, because there is no such fault for a light, etc. ⌘ ⌘

The opponent comes back to the charge raised in VP 05, namely that the Nyāya position that everything is established by epistemic instruments leads to an infinite regress. He rightly observes that such a regress only ensues if for every epistemic instrument we need a *new* epistemic instrument to know it, since in this case we would be compelled to continuously chase the chain of epistemic justification backward. If, however, we could use the same epistemic instrument both for knowing an epistemic object as well as for knowing the instrument itself, we could both adhere

110. See Siderits 2004.

to the principle of the universal scope of epistemic instruments and escape the infinite regress.

The opponent tries to establish this conclusion by appeal to an example. In darkness we produce a light in order to make things visible that are otherwise hidden to us. In order to see the light, however, we do not need a second light to see the first (and then a third to see the second, and so on, along an infinite regress), but the light itself simultaneously illuminates both the object and itself. The epistemic instruments are similar to a light, since as a light illuminates non-perceived objects and thereby makes them manifest, epistemic instruments make non-cognized objects manifest. For this reason, the opponent argues, the epistemic instruments are self-manifesting or self-establishing (*svayaṁsiddha*), thereby avoiding an infinite regress.

We should note that, by following this argumentative strategy, the opponent relinquishes the position suggested in the commentary to VP 05, that the epistemic instruments are established by epistemic objects. Nāgārjuna rightly pointed out that the opponent could not have both, epistemic objects as foundational establishers and a universal scope of epistemic instruments. The opponent now sets out to defend only the latter by introducing the example of the light.[111]

It is to be replied:

VP 07 The light does not illuminate, regardless of whether or not it is in contact with darkness.

111. Within Buddhist philosophical literature the example of the self-illuminating light is primarily employed in the discussion of two topics: concerning the question whether consciousness has the power to cognize itself (*svasaṁvedana*) and in the discussion of the antireflexivity principle (*svātmani kriyāvirodha*; see May 1959, 113–14n284; Schayer 1931, 19n14; Siderits 2007, 46–47; and Siderits and Katsura 2013, 89, 44–46, 77). All of Nāgārjuna's uses of this example belong to the second category. Apart from VV 33–39 Nāgārjuna discusses the example of the self-illuminating light also in MMK 7:8–12, even though in a slightly different context. In the context of the three characteristics of phenomena—origination, duration, and cessation—the question arises whether origination (*utpāda, skye ba*) originates, and the opponent argues that, like the light illuminating itself, origination brings about itself, as well as the object originating.

Does the light illuminate after entering into contact with darkness, or does it illuminate when it is not in contact? First of all, the light does not illuminate after being in contact with darkness, because there is no contact. Why is there no contact between light and darkness? Because of their mutual exclusion. If, where the light exists, darkness does not exist, how could that light dispel darkness or illuminate? However, if it is not in contact, it is like a sword without contact that cannot cut.

Nāgārjuna responds to the opponent's analogy of the self-illuminating light not by questioning the similarity between lights and epistemic objects, but by examining the more fundamental assumption that lights illuminate anything at all, whether it is themselves or other things. In VP 7–9, Nāgārjuna considers the difficulties with the light illuminating other things, and in VP 10–11, he analyzes the feasibility of a light illuminating itself.

It is plausible to assume that when one thing removes another thing, the two things stand in some kind of connection or contact, as when a farmer removes a stone from a field, or a polishing cloth removes a stain. So, if a light removes darkness, the light should also be in contact with darkness. Yet any kind of contact between two things presupposes that the things can coexist, like the farmer and the stone and the cloth and the stain. Yet, as Nāgārjuna points out, it is difficult to conceive of light and darkness in this way, since the existence of one at any place entails the nonexistence of the other: the existence of light in my room excludes the existence of darkness there, as the existence of darkness would exclude the existence of light. Since the existence of one entails the exclusion of the other, there cannot be a process in which both are involved, one bringing about the removal of the other. In the case of light and darkness, we are not dealing with two independent things,[112] but with a thing and its absence, and for Nāgārjuna absences are not fundamentally real. There is thus not much mileage in conceiving of illumination along the lines of two independent, ontologically substantial objects coming into contact.

112. This is already stressed by the Buddha himself: "The property of light is discerned in dependence on darkness"; *yāyaṁ...ābhādhātu ayaṁ dhātu andhakāraṁ paṭicca paññāyati* (*Saṁyuttanikāya, Nidānavagga, Dhātusaṁyutta*; Feer 1884–1904, 2:150).

Could it then be the case that light and darkness interact without contact? Nāgārjuna here uses the example of a sword, arguing that anything that does not touch its blade cannot be cut. In the same way, without some kind of causal connection between light and darkness, it is difficult to understand how one could remove the other. The example of the sword in this context is interesting, as the sword constitutes one of the stock examples in support of the antireflexivity principle: a sword cannot cut itself.[113] Direct reference to this example would not have been very helpful in the present context, since we would then be drawn into an unsatisfying discussion of whether an epistemic instrument is more like a light (so that the irreflexivity principle fails) or more like a sword, finger, or eye (so that the principle holds). Nāgārjuna rather questions the feasibility of the process said to underlie the example, instead of the applicability of the example itself.

It is interesting to note that, in refuting the light's power to illuminate both itself as well as other things, Nāgārjuna does not just focus on the first, which is the driving force behind the opponent's reply, but also argues against the second, the light's power to illuminate things other than itself. This is also made explicit in various commentaries on MMK 7.9, such as Buddhapālita's *Vṛtti*[114] and Chandrakīrti's PP.[115] This is curious for two reasons. First, in order to answer the opponent's reply, it would have been sufficient just to rule out the light's power to illuminate itself. Secondly, that a light cannot illuminate other things appears to be a highly counterintuitive position. Do we not continuously observe lights illuminating the objects around them?

113. For this simile see *Laṅkāvatārasūtra*, Sagāthaka 568, quoted by Chandrakīrti in MĀBh on verse 6:76, and the *Āryaratnacūḍasūtra*, quoted in Shāntideva's *Śikṣāsamuccaya* (Bendall and Rouse 1922, 221; Goodman 2016, 227–28), in Prajñākaramati's *Pañjika* on verse 9:17 of Shāntideva's *Bodhicaryāvatāra*, and by Chandrakīrti in PP on verse 1.1 of the MMK (Poussin 1903–13, 62–63; Ruegg 2002, 110–11). Other common examples include the finger that cannot point to itself (mentioned in these same passages) and the eye that cannot see itself.

114. "It is also untenable to say that it [the light] illuminates others. There is also no darkness in other entities where the light is placed." *gzhan dag snang bar byed do zhes gang smras pa de yang rigs pa ma yin te | mar me gzhan gyi bdag nyid dag la 'dug pa de la yang mun pa med de* (Saito 1984, 94:7–9).

115. "The light does not have the power to illuminate itself or other." *ato 'pi nāsti pradīpasya svaparātma prakāśakatvaṁ* (Poussin 1903–13, 152:1–2).

What Nāgārjuna has in mind when arguing against the view that lights can illuminate other objects is refuting one specific interpretation of how this illumination can proceed. This is the "worldly" understanding that illumination happens through the light's removal of darkness. This presupposes that light and darkness exist as two separate, independently existent entities, one of which removes the other, like a cat removes a mouse.[116]

Yet light and darkness do not exist independently, as light is just the absence of darkness and darkness is nothing but the lack of illumination by light. When Nāgārjuna claims that a light does not dispel darkness, he does not question that lanterns, butter lamps, and flashlights work at the empirical level, but the view that the illumination involved implies the interaction of two independent entities existing by *svabhāva*. But such interaction cannot take place, because the two entities in question are mutually dependent. This, however, does not entail that we cannot make sense of the interaction of light and darkness as interdependent objects.

Since Nāgārjuna wants to raise these general problems with the way illumination is conceptualized, he specifically discusses the view that lights illuminate other things, even though the opponent's argument is primarily based on the idea that they illuminate themselves. This raises the interesting question of whether, given his view of illumination, Nāgārjuna would still have wanted to maintain the parallelism between lights and epistemic instruments. He argues that the opponent is wrong about the properties he ascribes to lights (such as self- and other-illumination), but would he also want to say that he is wrong about comparing lights to epistemic instruments in the first place? If he does not, and if the analogy therefore still stands, we would have to accept that Nāgārjuna's criticism of the self- and other-illumination of lights also implies a criticism of the power of epistemic instruments to perceive themselves as well as other things. This would make sense from a Madhyamaka perspective. The illuminated corresponds to epistemic objects known by means of epistemic instruments; the

116. AK on MMK 7:9: "It is said 'Illumination occurs by the dispelling of darkness.' Moreover, because its own nature (*svabhāva*, *rang gi dngos po*) and the nature of another (*parabhāva*, *gzhan gyi dngos po*) with respect to the light is not made through that dispelling of darkness, therefore the light does not illuminate its own nature nor the nature of another, like cat and mouse." *mun pa sel bas snang byed yin zhes bya na | mun pa sel ba[s] de yang gang gi phyir mar me[s] rang dang gzhan gyi dngos po la mi byed pa de'i phyir mar mes rang gi dngos po yang snang bar byed pa ma yin la | gzhan gyi dngos po yang snang bar byed pa ma yin te | byi la dang byi ba bzhin no* (Huntington 1986, 310:6–11).

dark corresponds to whatever is not known by them. Like the illuminated and the dark, the known and the unknown exclude each other. As the notions of the illuminated and the dark do not make sense without each other, the idea of an uncognized world existing beyond the reach and wholly independent of our epistemic instruments does not make sense. If the unillumined does not exist by *svabhāva*, neither does the uncognized. We should therefore not consider the epistemic instruments as conveying knowledge about a world that exists independent of our epistemic capacities, as a self-existent, epistemically obscure object that is brought to knowledge by interaction with the luminous power of the epistemic instruments. As darkness is constituted by being the exclusion of illumination, the uncognized is constituted only negatively by what is not encompassed by the means of knowledge. The known and the unknown depend on each other, and as such, the parallelism with the light rules out the realist picture in which our tiny island of knowledge is surrounded by an ocean of unknown, but nevertheless self-sufficient and independently existent facts, some of which the prudent use of epistemic instruments can drag from the darkness of epistemic obscurity into the illumination of the known. Our search for knowledge does not resemble a quest with a flashlight in the attic, lighting up relics hidden in darkness since time immemorial, but more that of the author of the story, who, in telling the story and conveying information about a fictional world at the same time creates the reader's domain of ignorance, the set of all the questions we would like to ask about the world of the story, but which the story does not answer.

VP 08 **If it is said, "This is just like harm done by Rāhu"—it is not so, because of the inconsistency with the example.**

Harm done to their own body, etc., being seized after contact with the damage Rāhu did to Devadatta, etc.—with respect to this, there is no harm that darkness did to the light, so how could it be similar to damage done by Rāhu?

Rāhu, etc., acts on beings with a body, etc.; fire, rope, water, sickness, snakes, disease, etc., only cause harm to beings with a body. In respect to this, it does not exist even to a small amount for the light.

Therefore, this is clearly not a comparable phenomenon. Moreover, a light existing far away does not harm the body and sense of darkness, because those do not exist.

Therefore, for the example of Rāhu, as there is no contact it is not reasonable to establish the conclusion.

If, moreover, there would be illumination without contact with the light, the darkness contained in the caves of all mountains would be dispelled or illuminated from this very spot. But something like this is not seen in the world or asserted. ✠ ✠

The opponent now responds to Nāgārjuna's assertion at the end of VP 07, that a light that does not stand in contact with darkness cannot remove that darkness, by arguing that things that do not stand in contact with each other can still influence each other. If this argument were successful, one would then be able to infer that, even though illumination and darkness cannot stand in contact because they are mutually exclusive, light would still be able to influence (and thereby remove) darkness, even in the absence of contact.

VP 08 If it is said "This is just like harm done by Rāhu"—it is not so, because of the inconsistency with the example.

The example the opponent produces here is that of Rāhu, one of the nine planetary gods (*navagraha*). Attempting to drink of the nectar of immortality at the churning of the ocean of milk (*kṣīrodha*), Rāhu, originally an *asura*, was observed by Sūrya and Chandra, the gods of sun and moon, and subsequently punished by Viṣhṇu, who cut off his head. Viṣhṇu then made this (now immortal) head one of the planetary deities. Still holding a grudge against Sūrya and Chandra, Rāhu chases them through the sky, attempting to devour them, thereby giving rise to eclipses of the sun and the moon. The *Devaputtasaṇyutta* describes how Chandimā (Chandra) and Sūrya are captured in this way by Rāhu and subsequently released through the Buddha's intervention.[117] Rāhu, who can cover the sun and moon "with his hands, jaw, and tongue, and can even stuff his cheeks with them" (though he is apparently unable to obstruct their motion)[118] appears to fit naturally in the context of obscuration and illumination discussed in these verses. While Rāhu's obscuration of sun and moon apparently proceeds by his coming into contact with them, not all of his actions seem to require this kind of contact. Rāhu is also regarded as a generally malefic influence. One of the eight periods of the day (*rāhukāla*) is considered to be governed by Rāhu, and new projects should not be undertaken during that time.

When Rāhu exerts an evil influence on a person like Devadatta (a common placeholder name in Sanskrit texts, like Alice and Bob in English) he appears to do so without coming into direct contact with him.[119] The opponent suggests that this presents a model for the way illumination and light could interact, one influencing the other without any direct contact between the two.

Even though the example of Rāhu's influence appears fitting in the present context due to its close connection with matters of light and darkness, references to astrological or supernatural influence are not necessary as examples for interaction without contact. In commenting on the discussion of self-illumination in MMK 7:10, Chandrakīrti mentions three different apparent examples: knowledge removing ignorance, visual perception, and magnetism.[120] None of these involve any supernatural elements.

117. *Samyutta Nikaya* 2.9–10; Bodhi 2000, 144–46.

118. Bodhi 2000, 388n158.

119. Compare here the example of malevolent magic (*abhicāra*) mentioned in NS 5.1.8; Uddyotakara's *Vārttika* notes that "malevolent magic causing afflictions is observed to be efficient even without contact." *pīḍane abhicārād apraptya apy sādhakatvaṁ dṛṣṭam* (Nyaya-Tarkatirtha 2003, 1117:13–14).

120. "Perhaps you might think that even without contact knowledge destroys ignorance, the eye sees shapes, the magnet attracts iron." *atha manyase yathā'prāptāmevāvidyam jñānaṁ nihanti ('joms pa) aprāptameva rūpaṁ cakṣuḥ paśyati aprāptamevāyo 'yaskānto maṇirākarṣati* (Poussin 1903–13, 152:16–17). It is interesting to ask what kinds of contactless interaction Chandrakīrti had in mind when mentioning these examples. It seems clear that they are not all examples of the same kind. The eye sees shape without contact if "contact" is taken to mean "physical touch"; nevertheless, ancient Indian theories of perception do accept a causal connection between the physical sense organ and the object perceived. The removal of ignorance by knowledge appears to be a quite different case, as

> *Harm done to their own body, etc., being seized after contact with the damage Rāhu did to Devadatta, etc.—with respect to this, there is no harm darkness did to the light, so how could it be similar to damage done by Rāhu?*

Nāgārjuna denies that the example of Rāhu is an apt illustration of action without contact by pointing out that beings are harmed by getting into contact with the results of the evil influence Rāhu exerted on people like Devadatta. So harm done appears to require some kind of contact. In addition, if we accepted the opponent's model, we would have to assume that when a light is extinguished, darkness did some kind of harm to the light. But this is implausible given the discussion in VP 07. Darkness is a mere absence of light, and absences are not fundamentally real. For this reason, any apparent interaction between the two could not be used as a basis for arguing that either exists substantially. This is, after all, the motivation for introducing the discussion of illumination in the first place: to establish the self-sufficient status of the epistemic instruments in analogy with the self-illuminating power of light.

> *Rāhu, etc., acts on beings with a body, etc.; fire, rope, water, sickness, snakes,*[121] *disease, etc., only cause harm to beings with a body. In respect to this, it does not exist even to a small amount for the light. Therefore, this is clearly not a comparable phenomenon. Moreover, a light existing far away does not harm the body and senses of darkness because those do not exist. Therefore, for the example of Rāhu, as there is no contact it is not reasonable to establish the conclusion.*

The allegedly contactless influence of Rāhu on the beings he harms can only take place (like the allegedly contactless interaction between eye and object seen, or magnet and object attracted) because these are physical entities (or, in this case, living beings). It is only because these beings have bodies that the influences Rāhu produces can harm them, in the same way

---

one is just the exclusion of the other, so that any causal interaction would be prevented by the impossibility of their coexistence.

121. Some editions read *sprul* (*nirmita*, illusory magical creation) instead of *sbrul* (*nāga*, *ahi*, snake).

in which a fire, a rope, and so forth, cannot have any detrimental effects on nonphysical things. And while light is undoubtedly physical (though better conceived as a process of illumination than as a persistent object) its mere absence, darkness, is not, in the same way in which the hole in a bowl is not a physical thing.[122] Not being a physical thing, darkness does not have a body or sense organs, and for this reason Rāhu's influence on physical objects that do have these cannot be taken as a model of light's influence on darkness.

> *If, moreover, there would be illumination without contact with the light, the darkness contained in the caves of all mountains would be dispelled or illuminated from this very spot. But something like this is not seen in the world or asserted.*

This difficulty is also discussed by Nāgārjuna in MMK 7:11 and VV 39.[123] If absence of contact is understood not just as the absence of physical contact but as the absence of any causal influence, then it becomes difficult to explain what could keep such contactless interactions from occurring, why light does not dispel *all* darkness (and similarly, why knowledge does not remove all ignorance, why vision does not see every object, and why the magnet does not attract all pieces of iron).[124] A light does not illuminate a dark room next door because the wall blocks the light. But if the light would not even have to get into causal contact with the darkness next door, it now becomes difficult to see why the light does not go on there when it goes on here, since the wall could hardly block a contact that was not required in the first place.

122. Sorensen 2008, 88. One reason why we cannot equate the hole in a bowl with the physical object that is the collection of air that fills the hole in the (empty) bowl is the fact that if we place the bowl in a vacuum, the air is gone but the hole is still there. For a comprehensive discussion of the ontological status of holes and absences see Casati and Varzi 1994.

123. As well as by Āryadeva in his *Śataśāstra*. See Tucci 1981, 9.

124. See Chandrakīrti's commentary on MMK 7:11 in the PP (Poussin 1903–13: 153–54).

VP 09 **According to the treatise worldly people and investigators are clearly asserted to be in accord with Hari, etc.**

With respect to that, "worldly": from children, etc., up to cowherds; "investigators": Viṣhṇu, Īshvara, Brahmā, Kapilā, Ulūka, Vyāsa, Vasiṣhṭha, Vyaghrā, Samṛddha, Gagara, Māṭhara, etc. Those matters on which they agree are definitely established as examples.

Concerning Viṣhṇu, and so on: The mere absence of light is asserted to be darkness. Why is that? Because the absence of light is called darkness. The meaning of "here there is darkness" is "there is no light." Similarly, according to other investigators, what specific kind of thing exists as the substance of "darkness" does not exist for anyone.

For that reason, it is not established that "darkness is cleared away by the light." Therefore, the example, "the light clears away darkness," is not reasonable. Because that is not reasonable, the epistemic instrument is not established as exemplified. Therefore, there is no "epistemic instrument that establishes itself and others."

VP 09 According to the treatise worldly people and investigators are clearly asserted to be in accord with Hari, etc.

The meaning of this stanza and its commentary is unfortunately not as clear as we might wish it to be. To begin, the Tibetan has the expression *'jig rten pa'i spyod pa po*, "worldly agent"; Lindtner[125] convincingly argues this should rather be *'jig rten dang dpyod pa po*, "worldly people and investigators," in accordance both with the commentary as well as with the reference to "worldly people and investigators" (*laukikaparīkṣānāṁ*) in NS 1.1.25, a passage closely connected to the argument in the commentary.[126] The other two unclarities in this stanza are what treatise (*bstan bcos, śāstra*) is referred to, and what the reference to Hari is supposed to mean.

125. Lindtner 1986, 359n113.

126. See also Pind 2001, 161.

The treatise is probably an early version of the *Nyāyasūtra* that constitutes the basis of the arguments put forward by Nāgārjuna's opponent.[127] The Tibetan term *seng ge* translates the Sanskrit *hari*,[128] which can refer to a lion, but also functions as a proper name and as an epithet of Viṣhṇu, Shiva, or Brahmā.[129] Taking it in the latter sense, the stanza can be understood as saying that worldly people and investigators are asserted to be similar to Viṣhṇu, etc. As Viṣhṇu, Shiva, and Brahmā are mentioned in the commentary, this reading has the advantage of making it unnecessary to explain the reference to lions separately, as Tola and Dragonetti do.[130]

The passage can therefore be understood as saying that worldly people and investigators agree with Viṣhṇu. What they agree on becomes clear in the following commentary.

With respect to that, "worldly": from children, etc., up to cowherds; "investigators": Viṣhṇu, Īshvara (Shiva), Brahmā, Kapilā, Ulūka, Vyāsa, Vasiṣhṭha, Vyaghrā, Samṛddha, Gagara, Māṭhara, etc. Those matters on which they agree are definitely established as examples.

The commentary now gives a more detailed explanation of who the "worldly people" and the "investigators" are supposed to be. Worldly people include everybody included in an epistemic hierarchy with children at one end, and cowherds at the other. Cowherds are a common Madhyamaka example corresponding in epistemic status to the man on the Clapham omnibus: competent in negotiating the truths and conventions of everyday life, but without any theoretical sophistication. The meaning of "investigators" (*dpyod pa po*, *parīkṣā*) is spelled out by a list of names beginning with the Hindu triad (*trimūrti*) of Viṣhṇu, Shiva, and Brahmā, and continuing with an enumeration of ancient Indian scholars and sages.

127. Oberhammer (1963–64, 70) argues that the version of the NS Nāgārjuna would have known was a debate manual consisting mainly of the material contained in the first and fifth *adhyāya*. See also Lindter 1997, 358n114.

128. Sempa Dorje (1974, 29) reconstructs to *śāstre laukikaparīkṣākāṇāṁ haryādīnāmivābhimataḥ*.

129. See Boethlingk 1879–89, s.v. *hari*.

130. Tola and Dragonetti (1995, 105): "those who are philosophers among common people are said to be comparable to lions, i.e., are most important persons, whose opinion must be accepted."

These include Kapilā, the founder of the Sāṁkhya system, and Ulūka, better known as Kaṇāda, the founder of the Vaisheṣhika system. Vyāsa is a name applied in post-Vedic times to an arranger or compiler of particular works, and is perhaps here referring to the Vedavyāsa, the rishi (*ṛṣi*) who compiled the Vedas. Vasiṣhṭha is one of the seven sages (*saptaṛṣi*), sometimes considered as the compiler of the seventh *maṇḍala* of the *Ṛgveda*. Vyāghra ("the tiger") might refer to Vyāghrapāda, a devotee of Shiva usually depicted with tiger's feet[131] or to one of the compilers of the 97th hymn of the ninth *maṇḍala* of the *Ṛgveda*.[132] Gagara is possibly a misspelling of Garga; it might refer to another composer of a hymn from the *Ṛgveda*,[133] or possibly to the chief anstronomer at the court of the first universal ruler (*cakravartin*), Pṛthu,[134] who, with the *nāga* architect Śeṣa, introduced Nāgara architecture.[135] The name Māṭhara probably refers to a Sāṁkhya teacher and author of a commentary on the *Sāṁkhyakārikā*.[136] The identity of Samṛddha (*'byor ldan*) remains obscure. Mani[137] mentions a *nāga* of the same name, but given the other members of the list, this was probably not the intended referent. Kajiyama[138] refers to Bacot's[139] translating *'byor pa ldan pa* as Bhautia; Bhautya Manu is the ruler of the 14th and final cycle of creation (*manvatara*).[140]

That this list of "investigators" gives a plausible account of what Nāgārjuna's non-Buddhist opponents would have regarded as the main religious and philosophical authorities is confirmed by a passage from Āryadeva's *Śataśāstra*, in which an opponent suggests some of them as possible refer-

131. Prasoon 2009, 154. Kajiyama (1974, 389n13) suggests reading the name as *vyaghra* and as referring to Viṣhṇu.

132. Srinivasan 2011, 88.

133. The 47th hymn of the sixth *maṇḍala* is ascribed to Garga Bhāradvāja (Sarmah 1991, 123). See also Kajiyama 1974, 389n12.

134. Mani 1979, 280.

135. Stutley 1997, 94; Sarmah 1991, 127.

136. See Tola and Dragonetti (1995, 11–12) for a discussion of the difficulties of dating Māṭhara.

137. Mani 1979, 680.

138. Kajiyama 1974, 388n11.

139. Bacot 1930, 123.

140. Danielou 1964, 319.

ents for the term "blessed one" (*bhagavat*), which Buddhist authors use to refer to the Buddha:

> There are (some) men who say that Viṣhṇudeva is called the blessed one. Again (some) say that Maheshvaradeva is called the blessed one. Again (some) say that Kapila, Ulūka, Ṛṣabha, and other ṛṣis are all called the "blessed ones." How do you only say that the Buddha is the blessed one?[141]

The two lists of ordinary or worldly people (*laukika*) and trained experts or investigators (*parīkṣāka*) run in opposite directions: from the children upward to the cowherds, and from the creators of the universe all the way down to the philosophers. In asserting that these two opposed groups agree on what constitutes an example, the text makes a clear reference to NS 1.1.25, where the fifth of the sixteen Nyāya categories, the example (*dṛṣṭānta*), is defined.[142] The underlying idea is that if something is to serve as an example in a debate between two parties, it has to be understood by both parties, and it has to be understood in the same way. I cannot use the human brain as an example of an information processor to someone who believes it to be solely a cooling device.

Concerning Viṣhṇu, and so on: The mere absence of light is asserted to be darkness. Why is that? Because the absence of light is called darkness. The meaning of "here there is darkness" is "there is no light."

Nāgārjuna points out that the scholars and sages beginning with Viṣhṇu consider darkness as an absence of light. Indeed this conception was very widespread among thinkers of different schools, including the Vaisheṣhika,[143] Nyāya,[144] and Prabhākara Mīmāṁsā.[145]

141. Tucci 1982, 3.

142. "The topic on which worldly people and investigators are of the same opinion is the example." *laukikaparīkṣakāṇāṁ yasminnarthe buddhisāmyaṁ saḥ dṛṣṭāntaḥ* (Śāstrī 1998, 49:1).

143. *Vaiśeṣikasūtra* 5.2.19: *dravyaguṇakarmaniṣpattivaidharmyād abhāvas tamaḥ* (Chakrabarty 2003, 80).

144. Jhalakīkar 1996, s.v. *tamas*, 319–21; Potter 1995–, vol. 2, 614.

145. Keith 1921, 53.

> *Similarly, according to other investigators, what specific kind of thing exists as the substance of "darkness" does not exist for anyone.*

The translation of this sentence[146] is debatable. Tola and Dragonetti[147] translate it as:

> Similarly, for other investigators the thing called "darkness," of whatever description it may be, is not in any place.

Pind,[148] on the other hand, renders it as:

> Similarly, according to some philosophers there is a certain kind of substance (**vastu*) called "darkness," whereas no [such substance] exists according to other [philosophers].

What I take Nāgārjuna to be saying here is that some philosophers argue that there is no such thing as the substance (*dngos po*) of darkness. The difficulty I see with Tola and Dragonetti's translation (above)[149] is that I have been unable to find a supporting passage where *su zhig* means "somewhere" or "at some place"; the more common meaning is "somebody" or "someone."[150]

If we follow Pind's translation, Nāgārjuna would be distinguishing three kinds of philosophers:

1. Those saying that darkness is the mere absence of light (mentioned above).
2. Those saying that darkness is a substance.
3. Those saying that darkness is no substance.

146. *de ltar gzhan dag dpyod pa po la mun pa zhes bya ba'i dngos po ci 'dra ba zhig yod pa yin te | su zhig la yang yod pa ma yin no.*

147. Tola and Dragonetti 1995a, 62.

148. Pind, unpublished MS.

149. See also their commentary at Tola and Dragonetti 1995a, 105.

150. See Jäschke 1998, 573; Nagano 1997, 312. Tola and Dragonetti consider the Tibetan *su zhig la* to correspond to the Sanskrit *kutracit* ("somewhere"), based on the idea that it is a combination of *su zhig* (translating the Sanskrit *kecit* ["somethings"]; Chandra 1998, 2418) with a locative *la*.

Tola and Dragonetti[151] suggest that *dpyod pa po* could be a translation of the Sanskrit term *vicāra* or *vicāraṇa*, referring to investigators in general, or of *mīmāṁsā*, referring to this particular philosophical school. Interestingly the Bhaṭṭa Mīmāṁsākas did consider darkness to be a substance, a fact which appears to support Pind's translation.[152] The difficulty with this translation is not so much linguistic, but rather that it is difficult to see how it fits into the argument.

What Nāgārjuna infers in the immediately following passage from the different positions on the nature of darkness mentioned is that "for that reason it is not established that darkness is cleared away by the light." The justification for this is easy to see if Nāgārjuna tries to show that the investigators agree that darkness is not a real entity, either because it is merely an absence, or because it does not exist as a substance (*dngos po*). But if we follow Pind's translation, Nāgārjuna would have three classes of experts *disagree* about the nature of darkness: the Vaisheṣhika et al. say it is a mere absence, the (presumed) Mīmāṁsāka says it is a substance, and a third one says it isn't a substance. Unfortunately, it is not clear why this implies that "it is not established that darkness is cleared away by the light." One might want to say that Nāgārjuna could claim that mere absence and insubstantial darkness need not be cleared away, and substantial darkness could not be cleared away. But this would go against the idea that Nāgārjuna is here discussing a point on which all the investigators agree.

According to our reading, there are only two (congruent) positions mentioned here: that darkness is a mere absence, and that darkness is not a substance. These two are not necessarily coextensive; one might, for example, regard darkness as a property (and thus not as a substance) and believe that it is more than a mere absence.[153]

For Nāgārjuna both worldly people and trained investigators agree that darkness is not a self-sufficient, independently existent entity, since darkness

151. Tola and Dragonetti 1995a, 186n7.

152. Frauwallner (1973, 2:21): "[I]n the Mīmāṁsā school of Kumārila, however, the old view still asserts itself which understands darkness as an independent entity." Sharma (1991, 233): "Kumārila admits the nine substances of Vaiśeṣika and adds two more—darkness and sound—which are rejected by Prabhākara."

153. See Shrīdhara's position on darkness (Jha 1982, 20–21; Potter 1995–, vol. 2, 110, 589): "According to Shrīdhara, darkness, though not a substance is a special kind of colour, a positive entity (*bhāva*), because we always have a positive awareness of darkness."

is the mere absence of light. This is the everyday understanding of darkness[154] as well as the view of darkness on which philosophers who claim that darkness is a mere absence, or that it is not a substance, agree.

> *For that reason, it is not established that "darkness is cleared away by the light." Therefore, the example, "the light clears away darkness" is not reasonable. Because that is not reasonable the epistemic instrument is not established as an exemplified. Therefore, there is no "epistemic instrument that establishes itself and others."*

Yet if this is the case then we cannot hold that a light clears away darkness (and illuminates itself in the process), since a mere absence, a merely insubstantial thing, is not anything light can illuminate. The light can then not function as an illustration or example of an epistemic instrument's supposed cognizing of itself or others. Arguing that there are epistemic instruments that establish themselves as well as other things because there are lights that illuminate themselves as well as other things fails if we can show, as Nāgārjuna just argued, that no good ontological sense can be made of lights illuminating other things and dispelling darkness. In the following two verses, VP 10 and 11, Nāgārjuna will assess the other part of the example, i.e., the ability of a light to illuminate itself.[155]

154. Compare Chandrakīrti's PP on MMK 7:9: "In this world what is called illumination is the removal of darkness"; *iha prakāśo nāma tamasya vadhaḥ* (Poussin 1903–13, 151:13). Darkness and light are related in such a way that each is the exclusion of the other. See also Tucci's (1981, 22:6–7) Sanskrit translation of the *Tarkaśāstra*: "it is darkness insofar as there is the non-existence of light in darkness"; *andhakāre jyotiṣo 'bhāvaḥ tasmād andhakāraḥ.*

155. Note that there is a different way of understanding the argument in this passage, leading to the same conclusion as the one just presented, i.e., that the illumination by a light cannot serve as an example of cognition by an epistemic instrument. The idea is here that, since we know from NS 1.1.25 that an example is what experts and laymen agree on, and since they do not agree on the relation between illumination and darkness relative to the light, the light cannot constitute an example. The disagreement could either be construed as a disagreement between laymen and experts (if, e.g., the former believed illumination and darkness to be two substances acting on each other, while the latter rejected this view), a disagreement between the experts themselves (such as the substantialist view of darkness of the Bhaṭṭa Mīmāṁsākas and the non-substantialist view of the Vaisheṣhikas; see Bhaduri 1947, 6), or both. On the whole this interpretation strikes me as possible, though not as convincing as the one just presented.

Moreover,

VP 10 **The light cannot illuminate itself, because darkness does not exist.**

The light also does not illuminate itself. There is no darkness in the light—what shall it illuminate? "Light" and "illumination" are the same thing; darkness does not exist in that, because of their mutual exclusion.

In this and in the following verse, Nāgārjuna moves from the discussion of the light's ability to illuminate other things (discussed in VP 07–09) to its ability to illuminate itself. Establishing this point is obviously crucial, since the entire motivation for the introduction of the light example was to refute the criticism of the infinite regress brought forward against the Nyāya idea that everything is known by epistemic instruments. If a light were only able to illuminate other things, but not itself, it would be unclear how a light could ever be perceived, so that the illumination relation relative to a light would suffer from the same problem of infinite regression as the cognizing relation relative to epistemic instruments.

The key point made in the present passage in order to refute self-illumination is that illumination, i.e., the removal of darkness, presupposes the existence of darkness at the place to be illuminated. Yet if a light were self-illuminating this would imply that darkness was present within the light itself. Not only is this empirically problematic (when we inspect a light or a fire, we don't find any darkness hidden within it), it also clashes with the (as we saw in VP 09, widely accepted) conception of darkness as the absence or exclusion of light, for nothing can exist together with its own exclusion.

Nāgārjuna raises the same point in two other passages, MMK 7:9 and VV 37. In the former, the example of the light is not supposed to illustrate an epistemological point, but an ontological one, concerning the nature of origination (*utpādaḥ*). The opponent suggests that origination can bring about the object originating, as well as itself, and introduces the example of the light in MMK 7:8 to support this claim. It is interesting, however, that Chandrakīrti's discussion of this example in the PP gives a quotation from the *Ratnakūṭasūtra* that underlines the epistemological import of the example:

> [Light and darkness] both are empty.... Knowledge does not think "may there not be ignorance," [but] it is because of knowledge that ignorance is destroyed. Both cannot be grasped, like a flower in the sky, hence knowledge and ignorance are both empty.[156]

The fundamental idea underlying Nāgārjuna's discussion of the example of the light is that neither illumination and darkness, nor knowledge and ignorance, should be considered as two independent substances acting on each other in the processes of illumination and cognition, bringing about the destruction of darkness or ignorance, respectively. As mutually exclusive phenomena, they are interdependent and therefore empty.

⌘ Moreover,

VP 11 **Because of the contradictory consequence that darkness conceals itself.**

If the light illuminated itself and others, what would result with respect to the example? Because it is the opposite, darkness would conceal itself. If darkness concealed its own self, in that respect darkness would not be observed. To whom should it be replied? The word "if" is said with reference to those who themselves assert the statement "the light illuminates itself and others." Also, if it is itself concealed precisely by the very darkness itself, there is no illumination with respect to the light. ⌘ ⌘

In this verse Nāgārjuna discusses the second argument against the self-illumination of the light.

156. *ubhayaṁ pi śūnyaṁ... | jñānaṁ na kalpeti añānu no bhavet jñānaṁ pratītyaiva vinaśyate tamo* [Tib: *ye shes brten nas mi shes med par 'gyur*] | *bhayaṁ pi agrāhya khapuṣpasaṁnibhaṁ jñānaṁ tathājñānu bhayaṁ pi śūnyam*, (Poussin 1903–13, 156–157).

VP 11 Because of the contradictory consequence that darkness conceals itself.

If the light illuminated itself and others, what would result with respect to the example? Because it is the opposite, darkness would conceal itself. If darkness concealed its own self in that respect darkness would not be observed.

Again, we find a discussion of this point both in the MMK and in the VP.[157] The argument sets out to establish that if some object's power (such as the light's power to illuminate) acted on the object itself, the opposite power of the opposite object (in this case, the power of darkness to conceal) would also act on the opposite object itself.

In his discussion of MMK 7:12, May[158] points out that this argument is an "application de la loi de solidarité des contraires" (the law of correspondence of contraries), "qui constitue un des instruments importants de la dialectique Mādhyamika."[159] This law, referred to by Schayer[160] as the "*pratidvandvin*-Gesetz der mahāyānistischen Metalogik" states that if some object is irreal, its opposite must be irreal too, and if some object is real, its opposite is also real.[161]

Of course the point at issue here is not just that if light exists, darkness exists as well (the existence of both is not disputed), but if light has an essential property, such as acting on itself according to its nature, which is illumination, so will darkness, thus acting on itself according to *its* nature, which is obscuration.

Like the opponent described by Chandrakīrti, who argues that, since the opposite of samsara (nirvana) exists substantially, so does samsara

157. MMK 7:12 and VV 36. On the latter, see Westerhoff 2010, 76–77.

158. May 1959, 11n299.

159. May 1959, 66n68.

160. Schayer 1931, 36n29.

161. Schayer 1931, 95. May (1959, 16): "Le *principe de solidarité des contraires* permet au Mādhyamika de renvoyer dos à dos des thèses out des catégories opposées. En effet, si A n'existe pas, son contraire n'existera pas non plus. Les contraires sont solidaires dans l'existence ou l'inexistence, et non opposés comme nous avons l'habitude de le penser." See also Chandrakīrti on MMK 2:15: "If the opposite exists, it exists, like darkness and light"; *yasya ca pratipakṣo'sti, tadasti ālokāndhakāravat* (Poussin 1903–13, 101:13–14).

itself,[162] the opponent here uses the *pratidvandvin* principle (which Nāgārjuna endorses) with a false premise, claiming that:

> The opposite of darkness, light, acts on itself, therefore darkness too acts on itself.

Yet if darkness "acts on itself," darkness would be self-concealing and therefore could not be observed. But we all know that darkness can be observed; the opponent's position leads to a consequence that contradicts our experience of the world, in which we can perceive darkness. Nāgārjuna can then use this absurd consequence as a basis of a *modus tollens*, arguing that, since we observe darkness, we have to reject the initial premise that led to this consequence, namely that light illuminates itself.

> *The word "if" is said with reference to those who themselves assert the statement "the light illuminates itself and others." Also, if it is itself concealed precisely by the very darkness itself, there is no illumination with respect to the light.*

Nāgārjuna points out that the peculiar consequence of the self-concealment of darkness only applies to those who believe that lights are self-illuminating and other-illuminating. Moreover, the alleged unobservability of darkness is not only in conflict with our perception of the world around us but also leads to further problems if we agree to the "worldly" understanding that illumination happens by the light-dispelling darkness, for if darkness cannot be seen there is nothing for illumination to dispel in order to let us see an object hidden in darkness. Things would be permanently visible and illuminated, since the darkness obscuring them would itself be invisible.[163] It appears as if the assumption of self-illumination not only leads to views that conflict with everyday experience but also implies that illumination of any kind, whether self-illumination or illumination of other objects, cannot come about in the first place.

162. *asti ca saṁsārasya pratidvandvi nirvāṇam | tasmādasti saṁsāra iti* (Poussin 1903–13, 287:16–17).

163. This is pointed out in the AK (Huntington 1986, 312:9–11) and by Buddhapālita's comments on MMK 7:12 (Saito 1984, 96:8–10).

⌘ Moreover,

VP 12 Epistemic instrument and epistemic object are not established in the three times.

Is the epistemic instrument prior or posterior to the epistemic object, or are epistemic instrument and epistemic object simultaneous?

With regard to that, if the epistemic instrument is prior to the epistemic object, due to what is that called "epistemic instrument"? There is no existent epistemic object by which it is an epistemic instrument and something that is ascertained by an epistemic instrument.

On the other hand, if it is later, how does it become an epistemic instrument for the existent epistemic object? The non-arisen is not suitable as an epistemic instrument for something arisen, since there is the contradictory consequence that a hare's horn could even be an epistemic instrument, and because the arisen and the non-arisen do not dwell together.

Nor is it the case that they are simultaneous; for example the simultaneously arisen horns of a bull are not suitable as cause and effect. ⌘ ⌘

VP 12 Epistemic instrument and epistemic object are not established in the three times.

Is the epistemic instrument prior or posterior to the epistemic object or are epistemic instrument and epistemic object simultaneous?

In this verse Nāgārjuna examines the three possible temporal relations in which the epistemic instruments and epistemic objects could stand: the instruments could be earlier than the objects, they could be later, or they could exist at the same time.[164] This argumentative pattern (sometimes referred to as the *traikālyāsiddhi* argument) is encountered frequently in

164. Compare Vātsyāyana's commentary on NS 5.1.18. See also Kajiyama 1991, 110.

Madhyamaka literature and applied to a variety of phenomena,[165] such as causation[166] and negation.[167]

> *With regard to that, if the epistemic instrument is prior to the epistemic object, due to what is that called "epistemic instrument"? There is no existent epistemic object by which it is an epistemic instrument and something that is ascertained by an epistemic instrument.*

Epistemic instruments depend on epistemic objects, not just for being called "epistemic objects," but also for their existence. This is because it is hard to make sense of something as a means of cognitive access without there being what it is supposed to be a means of access to. The difficulty is similar to an irregularly shaped piece of metal being useful as a screwdriver without there being any kind of screw it could be operating on. Even the most bizarrely shaped piece might be a perfectly feasible screwdriver, given a sufficiently bizarre screw. And the existence of the screw is not just necessary for *calling* the piece of metal a screwdriver, it would not *be* a screwdriver in the absence of a screw to drive, but just an irregularly shaped piece of metal. Assume we found such a piece of metal in an archaeological excavation, and it turned out to be the perfect instrument for loosening a certain type of modern screw. It would be strange to use this as a justification for referring to the piece of metal as an "ancient screwdriver," given that the type of screws did not exist when the piece of metal was shaped. The exact same problem, Nāgārjuna argues, is faced by one who argues that epistemic instruments can exist before the epistemic objects they are supposed to access exist. While there is no epistemic object around, it is very hard to assess the suitability of anything as a cognitive means for knowing that object, or even make sense of what it would mean to say that an epistemic instrument existed at that time.

165. See Siderits and Katsura 2013, 8.

166. ŚS 6; Lindtner 1982, 221:16–22; Della Santina 2002, 155. As such, the response given by Vātsyāyana in his commentary on NS 5.1.19, which draws an analogy with causation, would not be regarded as satisfactory by the Mādhyamika.

167. VV 20; see Westerhoff 2010, 123–29. For a very detailed comparison of the use of the *traikālyāsiddhi* argument in the VV and NS, see Meuthrath 1999, 29–58. Another example of the *traikālyāsiddhi* argument applied to epistemology can be found in Āryadeva's *Śata-śāstra* (Tucci 1981, 50–51).

Similar arguments are employed by the Mādhyamika to establish that a cause cannot be temporally prior to its effect, and that a negation cannot be prior to what it negates. In the former case, the difficulty is that only the existence of the effect lets us gather the diverse collection of events and states of affairs into a unitary causal field; in the absence of the effect, there is simply no justification why some event should be regarded as forming part of the causal field, while another should not be.[168] In the latter case, it is necessary to remind ourselves that each negation is the negation of some content (in the same way in which every assertion is the assertion of some content), which entails that it cannot exist while its content does not yet exist.

It is interesting to note that the very same difficulty concerning the possibility of temporal relations between epistemic instruments and epistemic objects is also raised by an opponent in the NS.[169] However, the arguments presented in order to undermine the three different relations differ from the ones presented here. They are aimed specifically at pointing out inconsistencies between the assumption of temporal relations between epistemic instruments and objects and other Naiyāyika tenets.[170] Thus, in order to argue that the epistemic instrument cannot exist before the effect, the opponent does not raise the point that the instrument existentially depends on the object, but notes that for the Naiyāyika, perception consists of contact between the sense-organ and the sensory object.[171] Perception is of course one of the epistemic instruments, so it is unclear in this particular case how there could be a form of contact between an object that exists now (the epistemic instrument) and one that only exists in the future (its object).

> *On the other hand, if it is later, how does it become an epistemic instrument for the existent epistemic object? The non-arisen is not suitable as an epistemic instrument for something arisen, since there*

168. See Westerhoff 2009, 95–99.

169. NS 2.1.8–11. Vāchaspati Mishra identifies the opponent as a Mādhyamika (Ruben 1928, 22). Bronkhorst (1985, 107; who offers a very different reading) claims that the arguments presented could equally come from a Sarvāstivāda source.

170. See Meutrath (1996, 42–44) for a discussion of the idea that different types of *traikālyāsiddhi* arguments are being discussed in this section of the *Nyāyasūtra*.

171. NS 1.1.2, 2.1.25.

> *is the contradictory consequence that a hare's horn could even be an epistemic instrument, and because the arisen and the non-arisen do not dwell together.*

In the reverse scenario, where the epistemic instrument is later than the epistemic object, there is going to be a time when the object exists, while the instrument does not yet exist. Nāgārjuna identifies two difficulties with this. First of all, as future objects do not exist in the present, the epistemic instrument for apprehending some object will be nonexistent while the object exists. Not only is it unclear how a nonexistent thing could fulfill any functional role, such as giving us cognitive access to some object, there would also have to be a way in which we could distinguish epistemic instruments from epistemic non-instruments that also happen not to exist. Hares do not have horns, thus a hare's horn can carry out the very same functions as a (nonexistent) epistemic instrument, namely none at all. Yet it sounds distinctly odd to say that it is things like hare's horns, present kings of Nepal, and square circles that guarantee our epistemic access to the world. Secondly, and this consideration also applies to the previous section, if the epistemic instruments and epistemic objects are located at distinct points in time, presupposing the theory of momentariness, that which exists at one point will not exist at any other point. For this reason, instruments and objects could never come together in a way that allows us to gain cognitive access to the world.

In order to refute the supposition of temporal priority of the object over the instrument, NS 2.1.10 points out an inconsistency with the Nyāya assumption that objects are cognized by epistemic instruments.[172] If the objects are established by the instruments, supposing that the instruments exist only after the objects implies that the objects must have previously been established in some way (without the instruments) in order to exist.

> *Nor is it the case that they are simultaneous, for example the simultaneously arisen horns of a bull are not suitable to be cause and effect.*

The only remaining possible temporal relation between epistemic instruments and epistemic objects is that they exist at the same temporal point.

172. *pramāṇataścārtha pratipatteḥ* (NS 4.2.29).

Nāgārjuna notes that this causes difficulties for our assumption that there is a causal relation between the two. Perception, the first epistemic instrument, is the effect of contact between an epistemic object and a sense-organ.[173] Object and sense-organ constitute the cause, which would have to be regarded as simultaneous with an instance of the resulting epistemic instrument.

But we usually take the effect to be something that exists *after* the cause. It seems that our conceptualization into causes and effects loses its footing when we consider simultaneous events. We can argue that Peter going up the see-saw causes Paul to go down, but we might equally claim that Paul's going down causes Peter's going up—an unwelcome consequence if we also consider causation to be asymmetric. In this context, it is also worthwhile to remind ourselves of the Humean point that, since a cause's effect is another effect's cause, the simultaneity of causes and effects implies that the entire causal chain is telescoped into one instance, so that everything would happen at once.

NS 2.1.11 identifies the difficulty of the simultaneous existence of epistemic instruments and objects with the Nyāya assumption that simultaneous perceptions are impossible.[174] For if an epistemic object, such as a rose, existed at the same time as the perception of its color and existed at the same time as the perception of its smell, identity being transitive, both perceptions would be simultaneous. Yet this contradicts the Nyāya view that such perceptions are only possible in succession.

NS 2.1.15 argues against the rejection of the three possible relations between epistemic instruments and objects by mentioning the example of the drum established from its sound.[175] The idea is here that an earlier existent object (the drum) can be known by something that exists only later (the sound that it makes when beaten). The second possibility, that the object exists before the instrument, thus seems to be possible.[176]

173. NS 1.1.4: "Perception is knowledge that arises from the contact of a sense-organ with the object"; *indriyārthasaṁnikarṣotpannaṁ jñānam...pratyakṣam.*

174. NS 1.1.16. For a different interpretation of NS 2.1.11, understanding it as an argument against the exclusive existence of the present moment, see Bronkhorst 1985. A criticism of this interpretation is in Meuthrath 1999, 34–35.

175. *śabdād ātodya-siddhivat.*

176. Vātsyāyana points out that the other two temporal relations are possible as well; the epistemic instrument can exist before the object, as the light of the sun can exist before the things it illuminates, and instrument and object can exist at the same time, like fire that is inferred from smoke.

Meutrath[177] raises the point that the difficulties with possible relations between the epistemic instruments and objects brought forward by the opponent in NS 2.1.9–11 trade on an equivocation between "different modes of being of an object," namely its existence and its being known, a mistake facilitated by the use of the term *siddhi*, an expression that can denote both ontological "establishment" (existence) as well as epistemological "establishment" (being known). The drum example would then be considered as underlining the point that the order of existence (first drum, then sound) can be different from the order of cognition (first sound, then drum) and that the difficulties raised for the temporal relations between the two disappear once these two orders are distinguished.[178]

There is reason to be skeptical, though, that the distinction between "being" and "being known" is sufficient to defuse the *traikālyāsiddhi* argument in all its manifestations. In response to the criticism of the first possible temporal relation, that epistemic instruments cannot be prior to epistemic objects since they would otherwise not be instruments of anything (Nāgārjuna's point), and cannot stand in any relation of contact with the yet nonexistent epistemic object (the point of NS 2.1.9), the Naiyāyika defender would reply that in fact this is a case in which the epistemic instrument exists as an object (like the sun before it illuminates a yet-to-be-made thing), though it does not yet exist as an object that produces knowledge, i.e., as an epistemic instrument. The danger with this reply is that it makes "being an epistemic instrument" a relational property, a property not solely based in the individual that has it, but something that essentially involves another thing, in this case the object to be cognized. In the absence of an object to be known, everything could be an epistemic instrument (just as everything could be a screwdriver if we don't know what the screw is going to look like), and for this reason nothing will be an epistemic instrument intrinsically. Any closed list of epistemic instruments would lose much of its point, because any outlandish procedure might turn out to be an epistemic instrument if the right kinds of objects come along.

In response to the second possible temporal relation, that the instrument cannot be posterior to the object, the defender points out that all

177. Meutrath 1996, 41n123, and 1999, 42n149.

178. See also Oetke 1991, 21.

sorts of things can exist, even though they are not yet known (as the silent and unseen drum). In these cases, the epistemic object seems to exist first, yet our means of epistemic access to it, the epistemic instrument, only comes into existence later. While this is a good reply to the opponent's criticism in NS 2.1.10, it is not so clear whether it manages to dispel Nāgārjuna's worry. This is obvious if we accept the theory of momentariness (as a Mādhyamika would), for in this case, by the time the epistemic instrument comes into existence, the epistemic object will already have passed out of existence. For this reason, the two could never come together in a knowledge-producing contact. Yet even if we do not presuppose the theory of momentariness, the strict division between ontological and epistemological establishment this defense implies is likely to prove problematic. For the critic might point out that it is not sufficient to show that an object like the drum can exist before *some* of the epistemic instruments accessing it (such as its auditory or visual perception). Rather, one would have to establish that it can exist prior to *any* means of epistemic access, that is, in the absence of any way of getting to know it by inference, testimony, or likeness. Given the Nyāya assumption that all epistemic access happens via the epistemic instruments, one would thus be committed to the existence of objects that are, at a specific point in time, completely unknown and unknowable. This sits rather uneasily with Nyāya epistemic optimism, which regards the world as a whole as knowable.[179]

Regarding the third possible temporal relation, that of simultaneity of epistemic instruments and objects, differentiating between epistemological and ontological establishment helps in addressing the problem of simultaneous perceptions raised in NS 2.1.11. The Naiyāyika could point out that in fact we are dealing with two epistemic objects, the rose's color and its smell, and of these only one exists as epistemically established at any one time, while both are ontologically established at the same time.[180] While perceiving the rose's color, its smell exists unperceived, and vice versa. All

179. "According to Nyāya ontology, all things are knowable, and hence knowability characterizes everything and absence of knowability characterizes nothing." (Matilal 1968, 93) "The Naiyāyika affirms his complete confidence in the faculties of man to know the world. He even goes further and asserts that not only is there nothing which is unknowable, but also, given a proper method of knowing, there is nothing which cannot be known by men." (Junankar 1978, 486)

180. Meuthrath 1999, 45.

the Naiyāyika has to commit to here is that some object is unknowable for a certain person at a certain time (because no more than one perception "fits in" at any one time), but not that any objects are unknown (or unknowable) *tout court*.

Yet this differentiation does not help to dispel Nāgārjuna's worry, at least if the principle of momentariness is assumed. Pointing out that the epistemic instrument (in this case, the perception) is epistemologically established, while the epistemic object is ontologically established, does not help to resolve the difficulty of how the two could on the one hand be simultaneous, yet on the other hand stand in a cause-effect relationship.

It is objected:

VP 13 **The negation is not reasonable, because the epistemic instruments and epistemic objects are not established in the three times.**

It is claimed that the epistemic instruments and epistemic objects are not established in the three times. So is your statement, which is the negation of epistemic instrument and epistemic object, prior to or posterior to the object to be negated or is it simultaneous? That negation is not established in the three times.

Because the object to be negated does not exist, how can your words negate, and how is the negation of that established?

On the other hand, if you say that the negation is established, if a similarity in meaning to the investigation of the three times is established, the epistemic instrument and epistemic object are established, or the difference has to be asserted.

Therefore, if the object of negation and what negates are not established in the three times, it is like that, and the negation is also not established.

VP 13 The negation is not reasonable because the epistemic instruments and epistemic objects are not established in the three times.

The preceding verse VP 12 discussed the problem of the relation of epistemic instruments and objects to the three times also raised in NS 2.1.8–11. VP 13 continues the discussion with a point also raised in the directly following verse of the *Nyāyasūtra*,[181] namely the question of whether the negation of the existence of epistemic instruments and objects in the three times entails problems for the very possibility of asserting any kind of negation.

> *It is claimed that the epistemic instruments and epistemic objects are not established in the three times. So is your statement, which is the negation of epistemic instrument and epistemic object, prior to or posterior to the object to be negated or is it simultaneous? That negation is not established in the three times.*

The opponent points out that if we assume that there is no conceivable way in which the notions of epistemic instruments and objects can be arranged in a temporal order of "before," "after," and "at the same time with," there is nothing stopping us from applying the very same reasoning to negation and whatever it negates. The same issue is raised in a more detailed manner by the opponent in VV 20, and there as well as here, it makes sense to conceive of negation as an action that is applied to a thesis in order to refute it, rather than as an atemporal logical operator applied to an atemporal proposition.[182]

As before, there are three possibilities to consider:

1. The negation exists before the negated object.
2. The negation exists after the negated object.
3. Negation and negated object exist at the same time.

1. The opponent focuses on the first possibility:

> *Because the object to be negated does not exist, how can your words negate and how is the negation of that established?*

181. NS 2.1.12: "When it is not established in the three times the negation is unaccomplished"; *traikālyāsiddheḥ pratiṣedānupapattiḥ.*

182. See Westerhoff 2010, 123–29.

If the negation exists first, before the object to be negated, we would have to assume that there can be a negation that does not (yet) negate anything. The difficulty with this is that, in the same way in which the epistemic instrument depends on the epistemic object for its existence, we cannot have a negation, understood as a cognitive operation applied to some content, existing prior to its content, without it being the negation of anything. If we do not think of negation as an abstract logical operator (in which case the issue of the temporal relation between it and its content would not arise in the first place),[183] the idea of a contentless negation would be as peculiar as a contentless breaking, a breaking that is not the breaking of a particular clay pot or porcelain vase but a mere breaking without anything broken.

If the object to be negated does not exist, the words expressing the negation do not express any content and are unable to establish the negation of the object to be negated. One might want to object here that there can be empty expressions (such as "the present king of Nepal") that are nevertheless not devoid of content, and as a consequence their negations are not contentless either. But this reply is not available to the Naiyāyika who claims that only existent objects can be negated.[184]

Even though the remaining two possible temporal relations are not discussed explicitly here, consideration of the autocommentary on VV 20 gives us a fairly good idea of what Nāgārjuna's opponent would have had to say about these.

2. The opponent is likely to argue that if negation came after the object negated, it would already be too late. For if the negated object is already established, what is the point of the negation? Of course negations such as the denial that rabbits have horns are perfectly meaningful to us, and we do not think that in some contradictory manner they say that there are horned rabbits, and then take it back. Moreover, the Naiyāyika need not understand such a negation in this way, but could rather view it as an assertion that the property of having horns and the property of being a rabbit

183. Oetke (1991, 14–15) argues that since the relata of negations should be understood in precisely this way, the objection raised in NS 2.1.12 does not get off the ground. I have some doubts about the usefulness of assessing the Nyāya analysis of negation by using the view of negation found in contemporary philosophical logic as a yardstick.

184. See Matilal 1985, 52, 79; and Tola and Dragonetti 1995a, 109. See also VV 11 (Westerhoff 2010, 109–16), and VV 15 (Westerhoff 2010, 118).

are never coinstantiated. Both these properties are individually instantiated, and for the Naiyāyika every sufficiently simple property would have to be, since for him, absences are exclusively local absences of existent objects. Claiming that there is no pot in the house can only mean that the pot is at some other location, not that there are no pots *tout court*. But this means that at the most fundamental level of epistemic contact with the world, negations can never pertain to something that has already been apprehended by an epistemic instrument, since, once it has been established, this establishment cannot be reversed by applying the operation of negation. That negations come after the objects they negate is only an appearance, because in these cases the objects are not real objects but merely disguised claims about coinstantiated properties.

3. If negation is understood as an action applied to a thesis, rather than as an atemporal operation, it is understood in causal terms. However, as we saw in the discussion of VP 12, the assumption that cause and effect are simultaneous leads to a variety of difficulties.

Now if negation cannot be conceived of as operating within the framework of "before," "after," and "at the same time as," it becomes unclear in general how it can form part of our argumentative practices (which do operate in this framework), and in particular how the Mādhyamika could successfully negate the establishment of epistemic instruments and epistemic objects in the manner described in VP 12.

On the other hand, if you say that the negation is established, if a similarity in meaning to the investigation of the three times is established the epistemic instrument and epistemic object are established, or the difference has to be asserted.

If the negation of the epistemic instruments and objects is successful, on the other hand, and if this negation derives its justification from difficulties of relating the instruments and objects by the relations "before," "after," and "at the same time as," then it is similarly problematic to relate the negation and the negated objects by these temporal relations. If the Mādhyamika does not want to accept this consequence, he would have to point out what specific difference there is between the pair "epistemic instrument / epistemic object" and the pair "negation / object of negation," such that the former cannot be located in the framework of "before," "after," and "at the same time as," while the latter can. But, the opponent argues, no indication of such a difference has been provided.

> *In that way if the object of negation and what negates are not established in the three times, it is like that, and the negation is also not established.*

For this reason, the opponent argues, the Madhyamaka reasoning is self-defeating, because in attempting to negate the establishment of the epistemic instruments and objects, it deprives itself of the conceptual resources to carry out this very negation.[185] Since the attempted negation fails, both the epistemic instruments and the epistemic objects have to be regarded as existing.

Tola and Dragonetti[186] point out that the opponent is here using a debate move (called *matānujñā*) that the Naiyāyikas themselves regard as deficient.[187] Such a move occurs if some debater A is criticized for a mistake in reasoning and replies to his opponent B that B makes the very same mistake. By doing so, A has accepted that he himself made this mistake. Here the Mādhyamika criticizes the opponent's epistemological position by accusing him of being unable to account for the temporal relation of the epistemic concepts employed. The opponent replies that the Mādhyamika is himself unable to account for the temporal relations between the argumentative resources he employs, thereby admitting that the original criticism against the opponent was justified.

The resulting dialectical situation is interesting. On the one hand, the Mādhyamika can argue that by the Naiyāyika's own understanding of the *matānujñā* debate move, his criticism has been accepted. The Naiyāyika is likely to reply, on the other hand, that since the issues of the temporal relations for the pair "epistemic instrument / epistemic object" and the pair "negation / object of negation" are intrinsically linked, the Mādhyamika would never be able to prove his negative point, if it were true. There are at least two different ways in which the Mādhyamika could defend himself

185. As is pointed out in NS 5.1.20: "From the fact that the negation is unaccomplished [it follows that] what is to be negated is not negated"; *pratiṣedhānupapatteśca pratiṣedhavyāpratiṣedhaḥ*.

186. Tola and Dragonetti 1995a, 189n5.

187. NS 5.2.20.

here. Firstly, he could point out that again the Naiyāyika would accept an example of an unknowable truth (as the Mādhyamika's negative point that the epistemic instrument and object cannot be related by temporal relations would be such that it could not be established by reasoning, and it presumably could not be established by the other epistemic instruments either).[188] Secondly, the Mādhyamika could argue that the kind of establishment in the three times that the Naiyāyika demands for the epistemic instruments and objects, and the kind of establishment that the Mādhyamika demands for the negation and negated objects are fundamentally different, insofar as the former is a substantial or ultimate kind of establishment, whereas the latter is only a conventional kind of establishment. According to the Mādhyamika, only the former but not the latter can be obtained.

⁜ It will be replied:

VP 14 **It is not the case that "if the negation is established, the epistemic instruments and the epistemic objects are established as well," because of the previous assertion.**

You cannot object that there are epistemic instruments and epistemic objects because of the investigation of the three times, and because of the negation. Why is that? Because of the previous assertion. Just now you claimed that "epistemic instruments and epistemic objects are not established in the three times." Following that statement, and having seen this defect, after thorough investigation one cannot say that "the negation is also not established by that destruction." ⁜ ⁜

VP 14 It is not the case that "if the negation is established the epistemic instruments and the epistemic objects are established as well," because of the previous assertion.

188. Compare the discussion of VP 12, as well as Oetke 1991, 15.

> *You cannot object that there are epistemic instruments and epistemic objects because of the investigation of the three times, and because of the negation.*

In this verse we find Nāgārjuna's Naiyāyika opponent introducing a new argument for the existence of epistemic instruments and epistemic objects. He argues as follows: "Let's accept that the epistemic instruments and objects do not exist, because their temporal relations relative to the three times cannot be consistently analyzed, as suggested in VP 12.[189] But we know that in the Nyāya framework, negations are only ever reports of local absences, since there must be something for the negation to work on.[190] So if the argument from the three times manages to negate the existence of the epistemic instruments and objects, they must exist somewhere, and for this reason their existence has been established."

> *Why is that? Because of the previous assertion. Just now you claimed that "epistemic instruments and epistemic objects are not established in the three times." Following that statement, and having seen this defect [of your reasoning], after thorough investigation one cannot say that "the negation [of the epistemic instruments and epistemic objects] is also not established by that destruction [of them]."*

Nāgārjuna objects to the claim that the "destruction" (*'jig pa*) of the epistemic instruments and epistemic objects via the argument from the

189. We can understand the argument here in two ways: (1) The opponent realizes the difficulties posed by his rejection of negation, mentioned at the end of our commentary on VP 13. (2) The opponent attempts to construct a dilemma, arguing that either there is no negation of the epistemic instruments and objects (VP 13, the first horn), in which case Nāgārjuna is refuted by inconsistency, since he wants to negate these categories, or there is such a negation (VP 14, the second horn), in which case he is refuted by the specific Nyāya understanding of negation. The phrase "wanting to give up your own fault" (*rang gi skyon spang bar 'dod pa*) in the autocommentary on VP 15, speaks in favor of the first alternative.

190. "One may point out that properties like absence of red-color, which Nyāya urges us to construe as separate properties, are always dependent upon some counterpositive properties." (Matilal 1968, 93) "[W]e cannot negate a non-entity whatsoever,...in all negations that we can speak of, the negatum (*pratiyogin*) cannot be a nonentity (*alīka*)." (Matilal 1985, 79) Thus the negation asserting the absence of red depends on the presence of red (its "counterpositive," *pratiyogi*; see Ingalls 1951, 55) elsewhere, and, more generally, the negation of anything necessitates its presence elsewhere.

three times would be unable to establish their negation, since the peculiar Nyāya understanding of negation manages to reintroduce their existence through the back door. The reason he gives for that is "the previous assertion" (*sngar khas blangs pa*). This is somewhat elliptical, but can be easily unpacked. The "assertion" Nāgārjuna has in mind here is the opponent's acceptance for the sake of argument that the epistemic instruments and objects are in fact refuted by the argument from the three times. But it is due to the nature of the refutation accepted here that the next Nyāya move, claiming that the existence of the refuted object must be presupposed for the refutation to make sense, cannot work. This is because the negation of the epistemic instruments and epistemic objects cannot be in any sense construed as a "local" negation, like the negation of a pot being in the house, or a man being in the garden. The set of the three times is comprehensive; once it has been demonstrated that something does not exist in the past, in the present, or in the future, there is no possibility for it to be located somewhere else. Having asserted its absence in the three times, there is literally nowhere to put the contrapositive, i.e., its presence.[191] It must therefore be regarded as nonexistent *tout court*, not as nonexistent relative to some temporal or spatial location. For this reason, the Naiyāyika is unable to consider the absence established by this kind of negation as entailing a presence somewhere else.

VP 15 **If epistemic instruments and epistemic objects are said not to be established, the debate is finished at the same time as this assertion.**

Why is that? You, who are self-satisfied and foolish, object, just when the epistemic instruments and epistemic objects are not established in the three times, saying that the refutation and the words refuting are also not established. At that time, is it not the case that you, now wanting to give

191. We have noted already that negation in this context is to be understood as a linguistic or mental act, not as a logical operation conceived as an abstract object. For this reason, arguing that if negation is not located in the three times, it must be located outside of time (as abstract objects are usually understood to be), is not going to be successful in this context.

up your own fault, assert the nonexistence of the epistemic instrument and epistemic object? Because epistemic instruments and epistemic objects do not exist, you object by asking, "What is this refutation?" As it has been said that epistemic instruments and epistemic objects do not exist, and subsequently that the refutation is refuted, the debate is already finished when the first assertion is made.

> *VP 15 If epistemic instruments and epistemic objects are said not to be established, the debate is finished at the same time as this assertion.*

In this verse Nāgārjuna sets out to refute both of the opponent's arguments from the preceding verses VP 13 and 14. In VP 13, the opponent pointed out that rejecting the establishment of the epistemic instruments and objects by the argument from the three times suggested by Nāgārjuna in VP 12 would simultaneously reject the possibility of asserting any negations at all. In VP 14 he noted that even if one were tempted to endorse this rejection, the negation would, via the specific Nyāyā understanding presupposed, entail the establishment of the epistemic instruments and objects, contrary to Nāgārjuna's intentions.

> *Why is that? You, who are self-satisfied and foolish object, just when the epistemic instruments and epistemic objects are not established in the three times, saying that the refutation and the words refuting are also not established.*

The term translated here as "foolish" (*lha rnams dga' ba*, itself a translation of the Sanskrit *devānām priya*), which also occurs in VP 53, is interesting. It literally means "beloved of the gods"; Aśoka famously used to refer to himself by the (Prakrit) term *devānaṁpiya* or its variants. Its Chinese translation (天愛, *tian ai*) is sometimes used as a name for the Buddha.[192] Later, the phrase has been the subject of a semantic shift from

192. The phrase appears seven times in 佛說佛名經, *Foshuo Fomingjing*, "The Buddha Names Sutra," (T.14.440), said to have been translated by Bodhiruci around 510–20 and once in 現在賢劫千佛名經, *Xianzai xian jie qien foming jing*, "Thousand Buddha Names in the Present Era of the Worthies" (T.14.447a). There is, however, the strong possibility that both are apocryphal texts written in China. I thank Dan Lusthaus for this information.

an auspicious epithet to a pejorative term referring to a stupid person or a fool. An underlying reason might have been the idea (present in India, as well as in the West) that fools are those whom fortune favors, so that particular care from the gods might be indicative of less than impressive intellectual abilities. Yet there is no consensus on (and considerable discussion of) the origin and motivation of this shift.[193]

In this passage Nāgārjuna first reminds us of what happened in VP 13. The opponent objected that if we were convinced by a refutation based on the three times in general, there would be no reason why this should not apply to the mental act of negation (*dgag pa*), and to the words expressing it (*'gog par byed pa'i tshig*). This is, of course, just the point Nāgārjuna's opponent makes in VV 20, where he argues for the impossibility of a refutation or negation since there is a difficulty in establishing a temporal relation between the negation and whatever it negates.[194]

> *At that time is it not the case that you, now wanting to give up your own fault, assert the nonexistence of the epistemic instruments and epistemic objects? Because epistemic instruments and epistemic objects do not exist, you object by asking "What is this refutation?"*

Nāgārjuna now summarizes the opponent's move from VP 14. Realizing the potential difficulties with his position in VP 13,[195] in VP 14 he accepts the non-establishment of the epistemic instruments and objects, at least for the sake of argument. But then he asks what this refutation could possibly be if it were a refutation of nonexistent objects—for the Naiyāyika statements about absences have to be construed as referring to existent things that are absent to be meaningful at all.

193. See Palsule 1971 for further discussion, and Cardona 1976, 353n408 for additional references.

194. If the negation existed before the object it negates, there would be nothing for it to negate, and if it existed later, the negated object could not be refuted anymore, since it already exists. Negation and negated object also cannot be simultaneous, since the operation of the former on the latter is regarded to be a causal process, and in such processes the cause exists first, and the effect only exists subsequently. See Westerhoff 2010, 123–26.

195. Mentioned at the end of our commentary on VP 13.

As it has been said that epistemic instruments and epistemic objects do not exist, and subsequently that the refutation is refuted, the debate is already finished when the first assertion is made.

The opponent has first hypothetically accepted the argument from the three times in VP 13, agreeing that the epistemic instruments and epistemic objects are not established. In VP 14 he then turned around to argue that this very negation is not established. But, as Nāgārjuna points out, the debate has already been finished at step one, when the establishment of the epistemic instruments and objects has been denied.[196] This is because the opponent's initial agreeing to the refutation of the establishment of the epistemic instruments and epistemic objects for the sake of argument presupposes that a negation can be successfully applied to an object. He cannot subsequently deny the feasibility of negation without contradicting himself.

VP 16 **If it is said, "In case there is no negating, 'negation' does not exist"—that is not so. The conceptual thought of something non-established is rejected.**

It is like the following example: Some body of water is not very deep, and someone actually thinking that it is deep develops fear. In order to remove that one's terrifying fright, another, out of his knowledge, says to the first one: "This body of water is not deep."

Because it is reasonable, in order to clear away one's thought concerning the nonexistent, even though the object of negation does not exist, the negation is accomplished by asserting the object of negation.

Moreover, if one asserts a comparable mistake, by the assertion of the comparable mistake itself, the debate is finished. Having said that, another objection will be made.

196. See Lindtner 1997, 274.

VP 16 If it is said: "In case there is no negating, 'negation' does not exist"—that is not so. The conceptual thought of something non-established is rejected.

Tola and Dragonetti[197] consider the phrase *dgag par byed pa med na* as a translation the Sanskrit *pratiṣeddhum abhāve sati* and translate it as "when nonexistence is to be negated."[198] The Tibetan we have would be a strange way of rendering the Sanskrit, yet the autocommentary makes clear that something along these lines must be what is meant here. Perhaps there is a way of getting to this point even by following the translation given here, which is somewhat closer to the Tibetan text. The opponent employs the antecedent "there is no negating" (*dgag par byed pa med*) in order to refer to cases where the operation of negating cannot take place, because there is no object for the operation to operate upon. If there is no operation of negating, there is also no negation. Note that the opponent now employs a different argumentative maneuver in order to refute Nāgārjuna's negation of epistemic instruments and objects in the three times. Instead of stating (as he did in VP 14) that their negation must entail their existence, he is now arguing that if we do not want to presuppose their existence (and Nāgārjuna certainly does not want to do this), the negation cannot even obtain, since there is nothing for it to operate on. Nāgārjuna objects to this argument by proposing a different way to conceive of scenarios where the object of negation is lacking, namely as cases where a specific *thought* (*rtog pa*) about the object of negation is to be rejected. An example in the autocommentary spells out this thought in more detail.

Tola and Dragonetti[199] assert that, according to the opponent, if "the negation of *pramāṇa* and *prameya* is accepted, we must accept also the existence of the negated *pramāṇa* and *prameya*." What they mean here is that the epistemic instruments and objects must exist somewhere for the operation of negation to operate on them. If the opponent is a Naiyāyika (which their reference to VV 11, interpreted by them as the Naiyāyika speaking, suggests), it is clear what the opponent's point would be: that

197. Tola and Dragonetti 1995a, 189.

198. Kajiyama (1974, 390n23) changes *dgag par byed pa med na* to *dgag par bya ba med na* ("if there is no object of negation...").

199. Tola and Dragonetti 1995a, 110–11.

negating something commits us to the existence of the negated thing elsewhere. If the presence of the pot on the table is negated, it commits us to the existence of the pot elsewhere. Similarly, if we negate the existence of the epistemic instruments and epistemic objects in the three times (as Nāgārjuna did in VP 12), we would then be committed to their existence outside of the three times, and since both are intrinsically bound up with causal relations, which must exist in time, this position appears absurd. So the Naiyāyika would respond that the negation of their existence in the three times must be given up.

> *It is like the following example: Some body of water is not very deep, and someone actually thinking that it is deep, develops fear. In order to remove that one's terrifying fright, another, out of his knowledge, says to the first one: "This body of water is not deep."*

Nāgārjuna responds by pointing out that all the negation of some thing commits us to is the existence of the thought (*rtog pa*) of that thing. The negation of the existence of a deep river is asserted for the benefit of someone who believes there is a deep river, and only commits us to the existence of that belief. The purpose of the negation is removal of the thought, and thereby the removal of the painful mental states it gives rise to.[200]

An illustration of the same point frequently employed in Madhyamaka literature are the illusory strands of hair (*keśoṇḍuka, skra shad*) caused by vitreous floaters (*timira, rab rib*).[201] Only those suffering from this particular eye condition will see individual strands of hair, e.g., in an empty bowl. Someone may correct their mistaken belief by pointing out that there are actually no hairs in their bowl, without being thereby in any way committed to the existence of hairs. Even in a universe devoid of real hairs, the statement "there are no hairs in your bowl" could still be meaningful in order to remove the mistaken belief in apparent hairs. Such a statement would not require the existence of real or apparent hairs elsewhere, but only the *thought* of their existence in order to be meaningful.

200. Compare VV 13.

201. ŚS 66; Chandrakīrti's PP on MMK 15:11 (274:1), 18:9 (373:2–6), 23:7 (457:10), MĀ 6:29, MĀBh 106:10–110:3. See also Anne MacDonald: "Seeing Things: The *Timira* Disorder" (forthcoming).

Because it is reasonable, in order to clear away one's thought concerning the nonexistent, even though the object of negation does not exist, the negation is accomplished by asserting the object of negation.

This passage makes it clear that all that is necessary for successful negations is the assertion of mere words (*brjod pa*) to which the negation can become attached. No ontological commitment to the object of negation having to exist in some form or other as the referent of these words is necessary.[202]

Tola and Dragonetti[203] assert that the opponent's position has the "logical defect of deduc[ing] the impossibility of the negation of the deep river from the nonexistence of the deep river." The Naiyāyika might respond to this as follows. It is possible, he will argue, to negate the deep river, even though there is no deep river. We simply observe that there is a river there, but that the property of deepness does not inhere in it, but elsewhere (such as in a ravine). As such, the argument continues, the example of the river does not show that there is anything wrong in general with the Nyāya conception of negation that would lead to undue limitations regarding what it can negate.[204] But in this case there is then nothing wrong with Nāgārjuna's initial refutation of the epistemic instruments and objects, or the assumption that these do not exist. Their negation might similarly be construed as pointing out that various individually instantiated properties are not coinstantiated.

Moreover, if one asserts a comparable mistake, by the assertion of the comparable mistake itself, the debate is finished. Having said that, another objection will be made.

The aim of this very compressed statement is to bring the discussion back from the example to the main topic. Nāgārjuna points out that if the opponent asserts a mistake comparable to the one underlying the assertion that a nonexistent deep river cannot be negated, namely the mistake

202. Kajiyama (1974, 196) points out that the negation used in such cases is merely a negation for the sake of argument (仮に), not a negation simpliciter.

203. Tola and Dragonetti 1995a, 111.

204. See Westerhoff 2010, 111.

assuming that nonexistent epistemic instruments and objects cannot be negated, the debate is finished. This is because the opponent relies on a mistaken assumption; it is mistaken because it has just been shown that the nonexistence of something does not show that it cannot be meaningfully negated. For this reason, the opponent's attempt to demonstrate that Nāgārjuna's negation of the epistemic instruments and objects is either self-refuting (because it entails their existence) or meaningless (because it does not make sense to talk about negations of nonexistent things) must fail. The opponent immediately raises another objection in the following verse.

It is objected:

VP 17 **Perception, and so forth, exist. On the basis of what? Because of correct knowledge.**

If you say: "With regard to this, having cognized the object of perception, understanding of the qualities of action and nonaction is correct knowledge. The remainder is also similar. Therefore, the epistemic instruments and epistemic objects exist."

In this verse the opponent provides a brief description of a two-stage model of the acquisition of knowledge endorsed by the Naiyāyikas, using the example of perception.

1. At the first stage, sensory perception by a sensory organ takes place.[205] At this point only the object of perception is apprehended; there is no presupposition that this perception constitutes knowledge. Our perception of water in the distance might in fact be caused by a mirage. In this case we would not *know* that there is water in front of us.

2. At the second stage, we observe the functions the perceived object can fulfill and those that it cannot fulfill (*bya ba dang bya ba ma yin pa'i yon tan, kriyākriyāguṇa*).[206] The ability to successfully fulfill a function

205. To support this interpretation Kajiyama (1974, 390n25) changes *mngon sum gyi* to *mngon sum gyis.*

206. At the very beginning of his *Bhāṣya* on NS, Vātsyāyana points out that without epistemic instruments, there is no cognition of an object, and this cognition is in turn necessary

(*pravṛttisāmarthya*) of real water and of water in a mirage differ. Mirage water can be used to produce a visual impression of water, but not for irrigating fields. On the basis of knowing an object's function, correct knowledge of that object is gained.[207] The correctness of the perception achieved in stage 1 is established by the fact that it provides the basis for successful action:[208] unreal water cannot be drunk, but real water can be.[209]

---

for any successful activity involving the object (*pramāṇam antareṇa nārthapratipattiḥ, nārthapratipattim antareṇa pravṛttisāmarthyam*).

207. We should note that at this point we are only dealing with an epistemological account of correct knowledge (describing how it is gained) and not with an ontological one (describing what it is). For the Naiyāyika, truth is constituted by a correspondence between our representation and the world, not by the mere practical utility of certain beliefs. Compare Chatterjee (1978, 77): "According to Nyāya, knowledge is just the manifestation (*prakāśa*) of objects.... The truth and falsity of knowledge depend respectively on its conformity and non-conformity to objects or facts."

208. Sinha (1969, 211): "The knowledge 'this is water' is valid, if it leads to fruitful activity, if it prompts activity which quenches thirst. A judgement is true, if it has the capacity for prompting fruitful activity. If it does not prompt fruitful activity, it is invalid. The judgement 'this is silver' is invalid, if it cannot lead to fruitful activity. A shell mistaken for silver cannot come to practical use." Chatterjee (1978, 79): "Generally speaking, the Naiyāyikas maintain that the truth and falsity of knowledge are known by certain external conditions other than the conditions of knowledge itself (*parataḥ prāmāṇyāprāmāṇyajñapti*).... What, then, are the external conditions of the knowledge of validity or invalidity of knowledge? The Naiyāyikas answer that both are known by inference. While knowledge may be internally perceived, its validity or invalidity is to be *inferred* from such extrinsic conditions as its capacity or incapacity to produce successful activity (*pravṛttisāmarthya*)." Chatterjee and Datta (1950, 198–99) give the example of the cognition of a white powder believed to be sugar, and the necessity of a taste-test to ascertain the truth of this belief. They conclude that "the test of the truth or falsity of knowledge is the success or failure of our practical activities in relation to its object (*pravṛtti samārthya* or *pravṛtti samvāda*). True knowledge leads to successful practical activity, while false knowledge ends in failure."

209. Bijalwan (1977, 55–56): "If people try for an object and obtain it, they do not feel the necessity of examining the truth of the experience again. For instance, a man sees water and judges it as water. This judgement prompts him to move, but he also knows that similar judgement takes place even when he misapprehends the mirage for water. So, along with the judgement that 'this is water' a doubt about its validity also arises in his mind. This doubt is removed by quenching thirst or by bathing, i.e., by practically experiencing the presence of water. Here no further test is required to verify the practical experience. If, on the other hand, his knowledge turns out to be illusory, then it is a case of an extrinsic test of the invalidity of cognition." For the Nyāya discussion of whether knowledge bears its probative force intrinsically (*svataḥ-prāmānya*) or acquires it from external factors (*parataḥ-prāmānya*) more generally, see D'Almeida 1973, 46–62.

In the same way, knowledge is acquired by the three other Nyāya means of knowledge: inference, likeness, and testimony. At first a belief is inferred, established by likeness, or taken from testimony. In order to qualify as knowledge, this belief then has to be able to guide us to successful actions.

The opponent now points out that because we are able to arrive at correct knowledge through this two-step procedure, and because this correct knowledge must have come from somewhere, and must be knowledge of something, the epistemic instruments and the epistemic objects have to exist. Of course this is only a problem for Nāgārjuna if the opponent means by this (as he in fact does) that epistemic instruments and objects exist by *svabhāva*. If this kind of existence were implied, the opponent would have an epistemological argument based on a highly intuitive premise (namely that we have reliable knowledge of our surroundings) to reject the Mādhyamika's central conclusion (that nothing exists by *svabhāva*). It is therefore this kind of existence that Nāgārjuna needs to reject in the following discussion.

⌘ It is to be replied:

VP 18 **Even though perception, etc., is established, an epistemic object is not reasonable.**

If one says that, it has to be replied: If the epistemic instruments, perception, and so forth, are established, it should be objected, "What is the other, the object that is the epistemic object?" Because, even though potness is perceived, the pot is not perceived. When the sense faculty and the object toward which the sense faculty is wholly directed have been perceived, a sense-faculty sign (*dbang po'i rda*) is made for the visual sense faculty. Regarding that, the object to which it is wholly directed, that is what is perceived. Also, it depends on conditions like light, etc.

Therefore, if potness, etc., is fully established as perceived, what will become of the object that has become an epistemic object of which there is an epistemic instrument?

Similarly, there is the inference from the connection of fire and smoke, which has perception as a precondition. Therefore, if "inference" comes about, what will become of the other, the object of inferential activity of which there is an inference? The remainder is also similar. ⌘ ⌘

Even though the meaning of this verse is relatively clear (it provides a reply to the opponent's position from VP 17, pointing out that even if we have "correct knowledge" (*yang dag par rtogs pa*) and with it the epistemic instruments that generate it, this does not automatically give us epistemic objects), the details of the argument Nāgārjuna presents in the autocommentary in order to support this reply are less perspicuous.

It is not possible to make the meaning of the Tibetan explicit without a significant amount of translator's interpolations, yet in order to supply these one already has to have a fairly secure understanding of what the argument in question is. Tola and Dragonetti[210] solve this difficulty very well and present an interpretation that provides a coherent account of what the Tibetan appears to be saying, yet at the same time (some might say incongruously) putting a strong Yogāchāra spin on the passage. We will here consider an alternative translation that sets out to read Nāgārjuna's argument in a somewhat different way.

> *VP 18 Even though perception, etc., is established, [the assumption of] an epistemic object is not reasonable.*
>
> *If one says that, it has to be replied: If the epistemic instruments, perception, and so forth, are established it should be objected "What is the other, the object that is the epistemic object?" Because even though potness is perceived the pot is not perceived.*[211]

Note that the "that" does not refer to VP 18 but to VP 17. Nāgārjuna is speaking here, offering a reply to the opponent who maintains that the existence of correct knowledge entails the existence of epistemic instruments.

In contrast with Tola and Dragonetti, we do not translate the phrase *bum pa nyid* as "the pot itself" (*ghaṭa eva*) but consider it as the Tibetan

210. Tola and Dragonetti 1995a, 67–68.

211. Kajiyama (1974, 391n27) amends the Tibetan from *bum pa ni ma yin te* to *gsal bya ni ma yin te*, replacing the final reference to a pot by reference to epistemic objects (*prameya*).

rendering of *ghaṭatva*,[212] "pot-ness," the generality (*sāmānya, jāti*) that the Naiyāyikas considered to be present in all pots.

Thus understood, the passage connects with the Nyāyā theory of perception as happening in two stages. According to this theory, any sensory perception has a first stage of nonconceptual perception (*nirvikalpa*), which comes into contact with the generality instantiated by the object, followed by a conceptual (*savikalpa*) stage.[213] According to the Naiyāyika, generalities are grasped as "epistemic firsts"[214] and constitute an indispensable precondition for perception taking place.[215]

Dasgupta explains:[216]

> Thus in perception the proper contact of the visual sense with the object (e.g. jug) first brings about a non-intelligent, non-apprehensible indeterminate consciousness (*nirvikalpa*) as the jugness (*ghaṭatva*) and this later on combining with the remaining other collocations of sense-contact, etc., produces the determinate consciousness: this is a jug. The existence of this indeterminate state of consciousness as a factor in bringing about the determinate consciousness, cannot of course be perceived, but its existence can be inferred from the fact that if the perceiver were not already in possession of the qualifying factor (*viśeṣanajñāna* as jugness) he could not have comprehended the qualified object (*viśiṣṭabuddhi*) the jug (i.e., the object which possesses jugness).

Nāgārjuna's criticism is that even if an epistemic instrument such as perception is established for the Naiyāyika, perception does not get us into contact with the epistemic instrument's complementary "other," the epistemic instrument's object. For what perception acquaints us with, at

212. As does Yamaguchi 1944, 127.

213. Vāchaspati Mishra traces this distinction to NS 1.1.4 and its characterization of perception as inexpressible (*avyapadeśyam*) and determinate (*vyavasāyātmakam*). See Chatterjee 1978, 195n2; and Phillips 2012, 33–34.

214. Matilal 1986, 421.

215. Chakrabarti 2000, 5. See also Phillips 2001, and Chakrabarti 2001.

216. Dasgupta 1922, vol. 1, 412.

least in its first stage, is only the generality that the object instantiates, not the object itself.

> *When the sense faculty and the object toward which the sense faculty is wholly directed have been perceived, a sense-faculty sign (dbang po'i rda) was made for the visual sense faculty. Regarding that, the object to which it is wholly directed, that is perceived. Also, it depends on conditions like light, etc.*

Tola and Dragonetti[217] render the phrase *dbang po la rab tu phyogs pa'i don gang yin pa de ni mngon sum yin par byas nas* at the beginning of this passage as "because (only) that which is the correspondent object of a sense-organ is perceived." Their commentary then gives this passage a strong Yogāchāra reading[218] by understanding it along the lines of Vasubandhu's denial that extra-mental objects such as atoms can constitute epistemic objects.[219] This interpretation, for which the addition of the word "only" (not in the text, but a translator's addition) is crucial, reads Nāgārjuna as saying that even if there are epistemic instruments that produce "correct knowledge" (*yang dag par rtogs pa*), these do not provide epistemic objects understood as external objects, but merely mental representations. The argument they attribute to Nāgārjuna in support is that since "perception is a mental process, its counterpart can only be something mental."[220]

Note, however, that there is also another way of interpreting this passage. Nāgārjuna has just objected that the opponent's epistemic instruments do not acquaint us with epistemic objects, but only with generalities. For this criticism to make sense, the conception of generality employed here cannot be that of the fourth category (*padārtha*) of the *Vaiśeṣikasūtra*, a conception that is taken on board by the Naiyāyikas and considered to constitute

217. Tola and Dragonetti 1995a, 67.

218. This interpretation is later employed to question Nāgārjuna's authorship of the VP by locating it "after the appearance of the Yogācāra school more or less in 350 A.D." (Tola and Dragonetti 1995a, 12–13).

219. Tola and Dragonetti 1995a, 190n1. See also Lindtner (1986, 274) for an interpretation that goes in a similar direction.

220. Tola and Dragonetti 1995a, 112.

a class of mind-independent, objectively existent objects.[221] Such generalities would clearly qualify as epistemic objects.

Rather than as an entity "out there," such a general potness (toward which the sense-faculty is directed (*rab tu phyogs pa*), as the Naiyāyika claims) is to be understood as a sign[222] used by the sense-faculty (*dbang po'i rda*), superimposed by the conceptualizing mind in grouping together a multitude of distinct particulars.[223] This perceived generality is no objectively and independently existent component of the world, but an entity that is dependent on a variety of mental factors (such as conceptualization) as well as on nonmental factors (background conditions that render it perceptible, such as light, absence of obstructions, a functioning eye, and so on).

> *Therefore, if potness, etc., is fully established as perceived, what will become of the object that has become an epistemic object of which there is an epistemic instrument?*

Nāgārjuna's argument has proceeded in two stages: first he pointed out that, according to the opponent, perceptual contact with the world apprehends generalities in the first instance, rather than the instantiating particulars. Second, he argued that no mind-independent existence can be given to these generalities. It is now important to point out that once our perception has put us in contact with something as inextricably bound up with conceptualization as a generality, it is hard to see how we can proceed from there to the objectively existent object the Naiyāyika opponent demands—for if the generality is a mere conceptual fiction, it will not be possible to find an individual in the world in which this generality inheres. We have to ask ourselves what will become of the epistemic object that is this generality—will it somehow give rise to the cognition of another epistemic object, a mind-independent individual? Given its status as a mere mental creation, it is difficult to see how this could be so.

221. See Halbfass 1992, 113–37; and Siderits et al. 2011, 5–8.

222. *saṁketa*. Yamaguchi 1944, 127.

223. See Siderits et al. 2011, 12. Note that this interpretation does not presuppose the existence of the entire Buddhist *apoha* theory, which constitutes a considerably later development. All that is required here is the assumption that, for Nāgārjuna, generalities are not objectively existent but mind-dependent entities.

Similarly, there is the inference from the connection of fire and smoke, which has perception as a precondition. Therefore, if "inference" comes about, what will become of the other, the object of inferential activity of which there is an inference? The remainder is also similar.

Because the remaining three epistemic instruments accepted by the Naiyāyika—inference, likeness, and testimony—presuppose perception (for a cognition of the subject of inference, the relata of likeness, and the source of testimony to arise), the point Nāgārjuna has just made about perception (and more specifically about visual perception) generalizes. If perception only puts us in touch with the generality, and not with the object, the same holds for inference, likeness, and testimony. Thus, even though we may be able to establish perception and other epistemic instruments that produce the "correct knowledge" (*yang dag par rtogs pa*) mentioned in VP 17, this does not give us the kind of epistemic objects existing by *svabhāva* that the Nyāya opponent demands.

It is objected: "As regards the pot, its mental cognition is the epistemic instrument and the pot is the epistemic object."

If one says this, it is to be replied:

VP 19 **Because of that being a condition it is also neither knowledge nor object of knowledge.**

Because it is asserted that the mental cognition arises from the conjunction of sense-organ and object, the pot is in fact a condition. Therefore, the mental cognition is not an epistemic instrument, and the pot is not an epistemic object.

It is objected: "As regards the pot, its mental cognition is the epistemic instrument and the pot is the epistemic object."

This verse continues Nāgārjuna's point that the existence of epistemic instruments does not automatically supply us with epistemic objects. In VP 18 Nāgārjuna observed that the best we can hope for is that epistemic instruments acquaint us with generalities, entities that are so heavily bound up with conceptualizations as to render them practically useless for the opponent's realist project. In this verse, the opponent tries out a new idea. Let us assume, he proposes, that our mental cognition (*blo*, *buddhi*) of some thing is the epistemic instrument that generates knowledge of that thing, and the epistemic object is just that thing itself.

> *VP 19 Because of that being a condition it is also neither knowledge nor object of knowledge.*

The first part of this conditional statement, *de rkyen du gyur pa nyid yin pa'i phyir*, can be understood in two different ways, either as "Because that has a condition..." or "Because that is a condition [of something else]...." The first reading is supported by the version of VP 19 we find in the VS (*de'i rkyen can yin pa'i phyir*); this is also the way Sempa Dorje's reconstruction understands it (*tat-pratyaya-nibhandanatvāt*).[224] The second one is favored by Tola and Dragonetti,[225] who translate it as "because it (the pot) is (only) a determining condition...," and is also adopted in the present translation. It is evident from the commentary on this verse (*de'i phyir bum pa ni rkyen du gyur pa nyid yin pa*) that the pronoun *de* (*tat*) refers to the pot (*bum pa*, *ghaṭa*). Now, while Nāgārjuna would of course affirm the statement implied by the first reading (that a pot is arisen on the basis of conditions), the second reading in fact makes better sense in the context of the present argument.

Nāgārjuna wants to argue that the mental cognition of the pot is something that only arises as a result of a complex set of conditions,[226] one of which is the pot. From this he infers that the mental cognition (*blo*, *buddhi*) of the pot is not knowledge (*shes pa*, *jñāna*)—which, as the commentary makes clear, is here used as coextensive with "epistemic instrument" (*tshad ma*, *pramāṇa*)—while the pot itself (*bum pa*, *ghaṭa*) is not an object of knowledge (*shes bya*, *jñeya*), here used as coextensive with "epistemic object" (*gzhal bya*, *prameya*).

224. Sempa Dorje 1974, 31.

225. Tola and Dragonetti 1995a, 68.

226. This view is shared by many Indian epistemologists, Buddhists and non-Buddhists alike. See Reat 1993, 10, 62–63; NS 2.1.20–27.

For the mental cognition of a pot to arise, we would say that we need a functioning eye, light rays hitting the retina in the right way for the right length of time, processing of the incoming information by the relevant areas of the brain, lack of any other interfering stimuli, a physical object that is the source of the light rays, and so forth.

> *Because it is asserted that the mental cognition arises from the conjunction of sense-organ and object, the pot is in fact a condition. Therefore the mental cognition is not an epistemic instrument and the pot is not an epistemic object.*

From the fact that mental cognitions like that of the pot depend on conditions, Nāgārjuna draws two conclusions: first, that the mental cognition of a pot is not an epistemic instrument, and second, that the pot itself is not an epistemic object.[227]

The first conclusion might be more obvious to us than the second. The role of an epistemic instrument is to acquaint us with some object of knowledge, in much the same way in which, e.g., a motion detector tells us that there is a moving object in its range. But the mental cognition of a pot cannot be such an instrument, since its very existence depends on a web of conditions of which the pot is a part. If there were no pot, there would be no mental cognition of it. Yet an epistemic instrument should exist, whether or not the thing it is supposed to detect exists. This disqualifies the mental cognition of something as an epistemic instrument.[228] This argument can now be continued in two directions, either as saying that mental cognitions are an unsuitable candidate for epistemic instruments, or as pointing out that the opponent's idea of two distinct sets of entities, some epistemic instruments "in here" and epistemic objects "out there," leads to problems as soon as we realize the interdependence between plausible

227. See Lindtner 1986, 274.

228. Tola and Dragonetti (1995, 113–14) read Nāgārjuna's reasoning differently, in a way that effectively provides a single argument for both conclusions. They argue that because the mental cognition of the pot depends on various conditions, only one of which is the pot, the mental cognition of the pot might equally be considered to be an epistemic instrument of another of the conditions, such as the light rays, and intact sense-organ, and so forth. As such, it cannot be considered to be an epistemic instrument *of the pot*, and the pot cannot be considered to be an epistemic object (since the light rays, etc., might in fact be the object of the mental cognition of the pot.)

candidates for the two (such as a pot and its mental cognition). Nāgārjuna wants to extend the argument in the latter, more general direction.

But what about the second conclusion? Why is the pot not an epistemic object? Haven't we agreed that the presumed epistemic instrument, the mental cognition of the pot, is dependent on a variety of conditions, one of which clearly has to be *the pot*? And what else could this be but an epistemic object?

Nāgārjuna's point here is that the dependent relations between epistemic instruments and objects run both ways; the two players in the epistemic game form a mutually constitutive pair. What makes a pot a pot is essentially dependent on its relation to various epistemic functions. A pot is a piece of matter carved out of the complex that is the world by discerning minds. Imagine a clay container with a clay lid standing on a block of clay. The container and its lid form a unity (which we refer to by the term "pot"), while the container and the block do not. There is no difference between the spatio-temporal relations between container and lid and container and block (each can be moved independently of the other), and no way of telling, independent of human interests and concerns, which of those are essentially connected, and which are juxtaposed merely by accident. We need our epistemic faculties in order to tell which subset of the three clay objects in front of us constitutes *the pot*. Similarly, just from the perspective of material constitution, it is impossible to tell which portions of the universe count as pots, as pots can be made of nearly any kind of material, and don't have to have a specific shape, size, weight, and so on. It is only once our cognitive faculties enter the stage, in interacting with the world in certain ways (catching liquid, drinking, and so forth) that pots make an entrance.[229] It is for this reason that Nāgārjuna argues that the fact that pots and the minds knowing them form a web of conditions implies the impossibility of their existing as objects independently of the set of epistemic instruments.

229. Of course pots are artifacts, and it is obvious that we cannot make sense of what an artifact is without giving some account of the human thoughts and intentions that went into producing it. Yet Nāgārjuna (unlike Searle 1995, 185–186) wants to extend this reasoning to all objects, including such nonartifacts as Mt. Everest, electrons, or the sun. They all depend on conceptualizations, and since such conceptualizations are essential parts of our means of epistemic access to the world, these epistemic objects all depend on epistemic instruments. For further discussion of this point, see Westerhoff 2009, 177–179.

Moreover,

VP 20 **The mental cognition is not an epistemic instrument, because it is explicitly declared to be an epistemic object.**

Because for you a mental cognition is said to be an epistemic object. Why? Because the self, body, sense faculties, objects, mental cognitions, minds, activities, faults, future lives, fruits, suffering, and liberation are said to be epistemic objects. Therefore, the two also don't exist.

Here Nāgārjuna introduces a second argument against the opponent's suggestion from VP 19, that mental cognitions could constitute epistemic instruments.

> *VP 20 The mental cognition is not an epistemic instrument, because it is explicitly declared to be an epistemic object.*

He points out that the opponent's assertions are contradictory, since he explicitly subsumes mental cognitions among the epistemic *objects*, not among the instruments.

> *Because for you a mental cognition is said to be an epistemic object. Why? Because the self (ātma), body (śarīra), sense faculties (indriya), objects (artha), mental cognitions (buddhi), minds (manas), activities (pravṛtti), faults (doṣa), future lives (pretyabhāva), fruits (phala), suffering (duḥkha), and liberation (apavarga) are said to be epistemic objects.*

Nāgārjuna refers here to a list of epistemic objects found in NS 1.1.9,[230] pointing out that this shows that the Naiyāyika opponent himself regards mental cognitions (*buddhi*) as belonging to the set of epistemic objects. So how could they also be epistemic instruments?

230. *ātmaśarīrendriyārthabuddhimanaḥpravṛttidoṣapretyabhāvaphaladuḥkhāpavargās tu prameyam.*

The Naiyāyika admits that the same thing can be both epistemic instrument and epistemic object.[231] The same object can be used on a pair of scales to determine the weight of something (thus acting as an epistemic instrument providing us with knowledge of the weight of something) or as something that has its own weight determined (thus acting as an epistemic object about which we gain knowledge). Note that this is not the same point that Nāgārjuna raised in VP 02,[232] regarding the mutual existential dependence of epistemic instruments and objects. The point made here is the stronger one that relative to context *the very same thing* can function as either an epistemic instrument or as an epistemic object.

However, what Nāgārjuna would want to point out here is that if anything can have the double role of being an epistemic instrument and an epistemic object depending on context, it cannot have any of these properties intrinsically, since to do so would precisely mean to have them independent of context. Yet the Naiyāyika opponent is committed to the view that the epistemic instruments and objects have their properties in precisely this way, and for that reason his subsuming the alleged epistemic instrument, mental cognition, among the epistemic objects constitutes a real problem.

Therefore the two also don't exist.

This final sentence draws the conclusion from the discussion that began in VP 17 with the opponent's claim that, because there is correct knowledge, there must be its instruments and objects.[233] Yet, as Nāgārjuna has argued in the following three verses, VP 18–20, if "the two," i.e., epistemic instruments and their objects, are considered according to the Nyāya specification as distinct and mutually independent entities that exist substantially, so many problems follow that we are better off rejecting this notion.

This long discussion of epistemic instruments and objects, which shows considerable similarity to the discussion of the same topic in VV 5–6, 30–51, has as its main purpose the demonstration of the extent to which

231. *prameyatā ca tulāprāmāṇyavat.* NS 2.1.16.

232. This issue is also addressed in detail in VV 42–48. See Westerhoff 2010, 82–88.

233. As Tola and Dragonetti (1995, 114) point out, this sentence can also be considered as the conclusion of the entire discussion of the two Nyāya categories presented so far.

the Nyāya construal of these notions presupposes a conception of intrinsic existence or *svabhāva*. At the same time, Nāgārjuna sets out to present an alternative way of understanding these key epistemological concepts that is compatible with the theory of emptiness. For this reason, he stresses their dependently arising nature, rejects the example of the light as an attempt to establish the epistemic instruments as self-validating, and points out that the understanding of epistemic instruments and objects as intrinsically existent leads to inconsistencies when considering their temporal relations. His aim is not to argue that Mādhyamikas should not refer to such epistemological notions, or should not refer to them in arguments, but that they should avail themselves of suitably reformulated versions that do not make the problematic presuppositions that characterize the Naiyāyika understanding of them.

It is objected: "That very thing that is an epistemic instrument is an epistemic object. If that is said there is a doubt. Because there is a doubt the pair of epistemic instrument and epistemic object is established. The category 'doubt' clearly exists, it is not about an unreal thing." It is to be replied:

VP 21 **No doubt arises regarding what is conceived or what is not conceived, because of the very existence and nonexistence.**

In this context, does doubt arise regarding a conceived object or a nonconceived object or a seemingly conceived object? Doubt arising regarding a conceived object is not reasonable, and it is also not reasonable that doubt arises regarding a nonconceived object. Also, there is no third "seemingly conceived" object. Therefore, there is no doubt.

It is objected: "That very thing that is an epistemic instrument is an epistemic object. If that is said there is a doubt. Because there is a doubt the pair of epistemic instrument and epistemic object is established. The category 'doubt' clearly exists, it is not about an unreal thing (mi bden pa'i don, abhūtārtha)." It is to be replied: ...

The discussion of the preceding verse, VP 20, introduced the idea (supported by NS 2.1.16) that, depending on one's perspective, the very same thing could be both, an epistemic instrument and an epistemic object. This idea was raised by the Naiyāyika to defend himself against Nāgārjuna's criticism and is in turn attacked in the further development of the discussion. Therefore, both parties agree that there is an issue to be discussed here, a subject on which both have different ideas. But now the opponent replies by saying that if there is such a doubt,[234] the subject of the doubt—the subject on which both parties have different ideas—must be a real thing (*bden pa'i don*, **bhūtārtha*); otherwise the doubt wouldn't be real either.[235] This subject is, of course, the pair of epistemic instruments and objects. So, despite Nāgārjuna's denial, both of them do, after all, exist.

This reply also constitutes an elegant way of connecting the discussion of the first two Nyāya categories with the discussion of the third, that of doubt (*saṁśaya*, *the tshom*). We noted earlier that one way of understanding the order of the sixteen Nyāya categories is in terms of the successive steps in a debate. The third category, doubt, marks the start of the debate proper. Having apprehended some epistemic object by the epistemic instruments (the initial two categories), doubt can enter the stage.

Doubt can take different forms. We may know, for example, that an object has one property, but be uncertain about whether it also has another. If we see a pole-like object in the mist, we are certain about its apparent shape, but in doubt as to whether it is alive (in case the thing we see is a man) or not (if it is a column). Or two people may hold conflicting opinions, and, being unable to decide the matter for ourselves, we are uncertain which one is correct.

234. It is worth pointing out that even if there is no doubt in the mind of the two disputants, since each believes his position to be wholly true, and that of the opponent to be wholly false, there is certainly doubt in the mind of the audience that is confronted with their conflicting viewpoints but is not able to decide between them. See Vidyabhusana 1971, 103–04; NS 2.1.5–6; Jha 1939, 109–10, 114.

235. There is a parallel here with Nyāya arguments based on negation, which argue that since the negation exists, the object of negation must exist as well (see note 190 on p. 88 above; see also VV 12, 61–64; Westerhoff 2010, 109–16). In both cases we have the move from existence of a propositional attitude accepted by both parties in the debate (such as negation or denial, or doubt) to the existence of the object of this attitude.

Vātsyāyana distinguishes five different kinds of doubt.[236] What is common to all of them is that they describe a mental state that alternates between two conflicting notions relative to the same object. Regarding the pole-like object, the mind oscillates between attaching the property 'man' or 'column' to it, just as, if we hear two conflicting arguments on whether there is life after death, we will be undecided about classifying a recently deceased as existent or as nonexistent.[237]

The third kind of doubt, resulting from a divergence of opinions, is the most relevant in the context of the present discussion. Vātsyāyana characterizes it as follows:

> Doubt arising from contradictory opinions: By "contradictory opinions" one understands contradictory notions entertained regarding a unique object; such contradictions are incompatible affirmations for which it is impossible to coexist. For example, one says that the self exists, another says that it does not exist; since existence and nonexistence are impossible at the same time at the same place, and since there is no other means of proving one or the other the impossibility of deciding the matter in this case is called doubt.[238]

In the present verse, "contradictory notions" are entertained regarding the question of whether the very same thing can be both an epistemic instrument and an epistemic object, which the Naiyāyika affirms but which Nāgārjuna denies.

> *VP 21 No doubt arises regarding what is conceived (dmigs pa, upalabdha) or what is not conceived, because of the very existence and nonexistence.*

236. See Jha 1984, 299–302.

237. See Chatterjee 1978, 28.

238. *vipratipatter iti | vyāhatam ekārthadarśanaṁ vipratipattiḥ vyāghātaḥ virodhaḥ asahabhāva iti | astyātmā ityekaṁ darśanam nāstyātmā ityaparam | na ca sadbhāvā 'sadbhāvau sahaikatra saṁbhavataḥ | na cānyatarasādhako hetur upalabhyate tatra tattvānavadhāraṇaṁ saṁśaya iti* (Śāstrī 1998, 47:3–5); see also Jha 1939, 55. Note that the example given here is that of a debate between an orthodox (*astika*) philosopher who affirms the existence of a soul (*ātman*) and what is probably a Buddhist opponent, who denies its existence.

> *In this context, does doubt arise regarding a conceived object or a non-conceived object or a seemingly conceived object? Doubt arising regarding a conceived object is not reasonable, and it is also not reasonable that doubt arises regarding a non-conceived object. Also, there is no third "seemingly conceived" object.*[239] *Therefore there is no doubt.*

Note that Nāgārjuna does not reply to the opponent by arguing that it can be the case that even though we entertain a doubt regarding *x*, there is no *x*. To pick an example close to that of the opponent, we can doubt whether *piśāca*s and ghouls are identical without being committed to the existence of either. Rather, in line with the intention of the VP to crush all of the Nyāyā categories, Nāgārjuna develops an argument that doubt does not exist.

The argument is set out as a dilemma. Whatever is the object of doubt is either something grasped by the mind via the five senses or the mental faculty, or it is something not grasped in this way. Assume it is grasped by the mind. In this case, there is something in front of the mind's eye, so doubts about its existence are misplaced. How can we doubt something is there at the same time as apprehending that very something? On the other hand (taking the second horn of the dilemma), if it is *not* grasped by the mind, there is nothing to doubt there in the first place. How can we be in two minds about the existence of something we have just assumed is not even there? For an unperceived object, that is, for an object of which we have no representation at all, there is no possibility of asking "does it have this property or not?" since we don't have the representation required for even formulating this question. There is nothing "it" refers to.

The opponent now objects that neither of these cases is in fact what he is talking about. There is a third possibility, and for this reason Nāgārjuna's dilemma argument is deficient. This is the "seemingly conceived object" (*dmigs bhzin pa'i don*). This, the opponent would point out, is the case where doubt really arises. We come across a rope in the dark and

239. Kajiyama (1974, 199) reads this passage somewhat differently by understanding the term *bzhin* in *dmigs bzhin pa'i don* not as indicating likeness or similarity (as understood by Tola and Dragonetti [1995, 69] and in the present translation), but as indicating a continuous tense ("the object that is presently being conceived"), allowing us to draw a parallel with the structure of MMK 2.1, where three alternatives ("the path traversed," "the path not yet traversed," "the path presently being traversed") are rejected.

seemingly conceive of a snake, or a stick half submerged in water and seem to apprehend a bent stick. On the basis of this, we then develop a doubt in our mind, asking, "Is this really a snake?" or "Is this stick really bent?"

Nāgārjuna replies by categorically denying the existence of such a third kind of "seemingly conceived" objects, unfortunately without giving any reason. We can try to construct the underlying reasoning as follows, however. In the case of perceptual illusions, there are only two alternatives: either one is taken in by the illusion, or one is not. If one is, there is the mental cognition of the snake or the bent stick, and *ex hypothesi*, this is perceptually indistinguishable from cases where real snakes and bent sticks are involved. It is not the case that we somehow only half-perceive the snake, with the rope shining through just beneath the surface of the perception. If one is not taken in by the illusion, on the other hand, one does not perceive any snake or bent stick at all, though one does perceive a rope or a straight stick. So there is either a definite perception of some content, or no perception of it whatsoever. In neither case is there room for doubt. We can make sense of doubt by understanding it as a superimposition on a definite perception, when two rival interpretations (man or column) compete with each other relative to a given perception (a shape in the mist). But while such an understanding may provide us with some conception of doubt, it is clear that (given its relational status as a mental superimposition) it is very far from being an example of the kind of categories existing *svabhāvatas* that the Naiyāyika envisages.

It is objected:

VP 22 **Doubt exists, because of the lack of dependence on distinguishing features.**

Concerning this, for one apprehending a tree trunk or a man, the doubt arises: "Is what is apprehended a man, or rather a tree trunk?"—because he has seen it from a great distance.

At the time when the distinguishing features—birds building a nest or deer rubbing against it—are seen, it becomes certain: "This is a tree-trunk," and, in case it is otherwise, because the action of turning the head, moving the hand, etc., are seen, the mental conception of a man arises.

Moreover, because of the very existence and nonexistence, it depends on the distinguishing features; if it is other than this, it is doubt. Therefore, doubt exists.

It is objected

VP 22 Doubt exists, because of the lack of dependence on distinguishing features.

This *sūtra* presents us with a translational problem, as different recensions differ about the presence of a negative particle. Derge and Choney read the beginning of VP 22 as *the tshom ni yod pa ma yin te* ("There is no doubt..."), while Peking and Narthang read *the tshom ni yod pa yin te* ("Doubt exists...").

Tola and Dragonetti adopt the former reading and add the following peculiar comment:

> A literal translation of the Sūtra would be: "The doubt would not exist, if there were not reference to peculiarities": *nāstyeva saṁśayo viśeṣānapekṣāt*, being the meaning that whenever there is not reference to peculiarities, doubt does not occur and *contrario sensu* that whenever there is reference to peculiarities doubt does occur.[240]

Yet the principle *a contrario sensu*, appealed to here, is not a valid rule of inference.[241] From the statement, "The plant would not grow if the sun were not shining," we cannot infer that if the sun were shining, the plant would grow (we might be in a desert, with plenty of sun but no water); all

240. Tola and Dragonetti 1995a, 69n1.

241. *Contrario sensu* is a (contested) principle of legal interpretation used to make claims about what happens in the case of not-A on the basis of information that if A, then B. For example, it might be employed in arguing that the principle that no law may be applied retroactively if it harms someone allows us to claim that laws that benefit someone may be applied retroactively. While the principle can sometimes be useful in trying to determine the lawmaker's intent (in cases where not-A is not explicitly mentioned), the move from "If A, then B" to "If not A, then not B" is of course formally invalid.

we can infer is the contrapositive, namely that if the plant grows, the sun was shining. Similarly, what we can infer in the present case is not that if there is reference to peculiarities, there is doubt, but just that if there is doubt, then there is reference to peculiarities.

As the end of the commentary makes clear, this *sūtra* argues for the existence of doubt, so it must be the opponent speaking. The opponent speaks from the very beginning of the passage, as is indicated by the phrase "it is objected" (*smras pa*).

We should therefore not understand VP 22 as giving an argument for the nonexistence of doubt ("There is no doubt, because..."). Rather than following Tola and Dragonetti's interpretation, a more straightforward way of understanding the passage can be obtained if we adopt the second reading, found in the Peking and Narthang recensions that omit the negation, understanding VP 22 as providing a reason for why doubt exists.[242]

> *Concerning this, for one apprehending a tree-trunk or a man*[243] *the doubt arises "Is what is apprehended a man, or rather a tree-trunk?" because he has seen it from a great distance.*
>
> *At the time when the distinguishing features, birds building a nest or deer rubbing against it, are seen, it becomes certain "This is a tree-trunk," and, in case it is otherwise, because the action of turning the head, moving the hand, etc., are seen, the mental conception of a man arises.*

The opponent argues against Nāgārjuna's position in VP 21 and for the existence of doubt by pointing out that there are certain perceptions that do not depend on ascertaining the distinguishing features of two objects, but only perceive what is common to the two, not what makes each of them unique. Examples include seeing an object far away, without seeing whether it is a man or a tree, seeing a letter in the bottom line of an optician's chart, but not seeing whether it is an O or a Q, and hearing a voice next door, but without perceiving whether it originates from a person or

242. Sempa Dorje (1974, 32, line 2) adopts this reading and reconstructs as *astyeva saṁśayaḥ viśeṣānapekṣatvāt.*

243. Vātsyāyana also mentions the example of the man (*puruṣa*) and the tree trunk (*sthāṇu*) in his commentary on NS 1.1.23 (Śāstrī 1998, 46).

from a TV set. Once we manage to perceive the distinguishing features (bird nesting in the tree, head and hands on the man, etc.), our mind settles for one interpretation of the perceptual data, but before that, we were in a state of doubt, unable to say which of a set of objects was actually in front of us. Doubt arises because only the *common* features of two objects are perceived; once the *distinguishing* features are perceived, the doubt ceases. The ending of doubt is the perception of distinguishing features, so doubting is the mental act of searching for distinguishing features.

The situation described by the opponent is extremely common. Our mind is continually trying to come up with a single interpretation of the mass of sensory data coming in through our senses. Often the context of information provided by one sense or by all the senses together makes this less daunting a task than it would otherwise seem. But this does not imply that a conflict of alternative interpretations and its subsequent resolution described by the opponent is not a frequent occurrence in our cognitive lives. For this reason, the opponent argues, doubt is similarly frequent in our cognitive lives.

> *Moreover, because of the very existence and nonexistence it depends on the distinguishing features; if it is other than this it is doubt. Therefore, doubt exists.*

Having a certain, non-doubting cognition depends on the presence of distinguishing features in the cognition. If the features exist in cognition, the presence of the object (such as a man or tree) is perceived; if they do not exist, its absence is perceived. If we see the object in the fog move its arms, we perceive it to be a man, since one of its distinguishing features is present; if it appears not to be solid but translucent, we perceive that there is no man there, because a distinguishing feature is lacking. In the remaining cases, where the distinguishing features neither clearly exist nor clearly fail to exist, doubt arises about what it actually is that we are perceiving. Since there are such cases, the opponent concludes, doubt exists.

⁜ It is to be replied:

VP 23 **There is no doubt that depends on distinguishing features, because of the previous negation.**

"Because there is no doubt regarding existence and nonexistence"—with this statement it was indeed denied previously. Why? Because one has observed the sign of birds' nests built in trees, etc., [thinking] "There is a tree there." There is no doubt in the mind, because it is indeed thoroughly known in the way it is.

Similarly, with respect to "This is a man," by observing the sign of the head turning, etc., "This is indeed a man." Because thorough knowledge of the way it is arises, there is no doubt, because there is knowledge of the way it is.

On the other hand, if there is no sign of knowledge of the way it is, there is no doubt of it not being understood. The meanings of "not certain," "not understood," "not grasped," "not known," and "not seen" are not different—they are synonyms of ignorance, because they are the opposite of knowledge.

It is explained by saying: Depending on distinguishing features, it will be known, and for distinguishing features that are not seen, it will not be known. If turning the head and moving the hand, etc., are seen, there will be no doubt. If there are no distinguishing features, there will only be ignorance. It will be like this: If there are distinguishing features, there will be knowledge; if there are not, there will only be ignorance. Because with respect to this, there is no third understanding. There is no doubt regarding the simultaneity of existence and nonexistence of the distinguishing features. ⁜ ⁜

It is to be replied:

VP 23 There is no doubt that depends on distinguishing features (viśeṣāpekṣaḥ), because of the previous negation.

In this verse, which concludes the discussion of doubt, Nāgārjuna replies to the opponent's criticism from VP 22. He notices that the "previous negation" (the one made in VP 21) is also sufficient to defuse the new case for the existence of doubt, based on distinguishing features the opponent has introduced in VP 22.

> *"Because there is no doubt regarding existence and nonexistence"—with this statement it was indeed denied previously. Why? Because one has observed the sign of birds' nests built in trees, etc., [thinking] "There is a tree there." There is no doubt in the mind, because it is indeed thoroughly known in the way it is.*
>
> *Similarly, with respect to "This is a man," by observing the sign of the head turning, etc., "This is indeed a man." Because thorough knowledge of the way it is arises, there is no doubt, because there is knowledge of the way it is.*

The previous negation Nāgārjuna refers to is the rejection of doubt, applying either to the existence of something grasped by the mind (which is present to the mind, and therefore not subject to doubt) or to its nonexistence (for something not present to the mind cannot be doubted). But, as he points out now, this dilemma is equally present in the case the opponent mentions. If the distinguishing features of an object that characterize it as either tree or man are observed, there is no doubt concerning the object's nature. The observer will firmly hold the belief "this is a tree" or "this is a man."

> *On the other hand, if there is no sign of knowledge of the way it is, there isn't the doubt of it not being understood for the two. The meanings of "not certain," "not understood," "not grasped," "not known," and "not seen" are not different, they are synonyms of ignorance, because they are the opposite of knowledge.*

If, on the other hand, the distinguishing features are not observed, there is no doubt in relation to the pair of tree/man either—we are now just dealing with a case of ignorance of whatever it is that is in front of us. Characterizing the situation as a case of doubt presupposes that the two alternatives mentioned are the most probable, or indeed the only possible ones. Yet this is not the case, as the possibilities of what the appearance's real nature is are endless: a column, a statue, a bear, a short chimney, rising smoke, a hallucination, and so on. As such, the situation is better described as one of ignorance, not as one of doubt.

It is explained by saying: Depending on distinguishing features it will be known and for distinguishing features that are not seen it will not be known. If turning the head and moving the hand, etc., are seen there will be no doubt. If there are no distinguishing features there will only be ignorance. It will be like this: If there are distinguishing features there will be knowledge, if there are not there will only be ignorance.

Nāgārjuna points out that there are only two possibilities: either there is knowledge—in this case, we observe the distinguishing features and are aware that what we are dealing with is a man or a tree; or there is ignorance —in this case, we are not aware of such features. Doubt as a third possibility does not appear to fit into this scheme.

Because with respect to this there is no third understanding, of the simultaneity of existence and nonexistence of the distinguishing features, there is no doubt.

Taking up the point from the end of the discussion of VP 21, Nāgārjuna points out that for the opponent's doubt to exist, there would have to be a mysterious third way, an understanding that incorporates both—the existence of the distinguishing features of a tree, to ensure that we are actually dealing with a case of doubt whether something is a tree or something else (rather than a case of doubt about whether something is, say, a bear or a statue), and simultaneously the absence of these features (for otherwise our cognition would establish it as a tree, and doubt would no longer be possible).

It is useful to reflect for a bit on the philosophical purpose Nāgārjuna's refutation of doubt can be considered to have. Would we have to criticize a Mādhyamika who says he doubts it is going to rain in the afternoon by telling him that he either knows it is going to rain or he is in a state of total ignorance concerning the weather? What is wrong with merely probabilistic beliefs that express our degrees of belief in two mutually incompatible outcomes?

It is important to be clear about what kind of doubt constitutes the target of Nāgārjuna's criticism. The doubt his opponent has in mind is object-directed, and as such, the existence of doubt brings with it the existence of the intrinsically existent object the doubt is about. Yet, as Nāgārjuna insists, there is no "'seemingly conceived' object" (*dmigs bzhin zhes bya ba'i don*) and no object that simultaneously has and lacks the distinguishing qualities. There is either the perception of something, such as a man or a tree (whether this is real or illusory) or the absence of such a perception, in which case there is ignorance. We can alternatively conceive of doubt as a higher-order cognitive function, the result of harmonizing conflicting perceptual information. If we perceive a tree, and then subsequently perceive it to move about, we might question the veracity of our first perception, since the two properties are incompatible. In the absence of any further information, we may then conclude that we are in fact ignorant about what we saw earlier on.

According to the picture Nāgārjuna presents here, perceptions are always perceptions of something specific. We do not hear a certain sound and doubt what we hear, we hear it *as* the sound of rain or *as* the sound of bacon frying in the pan, or even just as a sound with a specific duration, pitch, and so forth. In the case of conflict, we may of course later give up some of the beliefs based on these perceptions.

So the Mādhyamika can have it both ways. Concerning the object-directed doubt his opponent talks about, a doubt that entails the intrinsic existence of the doubted object, he can explicitly deny that any such thing exists. Yet he can still give an account of doubt-talk in terms of giving up beliefs based on perceptions that we earlier took to be veridical. This latter point is important. The Mādhyamika wants to be able to give an account of conventional reality, and doubt-talk is certainly (we might even say indubitably) part of the equipment we use in order to speak about knowledge, a notion that forms an essential part of conventional reality.

It is also worthwhile to consider Nāgārjuna's denial of "seemingly conceived" objects in the wider context of Madhyamaka thought—for the appearance-reality distinction that this example implies is not something that coheres very well with the Madhyamaka view. While systems such as the Abhidharma can be successfully interpreted in the light of such a scheme (where conventional truths constitute the appearance, and ultimate truths the reality), the Mādhyamika's assertion of the emptiness of emptiness contradicts such a view, since this implies that ultimate truth ("reality"), namely emptiness, possesses the key characteristic of conventional truth ("appearance"), namely being empty. Substantially existent objects (objects existing *svabhāvatas*) are either conceived (if we are dealing with the conventional, unenlightened perspective)[244] or they are wholly absent (with the ultimate, enlightened perspective), but it is not the case that we merely *appear* to conceive them, but do not really conceive them. The dilemma Nāgārjuna describes in the case of individual perceptions can equally be applied to the case of knowledge of the two truths.

It is objected:

"There is a doubt concerning the purpose, the purpose regarding which certain knowledge does not arise for us." It is to be replied:

VP 24 **Because of existence and nonexistence there is no purpose.**

You say that "the object for which one acts, having aimed at it, is the purpose," as the potter acts for the sake of the pot. If the pot existed in the clay, his action would be pointless at that time. Or else, if it did not exist [in the clay], there can be no acting on it because of its nonexistence, as in the case of sand.

It is objected:

"There is a doubt concerning the purpose (dgos pa'i don, prayojanārtha),[245] *the purpose regarding which certain knowledge does not arise for us."*

244. The reader will be aware that for some interpretations of Madhyamaka, *svabhāva* does not even exist at the conventional level. We will ignore this complication at this point.

245. It is unclear whether the phrase *prayojanārtha* (*dgos pa'i don*) means anything more than just *prayojana* (*dgos pa*). Sempa Dorje (1974, 32) reconstructs *dgos pa'i don* to *prayojana*; other uses of the terms (e.g., Vasubandhu in the *Vyākhyāyukti* [Nance 2012, 115]) do not seem to mean anything more than just "purpose." We have therefore rendered *dgos pa'i don* in this way.

The discussion now moves on to the fourth Nyāya category, that of purpose (*prayojana*). Once more the exchange is set up in such a way as to connect it with that of the previous category, doubt (*saṁśaya*). The notion of purpose that the opponent has in mind here is the purpose of a debate, i.e., the establishment of a conclusion. An argument is constructed because there is no certain knowledge (*shes pa nges pa*) with regard to a specific statement on which the two disputants disagree. The opponent points out that if there is no knowledge of the statement to be established by the debate, there must be doubt. For this reason, the existence of doubt, a problem discussed in the previous three verses, is established, after all, by the fact that debates have purposes. It is interesting to note that the opponent's argument for the category of purpose is not based on the function it fulfills in the process (beginning with epistemic instruments) that leads up to a debate (for example, by pointing out that if there were no purpose, nobody would be motivated to start a debate), it is rather introduced in order to support the existence of the previously discussed category of doubt.

VP 24 Because of existence and nonexistence there is no purpose.

Nāgārjuna responds to this in line with his general purpose of the rejection of all the Nyāya categories in this treatise. There is no such thing as a purpose, and for this reason the opponent's justification for the existence of doubt disappears. The form of the reason for the rejection of purpose is the same as the one we encountered in VP 21, where doubt was rejected: there isn't any, "because of existence and nonexistence."

You say that "the object for which one acts, having aimed at it, is the purpose," as the potter acts for the sake of the pot. If the pot existed in the clay, his action would be pointless at that time. Or else, if it did not exist [in the clay], there can be no acting on it because of its nonexistence, as in the case of sand.

In Nāgārjuna's response to the opponent's assertion that the purpose exists, Nāgārjuna cites the definition of purpose we find in the NS.[246] Any

246. 1.1.24: *yam artham adhikṛtya pravartate tat prayojanam.* Śāstrī 1998, 48; Williams 1978, 287; Pind 2001, 63.

activity requires some end for which the activity is carried out.[247] In the most general sense, these ends can be the acquisition of pleasure and the avoidance of pain; in a more specific sense, such "purposes" also include intermediaries, the gaining of which is considered to bring about pleasure or the avoidance of pain.[248] Thus the potter, for example, gains pleasure from fulfilling his desire to make a pot, and it is this pot which brings about this pleasure.

When analyzed, the ontological status of such a purpose is somewhat perplexing, however. Clearly if the pot already exists, the potter is not motivated to make it again. Yet if it does not exist, it is unclear how such nonexistent objects can enter into causal relationships, acting as the cause of the potter's pot-making.

Note that we cannot simply resolve this problem by assuming that the pot in question is an intentional object and thus "merely representational."[249] This will not give us a sensible interpretation of the Nyāya definition of purpose, since it is not the representation or idea of the pot that the potter wants to make and sell, but the pot itself.[250] Our intentions are not merely directed at an intentional object but at what this object stands for. What it stands for, however, cannot already exist; otherwise there would be no point in carrying out the supposedly purposeful action that is intended to bring it into existence.

Nāgārjuna refers specifically to the potential existence of the pot in the clay, and its absence in sand[251] (as one can make a pot from the former, not from the latter), and thereby connects his reply with the familiar

247. There is an obvious parallel between the argument here and the argument from a negation to the existence of the negated that we find, e.g., in VP 14. In both cases we have a certain kind of mental operation or mental function (the operation of negation in one case, that of "aiming" [*adhi-√kṛ*] in the other), together with the claim that its existence entails the existence of its object.

248. Chattopadhyaya and Gangopadhyaya 1967–76, vol. 1, 98–99.

249. As suggested by Pind (2001, 163–64).

250. It is therefore unclear to me why Pind (2001, 164) considers Nāgārjuna's argument in this verse to be a sophism.

251. Not only are there no pots in sand, there is no oil either, as the popular Sanskrit maxim *sikatātailanyāya* informs us. This "sand-oil" is a common illustration of something a cause cannot produce, and therefore, more generally, of a nonexistent object. See Jacob (1907–11, 147) for some illustrations of the use of this maxim.

Madhyamaka discussion of the relation between cause and effect.[252] In this discussion, the Mādhyamika points out that if the effect were contained in the cause in any straightforward way, there would be nothing for the causal process to bring about. If, on the other hand, cause and effect were intrinsically distinct, it would be difficult to explain why certain causes can only produce certain effects (since, for example, oil and sand would be as unrelated as oil and sesame seeds).

Even without bringing in the notion of momentariness, the Mādhyamika can argue that the purpose—the object to be brought about—does not yet exist. This leads to problems for the opponent's claim that because debates have purposes, and because the purpose of a debate is the resolution of doubt, whatever is resolved by it, namely the doubt, must exist. If there is no purpose *before* the debate, this reasoning cannot be used to show that doubt exists, and *after* the debate no room for doubt will remain.

Fortunately, this does not mean that the Mādhyamika cannot differentiate between purposeful and pointless activities. But for him the purpose cannot be more than a mere *ens rationis*; it cannot exist with *svabhāva*, but must be a mind-made thing, a projection into the future. In the same way in which the Mādhyamika argues that the existence of a negation does not entail the existence of a negated thing, the fact that an action is goal- or purpose-directed does not mean that there is (or ever will be) such an independently existing object that is this purpose. We can argue that when the potter sets out to make a pot, he puts together in his mind various properties of already existent pots (the shape of this one, the color of that one, the texture of a third...) and sets out to create a new pot that combines them all for the first time. But such a pot does not exist at the time when the potter starts working, and even if it never exists, say, because the potter gives up on the project, this does not mean that his attempt to make it was an action without purpose. For this reason, Nāgārjuna does not reject the general possibility of making sense of talk about purposes, but the specific kind of object-directed purposes the Naiyāyika has in mind.

It is worthwhile to mention finally that Nāgārjuna's rejection of doubt also has a soteriological purpose. Narrowly understood, the "purpose" the Naiyāyika talks about in his account of the sixteen categories is the removal of doubt, since this is the aim of two disputants entering into a debate.

252. Westerhoff 2009, 102–12.

But there is a wider understanding of purpose that is also discussed by the Nyāya commentators, namely whatever motivates people to *any* kind of activity—the desire to acquire pleasure and avoid pain.[253] In short, purpose is what keeps the wheel of cyclic existence turning. Nāgārjuna's rejection of object-directed purposes can therefore also be understood as pointing toward a soteriological claim—toward a rejection of substantially existent causes of samsara.

It is objected:

VP 25 **There is no acting on sand, because the example exists.**

If one says that "It is just as when the purpose is a cloth, there is acting on threads, etc., but not on blades of grass,"

Once again this verse serves as a connecting point between the previously discussed Nyāya category (*prayojana* or purpose) and the next (*dṛṣṭānta*, the example).

It is objected:

VP 25 There is no acting on sand, because the example exists.

Tola and Dragonetti[254] translate this verse with a large amount of interpolations, rendering it as:

253. Chattopadhyaya and Gangopadhyaya (1967–76, vol. 1, 11): "It is incentive [i.e., purpose] that leads living beings to activity. In a living being a specific knowledge leads to a specific desire; that specific desire leads to motivation, which again results in the final activity. Traditionally, four incentives are mentioned, namely *dharma*, *artha*, *kāma*, and *mokṣa*. Uddyotakara, however, critically shows that the main incentives of the living beings are the attainment of pleasure and the avoidance of pain, because these alone are the basic causes of their activities. According to Vātsyāyana, incentives include also the undesirable objects, i.e., the objects shunned. For, being of the nature of pain or the cause thereof, the undesirable objects too induce the action of avoiding them."

254. Tola and Dragonetti 1995a, 70.

> In regard to sand action does not exist, but (the purpose of action exists) because there are examples (that demonstrate its existence).

Apart from noting that it is unclear where the adversative "but" is coming from, we here assume that the verse is comprehensible without interpolations, along the lines of our translation just given.

The opponent clearly agrees with Nāgārjuna's point from VP 24, that using sand in order to create a pot is not a purposeful activity. The point he makes here is that if there were no purposes at all, all activity would be similarly without purpose, and for that reason there would be no explanation of why people didn't try to make a pot out of sand, rather than out of clay.[255] But in fact there are examples of purposeful actions, and because there are these examples, other actions are purposeless (such as making a pot from sand), and for this reason nobody undertakes them.

> *If one says that "It is just as when the purpose is a cloth, there is acting on threads, etc., but not on blades of grass,"*

This point is further explained in the commentary. The reason that nobody tries to make a piece of fabric from blades of grass is that there is a purposeful action operating on threads, which results in a piece of fabric. In contrast, using grass to make a cloth is without purpose, and for this reason nobody tries to do so. It is therefore because there are examples of purposeful actions that we can explain someone's behavior in choosing some routes but not others to bring about a result. It is only because there are these examples that a second class of actions without purpose can be defined as a contrast. Given the crucial role these examples play in explaining the world around us, the opponent argues, there are good reasons for assuming that examples exist, and this constitutes a reason to believe in the existence of the fourth Nyāya category, the category of examples.

255. Compare the Madhyamaka position that if there are no causal connections, any cause could bring about any effect (Westerhoff 2009, 112).

⌘ It is to be replied:

VP 26 **Like that, moreover, there is similarity with the previous one.**

⌘ ⌘

Nāgārjuna disagrees with the opponent's view that the example of the cloth, threads, and blades of grass makes a point that differs from the one made by the example of the pot, clay, and sand, introduced by the opponent in VP 24. This verse is not elucidated by any further commentary, but fortunately its meaning is relatively transparent. It is not clear, Nāgārjuna points out, why the difficulty discussed there (that the aim of the action either already exists, in which case it can have no purpose, or fails to exist, in which case the action is aimed at nothing) is not equally applicable in the case of the cloth. Moreover, the Mādhyamika would want to point out here, the opponent's worry that for Nāgārjuna there is no distinction between actions with or without purpose, and therefore no way of explaining why cloths are not made from grass, and pots are not made from sand, is groundless. Nāgārjuna does not reject talk about purposes *tout court* but targets his refutation specifically at the Nyāya notion of object-directed purposes connecting an action with an entity that is more than a mere mental projection. But since the emptiness of causation does not mean that there is no causation (so that anything can follow from anything else), the absence of the kind of purposes the Naiyāyika has in mind does not imply the impossibility of making sense of conventions that appeal to purposes. Since it is therefore not necessary to bring in examples in order to make purpose-talk comprehensible (by introducing a contrasting class against which the purposeless actions could only be understood) the opponent's justification for the category of examples disappears.

⌘ Moreover,

VP 27 **Because there is no beginning and middle, the end also is not seen.**

How is the end (*anta*) seen (*dṛṣṭa*) by something by which the beginning and the middle of some things are not seen? If there is no beginning and middle, there is no end. Therefore, the example (*dṛṣṭānta*) does not exist.

In this verse Nāgārjuna continues the refutation of the fifth Nyāya category, that of an example (*dṛṣṭānta*). His argument is based on an analysis of the term *dṛṣṭānta*, comprised of *dṛṣṭa* (seen) and *anta* (end). Depending on what kind of nominal compound *dṛṣṭānta* is taken to be, it can be understood either as "the end that is seen" (taking it to be a *karmadhāraya* compound) or as "something of which the end is seen" (understanding it as a *bahuvrīhi* compound).

Nāgārjuna then argues that, since an end requires a beginning and a middle (we can't have the end of a row of men without there being also a beginning and a middle), and since neither of these are in sight, there cannot be an end, and thus no example (*dṛṣṭānta*) essentially involving such an end (*anta*).

This verse, as well as the very similar VP 32, seem to be prime examples of the "sophistries" with which some authors regard the VP as being filled. For them, Nāgārjuna's refutation appears to be based not on any substantive properties of the category of examples, but merely on the analysis of the Sanskrit *term* used for examples. Spotting the word *anta* in there is then seen as an excuse for plugging in the familiar Madhyamaka refutation of an "end."[256] This procedure seems to be not much better than replying to a criticism that some point is a red herring by pointing out that there is no water around, and so there can also be no herrings.

256. See, e.g., the commentary on VV 32b: "Because there is no beginning, where would middle and end come from?" (*āder asatbhāvāt kuto madhyaṁ kuto antaḥ*). Note in this context also Nāgārjuna's argument against the existence of the middle in the absence of beginning and end. In MMK 11:2a he asks: "How could there be a middle of that which lacks a beginning and an end?" (*naivāgraṁ nāvaraṁ yasya tasya madhyaṁ kuto bhavet*). Siderits and Katsura (2013, 123) explain the underlying argument as follows: "The middle is the midpoint in a series, equidistant from the endpoints of the series. But if the series goes on indefinitely in each direction, every point could be said to be equidistant from the ends of the series, which are infinitely far from any point. And if every point in the series could equally be called the midpoint, then none of them really is."

However, it is possible to develop a more sophisticated understanding of Nāgārjuna's argument. As a first step, it is important to note that Nāgārjuna's analysis of the term *dṛṣṭānta* was not made up by him, but is an understanding well documented in the Indian debate literature.

One example of such an etymological definition of the term can be found in Haribhadra's *Nyāyapraveśakasūtravṛtti*,[257] which points out that:

> So far as it leads to seeing the final meaning it is the example.

Kṣhīrasvamin's commentary on the *Amarakośa*'s entry on *dṛṣṭānta* notes:

> Its end (*anta*), or ascertainment, is seen (*dṛṣṭa*), hence *dṛṣṭa-anta*; an indication, an example. Like: "Here there is fire, due to smoke—like in the kitchen."[258]

As both these passages make clear, the "final meaning" or "end" that is understood (or "seen") through the example is the argument's conclusion ("conclusion" being, in fact, another meaning of *anta*).

The close connection of the example with the conclusion is also underlined by Vātsyāyana in his commentary on NS 1.1.1, where he states that:

> [W]hen there is an example, not otherwise, there is inference or testimony. It is thus on the basis of an example that reasoning proceeds; the opponent's position is to be refuted by showing that it is opposed to the example, one's own position is to be established through corroboration by the example.[259]

The example is therefore considered to be the means by which the conclusion (*anta*) of an inference is understood, this conclusion being either the refutation of the opponent's position or the establishment of one's own position.

257. *tathā dṛṣṭam artham antaṁ nayatīti dṛṣṭāntaḥ* (Dhruva 1930, vol. 14, 5).

258. *dṛṣṭo'nto niścayo'sya dṛṣṭāntaḥ, nidarśanam udāharaṇam yathā agnir atra dhūmān mahāsanavatvāt* (Oka 1913, 197).

259. *tasmin sati syātām anumānāgamau asati ca na syātām | tadāśrayā ca nyāyapravṛttiḥ | dṛṣṭāntavirodhena ca parapakṣapratiṣedho vacanīyo bhavati dṛṣṭāntasamādhinā ca svapakṣaḥ sādhanīyo bhavati* (Śāstrī 1998, 8:2–4).

Now if the "end" (*anta*) is to be understood as the conclusion of the inference, what is the beginning (*ādi*, *thog ma*) and middle (*madhyama*, *dbus*) supposed to be?

If we remind ourselves of the interpretation of the set of the sixteen Nyāya categories as describing successive stages in the course of a debate, we see that the example constitutes the fifth stage, following the perception of an epistemic object (*prameya*) by epistemic instruments (*pramāṇa*), and the opponent's raising of a doubt (*saṁśaya*) for a specific purpose (*prayojana*). It makes sense to identify the "beginning" with our acquaintance with the world via epistemic instruments and the "middle" with the opponent's intervention, raising a doubt with the purpose of refuting us.

As Nāgārjuna has refuted all of these previous four stages in the preceding verses, he is now asking how, in the absence of all of these, a conclusion could be established and how, *a fortiori*, there could be something by which this conclusion is understood, namely an example.

It is objected: "That thing on which laymen and researchers agree is the example, and, moreover, there are concordant and discordant examples." If that is said, it should be replied:

VP 28 **Because it is concordant, fire is precisely not an example of heat.**[260]

One does not say, "It is an example because it is concordant," because fire is not an example of heat. This is because there is no difference between established and establisher. If that very thing is established and that very thing is the establisher, how can the example exhibit a difference?

It is objected: "That thing on which laymen and researchers agree is the example, and, moreover, there are concordant (sādharmya) and discordant (vaidharmya) examples."

260. Our translation follows Sempa Dorje (1974, 33), who reconstructs this verse as *nāgnistejaso dṛṣṭāntaḥ, sādharmyāt*, rendering the first occurrence of the Tibetan *me* as *agni* (fire), and the second as *tejas* (heat).

The opponent now introduces a new reason for the existence of examples: They are simply the points of agreement between different kinds of people, the untutored persons concerned with everyday affairs (*laukika*, *'jig rten pa*) and experts with particular kinds of specialized knowledge (*parīkṣaka*, *dpyod pa po*). What the opponent has in mind here is of course the characterization of the example as that regarding which both layman and expert have similar ideas from NS 1.1.25,[261] which Nāgārjuna has already himself referred to earlier in the text, in the commentary on VP 9.[262]

The opponent specifically mentions two types of examples, concordant (*sādharmya*) and discordant (*vaidharmya*) examples.[263] In the classical Indian five-fold inference, the concordant example presents a case where the property to be established (*sādhya*) and the mark (*liṅga*) are coinstantiated in one object, while the discordant example is an object that instantiates neither. In the case of the well-known model inference, "There is smoke (*liṅga*) on the mountain, so there is fire (*sādhya*)," a concordant example is a kitchen (having both smoke and fire), while a discordant example is a lake (having neither).

Discordant examples will be addressed in the following verse, so let us here focus on the concordant ones. When we say that B is an example of A (that an elm is an example of a tree, that India is an example of a country with a long history), we mean that B is subsumed under A. The same applies to the concordant example in an inference; the kitchen is subsumed among the things that are characterized both by containing smoke and containing fire.

Yet this leads to the following problem: The equation of exemplification with subsumption allows us to move from:

> An elm is an example of a tree

to:

> An elm is a tree;

261. *laukikaparīkṣakāṇāṁ yasmin arthe buddhisāmyaṁ sa dṛṣṭāntaḥ.*

262. *'jig rten pa'i spyod pa po... | ...de dag don gang la blo mthun pa de ni dper rab tu grub pa yin no.*

263. See also the classification of examples in the *Upāyahṛdaya* ascribed to Nāgārjuna (Kajiyama 1991, 109; Gillon and Katsura 2016, 203–4).

and from:

> An elm is a tree

to:

> An elm is an example of a tree.

Since it is certainly the case that laymen and experts agree that an elm is an elm, we should be allowed to infer that an elm is an example of an elm. Yet this "perfect similarity" (*atyantasādharmya*) is specifically ruled out by the Naiyāyika. NS 2.1.42 states that there can be no similarity based on perfect resemblance,[264] as when we say that a cow is like a cow, to use Vātsyāyana's example.[265]

> *If that is said, it should be replied:*

> *VP 28 Because it is concordant, fire is precisely not an example of heat.*

> *One does not say, "It is an example because it is concordant," because fire is not an example of heat. This is because there is no difference between established and establisher. If that very thing is established and that very thing is the establisher, how can the example exhibit a difference?*

Nāgārjuna thus points out that if we allow concordant examples, such as fire being an example of heat, we are then also obliged to regard everything as an example of itself, which both contradicts the Naiyāyika's own explicit pronouncements and our intuitive understanding of what an example is for: to illustrate the unfamiliar (the thing to be established, *sgrub par byed pa*) by the familiar (the establisher, *bsgrub par bya ba*).[266]

264. *atyantaprāyaikadeśasādharmyādupamānā'siddhiḥ*. This *sūtra* is counted as 2.1.44 by Jha (1984, vol. 2, 816) and as 2.1.42 by Ruben (1928, 32).

265. *na caivaṁ bhavati yathā gaurevaṁ gauḥ iti* (Śāstrī 1998, 143:2).

266. Compare in this context the Nyāya definition of similarity (*upamāna*) as "the establishment of what is to be established through similarity with a well-known object" (*prasiddha-sādharmyāt sādhya-sādhanam upamānam*, NS 1.1.6). If example and exemplified were identical, the exemplified would be well-known (*prasiddha*) because the example is, in which case one would then not need the example in the first place, as the exemplified is already well-known in its own right.

Yet if both are identical, the example cannot do what it is supposed to do, namely bridging the difference between some thing that is known and one that is not yet known.[267] Every example should exhibit such a difference (*khyad par can*), yet if we have to regard everything as self-exemplifying, as Nāgārjuna argues here, many cases of "examples" would not do so.

VP 29 **Moreover, water is not an example of heat because it is a discordant example.**[268]

Water, which is subsumed under what is cold, is not reasonable as an example of heat. It is like saying, "Somewhere water is cold, for example, like heat."

Nāgārjuna now moves on to the discordant example (*vaidharmya*). The difficulty with concordant examples, pointed out in the previous verse, was that they oblige us to regard objects also as their own examples, a position explicitly rejected by the Naiyāyikas themselves. The difficulty with the discordant example is easy to see. The example mentioned by Nāgārjuna is water, "discordant" with heat since, according to the Vaisheṣhika metaphysics, which the Naiyāyikas accept, water is cold by nature.[269]

It is clear that, because of this difference in nature, water cannot be an example of heat, since otherwise, due to the symmetry of the exemplification relation, heat would also be an example of water and its coldness, which is absurd. In fact, the discordant example is not an example at all. While it is clear how fire can be seen as exemplifying heat, and a kitchen

267. Uddyotakara's remark in his *Vārttika* on NS 2.1.45, that we *do* appeal to such cases of perfect resemblance when saying, e.g., that "the battle between Rāma and Rāvaṇa is like the battle between these two heroes alone" (*yathā rāmarāvaṇayoryudhhaṁ rāmarāvaṇayoriveti* [Dvivedin 1986, 258:11]) does not really help here, because what we are really saying here is that there is *nothing at all* comparable to it.

268. The version of this verse found in VS has *gzi brjid* instead of *me*. Both terms can translate the Sanskrit *tejas*.

269. *Vaiśeṣikasūtra* 2.2.5 points out that coldness is the mark of water: *apsu śītatā*.

exemplifying a place where both smoke and fire exist, water does not exemplify anything with respect to heat, nor does a lake exemplify anything with respect to fire and smoke.[270] The exemplified is not in any way "illustrated, made intelligible, made known, set in a clear light"[271] by the discordant example, which has nothing in common with it. Nāgārjuna's criticism of the two types of example in this and in the preceding verse can therefore be summarized as the observation that concordant examples entail examples that are "too close" to the exemplified (namely the exemplified itself) and are therefore rejected, while discordant examples are "too far removed," since they do not exemplify anything with respect to the exemplified.[272]

Moreover,

VP 30 **If you say "It is from slight similarity"—this is not the case; it is like Mount Meru and a hair.**

One cannot say here that "it is an example from slight similarity." Why? In this world there is a slight similarity between Mount Meru and hairs, in terms of existence, unity, and corporeality. Moreover, a hair similar to Mount Meru is not well known.

Moreover,

VP 30 If you say "It is from slight similarity"—this is not the case; it is like Mount Meru and a hair.

270. The reason why the discordant example of the lake is used in the fire-smoke inference may be because the mist rising from a lake could be mistaken as a case of "smoke" without fire; but of course rising mist is no smoke.

271. Tola and Dragonetti 1995a, 120.

272. Note that this criticism does not on its own entail any problem with the *vaidharmya*'s role in five-membered inference. Independent of the role it plays there Nāgārjuna's point is that the *vaidharmya* cannot really be taken to be an example.

This verse can be regarded as a continuation of the discussion in VP 28, where Nāgārjuna began to discuss concordant examples. As we noted, there is a difficulty when example and exemplified share *all* properties, as in the case of something being an example of itself. The opponent is likely to reply that such complete similarity is neither necessary nor desirable. Example and exemplified should share some properties; they do not have to share a large range of properties, in fact exhibiting some "slight similarity" (*cung zad chos mthun pa*, *ekadeśasādharmya*) is sufficient.

Nāgārjuna's reply proceeds by mentioning the pair of Mount Meru (the enormous mountain located at the center of the world, according to classical Indian cosmology) and a hair. Tola and Dragonetti describe this illustration as "somewhat odd,"[273] as the opposition most commonly found in Indian literature is that between Mount Meru and the (very small) mustard seed (*sarṣapa*).[274] Yet the pair of Mount Meru and the hair seem to be equally suitable as two objects exemplifiying the two opposite ends of the spectrum of size, the very large and the very small.

One cannot say here that "it is an example from slight similarity." Why? In this world there is a slight similarity between Mount Meru and hairs, in terms of existence, unity, and corporeality.

The difficulty with the appeal to slight similarity that Nāgārjuna's example tries to bring out is that everything bears a slight similarity to everything else,[275] especially if we consider some very high-level concepts. Nāgārjuna introduces three very general properties that encompass a substantial portion of all there is: existence, unity (a property possibly even more inclusive than existence, since even if we include nonexistent objects, all of these must presumably be one thing [*gcig pa*, i.e., possess unity] to

273. Tola and Dragonetti 1995a, 192.

274. See, e.g., *Mahābhārata* 1.69.3; Lamotte and Boin-Webb 2003, 162; Uddyotakara *Vārttika* on NS 2.1.45: *yathā sarṣapasya tathā meroḥ* (Dvivedin 1986, 259:14–15); and Vāchaspati Mishra's *Vārttikatātparyaṭīkā* on NS 2.1.44: *tadidamāha na hi sarveṇa sarvam-upamīyate tathā sati sumerorapisarṣapeṇopamānapransaṅgāt* (Nyaya-Tarkathirta, et al. 2003, 528:17).

275. The *Bhāṣya* on NS 2.1.44, discussing resemblance (*upamāna*), one of the four epistemic instruments, points out the impossibility of conceiving of resemblance in terms of slight resemblance for this very reason: *ekadeśasādharmyāt upamānaṁ na sidhyati, na hi sarveṇa sarvam upamīyata iti* (Śāstrī 1998, 143:4–5).

qualify as an object) as well as corporeality (*lus can*, i.e., to possess a material form).[276] It is clear that, with properties such as these, we will find it impossible to come up with any two constituents of the world, no matter how diverse, that do not resemble one another in terms of some of these properties. But a relation that connects all pairs of objects in the world is not really worth talking about, since it does not tell us anything we did not already know. The reasons why it is interesting that Adam and Becca are married is because every person is not married to every other person. If I introduce a new social relation *R* between people, such that any pair of people stands in this relation, telling you that Adam and Becca are related by *R* is unlikely to be of much interest.

Moreover, a hair similar to Mount Meru is not well known.

Nāgārjuna here raises the additional point that, once we introduce this concept of slight similarity, it will no longer be the case that everybody, expert and layman, agrees on what resembles what. For, most laymen will deny that Mount Meru and the mustard seed have anything in common, or that a raven resembles a writing desk. This is because they do not regard the likeness between the two as significant. If the layman regards something as an example of something else, he holds that there is such a significant similarity between the two. But if the expert's understanding of resemblance is satisfied by the sharing of one property, and if this property can be a very high-level property, then mountains and mustard seeds do resemble each other, because they are (among other things) all existents, each of them is one thing, and they are all material. But this now leads to a problem for the Nyāya notion of examples and exemplification, since according to their understanding it is exactly this agreement between expert and layman that characterizes the example; and, in the case of Mount Meru and the mustard seed, the expert and layman will not agree.

276. Compare Tucci's Sanskrit translation of the *Tarkaśāstra* (Tucci 1981, 16:5–6), which mentions existence (*satya*), unity (*ekatva*), and knowability (*prameyatva*) as properties that cannot establish a similarity (*sādharmya*) between things.

⁘ "It is from major similarity"—if you say that, it has to be replied:

VP 31 **Precisely because of the previous negation it is not by major similarity.**

Here it does also not become a major dissimilarity. With respect to that, it is precisely not established by major similarity and dissimilarity. ⁘ ⁘

"It is from major similarity (prāyaḥsādharmya)"—if you say that, it has to be replied:

VP 31 Precisely because of the previous negation, it is not by major similarity.

In VP 28 and 30, Nāgārjuna has refuted the first two of the three ways of spelling out examples or similarities mentioned by the opponent in NS 2.1.42: perfect similarity (*atyantasādharmya*) and slight similarity (*ekadeśa-sādharmya*). In this verse he takes up the third: major similarity (*prāyaḥ-sādharmya, phal cher chos mthun pa*).

Perfect similarity is only obtained in the case of an object exemplifying itself. But in this case, the key function of an example (namely to show us something we don't know by reference to something we do know) appears to have been lost. Slight similarity, on the other hand, is vacuous, because any two things have *some* degree of similarity.

So what is wrong with the intermediate position, that exemplifier and exemplified share some but not all properties, thereby constituting a case of major, though partial similarity? Unfortunately, Nāgārjuna is not very explicit on this point; all he tells us is that the reason lies in the "previous negation" (*sngar bkag pa*). This, we may assume, is the negation of slight similarity from the preceding verse 30. One reason why this may be the case is that, if major similarity is just resemblance in respect of more properties, there does not seem that much of a substantial difference between slight and major similarity. For, depending on what we are allowed to regard as properties, and in particular if we are allowed to include negation, disjunction, and conjunction, we seem to be able to cook up an infinite number of resemblances between things: a raven is like a writing desk, not just because they both exist, are single objects, and are material. They are also both different from my pen, they are not the first two things I saw last Tuesday morning, they have the (conjunctive) property of being existent and material, and so forth. If a single slight resemblance did not serve our purposes, it is unclear how a large number of such resemblances would.

> *Here it also does not become a major dissimilarity. With respect to that, it is precisely not established by major similarity and dissimilarity.*

The final possibility Nāgārjuna discusses is a major dissimilarity (*prāya-vaidharmya, phal cher chos can mi mthun pa*). Tola and Dragonetti[277] suggest that "this *dṛṣṭānta* through partial dissimilarity is negated by Nāgārjuna because it is a kind of *vaidharmyadṛṣṭānta* which has already been negated." Yet this is a curious thing to say, since the reason Nāgārjuna rejected the discordant example in VV 29 is that it has no connection with the thing to be exemplified. Yet this would not be the case for something that is dissimilar in a major (but nevertheless only partial) way. It seems to be that the reason for the rejection of the major dissimilarity is not Nāgārjuna's rejection of complete dissimilarity from verse 29, but rather the rejection of partial similarity in the present verse. For how could it be the case that if partial similarity between two objects fails to establish an exemplifier/exemplified relation, partial dissimilarity succeeds? If the sharing of properties does not relate something to something else as an example, the failure to do so will not accomplish this either.

Once again it is worthwhile to reflect on Nāgārjuna's philosophical aim in rejecting the category of example. It would be peculiar if we had to assume that a Mādhyamika can never refer to examples, or cannot ever use them in his own reasoning. However, there is an understanding of examples that Nāgārjuna explicitly rejects, namely an understanding where the example is based on an objectively existent similarity between two objects, a mind-independent similarity that makes one thing an example of another, whether or not a mind is involved in the process.[278] But no such objectively

277. Tola and Dragonetti 1995a, 122.

278. It is interesting to compare Tversky's (1977) research on the influence of contrast sets on the judgment of similarity in this context. In this paper he tried to demonstrate that our judgment of whether A or B is more similar to C depends heavily on what the other members of the set A and B are drawn from are, and this in turn crucially depends on our

existent relation, whether it is that of total similarity, total dissimilarity, or partial similarity, can possibly do that job. The most plausible candidate is the last one (subsuming slight and major similarity), but even if partial similarity were sufficient for an intrinsically obtaining example-exemplar relation between two things, it would entail that everything is an example of everything else, since there is some similarity between any two things. What is important is that some similarities are more important or more salient than others, and it is among this subset of the partial similarities where we find cases of examples. But importance or salience are not found in the things but in the investigating mind. Nāgārjuna therefore points out that the *svabhāva*-entailing conception of examples has to be replaced by a modified one that does not have such commitments.

It is objected:

"For you what is established is said not to exist at all. There will be no argument with one who has no established conclusion." To this, it is to be replied:

VP 32 **If the beginning is not established, the end is also not established. If the beginning is not established, the pair of middle and end are not established.**

"For you what is established is said not to exist at all. There will be no argument with one who has no established conclusion (siddhānta, grub pa'i mtha')."

The translation of this passage[279] is not entirely straightforward. Our rendering follows Kajiyama,[280] having the opponent object that since the Mādhyamika rejects "what is established," which is here to be understood as "what is substantially (*svabhāvatas*) established," he will be unable to

---

interests. If our similarity judgments simply latched on to objective similarities in the world, this phenomenon would be hard to explain.

279. *khyod ni grub pa med pa nyid du brjod pa yin te grub mtha' med pa dang lhan cig smra bar bya ba ma yin no.*

280. Kajiyama 1974, 205.

accept a conclusion established in this very way. But if an opponent does not admit any established conclusion, there is no point in debating with him, since the entire aim of the debate is to establish either one's own or the opponent's *siddhānta*.

Tola and Dragonetti[281] translate this passage differently, rendering it as:

> You affirm that (the example) is not established (as existing) (*siddha*), but (this) must not be said (by you) together with (the statement of) the inexistence of the (category) 'accepted theory' (*siddhānta*).

They thus interpret the opponent's remarks as connecting VP 32 with the discussion of the example in verses 25–31. If the example is understood as "what is established" (*'grub pa*), as "the basis on which reasoning proceeds," as Vātsyāyana puts it in his commentary on NS 1.1.1, we can read them in the following way: Nāgārjuna has just refuted the fifth Nyāya category, the example, and is now setting out to refute the sixth, the established conclusion. But this appears to lead straight to a contradiction, since asserting the nonexistence of the "established" is precisely the assertion of an established conclusion, namely the conclusion that the example does not exist. So Nāgārjuna has just accepted (in conflict with his agenda of denying all sixteen categories) at least one established conclusion, and for this reason his plan, set out in VP 01, cannot be carried out.

Nāgārjuna's ensuing rejection of the established conclusion proceeds along the same lines as the rejection of the example in verse 27. The established conclusion (*siddhānta*) is understood as a *karmadhāraya* compound of *siddha* and *anta*, as the "end that is established."[282] The established conclusion is the end of a dialectical process that begins with our acquaintance with some subject-matter, some epistemic object, via the epistemic instruments, involves a doubting opponent and the motivation to refute his objection, and uses an example by which one's own position

281. Tola and Dragonetti 1995a, 74.

282. See Böhtlingk 1879–89, s.v. "das letzte Ziel." Compare also the etymological discussion of the 18th c. Tibetan author Könchok Jigme Wangpo, who argues that a *siddhānta* is *siddha* because it is "made firm, decided upon, or established in reliance on scripture and/or reasoning," and it is *anta* "because one will not pass beyond this conclusion" (Huntington 2003, 85n11).

is to be established.[283] The collection of these positions constitutes one's *siddhānta*.

As the Mādhyamika continues to point out, concepts (and their corresponding objects), such as "beginning," "middle," and "end," depend for their existence on one another. We cannot have one without the other. The same of course applies to the "end," which is the established conclusion of an inferential process. We cannot have the conclusion without the preceding steps leading to it. But Nāgārjuna has just refuted these "beginning" and "middle" steps, the Nyāya categories from epistemic instruments (*pramāṇa*) up to the example (*dṛṣṭānta*). Therefore, there cannot be any *siddhānta*. We should note also that if, as the Naiyāyika agrees, all these preceding steps are necessary for obtaining the established conclusion, Nāgārjuna cannot (against his own intentions, as suggested by the opponent) hold a conclusion (such as the nonexistence of the example) himself, as he has refuted all the preceding conditions that would justify his doing so.

What seems to be a more satisfactory conclusion, however, is to argue that what Nāgārjuna wants to show is that, because none of the steps leading to the established conclusion exists by *svabhāva*, the established conclusion itself cannot do so either. Rather than claiming that the Mādhyamika cannot hold any conclusion whatsoever, we would want to say that he cannot hold a conclusion that is established intrinsically.[284] This would then also show that the opponent's worry that arguing with somebody who accepts no conclusion is pointless is unfounded: Nāgārjuna does not reject any conclusion or *siddhānta*, but only conclusions of a certain kind. Such conclusions would have to be considered as assertions interpreted according to a semantics based on correspondence with a mind-independent world. Nāgārjuna rejects such a semantics in favor of a purely convention-based one. If such a correspondence-based semantics is not successful in interpreting the foundation of an established conclusion, consisting of *pramāṇa*, *saṁśaya*, *prayojana*, and *dṛṣṭānta*, it will also not be adequate to understand the *siddhānta* in this way.

283. *svapakṣaḥ sādhanīyo*. Vātsyāyana on NS 1.1.1; Śāstrī 1998, 8:4.

284. I would therefore propose that this rejection of the *siddhānta* should be interpreted along the same lines as the rejection of the *pratijñā* in VV 29, as the rejection of a conclusion or thesis that is to be interpreted according to a realist semantics. See Westerhoff 2010, 64–65, for more details.

⌘ It is objected:

"Without parts, there is no proof, and there is no speech of yours that has parts. Therefore, all of it is refuted, precisely because it lacks connection. Because of this it is evidently necessary to speak, having understood it as having parts. Otherwise a refutation is not possible."

It should be replied:

VP 33 **Because there is no whole, there are no parts.**

In this respect, because there is no whole for the parts—the thesis, the reason, the example, the application, and the conclusion—there are no parts. ⌘ ⌘

It is objected:

"Without parts, there is no proof, and there is no speech of yours that has parts. Therefore, all of it is refuted, precisely because it lacks connection. Because of this it is evidently necessary to speak, having understood it as having parts. Otherwise a refutation is not possible."

Nāgārjuna now moves on to the refutation of the seventh category, the constituents of an argument (*avayava, yan lag*). Before he has even stated his reasons for doing so, the opponent immediately raises an objection, namely that, without such constituents or parts, we cannot have a proof (such as the five-membered syllogism) since proofs are essentially partite. This objection also manages to connect this verse with the preceding one dealing with the established conclusion (*siddhānta*). For if Nāgārjuna wanted to present a proof, he would have to accept its parts, and accepting these entails the existence of an established conclusion, denied in VV 32. A natural comeback for the opponent after Nāgārjuna's rejection of the *siddhānta* would have been to point out that it would automatically have to be assumed, whenever we accept the existence of proofs (and thereby also accept their constituents). Given Nāgārjuna's wholesale rejection of the Nyāya categories, the opponent could already then have anticipated Nāgārjuna's reply, namely the rejection of the constituents of arguments.

But in this case, the opponent points out, how can Nāgārjuna express any logically established conclusions whatsoever?

More importantly, unless there is something specific about parts *of arguments*, Nāgārjuna would presumably reject other, suitably similar parts, such as the parts of speech that constitute a sentence. In this case, it is difficult to see how Nāgārjuna manages to say anything at all, given that meaningful speech consists of words connected in the right way. But of course if there are no parts to be connected, there can be no connections, and therefore no meaning. It is then difficult not to see this position as self-refuting. In order to understand what Nāgārjuna had to say up to this point, we had to presuppose that his sentences were meaningful, and therefore composed of parts. If any of the preceding refutations of the Nyāya categories has been successful, it can only be so by having been presented as a piece of meaningful language. So if Nāgārjuna does not want to abandon these refutations, it is not really obvious how he can hold on to his rejection of parts. The Mādhyamika is caught in a dilemma: Either he denies the existence of parts, in which case there can be no linguistically expressed proofs, so that his arguments for universal emptiness cannot be expressed anymore, or, presupposing that his arguments do work, he will have to accept the existence of partite entities by implication and will thereby contradict his own position.

It should be replied:

VP 33 Because there is no whole, there are no parts.

In this respect, because there is no whole for the parts—the thesis (pratijñā), the reason (hetu), the example (udāharaṇa), the application (upanaya), and the conclusion (nigamana)—there are no parts.

After these objections to anticipated positions of Nāgārjuna, this verse confirms that he indeed wants to reject the constituents of arguments, based on a general mereological point about the rejection of the whole,[285] and, consequently, the rejection of the parts. He specifically notes that the

285. For Nyāya arguments in defense of the existence of the whole, see NS 2.1.32–33, 4.1.5–29.

parts of the five-membered syllogism, the canonical form of inference in the Indian theory of reasoning, fail to form a whole.[286]

There are two questions we have to answer here in order to understand Nāgārjuna's point: 1. Why does he deny the existence of wholes? 2. Why does the nonexistence of wholes entail the nonexistence of parts?

In line with the very condensed nature of VP and its autocommentary, Nāgārjuna does not give any argument for the rejection of wholes at this point. This is not very surprising, given that it is reasonable to expect that the justification for the rejection of wholes is known to an audience familiar with core Buddhist teachings. Already in the *Saṃyuttanikāya* we find teachings of the Buddha that are later synthesized in the famous simile of the chariot in the *Milindapañha*. There the monk Nāgasena explains to king Menandros that the existence of the chariot is a merely nominal one, that of an entity superimposed on a collection of individual parts:[287] the axle, the wheels, and so forth. This mereological reductionism is a familiar tenet of Abhidharma philosophy, and one that plays a crucial role in arguing for the doctrine of non-self on the basis of the idea that the only plausible candidate for a self is the person composed of the five psychophysical aggregates (*skandha*).

Yet Nāgārjuna's assertion that the nonexistence of the whole also entails the nonexistence of the parts that compose the whole[288] would have appeared very puzzling to an Ābhidharmika. Even if the complex whole exists only as a name, if we break it down, we will eventually have to hit

286. To understand the centrality of this form of inference, and the impact of Nāgārjuna's criticism, it is helpful to keep in mind its connection with the four epistemic instruments recognized by Nyāya: "According to the tradition, the first step (*pratijñā*) is said to be generated by verbal cognition; the second (*hetu*) is established by inference; in the third step, example is acquired through perception; and the fourth step is based on cognition of similarity. Since these four steps are established by four sources of true cognition admitted in the Nyāya school, the Naiyāyikas consider this five-membered argument as the demonstration par excellence (*parama-Nyāya*)." (Chatterjee 2011, 118–19)

287. In NS 4.2. 7–9, the opponent explores various possible ways in which whole and parts are related, arguing that they are all deficient and that therefore the Nyāya view of an existent whole must be rejected.

288. Compare Chandrakīrti's MĀ 6:161: "When the chariot does not exist, there is neither the whole nor its parts. As when the chariot has been burnt, there are no parts, when the fire of intelligence burns the whole, the parts are burnt as well." *sattvaṁ rathasyāsti na cet tadānīṁ vināṅgināṅgāny api santi nāsya | dagdhe rathe 'ṅgāni yathā na santi dhīvahnidagdhe 'ṅgini tadvad aṅgam ||* (Li 2015, 24).

some things that exist in a more substantial way. For the Ābhidharmika, these are the ultimately existent dharmas. So how do we address the second question, concerning the entailment between the nonexistence of wholes and the nonexistence of parts?

There are a variety of ways in which Nāgārjuna can justify his conclusion. Tola and Dragonetti present two possible ways of spelling out the argument. Firstly, if the whole is regarded as nonexistent, it would then be strange to assume that it has parts—nonexistent objects such as a city in the clouds or square circles don't have parts. Secondly, the parts of the wholes can be regarded as wholes that are nonexistent in relation to *their* parts, and so on.[289] Neither of these strikes me as wholly satisfactory. The first fails to take into account that the Mādhyamika does not want to put wholes in the same category as cloud-cities or square circles, i.e., things that are not even real at the level of conventional reality. Wholes are not ultimately real, but conventionally real, and thereby able to have parts. The second appears to beg the question against the atomist, who makes precisely the claim that, by a continued process of division of material objects, we will eventually reach some objects that do not stand in the relation of wholes to their parts, since they are impartite. To claim that the whole-part relation will continue all the way down is just a denial of that assumption, not an argument against it.

A better way of understanding Nāgārjuna's argument here is to take note of the fact that the Mādhyamika agrees with the Ābhidharmika in rejecting wholes as ultimately real: because they only exist in dependence, their existence is derived from the existence of their parts. The Mādhyamika points out that the same holds for the objects that the whole depends on, i.e., the parts. Even if there are impartite entities that all matter is composed of, they fail to be ultimately real, since the existence of each is dependent on that of some other. It can plausibly be argued that the best candidates for the ultimately existent dharmas of the Ābhidharmika are not material atoms but particularized property instances (sometimes called tropes or, more memorably, pins), such as the blueness of this mailbox or the shape of this apple. These pins then cluster together to form the familiar objects of our acquaintance. The important point to note here, though,

289. Tola and Dragonetti 1995a, 124. See also Tola and Dragonetti 1981, 275; and 1982, 129–31n6.

is that the identity of each particular pin is not due to some intrinsic property of its own (otherwise it would in turn be a bearer of properties, and hence not simple). Rather, it depends on what other pins it co-occurs with in a cluster, so that this red pin is distinct from that because the former occurs in a cluster with a square pin, while the latter occurs in a cluster with a triangular pin.[290] But if these pins are in this way dependent on other pins for their identity, they cannot be ultimately real. So, assuming that the opponent defends an ontology of pins, Nāgārjuna is justified in saying that the wholes are not ultimately real (because they depend for their existence on their parts), and the parts are not ultimately real either (because they depend for their identity on other parts).

Nāgārjuna will explain the matter in more detail in the following verses (the discussion of the constituents of an inference [*avayava*] extend from verse 33 up to verse 49), but it is worth noting already here the originality of Nāgārjuna's argument. While part-whole considerations are usually applied to composite material objects (such as chariots) or to physio-psychological complexes (such as persons), the argument is in this instance used to analyze structures, in particular logical inferences and pieces of language. Such an analysis is certainly in accordance with the intention behind the more familiar versions of the part-whole arguments. If there is any sense in which structures can be said to have parts, the same points that the Buddhist's analysis of material composites makes should apply to them. Yet it also raises the specter of inconsistency, for now the very means by which one carries out the part-whole analysis, namely logical and linguistic complexes, are subjected to a part-whole analysis themselves.

⌘ It is objected:

"The whole is established in the composite." It is to be replied:

VP 34 **Because it does not exist in each individually, it is also not established in the composite.**

290. Note that individuating the pins in terms of spatio-temporal location would not help to tell them apart independent of clusters. If pins really are the fundamental ontological category, the property of being at a particular spatial or temporal location should either be a pin itself or reducible to pins. See Siderits 2007, 189–91.

The assertion "The whole exists in the composite" is not correct. Because the whole does not exist in each individual part, it also does not exist in the composite.

In this verse, Nāgārjuna's opponent tries to refute his denial of the whole (and in particular the denial of the whole that is the five-membered syllogism) by arguing that the whole made up by some parts is just to be found in all the parts put together, i.e., in the composite (*saṁyoga*, *tshogs*) of the parts.

There are two ways in which we could envisage the whole existing in the composite: it could either exist "spread out" across all the parts, or it could exist in each individual part. In the first case, the whole of a chariot, for example, would occupy the same spatio-temporal location as the parts put together; in the second case, it would exist in each of the individual parts. The whole would exist in each wheel, the axle, and so forth, in the same way in which, for example, a proponent of universals would hold that the universal redness is wholly and completely present at the same time in the red fire extinguisher, the red flag, and the red tomato.

The first possibility is not explicitly mentioned by Nāgārjuna. The key problem for this account lies in its apparent inability to provide a satisfactory explanation of the whole/part relation, which is, after all, the aim of our present discussion. For if the whole is a separate entity from the parts put together, and if it exists in the same space as they do, it will be spatially spread out and will possess parts in turn. Only a part of the whole will exist in each part of the chariot—not, as the second possibility would assume, the entire whole in each of the parts. Note that these parts of the whole are distinct from the parts of the chariot. It will then be necessary to describe the relation between the whole and *its* parts, and in order to do so, we have to introduce a second-order whole that relates to the parts of the whole in the way the whole relates to the parts of the chariot put together. This will go on forever, and the analysis of the relation between the parts of the chariot and the whole they compose will be indefinitely deferred, since it will always be necessary to understand first the relation of some higher-order whole to its parts. The same applies to the five-part syllogism, at least when conceived of as a piece of language.[291] The whole will exist in each part of the syllogism and will have to be understood as having parts that are separate from the parts of the syllogism.

The second possible way in which the whole could exist in the composite, namely by existing in each individual part, is explicitly mentioned by Nāgārjuna. And it is clear why this should be the case, since this is the view of part-whole relations actually adopted by the Naiyāyika.[292] Nāgārjuna points out that this view is deficient, but does not give us any reasons for his view. Fortunately, the discussion of the Nyāya position by other Buddhist writers can give us some idea of what Nāgārjuna's reservations may have been. The main difficulty here lies with properties of the whole that we cannot plausibly ascribe to some (or indeed any) particular part.[293] To use an example familiar from the traditional discussion, if we have a cloth woven from threads of two different colors, say red and blue, the result will be a cloth of a color that changes between red and blue, depending on how the light falls on it. Yet we cannot ascribe this "variegated" color (*citrarūpa*),[294] which is a property of the whole, to any red thread or

291. Matters are more complicated if it is understood as an abstract object, but the conception of proofs and pieces of language as tokens rather than types is certainly present in Madhyamaka texts such as these (see, e.g., Westerhoff 2010, 46).

292. The Naiyāyika also takes this position to have important epistemological implications: "The whole, therefore, must be supposed to be revealed *entirely* even when a particular part is perceived. The whole, in fact is perceived whenever any part is perceived. Thus, for instance, when we see the front of a tree, we do not see only the front, but the whole tree in and through this part." (Bhaduri 1947, 239)

293. See Vasubandhu's *Abhidharmakośabhāṣya* 3, 100ab (Pradhan 1975, 189–90; Poussin and Pruden 1988–90, vol. 2, 492–93; Poussin and Lodrö Sangpo 2012, vol. 2, 1111–12). This appears also to be one of the problems identified by the opponent in NS 4.2.7–8. Vātsyāyana notes that, according to him, "the whole cannot reside in each one of the components because they are of different sizes" (*na tāvat pratyavayavaṁ vartate tayoḥ parimāṇabhedād*; Śāstrī 1998, 393:9). See also Āryadeva's *Śataśāstra*: "'If the whole is in the part, how is it that the head is not in the foot?' If there is a *dharma* which is the body, then in the parts such as the foot, and so on, does it exist as a totality or (does it exist) as a part? Now, if it exists as a totality, the foot must exist in the head: on account of the unity of that *dharma* which is the body." (Tucci 1981, 47–48) Another difficulty one might identify with the view that the whole exists in each part is that all the other parts then appear to be redundant, since only one part would already contain the entire whole. See Sen 1996, 161.

294. It is to be understood as a single, unified color, not as an assembly of mutually distinguishable colors. See Bhaduri 1947, 247. For further discussion of *citrarūpa*, see Grohma 1975, and Sen 1996.

any blue thread, that is, to any of the parts that make up the whole. But in this case, it is unclear with what justification we can still say that the whole exists in each of the parts. In the case of the syllogism, the difficulty for conceiving of the whole as existing in each of the parts is that the whole has a probative force that the individual parts lack.[295] All members of the syllogism put together establish the conclusion, but no individual part on its own does. If the conclusion "there is fire on the mountain" were already contained in the reason "because of smoke," it would follow absurdly that any presence of smoke (such as smoke emanating from a kitchen) established the existence of fire on the mountain.

Nāgārjuna can therefore argue that because the whole does not exist as spread out across the parts, and since it does not exist in each part separately, the whole does not exist in the composite, since these are the only two ways in which it could exist.

Moreover,

VP 35 **Because the whole is one there is the faulty consequence that all the parts are just one.**

There is this defect when it is not different. Or else, if one is different from the five parts, it follows absurdly that there are six.

In the preceding VP 34, Nāgārjuna explicitly addressed the difficulty of the location of the whole conceived as being separate from the parts. In this verse, he considers problems arising from there being a unified whole in the first place.

> *VP 35 Because the whole is one there is the faulty consequence that all the parts are just one.*

295. See also the first verse of the **Vyavahārasiddhi*: "One syllable (*yi ge, akṣara*) is not a *mantra*, but many syllables are not a *mantra* either. The syllables have ceased (*'gags pa, viruddha*), dependent on a name, that is also not non-existent"; *yi ge gcig sngags gang yang med* | *yi ge mang po gzhan yang med* || *yi ge 'gags pa rnams ming la* | *rten nas de ni med pa'ang min* | (Lindtner 1982, 97).

Accepting the opponent's view of the unity of the whole for the sake of argument, Nāgārjuna uses this in order to derive a series of unsatisfactory consequences. Nāgārjuna notes two different problems entailed by the assumption held by Nyāya and Vaisheṣhika that the whole is one single thing.

There is this defect when it is not different.

Unfortunately, Nāgārjuna does not tell us what "this defect," the first problem, amounts to, but it is not too difficult to see what he could have had in mind. If the unity of the whole means that it is just the same as all the parts, we face the problem that different parts that make up the whole can have mutually inconsistent properties. One part of the poker can be hot while the other is cold, but the very same thing cannot be hot and cold, since the same mass of molecules cannot move both faster and slower. Āryadeva's *Śataśāstra* raises the same point when he notes that:

> If the head, the feet and the other parts are not different from the body, the foot must be on the head, since both are not different from the body, just as Indra is Shakra, because Indra and Shakra are not different.[296]

If "body," "head," and "foot" were names for a single thing, we should be able to substitute them in non-intensional contexts. Yet substituting "foot" for "head" and "head" for "body," "the head is on top of the body" turns into "the foot is on top of the head," which is demonstrably false. The three terms therefore cannot all name the same thing.

Or else, if one is different from the five parts, it absurdly follows that there are six.

Other difficulties arise if we assume that the unitary whole is different from the parts.[297] Some of these difficulties concern the question of the

296. Tucci 1981, 40. Shakra (the Mighty) is an alternative name of Indra "just as 'Hesperus' is a common name of the planet Venus" (Daniélou 1964, 108).

297. See Halbfass 1992, 94–96.

location of the whole relative to the location of the parts, as was discussed in the previous verse.

In addition, if saying that the whole is one single thing means that it is different from the parts, in any place where there are *n* objects, there are in fact *n + 1* objects, each individual object plus the whole of all of them together. The Naiyāyika should be reluctant to assert this, since he claims there are five parts of a syllogism, not six. But, apart from such exhortations to doctrinal consistency, the distinction of the whole being different from the parts brings additional difficulties with it. First of all, what is to keep us from saying that there are really *seven* parts present here: the five parts of the syllogism acknowledged by the Naiyāyika, the whole of these parts together, and the larger whole of all the six parts together?[298] Once we go down this particular slippery slope, it is understandably difficult to stop, which means everything ends up having the same number of parts, namely infinitely many. Secondly, and perhaps more importantly, counting the whole in addition to the parts is not the way we count. If we put six eggs in a carton and ask people how many objects there are, few will reply that there are seven. The defender of this solution would thus at least have to provide us with some reason as to why the adoption of such a novel way of counting is advantageous.

A further difficulty with assuming a unitary whole that exists separately from the parts is its conflict with the principle of lightness. This principle says that, of two equally good theories, we should choose the one postulating fewer unobservable entities.[299] The whole is certainly unobservable, for all we ever perceive are the different parts related in a certain way, but not any entity over and above this.[300] Furthermore, reductionist theories claiming that there are *only* the parts in relation seem to be equally good in providing a theory of parts and wholes.

298. Note that the Naiyāyika would deny that these additional objects are actually substances. Yet this response is unlikely to have much traction for the Mādhyamika, as it relies on a distinction between entities that are natural kinds, and those that are not, and the Mādhyamika would deny that we can make sense of this without appealing to *svabhāva*.

299. Siderits 2007, 44–45.

300. See, however, the discussion in Uddyotakara's commentary on NS 2.1.33 (Dvivedin 1986, 241–43; Jha 1984, vol. 2, 744–49), setting out to refute the opponent who claims that the whole is not different from its parts because a difference between the two cannot be perceived by a scale, i.e., because whole and part have the same weight. See also Halbfass 1992, 107n31.

Moreover,

VP 36 **Because it is not established in the three times the whole[301] certainly does not exist.**

The thesis, etc., is arisen or nonarisen; and relative to the present ones, there are past, future, and present ones.[302] This does not withstand investigation, because it is not reasonable. Therefore, the whole does not exist, and the parts also do not exist.

The commentary on this verse is very condensed. In particular, the sentence:

> *The thesis (pratijñā), etc., is arisen or nonarisen; and relative to the present ones, there are past, future, and present ones*[303]

is barely comprehensible without interpolations in either Tibetan or English. Here is one possible way of spelling out what it means:[304]

> The thesis, etc., is arisen or nonarisen [at the same time as the whole, which is the entire syllogism], and relative to the present ones [i.e., the present parts], [the whole is] past, or [it is] future, and present ones [i.e., the parts are present].

Nāgārjuna points out that there are two main possibilities when considering the temporal relation between parts and whole. Either both have arisen at the same time, such that a whole and its parts are simultaneously

301. P and N read *yan lag can* (the whole) here; D and C read *yan lag* (the part). We follow the first reading.

302. In the translation of the commentary, the first and third occurrence of "*dang*" are understood in its *'byed pa* (division) sense, separating a term into several notions subsumed under it. In English we can render this sense both by "and" as well as by "or" ("the primary colors: red and blue and yellow" vs. "the primary colors: red or blue or yellow").

303. *dams bca' ba la sogs pa skyes pa dang | ma skyes pa dang | da ltar ba rnams la 'das pa dang | ma 'ongs pa dang | da ltar ba rnams.*

304. This interpretation accords with the one given by Tola and Dragonetti 1995a, 75.

both present, or both past, or both future, or they have arisen at different times. In this latter case, there are six different possibilities: the whole is past, and the parts either present or future; the whole is present, and the parts either past or future; or the whole is future, and the parts past or present.

The "parts" Nāgārjuna has in mind are of course still the five parts of the syllogism beginning with the thesis (*pratijñā*), and so forth, and the "whole" is the syllogism composed of them. In the commentary, Nāgārjuna distinguishes the two main possibilities, that the parts and whole either exist at the same times, or that they don't, and mentions two of the six remaining possibilities, that, relative to the presently existent parts, the whole is past, or that the whole is future and the parts present. When he claims that "it does not withstand investigation," I take Nāgārjuna to understand these two as representative examples of the set of six possibilities, and suggest that what he wants to say is that all the nine different possible temporal relations between part and whole do not withstand analysis, because none of them is reasonable. But, given that this list of possible relations is exhaustive, it is then difficult for the opponent to claim that the parts and whole exist in any way, at least as long as he assumes that they exist in time at all.

But what is the argument against the feasibility of any of the nine possible temporal relations? Unfortunately, the commentary does not tell us. Here is one way to understand how Nāgārjuna could argue, building on the discussion in VP 34 and 35.

If the parts and the whole have arisen at the same time, they may be either identical or distinct. If they have arisen at different times, they must be distinct, because otherwise the very same thing would exist at some time and fail to exist at the very same time. That the whole is past and the parts present, for example, means that the whole exists only in the past, but not in the present, otherwise whole and part would, after all, exist at the same time.

Nāgārjuna has argued against the possibility of a separately existing whole in VP 34 and 35, and has addressed specific difficulties with the view that the whole and its collection of parts are identical in VP 35.

If we rule out that whole and part are distinct entities, six of the possible temporal relations between them are refuted, namely all those that claim that part and whole exist at different times. But Nāgārjuna also rejected the possibility that the whole and the collection of parts could be identical.

Together these two refutations entail that part and whole also cannot exist at the same time. Since these are all the possibilities, as long as parts and wholes are temporal entities at all, they cannot stand in any temporal relation. But partite entities are just the things we suppose would stand in temporal relations. Therefore, Nāgārjuna concludes, there is something deeply problematic about postulating the existence of parts and wholes.

VP 37 **Nevertheless, that is also established like the *balbaja* grass.**

As an elephant cannot be bound by a single strand of *balbaja* grass, even though it can be bound by a collection of these, in the same way the whole exists in the collection of the proposition, etc.

VP 37 Nevertheless, that is also established like the balbaja grass.

In this verse the opponent introduces an analogy for another way in which the whole (the referent of "that" [*de*] in the verse) can be considered to exist. The *balbaja* grass (*eleusine indica*) is a coarse kind of grass used for plaiting that is traditionally used in Vedic rituals.[305]

> *As an elephant cannot be bound by a single strand of balbaja grass, even though it can be bound by a collection of these, in the same way the whole exists in the collection of the proposition, etc.*

The opponent uses the example[306] in order to argue for the existence of a whole, even though the whole does not exist in each and every part. But, the opponent claims, the whole could exist as the aggregate of all the parts. The example introduces an emergent property, that is, a property that is

305. Gonda 1985.

306. It is interesting to note that the same example of the *balbaja* grass is also raised by the opponent against the Vaibhāṣika theory of meaning in the *Abhidharmadīpa* (see Jaini 1959, 104).

had by an aggregate of objects (such as a bundle of strands of grass), even though it may not be had by any one of the members of the aggregate. A rope can hold back an elephant, even though none of the individual fibres that make up the rope can do so.[307] It is precisely because there is such a property that only emerges at the level of the aggregate, not at the level of the parts, that we have to take the whole seriously ontologically. The whole understood as the aggregate of the parts is the best answer to the question regarding what the emergent property is a property of. Similarly, a whole consisting of various propositions (or, in the present case, of the members of the syllogism) can imply a conclusion, even though none of the members implies the conclusion. The syllogism exists in the collection of its parts in the same way the inference exists in the set of the premises. Only by forming an aggregate of parts, the probative force of the syllogism or inference emerges, and it is for this reason, the opponent argues, that we have to accept the existence of the whole.

⁜ If this is objected, one should reply:

VP 38 **It is not the case, because it is similar to what is to be established.**

This is like a barren woman, or a blind man, and like the sand. If a single barren woman is not able to give birth to a son, similarly a collection of several thousand barren women cannot do so either. As for a single blind man, there is no power of sight, similarly for a multitude of thousands of blind men, there isn't the power of sight either. As there is no sesame oil in any single grain of sand, similarly it cannot be extracted from a collection of many, because of its nonexistence. ⁜ ⁜

VP 38 It is not the case, because it is similar to what is to be established.

Nāgārjuna responds to the criticism from the preceding verse by accusing the opponent of commiting a *sādhyasama* fallacy (*bsgrub par bya dang*

307. The same simile is used in the *Śataśāstra* (see Tucci 1981, 48).

mtshungs pa).[308] *Sādhyasama* is sometimes rather unsatisfactorily translated as *petitio principii*, but the difficulty with a *sādhyamsama* is not that it explicitly or implicitly assumes the conclusion to be proved (as would be the case with a *petitio*) but that its premises are only as certain as the conclusion (or even less certain than it is), so that we would proceed from doubtful premises to a still doubtful conclusion.[309] Matilal therefore renders this fallacy more precisely, though less concisely as "the fallacy of 'having the same predicament as the proposition to be proved.'"[310]

Nāgārjuna[311] as well as later Madhyamaka authors[312] refer to this fallacy in numerous instances. Buddhapālita in his commentary on MMK 4:8 explains the *sādhyasama* fallacy as follows:

> When a dispute and discussion in terms of emptiness has begun, someone may give a reply in terms of non-emptiness. Yet when making such an objection, all of this is not a reply. Why? Because of having the same predicament as what is to be proved. For example, if the thesis is, "All things lack intrinsic nature," in order to point out an example, when we establish that a cloth is empty of intrinsic nature, at this point someone may say "Warp and woof certainly exist"—this is a case of having the same predicament as what is to be proved. The very reasons by which the cloth is shown to be empty of intrinsic nature also establish warp and woof to be empty. Therefore the assertion that warp

308. This fallacy is defined in NS 1.2.8 as something to be proved that is not different from the conclusion (*sādhyāviśiṣṭaḥ sādhyatvāt sādhyasamaḥ*). See also VP 41 for another place where Nāgārjuna accuses the opponent of this fallacy.

309. To give an example: If somebody argues that murder is wrong because God forbids it, and then explains the divine prohibition by the fact that murder is wrong, we have a *petitio*. If a thief claims that a watch found in his possession was not stolen but appeared in his pocket due to quantum tunneling, we have a case of *sādhyasama*, because we doubt the reason (the occurrence of quantum tunneling in this instance) more than we doubt the conclusion to be established (that he did not steal the watch).

310. Matilal 1974, 215.

311. See, e.g., MMK 4:8, and VP 28, 69. On the latter, see Westerhoff 2010, 58, 126.

312. Further examples of the Madhyamaka discussion of this fallacy (especially by Chandrakīrti) can be found in Bhattacharya 1974. See also Bhattacharya et al. 1978, 112–13n3.

and woof are not empty has the same predicament as the cloth to be established.[313]

As Buddhapālita points out, we cannot establish that a cloth has an extrinsic nature by pointing out that the threads that make up the cloth do, since the arguments that cast doubt on the intrinsic nature of the cloth also cast doubt on that of the threads. The claim that the threads have an intrinsic nature is therefore no more certain than the claim to be established by the opponent (that the cloth does). It therefore cannot lead us from undoubted premises to removing the doubt from a currently doubted conclusion, and therefore counts as a case of *sādhyasama*.

> *This is like a barren woman, or a blind man, and like the sand. If a single barren woman is not able to give birth to a son, similarly a collection of several thousand barren women cannot do so either. As for a single blind man, there is no power of sight, similarly for a multitude of thousands of blind men there isn't the power of sight either. As there is no sesame oil in any single grain of sand, similarly it cannot be extracted from a collection of many, because of its nonexistence.*

Why does Nāgārjuna claim that the opponent is commiting the *sādhyasama* fallacy in the present case? The example suggested by the opponent is that of some object x that lacks the property P, while a collection or compound of objects of the same kind as x has P. The opponent takes x to be a strand of *balbaja* grass, while P is the property of being able to bind and wants to argue that x as a member of a syllogism and P as the property of proving the conclusion are related in the very same way.

What the opponent has in mind here as a property P are cumulative properties. A single marching man will not make a bridge collapse, but a

313. *stong pa nyid kyis brtsad cing 'gyed pa brtsams te yongs su gleng ba'i tshe gang zhig stong pa nyid ma yin pas lan 'debs shing smra bar byed pa de'i tshe de dag thams cad ni lan btab pa ma yin no | ci'i phyir zhe na | bsgrub par bya ba dang mtshungs par 'gyur ba'i phyir dang | 'di lta ste dper na dngos po thams cad ngo bo nyid stong pa'o | zhes dam bcas na dpe bstan pa'i phyir snam bu ngo bo nyid stong par sgrub par byed pa'i tshe gang zhig re zhig rgyu spun dag ni yod do zhes zer ba'i de ni bsgrub par bya ba dang mtshungs pa yin te | gtan tshigs gang dag nyid kyis snam bu ngo bo nyid stong par bstan pa de dag nyid rgyu spun dag stong pa nyid du rab tu sgrub par byed pa yang yin pas de'i phyir rgyu spun dag stong pa nyid ma yin par ston pa ni bsgrub par bya ba snam bu dang mtshungs pa yin no* (Saito 1984, part II, 64).

thousand marching men might. A milligram of a certain substance may not be poisonous, but a gram is. It is the accumulation of many different things that brings about the effect. Yet there are also cases of properties (noncumulative properties we might call them) where this is not the case. A thousand naked men won't make one dressed one; adding more false sentences to a set of false sentences won't produce a truth; and adding any finite number of objects to a finite set won't result in an infinite one.

The opponent thus wants to argue that the property of proving the conclusion is a cumulative property of the parts of the syllogism, a property that obtains when all of them act together. Nāgārjuna's reference to the *sādhyasama* fallacy points out that this assumption is as much in need of proof as the conclusion the opponent wants to establish, namely that the whole exists separately from the parts. It is in no way obvious that the syllogism's probative force emerges when all its parts are brought together (as the plait's binding force emerges when all the individual strands of *balbaja* grass are brought together); the situation might very well be one in which a noncumulative property is involved (where no reproductive force emerges from the accumulation of individually infertile women).[314]

It is precisely this idea that underlies Carroll's paradox, made famous through its description in Lewis Carroll's "What the tortoise said to Achilles."[315] The problem raised there is the following: Suppose you have two premises:

A: P and B: if P, then Q.

They do not imply the conclusion:

C: Q

unless you also have an additional premise:

D: if A and B, then C.

But once you realize the need for D, it is clear that we also need:

314. The *Śataśāstra* (Tucci 1981, 48) uses the same appeal to noncumulative properties to argue against atomism: "As no barren woman can have a son and none of the blind men can see *rūpa*, and no grain of sand can produce oil, they cannot do it, even when they are collected together; also the same is the case with regard to the atoms; because each one [of them] cannot [produce that effect], then many also cannot [do it]."

315. Carroll 1895.

E: if A and B and D, then C

...and so forth. No matter how many more premises we insert here, the probative force of the inference that results in the demonstration of C is never going to emerge, since there is always one more premise you need to add.

For the Carrollian, the whole, or the proof of the conclusion, is not to be found in the collection of the premises. He doubts the validity of the inference. But then, adding more premises asserting that certain inferential matters are valid will not have any effect, since they have to form part of a yet bigger inferential structure, which the Carrollian will again doubt. Adding more truth is like adding more sand to a heap in the hope that one will finally be able to extract oil from the result.[316]

For this reason, Nāgārjuna's criticism—that the opponent's assumption of the parts of the syllogism acting like the strands of *balbaja* grass is as much in need of an argument as the conclusion of the separately existing whole to be established—is justified.

Well then, if you think: "It is similar to the example of the barren woman, etc. The single *balbaja* grass by which a creature like a butterfly, etc., is bound has a power concordant with the nature of the *balbaja* grass. An elephant can also be bound by a collection of many." That is also not the case. If you ask why:

VP 39 **Because it is unreasonable.**

Even though this is a well-known example of a whole, it does not apply to wholes, because of the failure to abide together. The thesis, etc., or the syllables of that do not abide together at the same time or within the mouth. Therefore, the example of the *balbaja* grass is not reasonable. Because it is not reasonable, it is established that "the parts do not exist."

316. Collins (2002, 474) draws the following conclusion from Carroll's paradox (a view that coheres well with Nāgārjuna's rejection of wholes as mind-independently real entities): "Astonishingly, it turns out that mathematical proof as we learned it at school and as it is practiced by working mathematicians—the thing that we have conventionally thought of as the high point of rationality—is a polymorphic action, an action based on shared social ways of being in the world."

> *Well then, if you think: "It is similar to the example of the barren woman, etc. The single balbaja grass by which a creature like a butterfly, etc., is bound has a power concordant with the nature of the balbaja grass. An elephant can also be bound by a collection of many." That is also not the case.*

It appears to me that the easiest way of understanding this passage is by supposing that a negation got lost in the transmission of the opponent's first statement, which would really be supposed to mean that "it [the syllogism] is *not* similar to the example of the barren woman, etc., [for the following reason]."[317] This is because the opponent now explains the difference between the example of the *balbaja* grass and its cumulative property of binding, and the barren women, blind men, and grains of sand that do not cumulatively produce fertility, sight, or oil. This is the fact that the property of the whole under discussion is present to an extremely small extent in each part of the whole. Each individual strand of *balbaja* grass has a tiny binding power, sufficient just for a very light animal such as a butterfly, and when many of these are put together, the binding power is more significant and can bind larger animals, such as an elephant. It is for this reason that putting together many strands of *balbaja* grass produces a rope that has the power to bind, while many grains of sand do not produce any oil, because there is not the smallest amount of oil in any of them. It is the same, the opponent wants to argue, for the syllogism: each member has a small probative force, and once all the parts come together, this force is sufficient to establish the conclusion. This is the specific reason why in this case the whole is comparable to the *balbaja* grass and not to the heap of sand, as Nāgārjuna claimed in his *sādhyasama*

317. Tola and Dragonetti (1995, 127) interpret the passage as having the opponent say that his example of the *balbaja* grass is indeed like that of the barren women (to the extent that both involve talk about entities on the one hand and accumulations of such entities on the other) but that the example of the *balbaja* grass is also very different for the reason given in the following two sentences. The overall consequence of the difference in interpretation for the understanding of Nāgārjuna's argument is negligible, and both involve making certain changes to the text (the sense of opposition between the opponent's first and his next two sentences is not evident in the Tibetan), yet I consider my reading to provide an overall simpler explanation.

charge in the immediately preceding verse. The syllogism cannot be compared to the examples of noncumulative properties Nāgārjuna mentions because, in these cases, the parts do not have the property in question even to the smallest extent.

VP 39 Because it is unreasonable.

Even though this is a well-known example of a whole, it does not apply to wholes, because of the failure to abide together. The thesis, etc., or the syllables of that, do not abide together at the same time or in the mouth.

Nāgārjuna responds, criticizing the opponent's use of the example of the *balbaja* grass by arguing that it is not reasonably understood as a representative example of the wholes under discussion here. Nāgārjuna's attack on wholes is directed specifically at the supposed whole constituted by the five-fold syllogism. This syllogism, conceived of as a token event of a spoken sequence of syllables, not as an abstract pattern of reasoning expressed by such a token,[318] differs crucially from the plait of *balbaja* grass in that its parts do not coexist at a single time. When one part of the syllogism such as the reason (*hetu*) is mentioned, another one, such as the thesis (*pratijñā*) has already ceased existing, while the later parts are yet to be spoken and do not yet exist.[319] The same reasoning applies to the individual syllables that make up each of the five parts of the syllogism. They also do not coexist in time, but only when each individual one is spoken, nor do they coexist in space, as only the syllable currently uttered presently exists in the organs of speech production.[320]

318. The same understanding is employed in the opponent's argument in VV 1, when he argues that, because philosophical arguments are causally produced by the mechanism that generates human speech, they are empty. See Westerhoff 2010, 45–46.

319. How can the Mādhyamika still claim that a syllogism has a probative force? For him, an inference consists of a causal sequence of distinct mental events, each of which presumably has an impact on the content of its successor. Accepting momentariness, he will hold that the syllogism as a whole, i.e., the series of temporally distinct events, is a fiction; however, the inference can still be understood to have probative force, since the conclusion has the right kinds of causal antecedents.

320. The *Tarkaśāstra* points out that as soon as a word has left the mouth it ceases to be (*sarve śabdā yadā mukhān nirgatās tadā nāṣṭāḥ*; Tucci's translation in 1981, 8:16).

> *Therefore, the example of the balbaja grass is not reasonable. Because it is not reasonable, it is established that "the parts do not exist."*

Nāgārjuna therefore concludes that the example of the *balbaja* grass is not suitable to establish the existence of the syllogism as an example of a whole in separation from its parts. And, as Nāgārjuna pointed out in VV 33, if the existence of the whole is not established, that of the part is not established either.

It is, however, important to point out that Nāgārjuna's argument can also be understood here as making a stronger point, not just directed at ruling out the example of *balbaja* grass giving rise to a cumulative property, which is taken as implying a separately existing whole that has such a property. Rather, the "failure to abide together" need not just be understood as applying to the constituents of the syllogism, but applies equally to tables, chairs, and plaits of grass. Because of the theory of momentariness accepted by the Buddhist, only temporal parts of such temporally stretched-out phenomena exist at one time. Yet one might argue that we are only speaking of the whole table if we speak about the sum of its temporal parts throughout its existence. And if this is the case, the parts of this will never abide together, since by the time the present temporal part exists, the preceding part has already passed out of existence. In this way, Nāgārjuna could be understood as appealing to the principle of momentariness in order to argue against the existence of wholes more generally, not just against the existence of wholes that are syllogisms.

One objection that the opponent might have raised against Nāgārjuna's argument in this verse consists of pointing out the difference between the temporal words and syllables used in a sentence and the atemporal meaning they express.[321] Even though the syllables cannot all exist at the same time,

321. Raja (1969, 116–17): "He [Bhartṛhari] says that in meaningful language, linguists recognize two entities, both of which may be called words: one is the underlying cause of articulated sounds, while the other is attached to the meaning.... The former is the sound-pattern which is the external facet of the language symbol, while the latter is the semantic facet which expresses the meaning. Janus-like, words have two faces: the external face looks at the sound (*dhvani*), while the internal face looks at the meaning (*artha*). The underlying cause of the articulated sounds (*śabdānāṁ nimittaṁ*) is the sound-pattern which underlies instances of the utterance of the word; this abstract sound-pattern with the time-sequence still attached to it is called *prākṛta-dhvani* and is the external aspect of language. The internal aspect, which is directly attached to the meaning is the *sphoṭa*, which is the

their aggregate expresses a meaning that is unified and timeless. If we identify this abstract meaning with the whole, Nāgārjuna's argument against wholes from the theory of momentariness will only be successful in refuting the existence of a certain kind of temporal complex of syllables, but not in refuting the existence of a timeless whole.

It is unlikely that Nāgārjuna would have been convinced by this objection, though, not just because of difficulties with fitting abstract objects—such as this nonlinguistic meaning—into the Madhyamaka framework.[322] The main difficulty is the theory of momentariness that constitutes the background of Nāgārjuna's argument. As a universal theory, this is not just supposed to apply to the phonetic expression of words and syllables, or just to all concrete objects, but to all objects whatsoever. As such, there is no space for atemporal meanings or any other kinds of entities that are supposed to exist outside of time. What the defender of the sound/meaning distinction thus would have to do in order to make his objection convincing is to show why the Buddhist arguments in favor of momentariness[323] are unsatisfactory.

There is also another interesting criticism the opponent can raise in relation to Nāgārjuna's argument. He might point out that the idea of the nonexistence of the whole, which is the meaning of the sentence or the proof expressed by a sequence of syllables, is a *reductio* of the theory of momentariness. For if there are meaningful sentences and proofs, the opponent would claim, there must be some entity such as a temporally thick self that holds them. This is because, in order to understand them, the self has to be able to have a cognitive grasp of an entity lasting for many moments, and only a self that is itself in this way extended could do so. The Buddhist would have to respond that it is strictly speaking not the same cognitive agent or self that doubts whether there is fire on the hill, and is later convinced that there is, having observed the presence of smoke. All there is for him is a sequence of mind-moments that replace each other

---

partless, integral linguistic symbol." Tola and Dragonetti (1990, 98): "[W]ords and sentences have two faces or facets: one, the external phonetic face which is submitted to time and as such has sequence; the other, the internal semantic face, which is timeless and as such has no sequence."

322. On this, see Westerhoff 2009, 111–12.

323. On these, see Siderits 2007, 120–23.

in quick succession,[324] producing the mistaken impression that there is a persistent self present in understanding the premises and also present in understanding the conclusion. The appearance of a temporally extended self is for the Buddhist wholly compatible with its ultimate nonexistence.

Moreover,

VP 40 **For the parts as well there is the contradictory consequence of the existence of a part.**[325]

If the parts are establishers of a non-established object, is it not that those also are something established that establishes, or something non-established?

If something established is an establisher, another establisher exists for the establisher by which those also are establishers—because for those another also exists, there will be the contradictory consequence of an infinite regress.

Well then, if for those also another one does not exist, regarding the assertion that the whole is established by all these parts, "the difference and the impairment of the thesis" should be replied.

VP 40 For the parts as well there is the contradictory consequence of the existence of a part.

After a general mereological discussion applied to the parts of a syllogism in VP 33–39, Nāgārjuna now looks more specifically at the individual members of the syllogism. The present verse examines the first part of the five-fold syllogism (*pratijñā*, the thesis), though not in a very direct manner.

324. Compare Galen Strawson's (1997, 424) "pearl" view of the self, which sees it as "a gappy series of eruptions of consciousness from a substrate of apparent non-consciousness" (425).

325. The version of this verse from VS is a bit more comprehensive: "In the same way in which the whole requires the parts, for all parts there is the contradictory consequence of the existence of a part as well" (*yang yan lag can la yan lag dgos pa ltar | yan lag thams cad la yang yan lag yod par thal ba'i phyir ro*).

It might be useful at this place to remind the reader of the structure of this syllogism.[326] Consider the stock example of the five-fold inference:

1. Thesis (*pratijñā, dam bca'*): The hill has fire.
2. Reason (*hetu, gtan tshigs*): Because it has smoke.
3. Example (*udāharaṇa, dṛṣṭānta, dpe*): Whatever has smoke has fire, as in an oven.
4. Application (*upanaya, nye bar sbyor ba*): The hill has smoke invariably associated with fire.
5. Conclusion (*nigamana, mjug bsdu ba*): Therefore, the hill has fire.

The first member, the thesis, tells us what the subject of the inference is (*pakṣa*, the hill), and what is to be proved about it (*sādhya*, that there is fire on it). The reason then states the mark (*liṅga*, because of smoke). The third member asserts the universal relation between the mark (*liṅga*) and what is to be proved about the subject (*sādhya*) in the case of one specific instance (as in an oven, whenever there is smoke, there is fire). The application then notes the presence of the mark in the subject (*pakṣa*, the hill), and the conclusion restates that what is to be proved indeed applies to the subject of inference. Despite their identity in content, thesis and conclusion have different characters: the thesis is what is to be established, the conclusion is what is established after the intermediate members of the syllogism have been presented. They are related to each other like a bill and a receipt; even though both show the same amount, their status in financial actions is very different. One indicates an obligation to be fulfilled, the other records the fact that an obligation has been fulfilled.

One good way of understanding this five-fold structure is by regarding it not primarily as the Indian equivalent of the Aristotelian syllogism but as a representation of stages in a debate. Each member can then be understood as a reply to an implied opponent.[327] Spelling out the above sample syllogism in this way would look something like this:

326. For an excellent discussion of the Indian syllogism and various frameworks of interpreting it, see Ganeri 2002, 1–25.

327. Ganeri 2001, 10.

Opponent: *What is your thesis?*
1. Proponent: **That there is fire on the hill.**

Opponent: *Why?*
2. Proponent: **Because there is smoke on the hill.**

Opponent: *Why is this relevant?*
3. Proponent: **Where there is smoke, there is fire, as in the oven.**

Opponent: *How does this universal statement relate to the present case?*
4. Proponent: **One of the places with smoke is the hill.**

Opponent: *What does this imply?*
5. Proponent: **That there is fire on the hill.**

Let us now return to the text and to Nāgārjuna's refutation of the first member of the five-fold inference.

> *If the parts are establishers of a non-established object, is it not that those also are something established that establishes, or something non-established?*

The "parts" that are the primary object of discussion here are of course the parts of the syllogism (of which the thesis is one), which together establish something not yet established, in this case the cognition of the state of affairs in which the hill is qualified by contact with fire. We might then want to ask what established the establishers, and in reply two possibilities present themselves:

1. There is something else that establishes them, or
2. They are unestablished.

> *If something established is an establisher, another establisher exists for the establisher by which those also are establishers.*

It is necessary to unpack this sentence. Suppose some part of a syllogism, such as the thesis T, which is one establisher of the syllogism, was established itself. In this case, there would be another establisher T' "by which those parts of the syllogism like T are establishers." And for this T' there would be another establisher T'' in turn establishing *it*.

> *Because for those another also exists, there will be the contradictory consequence of an infinite regress.*

And of course this sequence continues without bound. Once we have postulated a second-order establisher, there is nothing stopping us from postulating third-, fourth-, and other higher-order establishers.

> *Well then, if for those also another one does not exist, regarding the assertion that the whole is established by all these parts, "the difference and the impairment of the thesis" should be replied.*

Nāgārjuna now examines the second possibility, namely that "for those establishers like the thesis, another establisher does not exist." There are two ways in which this could happen. Either

1. The establishers are not established at all, or
2. The establishers are not established by *another* establisher, that is, they are self-established.

Option 1 would not present a problem in the general mereological case. In an ontological system that allows for atoms (such as Nyāya), parts establishing a whole can themselves be mereologically unestablished, simply because there are no more basic parts to establish them. But we could only transfer this reasoning to compounds that are proofs if all the premises are axioms. In these cases, it is feasible to regard the premises as implicationally unestablished, since (if the axioms are independent from each other) there are no other axioms that imply them. But as not all proofs are of this nature, the point cannot be generalized.[328] In the case of the inferences considered by the Naiyāyika, it does make sense to ask how the thesis

328. This difficulty differs from the one mentioned by Tola and Dragonetti (1995, 129): "And as something non-established, the *pratijñā* would not have the capacity to establish the *avayavin*, the *nyāya*, what destroys the statement of the opponent: 'the whole is established through all the parts.'" It is not the case that a non-established thesis would somehow be impotent to play its part in a syllogism. The point is rather that playing such a part would either be pointless or lead to an infinite regress.

(that the hill has fire), the reason (that it has smoke), and so on, are each individually established. It would indeed be worrying if neither inference nor one of the other epistemic instruments were able to establish them.

This leaves us with option 2, i.e., the idea that the parts of an inference are self-established. Yet it is clearly problematic to say that the part of an inference that is the *conclusion* is self-established. If this were the case, what is the point of the inference? A similar difficulty arises with the first member of the Nyāya inference, the thesis, which is even defined by the Naiyāyika as something to be established,[329] and so can hardly be anything that is already self-established. Moreover, if it were, what need would there be to prove it by a syllogism? So assuming that all parts of an inference are self-established leads straight to a contradiction, since it implies that something to be established is already established.

Nāgārjuna points out that, as neither of these two options is satisfactory, the opponent has to reply by either stating the difference, i.e., by pointing out in which way the non-established thesis is different from the established remaining members of the syllogism, or by giving up his thesis that the whole is established by all the parts. The opponent could escape the charge of vicious circularity by claiming that only the thesis is unestablished, while the remaining members are established and can thereby establish it. This, however, is only a temporary solution, for the question of how the established members of the syllogism are established (by yet more propositions or by themselves) will immediately arise. Denying that there is a difference by claiming that the Naiyāyika thesis *is* like the other members of the syllogism established (and thus self-established, to rule out the infinite regress) means that the thesis has contradictory properties: it is defined as something to be established and yet is already self-established. As there are no things with contradictory properties, the thesis therefore cannot exist. This is not a consequence the Naiyāyika would be willing to endorse. It would also imply that he has to give up his thesis that the whole is established by all the parts. In order to advance any arguments at all, the Naiyāyika has to assume that the whole that is the syllogism exists. Yet it manifestly cannot be established by *all* its parts, since we were just forced to conclude that one of its parts, the thesis, does not exist.

329. NS 1.1.33: *sādhyanirdeśaḥ pratijñā.*

It is worthwhile to note to which extent Nāgārjuna's discussion in this verse is specifically concerned with the thesis. The thesis is, according to the Nyāya discussion, something to be established. As such, it is unestablished and needs other members of the syllogism to establish it. Nāgārjuna points out that all ways of trying to make sense of these establishers, the existence of which the thesis necessitates, end up in failure. If they are themselves unestablished, how can they establish something else? If they have infinitely many establishers behind them, we face the charge of an infinite regress. It is also no help to assume that they are self-established, because in many cases they manifestly are not. A statement such as "wherever there is smoke, there is fire" does not bring its own truth with it but is dependent on the world for its truth-value. Therefore, even though Nāgārjuna's argument here is not framed as an explicit criticism of the thesis, the first member of the syllogism, such an examination of the difficulties flowing from the nature of the thesis and its place in the syllogism is very much the driving force behind the argument in this passage.

Moreover,

VP 41 **Because the reason is different from the thesis or not different from it, it is no reason.**

Are the thesis and reason distinct or not? If they are distinct, what will be obtained? The thesis is: "The cloth is indeed white." Moreover, if you ask what the reason is: "Because of blackness," it is not asserted, because whiteness is not established by the proof "black."[330]

"Well then, if reason and thesis are not different, what is accomplished?" "The thesis is 'The cloth is white,' what is the reason?" Because of whiteness. That very thing is not the proof of that. This is similar to what is to be established.

330. The P and C editions of the VP lack this part of the autocommentary and instead simply state "Because if the thesis is a proof, it is not established by the whole" (*dam bca' ba ni sgrub byed na gang pos mi 'grub pa'i phyir ro*).

VP 41 Because the reason is different from the thesis or not different from it, it is no reason.

Nāgārjuna now moves to the discussion of the second of the five parts of the syllogism, the reason (*hetu, gtan tshigs*).

Are the thesis and reason distinct or not?

The structure of Nāgārjuna's criticism of the reason will be familiar to readers from his analysis of causation. One aspect of this analysis is the inquiry whether the cause is identical to the effect or distinct from it.[331] As the reason is considered to be what "brings about" or "establishes" the thesis,[332] it is natural to consider a similar scheme of analysis in this case.

If they are distinct, what will be obtained? The thesis: "The cloth is indeed white." Moreover, if you ask what the reason is: "Because of blackness." It is not asserted, because whiteness is not established by the proof "black."

Nāgārjuna first considers the distinctness of reason and thesis, and considers the example where the thesis to be established is the assertion "The cloth is white." A "distinct" statement, such as "Because it is black" will here not be able to act as a reason, because it contradicts the thesis to be established.

"Well then, if reason and thesis are not different, what is accomplished?" "The thesis is, 'The cloth is white,' what is the reason?" Because of whiteness. That very thing is not the proof of that. This is similar to what is to be established.

What, then, about the second alternative, that reason and thesis are not distinct? An example of this would be to support the thesis that the cloth is white by the reason "Because it is white." This obviously will not do,

331. MMK 20:19.

332. NS 1.1.34 defines the reason as "what establishes what is to be established by the similarity with the example" (*udāharaṇasādharmyāt sādhyasādhanaṁ hetuḥ*).

since if we are in any doubt about the truth of the thesis, and want to construct a syllogism to establish it, we will equally be in doubt about the reason here given to support it. Nāgārjuna rightly points out that we have here another case of the fallacy of "similarity with what is to be established" (*sādhyasama*).[333]

It is likely that Nāgārjuna's argument here appears to us as sophistical. It is certainly true that all the statements that can be offered as reasons for some thesis can be divided into two: those that say the same as the thesis, and those that say something different. The first can obviously offer no support. The latter can be divided into statements that directly conflict with the thesis (in the case of the example "The cloth is white," these would be statements like "Because it is black," "Because it does not exist," "Because no part of it is white," and so on) and those that do not ("Because it is Tuesday," "Because it has been bleached," "Because it is the only one left in a box of fabric samples we know to contain some white samples, but all other samples taken out were colored"). Now some of the second set of possible reasons will either make it more likely that the thesis obtains, or will even deductively entail the thesis. Nāgārjuna's argument appears to ignore these distinct potential reasons that are not in direct conflict with the thesis.

Despite this appearance, however, there is a substantial point behind Nāgārjuna's argument. He rightly points out that because the conclusion "The cloth is white" and the premise "The cloth is white" are identical, this is indeed a case of a "similarity with what is to be established." Yet it is also more generally the case that in *any* valid argument there is such a similarity between premises and conclusion, since the conclusion tells us nothing that was not already in the premises. In terms of information content, there will either be the same amount of information in the conclusion and in the premises put together, or there will be less information in the conclusion.[334] And this insight does not sit well with the Nyāya idea that the premise is something to be established (*sādhya*) and the reason the means of establishing (*sādhyasādhana*), at least if this distinction is supposed to be of substantial and not just of practical or transactional importance. The potter, wheel, clay, and so on, are all means of establishing

333. See VP 38 for an earlier example of this.

334. E.g., if we infer "It is raining or snowing" from the premise "It is raining."

a pot, yet they are no pot, neither individually nor collectively. But there is an important sense in which we have the same amount of information in front of us when we consider a set of premises and the conclusion they entail.[335] To this extent, we are justified in asking why we regard the premises as establishing and the conclusion as established, when, in the case of deductive inferences, both contain the same amount of information or, in the case of probabilistic inferences, the premises have the same or a lower probability than the conclusion.[336] This appears to suggest that the distinction between thesis / conclusion and reason / premises is merely a distinction *for us*, a distinction we draw between something to be established, which we do not yet accept, and something we accept, something we take as a starting point in the process of establishing it, even though the premises are, in fact, "similar to what is to be established," since there is the same informational content in both. Nāgārjuna is thus arguing against a view according to which anything could be a reason, a "means of establishing" by its very nature, rather than something that plays a certain role in our inferential practices but is not intrinsically different from the thesis to be established.

⁂ Moreover,

VP 42 **Because there is in turn no reason for the reason.**

No thing is "established by a reason." For a reason, another reason is obtained in turn, and for that again another. There is an infinite regress. Well then, if it is not asserted for a reason that another reason exists in turn, then there is no reason. Or, as in the case of the reason, everything would also be established without a reason. ⁂ ⁂

335. This is not the same as saying that knowing the premises is knowing the conclusion. Whether our knowledge is closed under logical implication is a moot point, and in the case of mathematical theories this is quite implausible. Knowing all of Euclid's axioms does not entail that I know all the truths of geometry.

336. Adams 1988, 21.

After criticizing the Nyāya conception of a reason (*hetu*) by discussing its identity or difference relative to the thesis (*pratijñā*) Nāgārjuna now investigates reasons in relation to *their* reasons.[337]

VP 42 Because there is in turn no reason for the reason.

No thing is "established by a reason." For a reason, another reason is obtained in turn, and for that again another. There is an infinite regress.

Nāgārjuna presents his opponent with a dilemma.[338] The first horn is constituted by the assumption that there has to be a reason for the reason itself, in which case there is no justification for not assuming a third reason for this second reason, and then we will have to assume a backward infinite sequence of reasons. This regress is vicious because the justification of each member depends on the one directly preceding it, so that ultimately nothing is justified.

This argument is mentioned in NS 5.1.9 as one of the irrelevant rejoinders (*jāti*) called *prasaṅgasama*.[339] It is characterized as the desire for a proof of what already has been proven.[340] Vātsyāyana discusses this primarily as a demand for a proof of the example (*dṛṣṭānta*), and points out in his commentary on NS 5.1.10 that one would no more require a proof for an example than a second light in order to illuminate a light one already has; the light (and the example) illuminates because it is the thing it is. It is unlikely that Nāgārjuna would be impressed by this reply, not only because of his detailed criticism of the analogy of the self-illuminating light in the VP and VV but also because not every reason can be considered as self-evident and therefore not in need of justification itself.[341]

337. For a discussion of these two reasoning patterns in Nāgārjuna's MMK, see Siderits and Katsura 2009, 132–33.

338. It is interesting to compare Nāgārjuna's argument here with that in VV 17–18 (Westerhoff 2010, 120–21).

339. See Oberhammer 1991, vol. 3, 83–85.

340. *sādhanasyāpi sādhanam vaktavyam iti prasaṅgena pratyavasthānaṁ prasaṅgasamaḥ* (Śāstrī 1998, 426:3).

341. We might be more successful in arguing that this is true for an example. If it required a reason itself, it would hardly be a good example (see Jha 1984, vol. 4, 1689); moreover, an example is usually known by perception, and we do not usually ask for our perceptions to

> *Well then, if it is not asserted for a reason that another reason exists in turn, then there is no reason. Or, as in the case of the reason, everything would also be established without a reason.*

But, and this is the second horn, if there is no reason for the reason, then there is nothing establishing or justifying it. So what gives us a reason to appeal to it in order to establish the thesis? And, if there is no need for such a justificatory reason in the case of the reason, why is there such a need in the case of the thesis? Could we, in this case, not just assume that *everything* is established without a reason?

What Nāgārjuna wants to establish in this passage is that there is nothing that is a reason by its own intrinsic nature (*svabhāva*). It is true that some statements, the axioms of a given theory, do not require reasons to prove them in turn. But this is not due to their self-evidence, or due to any other reason derived from their intrinsic nature. To regard something as an axiom is simply to regard it as established without proof, and then to use it to derive all other statements in the theory. This is not a fact about the statement itself, but a fact about our attitude toward it in requiring or not requiring justification.

The opponent who wants to avoid the infinite regress by understanding the reasons as not in need of justification in turn, and thus as axioms, has two options. He can either explain the special characteristics that distinguish the axioms from the statements requiring reasons, or he can assert that every statement could potentially be an axiom. The first is exceedingly hard to do, and our current understanding of axioms is certainly free from any demands of self-evidence, obvious truth, or cognitive transparency of them. But if we embrace the latter, and claim that "for all there would be establishment without a reason," we have given up seeing proofs as foundational enterprises. Rather than grounding our knowledge in something indubitable, all we in fact do is show interconnections between the various statements we accept. Yet the existence of such logical connections does not show that any group of them could by nature bear the weight of establishing or justifying all the other ones. "Being a reason" is not a property that makes its bearer cognitively or ontologically fundamental.

---

be backed up by reasons (see Oberhammer 1991, vol. 3, 85). But these considerations would not generalize to avoid problems if one were to require reasons for *probanda* in general.

Moreover,

VP 43 **Because thesis and reason do not exist, application (*nye bar sbyor ba, upanaya*) and conclusion (*mjug bsdu ba, nigamana*) do not exist.**

Similarly, precisely because thesis, reason, and example do not exist, application and conclusion do not exist either.

After discussing the thesis in VP 40, the reason in VP 41–43 and the example in VP 25–31, in this verse Nāgārjuna refutes the remaining two members of the five-fold syllogism, the application, which asserts the presence of the mark (*liṅga*) in the subject of inference (*pakṣa*), as well as the conclusion. He points out that the nonexistence of the first three members would entail the nonexistence of the final two. The reason for this is clear, since the Nyāya definition of the application refers to the example,[342] and that of the conclusion to the reason.[343] If the entities referred to in the definition of some term are themselves problematic the success of the definition is compromised. If someone should define an office as the "Court Hairdresser to the present King of Nepal" we can infer from the fact that the present king of Nepal does not exist that there is no such office. In the same way, if the categories of example and reason are shown to be empty, we can infer that any categories that definitionally depend on them are equally empty.

Moreover,

VP 44 **There is no reason for the remainder.**

342. NS 1.1.38: "Application is the characterizing of what is to be established as similar or not similar with reference to the example" (*udāharaṇāpekṣas tathetyupasaṁhāro na tatheti vā sādhyasyopanayā*).

343. NS 1.1.39: "The conclusion is the restatement of the thesis through the assertion of the reason" (*hetvapadeśāt pratijñāyāḥ punarvacanaṁ nigamanam*).

In this case, if the thesis is established by the reason, there is the contradictory consequence that there is no reason for the establishers like the example, and so forth.

Having examined the five members of the syllogism individually, Nāgārjuna now looks at the interrelations between the different members. The reason's main purpose is to establish the thesis. It provides the answer to the question *why* the thesis obtains. But the reason does not establish the example. "Because it has smoke" does not support the claim that whatever has smoke has fire, as in an oven. Yet the example plays a key role in establishing the thesis, which is established via the similarity of attributes with the example.[344] However, as Nāgārjuna points out, there is no reason establishing this establisher. The opponent is thus left with a set of uncomfortable choices familiar from VP 42. Either the example and application are unable to prove the thesis (because they are unestablished themselves) or they are able to prove it, because they are in some way self-established or because there are reasons establishing it that are, however, not part of the syllogism. The first option would render the Nyāya syllogism inefficacious as a mode of inference, and the latter leads to the problem that we either do not know why the thesis in turn cannot, like the reason, simply be self-established (or, to put matters slightly differently, why the necessity of having to provide reasons stops after the example, but not after the thesis), or we end up with an infinite regress of reasons, because we then have to ask whether the reasons of the example, and so on, *themselves* have reasons. We should note, however, that the point Nāgārjuna makes in this verse differs from the one made in VP 42. There the focus was on whether the reason itself was to be considered as being endowed with a reason; here the question is whether members of the syllogism other than the thesis (in particular the example and application) would need to be provided with reasons in turn.

344. NS 1.1.34: *udāharaṇa-sādharmyāt.*

⁜ Moreover,

VP 45 **You may ask "What is achieved?" if the established is brought about by the reason. The example, and so on, are meaningless.**

If you think "It is established only by the reason," then the example, and so forth, are meaningless, because the aim is established only by the reason. ⁜ ⁜

The opponent now cannot respond to the difficulty raised in VP 44 by claiming that the example and application do not need a reason, because they are inferentially superfluous. This would amount to saying that all the actual work in the syllogism, transforming the thesis to be established into an established conclusion, is achieved by the reason. If "the established," i.e., the conclusion, were established solely by the reason, the remaining members of the five-fold inference would be meaningless and superfluous, as they are unnecessary for achieving the inference's aim, the establishment of the conclusion. This position is not available to the Naiyāyika since NS 1.1.32 clearly states that the syllogism consists of five members, not just of three.[345]

⁜ Moreover,

VP 46 **Or the reason is in fact meaningless.**

Well then, if you assert that the example establishes, at that time the reason will become meaningless. ⁜ ⁜

This verse continues with the opponent's idea, first mentioned in the preceding verse, that a single member of the five-fold syllogism may be responsible for all the inferential work. While in VP 45 the sole establisher was suggested to be the reason, it is now supposed to be the example, given

345. *pratijñāhetūdāharaṇopanayanigamanāny avayavāḥ.*

the central inferential role the Nyāya theory ascribes to it.[346] Yet the problem remains the same: if any one member of the syllogism has exclusive deductive powers, all the other members will become superfluous. If the example alone can establish the thesis, the reason will be superfluous, and if the reason alone can do it, the example is dispensable. None of these views is compatible with the Nyāya understanding of the five-fold inference, which regards all five members as contributing to a syllogism.

Alternatively, there might be the objection:

If you say that "there are reason and example for establishing the self"—it should be answered:

VP 47 **The self is not established.**

It is thought that it is established by the reason. It is like your stating: The thesis is "The self is permanent"; the reason is "Because it is incorporeal"; the example is "Like space." Being established by the reason, it is not permanent, because of impermanence. Because it is not by itself, there is no permanent substance. The reason and the example are also like that.

Objection: If you say that "there are reason and example for establishing the self"—it should be answered:

VP 47 The self is not established.[347]

The objection raised here is another attempt by the opponent to establish two key members of the five-fold syllogism, reason and example. This time he focuses on a particular example of an inference deemed sound by the Naiyāyikas, namely the demonstration of the existence of a permanent

346. NS 1.1.34: *udāharaṇa-sādharmyāt sādhya-sādhanaṁ hetuḥ.*

347. VS reads here, "There is no self, because it is not established" (*bdag med de | ma grub pa'i phyir ro*).

self.[348] The idea is that if this proof is accepted, all the constituents of the proof have to be accepted as well, so there is at least one instance of reason and example.

Variants of this argument pattern can also be found in the opponent's remarks in others of Nāgārjuna's works. In VV 19, the opponent points out that if Nāgārjuna accepts the soundness of his own arguments he has to believe in the existence of the reason.[349]

In the present case, of course, the opponent uses as an example an inference that Nāgārjuna (and other Buddhist philosophers) will not accept.

> *It is thought that it is established by the reason. It is like you saying: The thesis is "The self is permanent," the reason is "Because it is incorporeal," the example is "Like space."*

Uddyotakara's *Vārttika* on NS 3.1.20[350] spells out the argument in a bit more detail:

> Now the inference that the self is subject to arising and cessation cannot be right, as it is considered a substance, always incorporeal and uncaused, like space, etc.[351]

The Naiyāyika argues that the immateriality of the self places it outside of the range of causality, as causes and effects only operate on spatio-temporal phenomena. But to have a beginning or an end, a thing must have a *cause* that brings about that beginning or end. As the self, though existent, cannot have such a cause, it must be without beginning or end and therefore eternal.

348. See NS 3.1.1–30.

349. "If the reason exists, the 'absence of substance of things' fails to be accomplished" (*atha hetorastitvaṁ bhāvāsvabhāvyam iti anupapannam*). See Westerhoff 2010, 121–22.

350. This *sūtra* (*padmādiṣu prabodhasaṁmīlanavikāravat tadvikāraḥ*) is counted as 3.1.19 by Jha (1984, vol. 3, 1157) and as 3.1.18 by Ruben (1928, 61–62).

351. *athātmana utpattinirodhakāraṇānumānam tanna yuktaṁ dravyasya mataḥ sarvadā amūrtatvadakaraṇa ātmā ākāṣādivaditi* (Dvivedin 1986, 370:10–13). See Jha 1984, vol. 3, 1160.

Being established by the reason, it is not permanent,[352] *because of impermanence. Because it is not by itself, there is no permanent substance.*

Nāgārjuna's reply here is not simply that he rejects the Nyāya proof of the eternality of the self, and that there is thus no need to accept any of the constituents of that proof, such as the reason and the example. He makes the more sophisticated point that the subject of inference (*pakṣa*, the self) has the property to be established (*sādhya*) by depending on the possession of the mark (*liṅga*, incorporeality). This dependence is not just epistemological (we have to *know* that the self is incorporeal in order to know that it is eternal) but also existential (without the property of incorporeality, the self would not *be* eternal).[353] This entails that the self is not what it is all by itself (*rang nyid kyis med pa*), and this, Nāgārjuna argues, is sufficient for establishing its impermanence. His reasoning makes sense against the background of the fundamental Buddhist teaching of the three seals (*trilakṣaṇa*), stating that all phenomena are suffering, impermanent, and without self. These three characteristics are considered to be mutually co-implicative; anything that has one of them also has the two others. By showing that the eternality of the self depends on its establishment by the reason, Nāgārjuna argues that this eternality is not anything the self has intrinsically, by itself, by *svabhāva*. Thus its impermanence follows.

The reason and the example are also like that.

As the existence of the permanent self has been ruled out, it is no longer possible to base the existence of the thesis and the reason on an inference that is supposed to establish this nonexistent object. The opponent's reason for their existence therefore has to be rejected.

352. The P and N editions read here *bdag ni rtag pa ma yin te* ("The self is not permanent").

353. The Naiyāyikas accept the existence of corporeal and eternal things such as the *manas*, but this is permanent because it is also considered to be atomic, whereas all things with parts are considered as impermanent. The self's eternality is dependent on its incorporeality, as this means that it has no parts.

⌘ Moreover,

VP 48 **Because they are asserted one-by-one, they do not exist one with one another.**

At the time when the thesis is asserted, the reason, etc., do not exist and if the reason is asserted also the thesis, etc., do not exist. Therefore, the reason, etc., do not exist. ⌘ ⌘

We find here an argument resembling that in VP 39, based on the idea that because the elements of a semantic complex (in this case, an inference) are momentary, the complex, which depends on the existence of all the elements together, cannot exist.[354] The elements are produced sequentially, and because each ceases immediately after its production, when one element is produced, its predecessor has already ceased to exist. No two members of the sequence can coexist, and for this reason the entire inference, which depends on all members existing jointly, does not exist. But since each element only acquires its role via its place in the inference ("because of smoke" is not a reason in itself, but only in conjunction with

354. We also find this argument in the Tibetan version (the relevant passage is missing in the Chinese version) of the *Akṣaraśataka* attributed to Nāgārjuna in the Tibetan tradition and to Āryadeva in the Chinese tradition: "When there is the thesis the reason does not exist because it has not been produced. Similarly, when there is the reason the thesis does not exist, because it is destroyed. Therefore, when the thesis is nonexistent, of what is it a reason?" (*dam bca' ba'i dus su ni gtan tshigs yod pa ma yin te ma skyes pa'i phyir ro | de bzhin du gtan tshigs kyi dus su yang dam bca' ba yod pa ma yin te 'gag pa'i chos yod pa'i phyir ro | de'i phyir dam bca' ba'i dngos po med pa la 'di gang gi gtan tshigs su gyur*; P 5235 160a). See Gokhale 1930, 20n31; and Pind 2001, 166. See also the related discussion in Shāntarakṣhita's *Tattvasaṁgraha* 872–77 (Śāstrī 2006, 240–42; Jha 1986, 508–13). Compare Jha's interpretation of Vātsyāyana's criticism of the *nāstika* in commenting on NS 1.1.1 (Śāstrī 1998, 8:4–5: *nāstikaś ca dṛṣṭāntam abhyupagacchann āstikatvaṁ jahāti anabhyupagacchan kiṁsādhanaḥ param upālabheteti*): "There is yet another reason why importance has been attached to Example; it is through this that the position of the atheistic Bauḍḍha [sic] becomes doubly untenable. If the Atheist admits a corroborative example, he renounces his atheistic (Nihilistic) position (as by Nihilism, all things have merely momentary existence; and hence it is not possible for the Example, which must be in the form of something that existed in the past, to be present at the time that it is put forward); if, on the other hand, he does not admit an example, on the basis of what could he attach the position of his opponent?" (Jha 1984, vol. 1, 46–47)

a specific thesis, a specific example, and so forth) the nonexistence of the whole, the inference also entails the nonexistence of its constituents. This is why Nāgārjuna can conclude that "the reason, etc., do not exist."

Consider as an example trying to build an arch out of blocks of ice produced in a freezer. This requires that we put all the blocks together in a particular structure. Some blocks are not yet frozen and therefore not ready to use; others have already melted away because we have taken them out so early. The only block we can really work with is the one we have taken out of the freezer *right now*, but this on its own is unable to constitute an arch.

Alternatively, imagine that we write a proof on a slab of stone with a brush dipped in water. By the time we reach the middle of the proof, the inscription of the first premises will have evaporated already, so that we are never able to get the whole proof down on the slab at any one time.

Of course the Buddhist has to explain that we are still somehow able to make and understand inferences. To deny this would not be in accord with conventional reality. One way of solving this problem could go something like this: At each moment, we assume, only one of the five members of a syllogism can exist. Yet in the present moment, when, e.g., member 3, the pervasion, is perceived by the mind, there can be the memory of member 2 being perceived just before that, and of a memory of a memory of member 1.

The structure of this would look as follows:

t1: 1
t2: 2, mem(1)
t3: 3, mem(2), mem(mem(1))
t4: 4, mem(3), mem(mem(2)), mem(mem(mem(1)))
t5: 5, mem(4), mem(mem(3)), mem(mem(mem(2))), mem(mem(mem(mem(1))))

Even though the utterance of the thesis does not exist at time t2 anymore, there is still a substitute, the memory of the thesis coexisting with the reason at time t2. In this way, substitutes for all the members of the inference can coexist at one point in time, and the inference can be understood, even though the whole that is the inference never exists at any point in time.

It is of course essential for this understanding that, e.g., mem(1) is not identical with 1, since otherwise t5 would just be the coexistence of the five members of the syllogism that Nāgārjuna rejects. This identity could only be supposed if we considered mem(1) and 1 as being objects of the same (abstract) type. Yet, as we have seen numerous times before, the discussion of syllables, words, parts of an inference, and so on, is conducted in terms of concrete, spatio-temporal tokens of such syllables, etc., not in terms of types.

It is interesting to note, however, that a very similar argument would be available to Nāgārjuna even if the parts of an inference and similar objects were understood as types, i.e., as abstract objects. This is because the doctrine of momentariness does not just apply to perceived objects but also to the perceiving subject. As Nāgārjuna has just pointed out in VP 47, there is no permanent self. But if the self is momentary too, there is no single self that could hold all the five members of an inference simultaneously in front of its mind's eye, for as soon as the reason is understood, the mind-moment that understood the thesis has already ceased to exist. And if there is nothing at the ultimate level that exists throughout the inferential steps, there is also nothing at the ultimate level that could draw the required inference. As long as an inference is considered as something that establishes a conclusion in the mind of a particular person, we can then conclude that no inference exists at the ultimate level.

⌘ Here it is objected: "It is your thesis that 'all parts do not exist.' Therefore, because the thesis is asserted, the remainder is also established for you." It should be replied:

VP 49 **The syllables are also like this.**

That is also seen concerning the syllables that are the constituents of the non-established parts. Just because the syllables *pra*, *ti*, *jñā* do not coexist, the thesis does in fact not exist. Similarly, also regarding the syllable *pra*, because *pra*, etc., are uttered successively, the syllable *pra* does not exist. When arising from conditions such as wind and space, the effort of tongue, teeth, palate, lips, and so on, they do not exist with one another. ⌘ ⌘

Here it is objected: "It is your thesis that 'all parts do not exist.' Therefore, because the thesis is asserted, the remainder is also established for you."

The opponent points out that Nāgārjuna aims to establish a philosophical position, that of the nonexistence of parts, both generally and specifically in relation to the parts of the five-fold inference. As such, he is aiming at establishing a *thesis*, and a thesis can only be established by working through an inference that establishes the thesis as a conclusion. But once Nāgārjuna has accepted the inference, he has of course also accepted all the members of the inference, which makes his refutation of the parts of an inference inconsistent.

In fact, the opponent might point out, Nāgārjuna is facing a dilemma.[355] He claims that since the Mādhyamika asserts that everything is empty, there must be at least one nonempty thing, namely that assertion. If there is not, the assertion is empty too, and for that reason it cannot establish the Madhyamaka position. Since the only way to back up a thesis is by supplying the other four members of the syllogism, either Nāgārjuna contradicts himself, if he regards this thesis as established, because there must be one instance of a syllogism of which all the parts exist, or, if his thesis is not established, he cannot say what he wants to say, at least not in a context in which truth-bearing assertions and inferential support play any role.

It should be replied:

VP 49 The syllables are also like this.

That is also seen concerning the syllables that are the constituents of the non-established parts. Just because the syllables pra, ti, jñā do not coexist, the thesis does in fact not exist.

Nāgārjuna now points out that the considerations that applied to the constituents of the syllogism (the "non-established parts") also apply to their subsentential components. In the same way in which all the constituents of an inference do not exist at one time, all the constituent syllables

355. Compare the dilemma Nāgārjuna's opponent raises at the beginning of the VV (Westerhoff 2010, 43–54).

of any of these constituents do not exist simultaneously either, since when, for example, the second syllable of a word such as *pratijñā* is uttered, its first syllable has disappeared and its third syllable does not yet exist.

Similarly, also regarding the syllable pra, because pra, etc., are uttered successively, the syllable pra does not exist.

The same then applies to the constituents of a single syllable. That "*pra*, etc., are uttered successively" means that they, in turn, have components, not all of which can exist at a single time. There is good evidence that this passage is to be understood in this way. Consider the same argument being presented in the Tibetan version of the *Akṣaraśataka*, immediately following the passage cited in the commentary on the previous verse:[356]

> It is similar for the thesis as it is something that does not exist at a single time. When the syllable *pra* exists, the syllables *ti* and *jñā* do not exist. Similarly the letters *p*, *ra*, *a*, etc., do not arise simultaneously at one time either.[357]

When arising from conditions such as wind and space, the effort of tongue, teeth, palate, lips, and so on, they do not exist with one another.

Nāgārjuna here gives a list of the production-places of speech as understood in traditional Indian phonetics.[358] His point is that since the individual syllables are produced by successive and distinct sets of actions of the various production-places, they cannot all exist at the same time, but

356. This passage is also included in the Chinese version. See Gokhale 1930, 9.

357. *de bzhin du dam bca' ba la cig car med pa'i chos can gyi phyir te | gang gi tshe yi ge pra yod pa de'i tshe yi ge ti dang yi ge jñā yod pa ma yin no | de bzhin du dus gcig tu pa yig dang ra yig dang yi ge a la sogs pa rnams kyang cig car 'byung ba ma yin no* (P 5235 160a–b).

358. On these, see Allen 1953. Additional references are in Tola and Dragonetti 1995a, 195n2. Tucci (1981, 23–24) mentions a parallel passage in a work attributed to Vasubandhu. Compare also the reference in VV 1 to "the efforts made in the breast, throat, lips, tongue, root of the teeth, palate, nose, head" (*uraḥkaṇṭhoṣṭhajiḥvādaṁtamūlatālunāsikāmūrdhaprabhṛtisu* [Yonezawa 2008, 218:4]; *rkyen brang dang | lkog ma dang | mchu dang | lce rtse dang | so'i brun dang | rkan dang | sna dang | spyi bo la sogs pa dang | 'bad pa rnams la yang med* [Yonezawa 2008, 219:4–6; Westerhoff 2010, 45–46]).

only one after the other. This of course implies that the entire syllable, word, or sentence can never be present at any one time.

How is all of this a reply to the opponent who argues that because Nāgārjuna accepts a thesis, he also has to accept the existence of all the other members of the syllogism?

Tola and Dragonetti[359] suggest that Nāgārjuna replies to the charge of inconsistency claiming that he does, after all, hold a thesis (*pratijñā*) by pointing out that there is no *pratijñā* since its syllables do not coexist. How could he therefore hold a thesis? We should note in addition, however, that this reply does not imply Nāgārjuna getting caught on the other horn of the dilemma, that of the impossibility of making any substantial reply in a debate.[360] For Nāgārjuna will accept, his arguments in this verse notwithstanding, that we manage to communicate using syllables, and words and sentences built from these. The doctrine of momentariness does not refute this truth about conventional reality, but it stresses the contribution conceptual superimposition makes in order to create this reality. In order to understand the word *pratijñā* on hearing the syllable *ti*, we must contribute the syllable *pra* from memory and the syllable *jñā* by anticipation. In the same way, even though considerations of momentariness apply to all semantics complexes, including inferences, we are able to communicate inferences from one person to another, even though no more than one part of an inference is ever present at one time. The opponent is thus mistaken to assume that Nāgārjuna could not communicate a thesis, word, or syllable, even at the level of transactional reality, and would therefore be condemned to either inconsistency or silence.

Nāgārjuna's rejection of the sixth Nyāya category of "parts," *avayava*, of a syllogism in verses 33–49, uses a surprising variety of conceptual techniques familiar from Madhyamaka arguments (mereological considerations, the notions of identity and difference, existence in the three times).[361] The overall aim of these arguments should be understood in the same way as similar arguments applied to more familiar topics like material objects or persons, i.e., not as arguing that these objects do not exist at all, but that

359. Tola and Dragonetti 1995a, 132–33.

360. I disagree with Pind (2001, 166) who claims that Nāgārjuna's argument in this verse serves only "sophistical purposes."

361. Siderits and Katsura 2013, 8.

they are empty, devoid of *svabhāva*, and do not exist intrinsically. In the same way, Nāgārjuna's critique of the members of the syllogism is not supposed to show that syllogisms do not exist at all but that any substantialist understanding of them inevitably leads to problems. If Mādhyamikas are going to use syllogisms at all, they have to employ a suitably desubstantialized version that acknowledges their dependently arisen nature.

Objection: "Because if one examines it, there is a conjecture immediately afterward, for that reason the term 'hypothetical reasoning' exists.[362] Because that exists, others are established as well." If one says this, it is to be replied:

VP 50 **Hypothetical reasoning is also like doubt.**

Why is that? Is a known object analyzed, or is an unknown object analyzed? In regard to that, if it is a known object, what is analyzed? Or otherwise, if it is an unknown object, what is analyzed in that case? There is no third alternative.

Objection: "Because if one examines it, there is a conjecture immediately afterward, for that reason, the term 'hypothetical reasoning' exists. Because that exists, others are established as well."

Hypothetical reasoning (*tarka*) is defined in the *Nyāyasūtra* as a kind of reasoning employed "when the nature of a thing is not known."[363] Vātsyāyana describes this as reasoning inquiring whether some object has property *P* or not.[364] Both possibilities are examined, and once we realize that one of the two possibilities leads to difficulties,[365] the other one can be

362. *gang gi phyir brtags na de ma thag tu rab tu rtog pa de'i phyir rtog ge zhes bya ba'i tshig gi don yod pa yin no.* I consider *rab tu rtog pa* here to be a translation of *pratarka* (Böhtlingk 1879–89, vol. 4, 136: Folgerung, Vermuthung).

363. NS 1.1.40: *avijñāta-tattve arthe.* See Kang 2010, 5–7.

364. See also Guha 2012, 49; and Phillips 2012, 30–32.

365. Such a difficulty can, for example, consist in the fact that the position in question entails a contradiction. This explains why *tarka* is sometimes characterized as a *reductio ad*

considered as true. He considers as an example the question of whether an epistemic subject has the property of being produced. The affirmative answer, he argues, leads to problems, and for that reason we should conclude that the epistemic subject is not produced.

This form of reasoning can therefore be understood as a metatheory,[366] something that is not an epistemic instrument itself,[367] but which sets up a framework to determine which of the two contradictory options is actually supported by an epistemic instrument. On the basis of this, we can see how the present verse connects with the previous verses 33–49 on the members of the syllogism by describing the argumentative context in which the syllogism would be applied, namely in a situation where we employ some epistemic instrument (such as inference) in order to determine which of two contradictory possibilities does in fact obtain.

The opponent points out that if we examine any subject-matter to find out whether it has or lacks a certain property, we will often make a conjecture (*pratarka*) that one of the two alternatives is correct, before investigating which of the two is in fact the right one. But this just means that we are engaging in hypothetical reasoning (*tarka*). So the opponent can argue that not only the presence of the term *pratarka* (*rab tu rtog pa*) entails that of the term *tarka* (*rtog pa*), which forms a proper part of it, but that also the activity of supporting a conjecture implies that we are engaged in hypothetical reasoning. Moreover, since the set of sixteen Nyāya categories is not just a list of isolated items but a network of mutually connected notions, the presence of a single one cannot really be made sense of without the presence of all the others. For this reason, the opponent argues, the entire set of the Nyāya categories emerges naturally when we analyze the process of investigation.

If one says this, it is to be replied:

VP 50 Hypothetical reasoning is also like doubt.

---

absurdum (see Davies 1981, 106). Yet consistency is not the only consideration at issue. As Phillips (2012, 31) points out, *tarka* consists of "drawing out of implications of opposed views and testing them against mutually accepted positions (*siddhānta*), according to, broadly speaking, criteria of coherence but also of simplicity."

366. Guha 2012, 65.

367. Phillips 2012, 31.

> *Why is that? Is a known object analyzed, or is an unknown object analyzed? In regard to that, if it is a known object, what is analyzed? Or otherwise, if it is an unknown object, what is analyzed in that case? There is no third alternative.*

Nāgārjuna replies by pointing out that the same difficulties he identified in the case of doubt in VP 21 apply in this case, as hypothetical reasoning presupposes doubt.[368] In the case of doubt, the question arises whether the doubt concerns a conceived object (*dmigs pa'i don*) or a nonconceived object (*ma dmigs pa'i don*); in this case, it concerns the matter of whether a known object (*shes pa'i don*) or an unknown object (*mi shes pa'i don*) is analyzed in the process of investigation. In the case of a known object, analysis is pointless, because the object is already epistemically present. In the case of an unknown object, on the other hand, there is nothing present to the mind that could be analyzed in the first place.

It is instructive to read Nāgārjuna's position here as relating to the Madhyamaka view of metaphysical analysis aiming at an ultimately true theory. As all such attempts are argued by the Mādhyamika to lead to a contradiction, all we are left with is the conventional, transactional view of the world.

Chandrakīrti points out in the MĀ that:

> because if one analyzes things, apart from their own specific nature, nothing that abides can be found, for that reason the world's conventional truth should not be analyzed.[369]

368. See the definition of the following category, determination (*nirṇaya*), which succeeds hypothetical reasoning in the dialectical context, according to NS 1.2.41: "Determination is the ascertainment of an object through thesis and antithesis after an initial doubt," (*vimṛśya pakṣapratipakṣābhyām arthāvadhāraṇaṁ nirṇayaḥ*). See also Chattopadhyaya and Gangopadhyaya 1967–76, vol. 1, 129–30.

369. MĀ 6.35: *arvāṅ na tattvātmakarūpato 'mī sthitiṁ labhante pravicāryamāṇāḥ | yataḥ padārthā na tato vicāraḥ kāryo hi lokavyavahārasatye* || (Li 2015, 8). The *Bhāṣya* comments: "Worldly people see that 'if this exists, this arises,' one should make assertions through points of access such as this, which depend on others" (*jig rten pas yongs su mthong ba 'di yod na 'di 'byung ngo zhes bya ba 'di tsham zhig gzhan la rag las pa'i 'jug pa'i sgo nas khas blang bar bya ste*; Poussin 1912, 120:15–17). For a discussion of Chandrakīrti's "no-analysis" view, see Tillemans 2011.

Since this conventional truth is wholly transparent to us and thereby a known object (*shes pa'i don*), there is no point in any further analysis. Moreover, for the Mādhyamika, *no* conventional truth will be able to withstand analysis, i.e., none will turn out to possess an ultimately true core. We might therefore as well give up on the ontological project of finding such a core and settle for the unanalyzed conventional truth. There is also no point in analyzing an unknown object, and so Nāgārjuna's point here can be understood as rejecting any kind of analysis attempting to arrive at a truth at the ultimate level. He rejects an analysis that sets out to replace the truth of conventional reality with an ontological theory that proclaims to provide a more reliable understanding of what the world is really like *svabhāvatas*. He does not reject *tarka* as a category *tout court*; what is rejected is an understanding of *tarka* that is believed to supply us with insights into ultimate truths. *Tarka* can still be applied to investigate beliefs we hold at the level of the merely transactional and, in some cases, can provide a justification for changing them.[370] Once more, it is not the category as such but a specific interpretation of it that is rejected by Nāgārjuna's arguments.

Objection:

"Determination is the understanding of an object through investigation, justified ground is the reason for recognition, and hypothetical reasoning is the examination of the way things are for the sake of knowledge." If you say that, it has to be replied:

VP 51 **Since substance, existence, unity, etc., are neither distinct, non-distinct, nor both, there is no determination.**

Are existence, unity, roundness, redness, etc., identical or different with respect to a pot? Regarding this, if you say that they are identical, then where there is a single entity, any one among existence, etc., there is the capacity, like the Mighty, the Powerful, the Destroyer of Cities.

On the other hand, if they are different, this implies that the pot does not exist and is not unitary either. Nor is it round or red. You cannot say, "It is

370. Compare Tillemans 2011, 160n17.

an existent pot because it is endowed with existence." If something is endowed with something, that does not become that very thing. Therefore, because identity, difference, and both do not exist, there is no determination.

Objection:

"Determination (nirṇaya, gtan la phab pa) is the understanding of an object through investigation, justified ground (upapatti, 'thad pa) is the reason for recognition, and hypothetical reasoning (tarka, rtog ge) is the examination of the way things are for the sake of knowledge."

The opponent now considers the ninth Nyāya category, determination, in order to defend the eighth category, hypothetical reasoning, discussed in the previous verse. NS 1.1.41 states that "determination is the ascertainment of an object through thesis and antithesis after an initial doubt."[371] During the course of a debate, which is caused by a disagreement or doubt regarding a specific subject matter, the two contestants will present their reasons for the establishment of the thesis and the antithesis, respectively. The debate is concluded when the defense of one position is judged to be victorious, which then leads to the determination or resolution of the question that the initial doubt was concerned with.

The immediately following phrase (*ngo shes pa'i rgyu mtshan ni 'thad pa'o*) is understood very differently by Tola and Dragonetti. They translate it as "a cause of the defined ('determination') is admitted."[372] This leads them to explain Nāgārjuna's argument in the following way: Having defined determination, the opponent now points out that if we accept any such determination of a question through a debate, we must also accept "the cause of what is known," (or as they put it, the "cause of the defined," *ngo shes pa'i rgyu mtshan*), that is, whatever allowed us to arrive at this resolution in the first place.[373] Since there would have been no debate without an initial doubt, this doubt is one of the causes of the determination and

371. *vimṛśya pakṣapratipakṣābhyām arthāvadhāraṇaṁ nirṇayaḥ.*

372. Tola and Dragonetti 1995a, 81.

373. Tola and Dragonetti 1995a, 134.

therefore has to be accepted as well. But once we have accepted that, we also have to accept the reasoning that investigates both sides involved in such a doubt, and tries to determine the matter by finding out which is supported by better reasons. This reasoning is of course nothing else than hypothetical reasoning (*tarka*, *rtog ge*). The existence of hypothetical reasoning, it appears, has been thus defended.

In fact it seems to be more justified, however, to translate the phrase *ngo shes pa'i rgyu mtshan ni 'thad pa'o* in parallel with the other two phrases containing the emphasizing particle (*brnan pa'i sgra*) *ni*, that is as three consecutive definitions of determination, justified ground, and hypothetical reasoning.[374] In the case of the definitions of determination and hypothetical reasoning, the passages from the NS Nāgārjuna is referring to are evident; this is not the case with the definition of justified ground.[375] What the definition says is relatively clear, however: justified ground is what acts as the reason of the recognition of some object. The three definitions the opponent mentions form a reverse sequence. First, two contradictory possibilities are examined by hypothetical reasoning; a justified ground then presents us with a reason for recognizing one of the possibilities as the correct one, which then in turn leads to determination. And if we accept determination, the opponent points out, we also have to accept the various steps that lead to this determination; in particular, we have to accept hypothetical reasoning, contrary to what Nāgārjuna asserted in VP 50.

If you say that, it has to be replied:

VP 51 Since substance, existence, unity, etc., are neither distinct, non-distinct, nor both, there is no determination.

Nāgārjuna's argument appears to be a curious one, for he is addressing neither the categories of determination or of hypothetical reasoning directly, but raises instead an ontological point.

Are existence, unity, roundness, redness, etc., identical or different with respect to a pot?

374. Pind (2001, 162) renders the passage in this way.

375. See Pind (2001, 162–63) for some comments on this.

The point conforms to a familiar Madhyamaka form of argument concerning identity and difference,[376] in this case concentrating on the relation between an individual, a clay pot, on the one hand, and on its various properties, existence, individuality, round shape, red color, and so on.

It is interesting to note that the very same argument is discussed by Āryadeva in several places, in the *Catuḥśataka*,[377] the *Śataśāstra*,[378] and in the *Akṣaraśataka-nāma-vṛtti*.[379] The *Śataśāstra* and the *Akṣaraśataka-nāma-vṛtti* introduce the argument in the context of a debate with an opponent who defends the *ātman* by arguing that an *ātman* must exist since such things as pots can belong to it or can be known by it.

Nāgārjuna examines both alternatives of identity and difference in turn.

> *Regarding this, if you say that they are identical, then where there is a single entity, any one among existence, etc., there is the capacity, like the Mighty (Indra), the Powerful (Shakra), the Destroyer of Cities (Purandara).*

He argues that assuming the identity of an individual with any of its properties is problematic, since it entails that whenever the property is present anywhere, so is the individual. But this is absurd: just because a red color is present somewhere, this does not entail that there is also a clay pot. Matters are even more problematic if we consider very general attributes such as existence. If a pot exists, and if it is identical with existence, then whenever there is existence, "there is the capacity" of fulfilling a pot's function (such as holding water, and so on), and so everything would be a pot.[380] Similarly, if a pot is destroyed, because existence is destroyed along

376. See Siderits and Katsura 2009, 132–33.

377. CŚ 14:2–11 (D 3846, dbu ma, tsha 15a ff.).

378. Tucci 1981, 37–50.

379. This text is extant in Chinese (百字論, Taisho 1572) and Tibetan translations (*yi ge brgya pa shes bya ba'i 'grel pa*, D 3835, dbu ma, tsa 138b4–146b1) and ascribed to Āryadeva by the former and to Nāgārjuna by the latter. See Gokhale 1930, 9–10.

380. Āryadeva's *Śataśāstra* adds some more detail here (Tucci 1981, 37–38): "If so, all things such as a cloth and so on also must be a pot, because existence, unity and pot are one. In the same way, existence, unity, object, all must be pot. Now, the pot, the cloth, and all other things must necessarily be identical. And again because of the eternity of existence, unity and the pot must also be eternal. Moreover, if one says 'existence', then he would say [at the same time] 'unity', and 'pot'; then, since one is a number, existence and

with it, everything would be destroyed.[381] Moreover, if the individual and all its attributes were identical, they would not just characterize the individual, but would also characterize each other. Redness would be round and impermanence would be able to carry water. This is manifestly not the case, so we cannot assume the identity of an individual and its attributes.[382]

The example Nāgārjuna gives is a set of names all referring to the Vedic god Indra. Given that Indra, Shakra, and Purandara[383] are identical, whenever there is one, there is the other.[384] The identity of these three is unproblematic, unlike the identity of the pot and its properties.

> *On the other hand, if they are different, this implies that the pot does not exist and is not unitary either. Nor is it round or red.*

---

the pot must also be numbers. Moreover, if the pot is (the result) of five bodies, existence and unity also must have five bodies. If the 'pot' has shape and resistance, then, existence and unity also must have shape and resistance. Then if the pot is not eternal, existence and unity also must not be eternal." See also Āryadeva's *Catuḥśataka* 14:10: "If the characteristic of shape applied to all shapes without incongruity, why is one thing a pot and not the others?" (*gzugs rnams kun la gzugs nyid ni | mtshan nyid mi mthun ma yin na | gcig la bum pa yod 'gyur zhing | gzhan dag la min rgyu ci zhig* [D 3846, dbu ma, tsha 15b.]) Āryadeva's point is that if pot and shape were identical it would be hard to explain why other things, which also have shapes, are not pots.

381. *bum pa zhig na thams cad du 'jig par 'gyur te* (*Akṣaraśataka-nāma-vṛtti*, D dbu ma, tsa 141b). See Gokhale 1930, 20n33.

382. Āryadeva's *Catuḥśataka* 14:5ab: "When the shape is just whatever the substance is, why is then the shape not large?" (*gang tshe rdzas ci tsam gzugs na | de tshe gzugs chen ci ste min* [D 3846, dbu ma tsha 15b].)

383. This set represents a common example for a group of synonymous terms. The *Laṅkāvatārasūtra* (X:684) notes that "as in the world *hasta* is *kara* [both meaning 'hand'] so Indra is Shakra is Purandara" (*hastaḥ karo yathā loke indraḥ śakraḥ purandaraḥ* [Vaidya 1963, 152; Suzuki 1932, 276]). It is interesting to see that reference to *hasta* and *kara* can also be found in a parallel discussion in the Tibetan version of the *Akṣaraśataka-nāma-vṛtti*, D dbu ma, tsa 141b–142a. See Gokhale 1930, 20n33. See also *Laṅkāvatārasūtra* III: LXXVI (Vaidya 1963, 78; Suzuki 1932, 165–66; Red Pine 2012, 217–18; Tucci 1981, 40; Balcerowicz 2001, 105).

384. Another passage making the same point (though it uses another of Indra's names, Kaushika, instead of Purandara) can be found in the *Śataśāstra* (Tucci 1981, 37): "If existence, unity and pot are a unity, then, as Indra, Śakra and Kauśika are identical, and in the place where Indra is, there Śakra and Kauśika must also be, in the same way, in the place of existence there will then be unity and pot. In the place of unity there will be existence and pot. In the place of pot there will be existence and unity."

Now considering the second possibility, Nāgārjuna focuses on a notion of difference that entails mutual ontological independence: the pot does not depend on its properties, and the properties do not depend on the pot. Yet that means that there could be a pot separate from all its properties, separate from its color or shape, and also separate from unitariness and existence.[385] What such a pot would be like, and how it would differ from a similarly "independent" table, for example, is not at all clear. In addition, if the pot were separate from the property of existence, it would lack that property, and thereby fail to exist.[386]

> *You cannot say: "It is an existent pot because it is endowed with existence." If something is endowed with something, that does not become that very thing.*

The opponent now considers an alternative proposal combining the advantages of each of the previous ones. Unlike in the case of the first alternative, the pot and its properties are now not regarded as identical, and, differing from the second alternative, they are not entirely unconnected. Rather, the pot possesses or is endowed with its properties.[387] However, Nāgārjuna points out, that does not really solve the problem of

385. "As the sword and the sheath can be seen as existing separately, pot, existence and oneness ought to be seen separately." Chinese translation of the *Akṣaraśataka-nāma-vṛtti* XI (Gokhale 1930, 10).

386. See Āryadeva's *Catuḥśataka* 14:3: "Because the two are seen to have different properties, if the pot is different from existence, would existence not also be different from the pot?" (*gnyis mtshan mi mthun mthong nas ni | gal te dngos las bum gzhan na | ma yin de ltar dngos po yang | bum pa las gzhan cis mi 'gyur* [D 3846, dbu ma, tsha 15a]).

387. Chandrakīrti, commenting on Āryadeva's *Catuḥśataka* 14:2, notes that: "If, wanting to avoid that fault you imagine, for example, that a pot distinct from shape has shape, like Devadatta owning distinct cows, this is not reasonable. Is the pot having shape in this way distinct or not? If the pot was different from its shape it would be conceived independently from the shape. It is not that a Devadatta distinct from cows is not conceived as distinct from a cow. In the same way the pot, if it is conceived independently of the shape, is not conceived at all." (*ci ste nyes pa 'di spang bar 'dod nas dper na lha sbyin don gzhan du gyur pa'i ba lang dag dang ldan pa ltar gzugs las gzhan pa'i bum pa zhig gzugs dang ldan par yongs su rtog na 'di yang mi rigs te 'di ltar gzugs ldan bum gzhan yod min la gal te bum pa gzugs las gzhan du 'gyur na ni de gzugs la mi ltos par gzung du yod par 'gyur ro ba lang dag las tha dad pa'i lha sbyin ni ba lang las tha dad par mi 'dzin pa ma yin te de bzhin du bum pa yang gzugs la mi ltos par bzung du yod par 'gyur na 'dzin pa yang ma yin no* [D 3865, dbu ma, ya 209b]).

the second alternative, that of the difference of an individual and its attributes. For the possession of something does not in general entail that one is that very something: I have a pen, but I am not my pen. I can exist entirely without my possessions, and if the same is true of the pot, which possesses existence, unity, shape, and color, we still have the same problem of a nonexistent, nonunitary, shapeless, and colorless pot. Such a pot would function like a bare particular, an individual from which all properties it is "endowed with" have been abstracted.[388] Nāgārjuna explicitly rejects such bare particulars,[389] not only because it is unclear what such an individual would be like, but also, as Chandrakīrti points out,[390] because an infinite regress follows: if the bare particular is what it is because it has the property of bare particularness we have to postulate a second, even barer, particular that instantiates this property, and so on.

> *Therefore, because identity, difference, and both do not exist, there is no determination.*

Nāgārjuna therefore concludes that neither the two alternatives of identity and difference nor the third "combined" alternative manages to produce a satisfactory account. How does this ontological discussion connect with the Nyāya concept of determination? We recall that determination comes about once an initial doubt is resolved, after considering which of the pair of thesis and antithesis are established. Nāgārjuna has just given an example where neither the *pakṣa* (the assumption that the properties of the pot are identical with it) nor the *pratipakṣa* (the assumption that the properties of the pot are distinct from it) can be considered as the final true position, as both lead to absurd consequences. The Mādhyamika argues that this situation arises in all metaphysical disputes that somewhere presuppose the notion of intrinsic existence or *svabhāva*, i.e., in all debates that do not attempt to settle a question purely at the level of

388. Nāgārjuna therefore does not reject this alternative proposal, because he "handles the relation between an individual and a universal as if it were the relation between two individuals" (Tola and Dragonetti 1995a, 135). Even the defender of generalities, Nāgārjuna argues, cannot provide a satisifactory account of the identity or difference between an individual and its attributes.

389. MMK 5:1–3. See Siderits 2007, 188–89.

390. Poussin 1903–13, 130:11.

conventional truth, but are concerned with ultimate truth. As these are also the debates the Naiyāyika has in mind the Mādhyamika will point out that, in all cases that matter to his Nyāya opponent, there is no determination, because neither thesis nor antithesis can be accepted as the final truth.[391] An understanding of determination that considers it as a determination at the level of ultimate truth is therefore to be rejected. The possibility of having a suitably modified understanding of determination, one that decides between thesis and antithesis at the conventional level only, is left open.

Objection:

"Debate is what has proof and criticism by epistemic instruments,[392] does not contradict the established conclusion, is arisen from the five limbs, and encompasses a thesis and counterthesis. In this context, as you clearly assert the pot, etc., there is a position and an opposing position for you." It is to be replied:

VP 52 **The debate does not exist, since the expressing and expressed do not exist.**

The debate does not exist either. As determination does not exist, since for substance, existence, identity, etc., there is no difference or nondifference, in the same way, if the verbally expressed pot and the pot were

391. It is worthwhile to point out the difference between this interpretation and the one suggested by Tola and Dragonetti (1995, 134). According to them, each alternative individually rules out the existence of determination. If an individual and its attributes are identical, the determination of anything as anything would be impossible, because everything would be the same. And if an individual and an attribute such as existence were distinct, the individual would be nonexistent (since it could be without existence) and therefore, as nonexistent, could not be determined as being anything either. According to our interpretation, it is the impossibility to establish either the thesis of identity or the counterthesis of difference that indicates the impossibility of determination, which would involve such an establishment.

392. The Tibetan here reads *tshad mas sgrub par byed pa dmigs pa can*, which Tola and Dragonetti (1995, 174n2, 196n1) correct to *tshad mas sgrub par byed pa klan ka can*, following Kajiyama (1965, 147n178a; 1974, 395n59), in arguing that the translator misread *upālambha* (*klan ka*, criticism) as *upalambha* (*dmigs*). This amended reading is plausible, given the parallel with NS 1.2.1.

identical, like the word pot, the external object would also be established without depending on the collection of the lump of clay, wheel, water, etc. But one does not maintain that if "pot" is said the mouth is filled, and if "fire" is said the lips are burnt. If they are different, in case "pot" is said, a pot is not known for certain.

The opponent's objection closely follows the definition of debate in NS 1.2.1.[393] The first part of the definition given here only mentions epistemic instruments (*pramāṇa*), not hypothetical reasoning (*tarka*). Interestingly, the presence of *tarka* in the definition presented in NS 1.2.1 is regarded as a difficulty by the opponent in the discussion of this *sūtra* in Uddyotakara's *Vārttika*.[394] He points out that, since *tarka* is not one of the epistemic instruments, it is difficult to see how it could play any role in proof or criticism, the domain of the epistemic instruments *par excellence*. Uddyotakara replies by pointing out that hypothetical reasoning helps the epistemic instruments, by "investigating the real nature of the thing" over which the epistemic instruments range. The epistemic instruments then "come to determine the real character of the thing that has been duly investigated by the hypothetical reasoning."[395]

> *"In this context, as you clearly assert the pot, etc., there is a position (phyogs) and an opposing position (mi mthun pa) for you."*

The opponent points out that in his refutation of determination (*nirṇaya*) in the preceding verse, Nāgārjuna considered two contradictory positions concerning the example of a pot, namely the position that the pot was identical with its attributes, or that it was distinct from them. But this is nothing else but trying to settle whether a thesis or a counterthesis

393. "Debate encompasses the thesis and counterthesis by proof and criticism through epistemic instruments and hypothetical reasoning, without being contradicted by the thesis and being endowed with the five limbs." (*pramāṇatarkasādhanopālambhaḥ siddhāntāviruddhaḥ pañcāvayavopapannaḥ pakṣapratitpakṣaparigraho vādaḥ.*)

394. Jha 1984, vol. 1, 476–77.

395. *na brūmastarkaḥ siddhupālabdhayoḥ kāraṇam api tu pramāṇaviṣayavivecanāt tarkaḥ pramāṇānyanugṛhṇātīti tarkaviviktaṁ viṣayaṁ pramāṇāni pravartamānāni paricchindanti* (Nyaya-Tarkatirtha and Tarkatirtha 2003, 337:5–6; Jha 1984, vol. 1, 476).

are true. Nāgārjuna is therefore taking on board a key characteristic of a debate as defined in the NS and should accept the existence of the corresponding category.

Various modern commentators argue that the reading of the Tibetan should be changed,[396] so that it says instead:

> In this context, as you desire to eliminate the pot, etc., you embrace a counterthesis (*mi mthun pa'i phyogs, pratipakṣa*).

It is not too difficult to see why the opponent might want to say this. Nāgārjuna's arguments against wholes apply to all partite entities, including pots. As a consequence, Nāgārjuna holds a position opposed to that which one might initially think to be plausible, namely that there are wholes, such as pots, at the fundamental level of reality. Once we have this, we have a counterthesis that opposes the thesis that there are wholes, and then we seem to be already in the middle of a debate. As the opponent points out, it seems odd that Nāgārjuna asserts counterintuitive theses, appears to defend them by arguments, and still claims that debates do not exist.

It is to be replied:

VP 52 The debate (vāda) does not exist, since the expressing (vācya) and expressed (vācaka) do not exist.

Nāgārjuna responds by rejecting the category of debate, a category that depends essentially on linguistic exchange by denying the existence of linguistic signifiers and their significations.[397]

396. Instead of *'dir bum pa la sogs pa gsal bar 'dod pa khyod phyogs dang mi mthun pa yongs su 'dzin pa yin no* they suggest *'dir bum pa la sogs pa* ***bsal bar*** *'dod pa khyod* ***mi mthun pa'i phyogs*** *yongs su 'dzin pa yin no*. Tola and Dragonetti (1995, 82; following Kajiyama 1974, 395n61) suggest the first emendation; Kajiyama (1974, 395n62) also suggests the second emendation.

397. Note that apart from being a technical term for debate, *vāda* also has a more general meaning referring to assertions, speech, or talk (see Böhtlingk 1879–89, s.v.). The rejection of the latter more general notion presented here will therefore also be able to reject the more specific technical one.

> *The debate does not exist either. As determination (nirṇaya) does not exist, since for substance, existence, identity, etc., there is no difference or nondifference, in the same way, if the verbally expressed pot and the pot were identical, like the word pot, the external object would also be established without depending on the collection of the lump of clay, wheel, water, etc. But one does not maintain that if "pot" is said the mouth is filled, and if "fire" is said the lips are burnt.*

The same argument schema used in the discussion of VP 51, Nāgārjuna points out, can be applied to the relation between words and their referents. He begins by discussing the first alternative, the identity of words and referents. There are two immediate absurd consequences. First of all, it would be possible to make a pot without recourse to the usual pot-making paraphernalia such as clay, water, and so on. In fact, as the identity of words and referents is supposed to hold universally, not just for pots, any external object could be produced merely by naming it.

Secondly, if the word were really the same as the referent, wherever one is, the other should be. As traditional Indian phonetics tells us that some of the production places of speech, such as teeth, tongue, and palate, are located inside the mouth, when we say the word "pot," our mouth should be filled with the pot's clay, and when we say "fire," real fire should burn our mouth.

The same point is made in NS 2.1.53, where the potential powers of the word "food" to fill the mouth, "fire" to burn it, and "knife" to cut it are considered.[398] The Naiyāyika's criticism is here directed against the position of the *Mīmāṁsāsūtra*,[399] according to which there is a natural, not just a merely conventional, connection between a word and its referent.[400] If this natural (*autpattika*) relation is spelled out in terms of identity or

398. "And also because [the mouth] being filled, burned, or cut is not perceived, there is no natural relation [between words and referents]." (*pūraṇapradāhapāṭanānupalabdheśca saṁbandhābhāvaḥ.*)

399. Ruben 1928, 35. See also 190n134 for a summary of the Vaisheṣhika argument against the Mīmāṁsā position.

400. *Mīmāṁsāsūtra* 1.1.5: "There is certainly a natural connection between a word and its referent, its knowledge is through instruction, it is unerring regarding the non-perceived, it is an epistemic instrument according to Bādārayaṇa because it is independent." (*autpattikas tu śabdasyārthena saṁbandhas tasya jñānam upadeśo 'vyatirekaś cārthe 'nupalabdhe tatpramāṇaṁ bādarāyaṇasyānapekṣatvāt.*) See Sandal 1923, 2–3.

colocation, the Naiyāykika argues, it will entail all the absurd consequences of the thing existing where there is in fact only the word.

If they are different, in case "pot" is said, a pot is not known for certain.

Unfortunately Nāgārjuna is very brief when it comes to describing the absurd consequences of the second alternative, that of the nonidentity of word and referent, a position that we would presumably consider to be more intuitively convincing than that of their identity.[401] All he says here is that such nonidentity would entail that the referent is "not known for certain" (*nges par mi 'gyur*). We can elucidate this point somewhat by looking at some parallel passages in Nāgārjuna's other works.

Nāgārjuna uses the "fire" example also in verse 7 of the *Lokātītastava*:

> If name and referent were not distinct, the mouth would be burnt by fire; if they were distinct, there would be no comprehension—so you have said as a speaker of truth.[402]

The example is used once more in the *Mahāprajñāpāramitāśāstra*, sometimes ascribed to Nāgārjuna.[403] In regard to the absurdity of the difference between word and reference, it states:

> If [word and referent are] distinct, when one says "water," one should get fire.[404]

It becomes clear that the point Nāgārjuna is making in these passages is that if word and referent were substantially (*svabhāvatas*) distinct, there would be no way of getting from one to the other. Knowledge of the word would not lead to knowledge of the thing, there would be no

401. The situtation is therefore similar to that of the discussion of identity and difference of cause and effect: their distinctness is *prima facie* more plausible than their identity.

402. *saṁjñārthayor ananyatve mukhaṁ dahyeta vahninā | anyatve 'dhigamābhāvas tvayoktaṁ bhūtavādinā* (Lindtner 1982, 131).

403. *Da zhidu lun*, T 1509, p. 246, b6–8; Lamotte 1970, vol. 3, 1617–18. On the authenticity of this text, see Robinson 1978, 34–39, and Ruegg 1981, 32–33. I thank Stefano Zacchetti and Dan Lusthaus for their explication of this passage.

404. 若離, 說火時應得水, *Da zhidu lun*, T 1509, p. 246, b6–8; Lamotte 1970, vol. 3, 1617.

comprehension (*adhigama*) of the word's meaning, "fire" could refer to water, and, more generally, anything to anything else (which of course means that nothing refers to anything).

The passage from the *Mahāprajñāpāramitāśāstra* just cited is also interesting in spelling out the position behind the Madhyamaka rejection of the two alternatives:

> The ancient ones provisionally (**prajñapti*) established names to designate objects (**dharma*); people of later times know things (**vastu*) on the basis of these names.[405]

The conventional nature of the word-referent relation is also stressed in Diṅnāga's *Prajñāpāramitāpiṇḍārtha*, which points out that:

> Names are fabricated and expressible things are conceptually imputed; therefore one does not think that the connection between words and referents exists substantially.[406]

In fact, this text goes further by denying that it makes sense to speak of separately existent expressible objects in the first place:

> Therefore, the name is conceptually imputed in this world; there is certainly no expressible object. For this reason it is certain that referents are conceptually imputed according to their names.[407]

405. 亦不合, 亦不離, 古人假為立名以名諸法, 後人因是名字識是事, *Da zhidu lun*, T 1509, p. 246, b6–8; Lamotte 1970, vol. 3, 1618.

406. *kṛtrimaṁ nāma vācyāś ca dharmās te kalpitā yataḥ | śabdārthayor na sambandhas tena svābhāviko mataḥ*, 48 (Tucci 1947, 58). It is important to note that even though Nāgārjuna and Diṅnāga agree in saying that language cannot be directly grounded in an underlying reality, their reasons for *why* this is the case differ in crucial ways. For Diṅnāga, each fundamentally real object is unique, and since language operates by linking up shared characteristics, the fundamental objects are beyond its reach, as they do not have any shared characteristics. For Nāgārjuna, there are no fundamentally real objects, so they could not act as a ground for language. Both systems agree that, because of this inability of language to link up with the ground of reality, it can only gain its functionality by being grounded in conventions.

407. *atra tena yathā nāma kalpyate na tathāsti tat | vācyam vastu tato niṣṭhā yathā-nāma-artha-kalpanā*, 50 (Tucci 1947, 58). Also compare Nāgārjuna's statement in the *Acintyastava*

Rather, name and object arise in mutual dependence through the process of conceptual imputation.

Nāgārjuna thus responds to the opponent's charge that he is conducting a debate (and thereby accepting the Nyāya category *vāda*) by pointing out that because two key theories of semantics (assuming identity or difference between word and referent) lead to contradiction, debate, which is fundamentally a language-based endeavor, does not exist.

Tola and Dragonetti comment:[408]

> As a consequence of the previous argumentation, there is not the possibility of words related to objects and of objects related to words, and therefore, without words and objects, the debate is not possible either.

Even though Nāgārjuna says explicitly, and without any modifiers, that neither the expression, the expressed, nor debate exist,[409] it is tempting to insert some suitable modifiers here, having him say that there is no substantial (*svabhāvatas*) relation between words and referents, i.e., no relation that is not wholly explicable in terms of conventions. To assert any more would be dangerously close to a performative contradiction, since Nāgārjuna presumably wants his own statements in the VP and elsewhere to be conventionally meaningful. And in fact the denial of a substantial word-referent relation is all Nāgārjuna needs at this point, for it would be sufficient to refute the Nyāya conception of debate, which presupposes precisely the existence of such a relation.[410]

⁂ If you say: "There is the convention of the word as a signifying expression"—this is not so.

VP 53 **Because the ultimate is subject to analysis.**

---

that "nothing expressible is to be found isolated from the expression"; *abhidhānāt pṛthagbhūtam abhidheyam na vidyate* (Lindtner 1982, 152).

408. Tola and Dragonetti 1995a, 136.

409. *rjod par byed pa dang brjod bya dag med pa, rtsod pa yang med.*

410. See Westerhoff 2009, 191; and Westerhoff 2010, 64–65.

It is a tenet of yours that "who comprehends the sixteen categories is liberated," you who have fallen into the view of the foolish little Nyāya.

Since the sixteen categories, epistemic instruments, etc., are ultimate, precisely which reasoning will the intelligent ones realize?

Names that are self-made expressions are also seen to stand for things that are not real, such as "Devadatta" and "Indragupta."

If there were liberation by mere worldly convention, cowherds, etc., would also all be liberated. There would also be no distinctions between "intelligent ones" and "ignorant ones."

If you say: "There is the convention of the word as a signifying[411] *expression"—this is not so.*

Nāgārjuna's opponent replies to the argument from the preceding VP 52 by pointing out that the dilemma Nāgārjuna presented there is no real dilemma, because there is a way of passing between the two horns. It is not the case that the only two ways of producing a semantic theory are by taking words and referents to be identical (so that objects and the linguistic expressions they refer to are the same kind of thing) or by considering them to be intrinsically distinct (so that there is no way of getting from one to the other). There is a third possible position, namely one that asserts that word and referent, though separate, are linked by a network of conventions. This convention-based theory of semantics is explicitly discussed in NS 2.1.55, which points out that the connection between words and referents is based on agreement (*sāmayika*).[412] Such conventional agreements ensure that on saying "water," we do indeed get water, rather than fire.

411. *brda (saṁketa) byas pa'i brjod.*

412. *na sāmayikatvāc chabdārthasampratyayasya.* See also Vātsyāyana's commentary on this passage: "The restriction of a specific word to a specific meaning is not due to a natural relation. What it is due to? Convention.... What again is this convention? It is an agreement regulating expression and expressed saying 'this sort of thing is the meaning of this word.' When this is used there is the right conception of the object resulting from the expression. Otherwise, even though the word is heard, there is no understanding. This is inevitable, even for one who believes in such a natural relation. For ordinary people, the use of the convention comes from a conception of its ordinary employment.... Thus, because of that, there is no reason for inferring even the least remnant of a natural relation between words and objects." *na sambandhakāritaṁ śabdārthavyavasthānam | kiṁ tarhi | samayakāritam |*

VP 53 Because the ultimate is subject to analysis.[413]

Nāgārjuna replies that such a convention-based account of semantics is not the subject of his analysis. What his analysis concerns is a theory of semantics that treats semantic relations as something ultimate and hence nonconventional, as, for example, the views that word and referent are intrinsically (*svabhāvatas*) identical or distinct.

It is a tenet of yours that "who comprehends the sixteen categories is liberated," you who have fallen into the view of the foolish[414] *little Nyāya.*[415]

The opponent's "tenet" is a direct reference to the very beginning of the NS,[416] which asserts that the knowledge of the inner nature of the Nyāya categories leads to the highest goal of liberation (*niḥśreyasa*).[417]

The soteriological (and not just logical or epistemological) importance of the sixteen categories is stressed by the fact that the NS does not venture

---

...kaḥ punar ayaṁ samayaḥ | asya śabdasyedam arthajātam abhidheyam ity abhidhānābhidheyaniyamaniyogaḥ | tasminn upayukte śabdād arthasampratyayo bhavati | viparyaye hi śabdaśravaṇa 'pi pratyayābhāvaḥ | sambandhavādino 'pi cāyam avarjanīya iti | prayujyamānagrahaṇāc ca samayopayogo laukikānām | ...tad evaṁ prāptilakṣaṇasya śabdārthasambandhasyārthatuṣo 'pi anumānahetur na bhavatīti (Śāstrī 1998, 249:9–250:6).

413. *don dam pa* (*paramārtha*) *dpyod pa'i skabs* (*vicāraprakaraṇa* [Pind 2001, 157], *vicārasyaiva prastutatvāt* [Sempa Dorje 1974, 39]) *yin pa'i phyir ro.*

414. *lha rnams dga' ba* (*devāṇāṁpriya*). For further discussion of this term, see commentary on VP 15 above (pp. 90–91, and notes 192 and 193).

415. *rigs pa phra ba* (*nyāyasūkṣma*).

416. NS 1.1.1: *pramāṇa-prameya-saṁśaya-prayojana-dṛṣṭānta-siddhānt-āvayava-tarka-nirṇaya-vāda-jalpa-vitaṇḍā-hetvābhāsa-cchala-jāti-nigrahasthānānāṁ tattva-jñānān niḥśreyas-ādhigamaḥ.* It is therefore unclear why Williams (1978, 281) claims that "[t]he Naiyāyika needs his categories for the structure of the debate—the contention that liberation results from understanding them is at no point mentioned," as the reference to *niḥśreyasa*, the *summum bonum*, appears to do precisely that.

417. Bernard (1981, 21–22): "[Nyāya] teaches that the world consists of the uninterrupted flow of misapprehension, faults, activity, birth and pain. By the cessation of the flow of this chain of consequences will we be freed. The way to break this chain is to obtain a fuller understanding of the true nature of things. When this has been accomplished the faults which consist of a delusion causing us to like and dislike a thing will no longer exist. When this disappears, there will no longer be any desire which is the stimulus for all action. It is claimed that this will free us from rebirth, the cause of all sorrow and suffering, and enable us to achieve the supreme end of life."

to give a complete list of all the basic categories under which all epistemic objects could be subsumed; rather, it mentions only those that have soteriological import:

> Vātsyāyana points out that the list [of the twelve epistemic objects given in NS 1.1.9] neither is, nor is intended to be, an exhaustive enumeration of all possible objects of valid cognition; it is only a list of those facts which are believed to be *necessary* objects of cognition, that is, of which it may be said that they should be cognized correctly (*prameya*) for the achievement of that highest spiritual end which is characterized by the cessation of all suffering. It is also admitted by Vātsyāyana that, besides these twelve, there are countless other cognizables or reals, and that it is possible to classify them all under the six or seven heads recognized by the Vaisheṣhika.[418]

Bhaduri refers here to Vātsyāyana's commentary on NS 1.1.9,[419] where he points out that:

> there are also other epistemic objects, substance, property, action, generality, particularity, and inherence, and these will not be enumerated separately, hence what has been taught by the distinction is such that knowledge of its inner nature leads to liberation, and wrong knowledge leads to cyclic existence.[420]

418. Bhaduri 1947, 5. See also Bernard (1981, 26): "There are innumerable objects that might serve as the objects of right knowledge, but these twelve are especially listed because knowledge of truth about them is said to dispel all delusions and lead to salvation, while false knowledge concerning these topics holds man in the bondage of human sorrow and suffering. It is not the object of Nyāya to explain all that is known about these several topics...."

419. "Soul, body, sense-organs, objects, thought, mind, activity, defect, rebirth, fruit, pain, and liberation are the epistemic objects" (*ātma-śarīr-endriy-ārtha-buddhi-manaḥ-pravṛtti-doṣa-pretyabhāva-phala-duḥkh-āpavargās tu prameyam*).

420. *asti anyad api dravyaguṇakarmasāmānyaviśeṣasamavāyāḥ prameyam tadbhedena cāparisaṁkhyeyam asya tu tattvajñānād apavargo mithyājñānāt saṁsāra ity ata etad upadiṣṭaṁ viśeṣeṇeti* (Śāstrī 1998, 30:1–2; see also Jha 1984, 212).

Nyāya therefore does not regard itself as mere debate manual, or as an explication of logical and epistemological topics that forms a useful propaedeutic for conducting a philosophical dispute. It is rather a soteriologically effective system in itself,[421] and its exposition is governed not primarily by the structure of the logical and epistemological content it covers but by a focus on the soteriological efficacy of this content.

The term "little Nyāya" (*rigs pa phra ba, nyāyasūkṣma*) is discussed in more detail by Pind.[422] The term *sūkṣma* can be used in two different senses. It can mean "keen," "sharp," or "subtle," as well as "minute" or "little." In the present context, it is probably the latter that is intended. Pind notes that:

> it seems more likely that the Buddhists in the beginning used it ironically, if not derogatively, with reference to the smallness and insignificance of the NS, which originally may have been a debate handbook of fairly limited scope on the methodology of investigation.[423]

By characterizing Nyāya as "little," Nāgārjuna might be wanting to point out that mere knowledge of the canons of argumentation, even the knowledge of their inner nature (*tattvajñāna*), is not sufficient to bring about liberation.[424] As such, the epithet "little" would constitute a direct

421. Randle (1930, 47n2): "The Naiyāyika of course does not presuppose that a knowledge of the logical notions, which form fifteen out of these sixteen 'categories', constitutes the soul's salvation: but he is convinced that bad logic will incur damnation. The knowledge that constitutes salvation is knowledge of certain topics that fall under the category of 'objects of knowledge', notably the topic of the nature of the soul. The other fifteen categories constitute the equipment for getting and guarding right knowledge of this. So Vātsyāyana says: *ātmādeḥ khalu prameyasya tattvajñānān niḥśreyasādhigamaḥ*—the attainment of the highest good results from knowledge of the true reality of such objects of knowledge as the soul (NBh. p. 2 l. 16 on NS I.i.1). And he claims that the Nyāyaśāstra is the *ānvīkṣikī vidyā* traditionally spoken of as fourth among the branches of knowledge—(a) the three vedas (b) the science of wealth (c) politics, or the art of kingship (d) *ānvīkṣikī vidyā* (NBh p. 3 ll. 5–6). Without its treatment of the logical categories the Nyāyaśāstra would be just like the Upaniṣads i.e., it would be knowledge of the true self (*adhyātmavidyāmātram iyaṁ syād yathopaniṣadaḥ*). The Nyāya is therefore a system of applied logic: and its application is to the ontological problem of the soul."

422. Pind 2001, 157–60.

423. Pind 2001, 159–60. See also Lindtner 1982, 250n194.

424. See also Tola and Dragonetti 1995a, 197n5.

rejection of the Nyāya claim of the soteriological force of the system of the sixteen categories.

> *Since the sixteen categories, epistemic instruments, etc., are ultimate, precisely which reasoning (rigs) will the intelligent ones realize?*

For the Naiyāyika, the sixteen categories are ultimate reals. They include the Vaisheṣhika categories—substance (*dravya*), property (*guṇa*), action (*karma*), generality (*sāmānya*), particularity (*viśeṣa*), and inherence (*samavāya*)—listed in the *Vaiśeṣikasūtra* as the categories that are conducive to liberation.[425]

From the perspective of the Vaisheṣhikas themselves these categories exist at the fundamental level of reality:[426]

> These categories, or *padhārthas* as they are called, are believed by the Vaisheṣhika to be ultimate reals, absolutely objective facts. They are not products of thought; they are independent of all thought referring to them. It is an accident that there are conscious beings who cognize them, but this cognition makes no difference to their autonomous reality. They would exist as reals, even if there were not a single conscious mind to think of them. They are, therefore, not merely logical categories but ontological.

These realist assumptions can be extended to the remainder of the Nyāya categories, all of which have to be considered as existing at the ultimate level. Yet, Nāgārjuna objects, if matters are thoroughly analyzed by intelligent persons,[427] this turns out not to be the case.

425. *Vaiśeṣikasūtra* 1.1.4: "The knowledge of the inner nature of common and differing properties of categories, based on the particular attributes of those things, substance, property, action, community, invidividuality and inherence leads to the highest good." (*dharma-viśeṣaprasūtād dravya-guṇa-karma-sāmānya-viśeṣa-samavāyānāṁ padārthānāṁ sādharmya vaidharmyābhyāṁ tattvajñānān niḥśreyasam* [Chakrabarty 2003, 39–40].)

426. Bhaduri 1947, 3.

427. Nāgārjuna refers here of course to the Naiyāyika's Buddhist opponents. See Tola and Dragonetti 1995a, 197n7.

> *Names, which are self-made expressions (rang gis brda byas pa'i ming), are also seen to be for things that are not real (yang dag pa ma yin pa, abhūta), like "Devadatta" and "Indragupta."*

Nāgārjuna uses the example of two personal names, Devadatta and Indragupta, in order to argue that the referents of the names do not have substantial, nonconventional existence. There are at least two different ways of understanding the argument here. Firstly, the two names mean literally "god-given" and "protected by Indra." Nevertheless, when a person bears such a name, we do not assume that it was literally given by a god or literally protected by Indra. Rather, these names work as conventional designations to pick out some specific people. As such, the two names do not have real referents, that is, referents that actually have the attributes described in the names.[428]

Secondly, Devadatta and Indragupta are of course very common names, and particularly the former is often used as a mere placeholder to denote some person or other. If the specific meaning of the two names is not what the argument turns on, the idea might not just be that the names "Devadatta" and "Indragupta" pick out their referents by convention, but that the entity the name refers to—the person—is only conventionally existent too. This is because, according to the Buddhist understanding, a person is simply a particular division of the continuously changing stream of the psychophysical aggregates that constitute the five *skandha*s.

> *If there were liberation by mere worldly convention, cowherds, etc., would also all be liberated. There would also be no distinctions between "intelligent ones" (mkhas pa) and "ignorant ones" (rmongs pa).*

If, on the other hand, merely conventional truths would be sufficient for obtaining liberation, those who know this conventional truth of transactional reality, e.g., such ordinary people as cowherds, would all be liberated.

428. Tola and Dragonetti (1995, 137) read the argument in this way.

A parallel idea can be found in Vasubandhu's *Trisvabhāvakārikā*,[429] which lists four different arguments for Yogāchāra's mind-only thesis,[430] the last of which concerns the unwelcome consequence that if nonmental things existed, there would be "the occurring of liberation without effort" (*mokṣāpatter ayatnataḥ*). Tola and Dragonetti explain:[431]

> If things really exist, they would be known by ignorant people as they really are; it would happen then that the knowledge of ignorant people reaches truth without effort and therefore this knowledge would produce liberation, since it is the true knowledge. Consequently no special training would be necessary to be in possession of the supreme intuitive knowledge, which according to Buddhism is the only one which grasps the true reality of things and in consequence is the only one that is able to produce liberation."[432]

It is therefore apparent that the ultimate existence of the Nyāya categories is not just something that finds textual support on the basis of the tradition's own texts, but that there are also strong systematic reasons for this assumption: without the ultimate existence of the Nyāya categories, it would be difficult to explain their alleged soteriological force.

Moreover,

VP 54 **We see in many ways that names are used as signifying expressions.**

429. *Trisvabhāvakārikā* 35: *viruddhadhīvāraṇatvād buddhyā vaiyarthyadarśanāt | jñānatrayānuvṛtteś ca mokṣāpattir ayatnataḥ* (Mukhopadyaya 1939, 7).

430. There is no Indian or Tibetan commentary on this text, and interpretations (particularly those of verse 35) diverge. My interpretation follows Tola and Dragonetti (2004, 217), Anacker (2005, 297n6–9), and Brunnhölzl (2007, 495n212). For diverging readings, see Kochumuttom (1982, 123) and Garfield (2002, 150).

431. Tola and Dragonetti 2004, 217.

432. See also Sthiramati's *Ṭīkā* on the *Madhyāntavibhāga* 1.2 (Stcherbatsky 1936, 18).

It is like this: As the cow...is referred to by the names "gentle" and "noble," because of the divisions of the languages of the countries, the substances *piṇḍarasa* and acid, etc., the *Kadamba* tree, *shaloka*, etc., are like this.

It is like this. As the cow...[433] *is referred to by the names "gentle"*[434] *and "noble," because of the divisions of the languages of the countries, the substances piṇḍarasa*[435] *and acid,*[436] *etc., the Kadamba tree, shaloka,*[437] *etc., are like this.*

The translation of the commentary on this verse[438] is difficult due to the fairly obscure vocabulary used. Kajiyama[439] leaves this section untranslated, while Tola and Dragonetti[440] prefer to give a summary translation.

It seems clear that the commentary refers to the fact that the things can be given different names in different languages, a point that is also made by Vātsyāyana in commenting on NS 2.1.56:[441]

433. The meaning of [*la*] *ḍa mi ḍa* is unclear, though it probably refers to something else to which the terms "gentle" and "noble" also apply, possibly another kind of animal.

434. The Tibetan *sting ta* may be a faulty transcription of the Sanskrit *stimita* = "soft," "gentle."

435. See *Carakasaṁhitā* 6.2.1.40. The term denotes some form of liquid, possibly a broth (*rasa*) containing meat (*piṇḍa*).

436. *skyur rtsi* (Jäschke 1998, s.v. *skyur ba*). The *Mahāvyutpatti* (Sakaki 1916, 377, no. 5807) gives *nāgaraṅgaḥ* as the meaning of *skyur rtsi*. According to Franke et al., (2005–, vol. 5, 318) *nāgaraṅgaḥ* denotes a citrus fruit, *citrus aurantium* (bitter orange), or *citrus reticulata* (mandarin orange).

437. The meaning of *sha lo ka* is unclear. The term might denote another kind of tree.

438. *ba lang la ḍa mi ḍa la sogs pa ni sting ta* [C and D read *stigs ta*] *dang 'phags pa zhes ming du byas pa lta bu dang | de bzhin du yul tshig 'jig pa dag gis kyang piṇ ḍa ra sa dang skyur rtsi la sogs pa'i rdzas la tshogs can dang sha lo ka la sogs pa lta bu'o.*

439. Kajiyama 1974, 216.

440. Tola and Dragonetti 1995a, 83–84.

441. *ṛṣyāryamlecchānāṁ yathākāmaṁ śabdaviniyogo 'rthapratyāyanāya pravartate | svābhāvike hi śabdasyārthapratyāyakatve yathākāmaṁ na syād* (Śāstrī 1998, 151:2–3). See also Jha 1984, 845.

> Ṛṣis, Āryans, and barbarians use words for making known the meaning according to their wishes. If what makes the meaning of a word known did so naturally, it would not be according to their wishes.

The connection between a word and its power to denote a referent, Vātsyāyana continues,[442] therefore differs crucially from a connection like that between fire and its power to illuminate (which is the kind of natural relation that the Mīmāṁsāka believes to hold between words and referents). Fire always illuminates, whether lit by Aryan or barbarian, but a word, when uttered to speakers of another language, might denote something else, or nothing at all. This fact can only be accounted for by assuming that the connection between words and referents is convention based.

Due to the difficulties with translating this verse, it is not entirely clear whether Nāgārjuna just wants to point out that different people can have different names for the same thing, or also that the same name can denote different things for different people. As the multiplicity of referents for a single term is discussed in the next verse, we choose not to interpret it in this way. Be this as it may, in any case, it appears uncontroversial that the bottom line of this passage is that the cross-linguistic difference of word-referent pairs acts as a strong argument against the view that the relation between words and referents is in some way natural or based on the essence of things.[443]

⁜ Moreover,

VP 55 **Also because worldly experts see connections between expressions and many things to be expressed.**

442. *yathā taijasasya prakāśasya rūpapratyayahetutvaṁ na jātiviśeṣe vyabhicaratīti* (Śāstrī 1998, 151:3–4).

443. Bijalwan (1977, 230): "As regards the contention of the Mīmāṁsākas that the meaning of a word is that which has been used by the Āryans and that the meaning of the word which has been accepted by the non-Āryans is not real, Jayanta observes that this thesis cannot be established by any standard of judgment, and if the Mīmāṁsākas are bent upon sticking to this absurd hypothesis, they would have no other means than to take an oath to prove it."

Worldly experts connect the [Sanskrit] word "*go*" to many; it is also like the word "*hari*." The word "*go*" is involved with manifold kinds in the following way:

> Speech, region, ground,
> Light-ray, *vajra*, cattle, eye,
> Water, heavenly realm: by nine meanings
> The word "*go*" should be understood by the experts.

Similarly:

> Viṣhṇu, lion, elephant, frog,
> Sun, moonlight, monkey,
> Light yellow, parrot, Indra, snake,
> Should be understood as "*hari*" by the wise.
>
> Rāhu, the Abiding One, Viṣhṇu,
> Hari, Gopati, the Protector,
> Narasiṁha, Vāmana, the Snake,
> These are known as "Nārāyaṇa."

Other words should be conceived of in a similar way.

Similarly, in this context there are many referents for a single expression, and there are many expressions for each thing to be expressed as well. In the same way, the names Mighty One, Indra, Destroyer of Cities, Bringer of Sacrifices, Kaushika, and Shakra express a single referent. They are synonyms for the nonexistent, inexistent, and non-imputed.

Moreover, it is not established ultimately. Therefore, because the fault of mixing expressions and things to be expressed in many ways is apparent, it is not established because of its uncertainty.

Moreover,

VP 55 Also because worldly experts see connections between expressions and many things to be expressed.

Nāgārjuna continues his discussion of the connection between words and what words express that began with the discussion of the Nyāya category of debate in verse 52. He now concentrates on the consequences of the existence of homonyms and synonyms for our view of language.

> *Worldly experts connect the [Sanskrit] word "go" to many; it is also like the word "hari." The word "go" is involved with manifold kinds in the following way:*
>
> *Speech (vāc), region (diś), ground (bhū),*
> *Light-ray (raśmi), vajra, cattle (paśu), eye (akṣi),*
> *Water (vār), heavenly realm (svarga): by nine meanings*
> *The word "go" should be understood by the learned (medhāvin).*

Nāgārjuna here quotes a verse listing nine different meanings of the Sanskrit word "*go*." The verse is also cited in Vasubandhu's *Abhidharmakośabhāṣya*,[444] and a variant occurs in Amarasiṁha's *Amarakośa*.[445]

> *Similarly:*
>
> *Viṣhṇu, lion (siṁha),*[446] *elephant (kapi), frog (bheka),*
> *Sun (arka), moonlight (candra), monkey (kapi),*
> *Light yellow (kapila),*[447] *parrot (śuka), Indra, snake (ahi),*[448]
> *Should be understood as "hari" by the wise.*

444. *vāgdigbhūraśmivajreṣu paśvakṣisvargavāriṣu | navasvartheṣu medhāvī gośabdam upadhārayet* (Pradhan 1975, 81:2–3).

445. 3.3.25: *svargeṣupaśuvāgvajra diṅnetradhṛṇibhūjale | lakṣyadṛṣṭyā striyāṁ puṁsi gauḥ* (Sardesai and Padhye 2009, 112).

446. Narasiṁha, the fourth of the ten incarnations of Viṣhṇu (*daśāvatāra*), is half man, half lion.

447. The Tibetan has *ser skya*, a term that denotes a whitish or light yellow (see Jäschke 1998, s.v. *skya bo*; the term also collectively refers to the yellow-robed clergy and white-robed laymen). Its Sanskrit equivalent, *kapila* (see *Mahāvyutpatti*, Sakaki 1916, 241, no. 3464), however, appears to denote a red or brown color (Böhtlingk 1879–89, s.v. "die bräunliche oder röthliche Farbe"; Apte 1957: "tawny, reddish"). It is interesting to note that the sage Kapila, traditionally regarded as the founder of the Sāṁkhya school of classical Indian philosophy, is listed as an incarnation of Viṣhṇu in the *Bhāgavata Purāṇa* (1.3.10).

448. P and N read *rlung*, "wind," instead of *klu*, "snake." Both readings make sense as *anila*, "wind," is also listed as a synonym of "*hari*" in *Amarakośa* 3.3.175. Note, however, the close connection of Viṣhṇu and the snake, a connection so close that the king of snakes that Viṣhṇu rests on, Sheṣhanaga, is also sometimes regarded as an incarnation of Viṣhṇu himself (*Bhāgavata Purāṇa* 5.25.1).

This verse draws on a list of synonyms of the word "*hari*" that can also be found in Amarasiṁha's *Amarakośa*.[449] With the exception of *glang po*, "elephant,"[450] all of the eleven synonyms of "*hari*" given here come from the set of sixteen given in the *Amarakośa*. Interestingly, different Tibetan recensions make slightly different selections from the set; Derge and Choney choose *klu* (*ahi*), while Peking and Narthang take *rlung* (*anila*).

The examples of terms, "*go*" and "*hari*," have been chosen by Nāgārjuna for their multiplicity of meanings. Reference to contemporary dictionaries confirms the impression of the bewildering variety of meanings these terms encompass: the entry on "*hari*" in Apte (1957) takes up two whole columns, while that on "*go*" takes up nearly seven.

The connection of these two verses with the later *Abhidharmakośabhāṣya* and *Amarakośa* does not in itself make the ascription of the VP to Nāgārjuna questionable. The first verse is quoted by Vasubandhu from an earlier source that might well have been extant at Nāgārjuna's time. The second verse is not an actual quotation from the *Amarakośa*; it is rather plausible that there was an earlier list of synonyms of "*hari*" on which both the verse quoted by Nāgārjuna and the passage in the *Amarakośa* are based.

> *Rāhu,*[451] *the Abiding One,*[452] *Viṣhṇu,*[453]
> *Hari,*[454] *the Lord of Cowherds,*[455] *the Protector,*[456]

449. 3.3.175–76: *yamā'nilendracandrā'rkaviṣṇusiṁhāṁ'śuvājiṣu* | *śukā'hikapibhekeṣu harir nā kapile triṣu* (Sardesai and Padhye 2009, 134).

450. Note, however, that the term *kapi* can also mean "elephant" (Böhtlingk 1879–89, s.v.; see also Apte 1957, s.v. *kapila*).

451. See the remarks on VP 08 above. While I am not familiar with any instances where Rāhu is used as a name of Nārāyaṇa, there are numerous names of Nārāyaṇa that begin in *rāhu*, such as *rāhu-śatru*, "Rāhu's enemy," *rāhu-mūrdha-hara*, "Rāhu's decapitator," and *rāhu-bhedin*, "severing (the head of) Rāhu." We could thus understand the passage not as saying that "Rāhu...is known as Nārāyaṇa" but that "*rāhu-*~ ...is known as Nārāyaṇa."

452. The Tibetan term *gnas ldan* might refer to *paryavasthita*, "he who stands close," the 931st of the thousand names of Viṣhṇu listed in the *Viṣṇusahāsranāma*. In his commentary Śaṅkara explains this name by the fact that Viṣhṇu pervades the entire universe (Sastry 1927, 150).

453. Viṣhṇu is listed in the *Viṣṇusahāsranāma* as the second, 258th, and 657th names.

454. *hari*, the 650th name of Viṣhṇu.

455. *ban glang* translates the Sanskrit *go*, "cow." This presumably refers to the 495th and 592nd names of Viṣhṇu, *gopati*.

456. The Tibetan *skyong bdag* is likely to be a contraction of *skyong bdag po*, "the lord who protects," probably corresponding to *goptā*, the following 496th and 593rd names of Viṣhṇu.

Narasiṁha,[457] *Vāmana,*[458] *the Snake,*[459]
These are known as "Nārāyaṇa."

Nārāyaṇa is the 245th name of Viṣhṇu according to the *Viṣṇusahāsranāma*. The point made here differs from the one made in the preceding two verses. Nāgārjuna notes that "*go*" and "*hari*" are both homonyms (one sound, multiplicity of meanings), whereas the different names of Nārāyaṇa are synonyms (multiplicity of sounds, one meaning).[460]

Other words should be conceived of in a similar way. Similarly, in this context there are many referents for a single expression, and there are many expressions for each thing to be expressed as well.

The fact that one expression can denote many things, and that many different things can be denoted by a single expression, of course, not only applies to the words "*go*," "*hari*," and "*nārāyaṇa*," but is a fact about language more generally.[461] Nāgārjuna continues by giving another example for a set of synonyms, six different names of Indra.

457. *narasiṁhavapu*, the 21st name of Viṣhṇu.

458. In his fifth incarnation Viṣhṇu takes the form of a dwarf (*vāmana*). Vāmana is also the 152nd name of Viṣhṇu.

459. *vyāla*, the 92nd name of Viṣhṇu.

460. Tola and Dragonetti (1995, 138), however, comment: "The third quoted stanza presents another example which has not been announced together with *go* and *hari*. We understand this third example in the same way as the two previous examples: the different beings enumerated in the stanza are denoted by a single name: Nārāyaṇa." This seems to get matters exactly the wrong way around, as the terms listed in the third verse do not refer to "different beings" but rather are all names of Viṣhṇu.

461. It is of course also something that holds between languages. See, e.g., Jha (1984, 845): "(a) The word '*yava*' is used by the *Āryas* to express barley, and by the *Mlēchchhas* to express *long-pepper*; (b) the word '*ṭrivṛiṭ*' is used by *Ṛiṣis* in the sense of *nine hymns*, and the *Āryas* used it in the sense of a *particular creeper*."

In the same way the names Mighty One,[462] *Indra,*[463] *Destroyer of Cities,*[464] *Bringer of Sacrifices,*[465] *Kaushika,*[466] *and Shakra*[467] *express a single referent.*

As in the case of Nārāyaṇa, there are a variety of names for Indra, each of which emphasizes a different aspect of him, even though all refer to the same divinity.

They are synonyms for the nonexistent, inexistent, and nonimputed.[468]

The meaning of this sentence is not straightforward. Tola and Dragonetti[469] render it as:

> 'Inexistent', and 'nonexistent' and 'not known' are synonyms,

explaining that: "What is not known is considered not to exist."[470] They interpret the sentence as a continuation of the point made in the preceding sentence about the six names of Indra: in the same way in which there are synonymous names for Indra, there are synonymous terms for the nonexistent.

Yet translating *mi 'dogs pa* as "not known" is curious, since the verb *'dogs* does not mean "to know," but "to affix," "to bind something to something else," as well as "to impute" (as in the phrase *ming 'dags pa*, "to impute a

462. *nus ldan*, *śaktīvat*. All six names of Indra given here are included in the *Indrasahāsra-nāma*, a modern work by Kavyakantha Ganapati Muni, based on Vedic sources (Natesan 2003–07, vol. 3). The term *śaktivāt* is the 434th in this list.

463. The first name in the list.

464. *grong khyer 'jig*, *puraṁdara* (the 108th name).

465. *mchod sbyin*, *yajñavāhasa* (the 47th name).

466. The 230th name. See also the *Śataśāstra* (Tucci 1981, 37): "If existence, unity and pot are a unity, then, as Indra, Shakra, and Kaushika are identical, and in the place where Indra is, there Shakra and Kaushika must also be, in the same way, in the place of existence there will then be unity and pot."

467. The 405th name.

468. *med pa dang yod pa ma yin pa dang mi 'dogs* [P and N read *mdog*] *pa zhes bya ba'i ming gi rnam grangs yin no.*

469. Tola and Dragonetti 1995a, 85.

470. Tola and Dragonetti 1995a, 198n7.

name"). In addition, the syntax of the sentence may be taken to suggest that "nonexistent" (*med pa*), etc., are not regarded as synonyms of each other, but that all three are said to be synonyms of something else (namely the names mentioned in the previous passage). We therefore understand the sentence as saying the names Mighty One, Indra, etc., are synonyms for the nonexistent, inexistent, and nonimputed. Since for the Mādhyamika *everything* exists as the product of mental labeling, that is, as an imputed object, for them the term "nonimputed" has the same extension as "nonexistent." The reason Indra, etc., refer to something nonexistent is that the devotee conceives of these divinities as existent *independent of* human labeling, and therefore as *non*imputed. However, as the Madhyamaka arguments set out to show, nothing can exist in this manner. Nāgārjuna therefore does not want to say that referents of words *in general* do not exist, but that there can be no referents if we mistakenly assume that these referents exist in a self-sufficient, nonimputed way. If nothing exists that is nonimputed, then words cannot have (as one might naively assume them to have) a direct relation with the things they designate, since words separate from things do not exist.

Another way of interpreting this passage would be to understand it as a reference to the Vaisheṣhika idea that knowable (*jñeya*), nameable (*abhidheya*), and existence (*sattā*) are coextensive terms; this would then be saying that their term-negations are coextensive as well.[471] The difficulty with assuming that the original Sanskrit terms used here were *ajñeya*, *anabhidheya*, and *asattā* is that we would have to assume that the translator rendered the first two (fairly straightforward) terms mistakenly as *med pa* (instead of *shes bya med pa*) and *mi 'dogs pa* (instead of *brjod par bya ba med pa*; it is likely that *brjod par bya ba* (correctly) translates *abhidheya* in VP 56. That would be an uncharacteristically bad performance, even though it would have the advantage of making the reading of the text much simpler, simply saying that in the same way as the names "Mighty One," "Indra," etc., are synonyms, so are the terms "unknowable," "unnameable," and "nonexistent."

471. Prashastapāda in *Praśastapādabhāṣya* 11 points out that everything is real (*asti*), knowable (*jñeya*), and nameable (*abhidheya*): "All six categories possess reality, nameability and knowability" (*ṣaṇṇām api padārthānām astitvābhidheyatvajñeyayatvāni*; Bronkhorst and Ramseier 1994, 3).

Moreover, it is not established ultimately. Therefore, because the fault of mixing expressions and things to be expressed in many ways is apparent, it is not established because of its uncertainty.

What is not established ultimately is the word-referent connection. Such an ultimate establishment would, for example, be entailed by the kind of essential connection between a word and its referent we find with the Mīmāṁsākas. The relationship between words and referents is not one-to-one but "mixed": one word can pick out many referents, and one referent may be denoted by a multiplicity of words. Yet if a word expresses a thing's inner nature, because there is only one inner nature, there should also only be one word. Similarly, since cow, eye, water, etc., all have different natures, according to this semantic picture, they could not all be expressed by the word "*go*."[472] If the word-referent relation was instituted by nature and not by human convention, it is unclear why such "mixing" should be the case. The resulting uncertainty regarding the source of the word-referent relation therefore throws doubt on the possibility of its ultimate establishment.

⌘ Moreover,

VP 56 **Expression and expressed are neither established as identical nor as distinct.**

If they are identical, expression and expressed are not established, but if they are distinct, if the expression "pot" is applied, there is no certain knowledge of the pot. For that very reason, if being distinct, they are also identical, there is precisely the fault mentioned earlier. Therefore, debate is impossible. ⌘ ⌘

472. See *Mahāyānasaṁgrahabhāṣya* (Lamotte 1973, vol. 2, 118–19).

Moreover,

VP 56 Expression (brjod par byed pa, abhidhāna) and expressed (brjod par bya ba, abhidheya) are neither established as identical nor as distinct.[473]

Nāgārjuna again takes up a point from VP 52, where he argued against the identity and distinctness of the expression and the expressed.

If they are identical, expression and expressed are not established,

If there were no distinction between word and referent, it would not make sense to speak of language referring to the world, or, more specifically, of a word-referent relation, since this would be indistinguishable from the identity relation.

but if they are distinct, if the expression "pot" is applied, there is no certain knowledge of the pot.

If, on the other hand, there was no relation between expression and expressed, it would be unclear how we could get from one to the other, how uttering an expression like "the pot" could produce a belief about or knowledge of a pot in anybody.

For that very reason, if being distinct, they are also identical, there is precisely the fault mentioned earlier. Therefore, debate is impossible.

If some account of the relation between words and referents were to combine both ideas, arguing that they are distinct (in some way) and identical (in some other way), it would also combine the difficulties of either account.

473. In the VS, the *sūtra* between *sūtras* 55 and 57 is "Expression and expressed are neither established as identical nor as distinct" (*brjod par byed pa dang brjod par bya ba gcig nyid dang gzhan nyid du ma grub bo*). In the VP, this passage is missing. This passage should therefore be inserted after the introductory *gzhan yang* that follows the commentary on *sūtra* 55. As a consequence, what Tola and Dragonetti (1995, 44) identify as *sūtra* 56 is in fact part of the commentary on it. Sempa Dorje's reconstruction (1974, 40) identifies the *sūtra* correctly.

It is curious that Nāgārjuna here seems to repeat the argument he already gave in VP 52 in abbreviated form.[474] While difficulty resulting from the identity of expressing and expressed are here not described in detail, the problem connected with their distinctness, mentioned here, is the very same as in VP 52.

One way to explain this would be that in concluding the section on debate (*vāda*), Nāgārjuna also wanted to include the key argument concerning the identity and difference of expression and expressed mentioned in the commentary on *sūtra* 52 in an independent *sūtra*. In this way, he could both underline what his key argument against the existence of debate as envisaged by the Naiyāyika is and give this argument greater prominence by moving it out of the commentary to the level of the root text.

The discussion of *vadā* in verses 52–56 is used by Nāgārjuna to present a general critique of a realist understanding of referential relations. His refutation is directed at an understanding of debate that presupposes a view of language according to which words and their referents are either intrinsically the same or intrinsically different. Both alternatives, Nāgārjuna sets out to show, lead to difficulties. What this means is not that the Mādhyamika has to give up the notion of philosophical debate altogether, because it necessarily brings with it *svabhāva*-entailing consequences, but that the notion of language the Nyāya understanding of debate is based on has to be replaced by a different one. A realist semantics that settles the meaning and truth of statements by means of objectively existent word-world relations that connect mental entities "in here" with ultimate reals "out there," has to be replaced by one that settles questions of truth and meaning by appeal to human conventions—conventions that are changeable, mind dependent, and do not obtain, "no matter what."

VP 57 **Devious debate and mere refutation are similar.**

"Similar" means "in that way in which debate has been refuted." Because of that, devious debate and mere refutation do not exist.

474. It is unclear why Tola and Dragonetti (1995, 138) regard this as a "new" argument.

VP 57 Devious debate (brjod pa, jalpa) and mere refutation (sun ci phyin du brgal ba, vitaṇḍā) are similar.

The NS distinguishes three kinds of argumentational exchange (*kathā*).[475] They can most easily be distinguished in terms of their argumentative aims. *Vāda* aims at establishing the truth, *jalpa* at winning the debate by establishing one's own position, while *vitaṇḍā* tries to derive a contradiction from the opponent's thesis without attempting to establish one's own position.[476]

Jalpa shares the first and fourth characteristic of debate discussed in VP 52;[477] it provides proof and criticism by epistemic instruments and encompasses a thesis and counterthesis. Unlike debate, however, devious debate can avail itself of three sophistical techniques: equivocation,[478] false parities of reasoning,[479] and grounds of defeat.[480] In the context of a devious debate, the debater is therefore allowed to mislead his opponent by equivocations and false parities, and employ grounds of defeat, that is, attempt moves (such as contradicting himself, or shifting the proposition to be argued for) which, if correctly spotted by the opponent, would entail that he loses the debate. Whether the position defended is his own position is of secondary importance, as long as some thesis can be successfully defended and the opponent thereby defeated.[481]

Vitaṇḍā shares with *jalpa* the employment of sophistical techniques but is frequently regarded as worse, since, unlike *jalpa*, it does not even attempt to establish a position of its own. In this context, a debater is solely concerned with refuting his opponent by any licit or illicit means, without

475. NS 1.2.1–3.

476. Vidyabhusana 1971, 62–63.

477. Matilal 1985, 13.

478. *chala*. NS 1.2.11 distinguishes three varieties.

479. *jāti*. NS 5.1.1 distinguishes 24 kinds. Matilal (1985, 15) argues that the last two on this list, *nityasamā* and *kāryasamā*, may generate genuine philosophical puzzles, rather than being mere sophistries. On the former, see also Matilal 1971, 159–62.

480. *nighrahasthāna*. NS 5.2.1 lists 22 different types.

481. Ballantyne 1850–53, 38.

defending any positive thesis that could itself be the subject of an argumentational attack.[482]

We might wonder why a text like NS, which states at its very beginning that knowledge of the true reality (*tattvajñāna*) of the sixteen categories is a means to the highest good (*niḥśreya*) of liberation, discusses such sophistical debating techniques at all. These techniques, and the forms of debates utilizing them are, however, considered to be of purely propaedeutic value. Even though they are themselves unable to bear the fruit of right knowledge, but are better compared to thorny branches, such branches have their usage when it comes to the protection of sprouting seeds.[483] They are, as Matilal points out, "meant for the protection of one's learning when the learner is apparently a young beginner so as not to be swept away by some tricky debater into believing the false doctrine."[484] As Vātsyāyana and Vāchaspati Mishra point out in their commentaries, however, such sophistical techniques are solely to be used by the beginner, not by somebody who has already realized the true knowledge of the categories the Nyāya system aims at.

> *"Similar" means "in that way in which debate (vāda) has been refuted." Because of that, devious debate and mere refutation do not exist.*

Even though the three kinds of argumentational exchange distinguished by the Naiyāyika differ in their aims and in the types of argumentative techniques they employ, they are still sufficiently alike to allow Nāgārjuna's criticism of the first type (*vāda*), raised in verses 52–56, to apply to the other two types as well. If the refutation of the idea of a substantial word-referent relation, the key semantic theory standing behind the Nyāya conception of debate, affects our understanding of debate, it will also affect our understanding of devious debate and mere refutation.

482. See Matilal (1985, 14–19) for more discussion. Not all scholars see *vitaṇḍā* as wholly negative. Udayana distinguishes *vāda-vitaṇḍā* and *jalpa-vitaṇḍā*, the former involving an honest debater who genuinely does not have a position to defend, the latter a charlatan only intent on winning the debate (Matilal 1985, 16–17, 19).

483. NS 4.2.49: *tattvādhyavasāyasaṁrakṣaṇārthaṁ jalpavitaṇḍe bījaprarohasaṁrakṣaṇārthaṁ kaṇṭakaśākhāvaraṇavat.* Jha (1984, vol. 4, 1657) counts this *sūtra* as 4.2.50.

484. Matilal 1985, 15.

Objection: "You say that all are pseudo-reasons and that nothing has a refutation." It is to be replied:

VP 58 **Because the similar and the dissimilar do not exist, there is no pseudo-reason.**

If the pseudo-reason exists, is that due to similarity or due to dissimilarity? First of all, it is not the case that something becomes a pseudo-reason through similarity.

In the same way, if one tests the goldness in gold itself, that very gold is not thrown out; that is gold, not, however, pseudo-gold. In the same way, what is a reason is solely a reason, not, however, a pseudo-reason.

Similarly, something does also not become a pseudo-reason through dissimilarity. In the same way, how could a piece of dirt, and so forth, which is not gold, be pseudo-gold?

In the same way, what is not a reason is not a pseudo-reason, because it is not a reason at all. "Pseudo" is not that very thing, because it is its opposite.

Because an independent thing is transformed, it is not destroyed; because of the difference of its constituents, or, since the constituents are the same, the thought of that is the cognition itself.

If it is fully investigated, a "pseudo-reason" does not exist at all. Since there is no reason and another, third thing other than a reason is not plausible, therefore a pseudo-reason does not exist.

Objection: "You say that all are pseudo-reasons (hetvabhāsa) and that nothing has a refutation."

The opponent raises a point already made in the discussion of verse 32, namely that in the process of refuting the Nyāya categories, Nāgārjuna is implicitly implying (and thereby asserting the existence of) these very categories. In VP 41 and 42, he has rejected the existence of reasons (*hetu*), so that everything considered by him to be a reason has to be the mere appearance of a reason, but not a real reason—in other words, a pseudo-reason. Nāgārjuna has therefore affirmed the existence of at least one of the Nyāya categories, namely the category of a pseudo-reason.

NS 1.2.4 distinguishes five kinds of pseudo-reason. Vātsyāyana points out that what is common to all of them is that they lack the intrinsic characteristics of reason, yet appear to be sufficiently similar to a reason to be mistaken for one.[485]

Consider an example of the penultimate of the five kinds of pseudo-reason distinguished in the NS, *sādhyasama*.[486] The invalid inference, "Shadow is a substance (*dravya*), because it moves," appears structurally similar to the valid inference "There is fire on the hill, because there is smoke." Despite its being used in place of the reason, and thus appearing as the reason, however, "because it moves" is not really a reason. This is because this "reason" has the same epistemic status as the property to be proved. While the presence of smoke on the hill is established by perception, and can then be used as a *probans* to inferentially establish the presence of other qualities (such as fire), the movement of shadow is as contentious as its substantiality. For the Naiyāyika, a shadow is nothing but a sequence of absences (*asannidhisaṁtāna*) of light, and therefore not a moving thing. Consequently the pseudo-reason is unable to establish what it sets out to establish.[487]

Moreover, the opponent continues, since all refutation proceeds by means of reasons, if there are no reasons, there cannot be any refutations. Thus Nāgārjuna has undermined his own ability to refute the Nyāya categories. His position, the opponent claims, is therefore doubly problematic: not only does it affirm the existence of Nyāya categories in denying them, his rejection of the categories also deprives him of the very tools needed to achieve his argumentative goal.

It is to be replied:

VP 58 Because the similar and the dissimilar do not exist, there is no pseudo-reason.

485. *hetulakṣaṇābhāvāt ahetatvo hetusāmānyād hetuvadābhāsamānaḥ* (Śāstrī 1998, 72:7).

486. NS 1.2.8. For discussion of a later list of the five different kinds of pseudo-reason, see Vidyabhusana 1971, 438–42.

487. See Vātsyāyana's commentary on NS 1.2.8 (Śāstrī 1998, 77).

Nāgārjuna responds by rejecting the 13th Nyāya category, the category of pseudo-reasons (*hetvābhāsa, gtan tshigs ltar snang ba*). He does so by considering two mutually exclusive and jointly exhaustive possibilities: either the pseudo-reason is similar to the real reason, or it is not. Since either possibility leads to difficulties, Nāgārjuna argues, there must be some fundamental flaw inherent in the nature of a pseudo-reason.

> *If the pseudo-reson exists, is that due to similarity or due to dissimilarity? First of all, it is not the case that something becomes a pseudo-reason through similarity. In the same way, if one tests the goldness in gold itself, that very gold is not thrown out; that is gold, not, however, pseudo-gold. In the same way, what is a reason is solely a reason, not, however, a pseudo-reason.*

Nāgārjuna first considers the first horn of the dilemma, that pseudo-reason and reason are similar. A pseudo-reason cannot share the essential properties of a reason, because in that case it would just *be* a reason, in the same way in which any substance tested, and found to share the essential properties of gold is just gold, but not fool's (or pseudo-) gold.

> *Similarly, something does also not become a pseudo-reason through dissimilarity. In the same way, how could a piece of dirt, and so forth, which is not gold, be pseudo-gold?*

On the other hand, if something differs in its essential properties from gold, as, for example, a lump of dirt does, it will not even constitute a semblance of gold. As no one would mistake a lump of dirt for a lump of gold, there is no justification to refer to it as "pseudo-gold."

> *In the same way, what is not a reason is not a pseudo-reason, because it is not a reason at all. "Pseudo" is not that very thing, because it is its opposite.*

Nāgārjuna points out that the modifier "pseudo" (*ābhāsa*), like "alleged," "fake," "ersatz," and so forth, does not help to indicate a specific kind of thing referred to by the directly following term (as "golden" in "golden pot" helps to refer to a specific kind of pot). As an alleged fortune is not a fortune, a fake Rembrandt not a Rembrandt, and ersatz coffee not coffee, a pseudo-reason is not a reason.

We might suspect that Nāgārjuna is here putting up a false dilemma. Why argue that a pseudo-reason either shares all key characteristics of a real reason, or that it has no characteristics of a real reason whatsoever? Is there not a third possibility, a middle way Nāgārjuna overlooks, that a pseudo-reason could fail to have the essential characteristics of a reason (thus failing to be a reason), while displaying some of its accidental characteristics (thereby giving the appearance of being one)?

It seems as if following Nāgārjuna's argument we could just as well establish that there is no counterfeit money—since if we examine a suspicious banknote and find it to be genuine, it is obviously not counterfeit. Other objects, such as a piece of newspaper, for example, are equally obviously not money, and also not counterfeit money. Yet something has gone wrong here. What about pieces of paper that share some properties with a five-pound note (such as its size, color, or design) but lack a key property (being issued by the Bank of England)? Why can't we regard these as counterfeit banknotes?

It is instructive to compare the discussion of the example in verses 28–31 where Nāgārjuna argues in a similar way. Taking into account the discussion of verse 30 in particular, we should note that if *some* similarity with a real reason is sufficient for something being a pseudo-reason, there are going to be a lot of pseudo-reasons around, since arguably everything shares some properties with everything else. Is "baa-baa black sheep" a pseudo-reason? It certainly shares numerous properties with a real reason, such as "because of smoke"—it is formulated in English, consists of three expressions, begins with the letter "b," and so on. Yet once we go down that route, it is hard to conceive of anything that is *not* a pseudo-reason. In the same way, if *any* similarity with a five-pound note is sufficient to turn something into fake money, lottery tickets, stamps, postcards, and so on, could all be regarded as counterfeit money.

If we assume with the Naiyāyika (as Vātsyāyana's comment on NS 1.2.4 indicates), that there is some intrinsic characteristic, some *lakṣaṇa,* involved, it is apparent that any *x* that shares this characteristic is not a pseudo-*x*, but a genuine *x*. But locating the pseudo-*x*s among the countless things that do not share the characteristic is exceedingly difficult. Not everything that is not issued by the Bank of England is to be regarded as counterfeit money. It seems to be impossible to come up with any objectively determined, definite set of properties an object must have in order to be a pseudo-reason, or to be counterfeit money. Some non-reason may be accepted as a reason in one context, but not in another one; some object might be mistaken for or falsely claimed to be money in one situation, but not in another one. Nothing is a pseudo-reason or a false banknote just by itself, but only becomes so in the right kind of context.

So it does not seem to be the case that Nāgārjuna wants to rule out the existence of pseudo-reasons *tout court*, but that his argument is meant to show that if we assume an intrinsic characteristic of reasons, a *hetu-lakṣaṇa*, we cannot make sufficient sense of the idea of a pseudo-reason. The set of objects lacking this characteristic is just too diverse for all of them to count as pseudo-reasons, while at the same time there appears to be no stable set of properties something must have in order to be a pseudo-reason. All of this does not rule out the possibility of coming up with some alternative, Madhyamaka-compatible understanding of pseudo-reasons (and counterfeit currencies), but aims at showing the difficulties with the preferred Naiyāyika route.

> *Because an independent thing (rang gi rgyud, svatantra) is transformed, it is not destroyed because of the difference of its constituents (khyad par khams mi mnyam pa, dhātu-vaiṣamyatā), or, since the constituents are the same (khams mnyam pa, samadhātu), the thought of that is the cognition itself.*[488]

This passage is particularly difficult to understand. The modern secondary literature provides us with two very different ways of understanding it. Tola and Dragonetti render it as follows:

> As for (the hypothesis of) the transformation of a self-dependent (entity), (this one) cannot be destroyed through peculiarities unequal to its basis; or the representation of that (self-dependent

488. *rang gi rgyud yongs su 'gyur ba'i phyir khyad par khams mi mnyam pa nyid las mi nyams pa'am | khams mnyam pa las de'i blo ni shes pa nyid yin pa ltar.*

> entity), produced out of (peculiarities) equal to its basis, is indeed the cognition of it.[489]

The idea here seems to be the following: In the preceding passage of the commentary, Nāgārjuna has argued that neither something similar to the reason nor something dissimilar could be a pseudo-reason. Now he introduces a third possibility. Could some reason that existed intrinsically (*rang gi rgyud*) as a reason, which had been a reason as part of its intrinsic nature, be transformed (*yongs su 'gyur ba*) into a pseudo-reason—into a reason that was not really a reason but only appeared to be one? Nāgārjuna gives two reasons why this cannot happen:

1. The product of this transformation, the pseudo-reason would be characterized by peculiarities (*khyad pa*) or properties that are dissimilar (*mi mnyams pa*) to those that are instantiated by the basis (*khams*) or bearer of properties in the case of the untransformed, genuine reason. In fact, the properties of the transformed are not just dissimilar to those of the original, they would be directly contradictory. The original has the property of being capable of acting as a reason in an argument (that is what makes it a real reason), while the transformed has the property of being unable to do so (that is what makes it a pseudo-reason). But if it is part of the nature of the real reason to act with probative force in an argument, then this is a property it cannot lose. If we take this property away, we have not transformed it into something else, but have destroyed (*nyams pa*) the real reason and replaced it with a non-reason. For example, in the inference "there is fire on the mountain, because of smoke," "because of smoke" constitutes a real reason. If we transform this inference into "there is fire on the mountain, because the mountain can be perceived," we have something that due to its position in the inference still *appears* like a reason, but is as a matter of fact no reason. We are dealing here with a particular kind of pseudo-reason called *sādhāraṇa* in which the reason is too comprehensive to prove the point to be established: mountains with and without fire on them can be perceived, but only mountains with smoke on them also have fire on them.

2. Alternatively, suppose that the transformation did not actually replace any of the properties of the original with dissimilar ones but just added

489. Tola and Dragonetti 1995a, 86.

properties similar to the one instantiated in the basis or bearer of properties, or the real, untransformed reason (*khams nyam pa*)? If "similar" can here be taken to mean "not changing the object's nature," then it is clear that any representation (*blo*) of this "transformation" is just the cognition of the real reason itself (*shes pa nyid*), at least if we assume that the cognition makes the object's nature known. But if this is the case, we certainly haven't transformed a real reason into a pseudo-reason. The transformed may have some additional, "similar" properties over and above those of the original, but it is still a real reason, not a pseudo-reason, since its nature remains unaffected. An example of this would be the transformation of the inference "there is fire on the mountain, because of smoke and the smell of burning wood." Here the reason contains an additional property (which, as a matter of fact is also caused by the fire). But if the original reason proved the presence of fire, so will the transformed one. Because of this, we still have a real reason, not a pseudo-reason.

Because of these two reasons, Nāgārjuna concludes that it is not possible to transform a reason into a pseudo-reason.

Pind, on the other hand, offers a completely different reading of the passage. He translates it as:

> For (**hi*) the perception (**buddhi*) of the particular transformation of one's own mental series (**svasantānapariṇāmaviśeṣa*), which is not impaired (**anupahala*) because of the disequilibrium of the elements (**dhātuvaisaṁya*) or because of their equilibrium (**dhātusamya*), is like a cognition.[490]

This translation is based on the assumption that the Tibetan *rang gi rgyud yongs su 'gyur ba'i phyir khyad par* is "incomprehensible," that the word *phyir* should be deleted, and that the correct reading is *rang gi rgyud yongs su 'gyur ba'i khyad par*. This would allow us to understand the phrase as a direct translation of the Sanskrit term *svasantānapariṇāmaviśeṣa* = "a special transformation of one's own mental series."[491]

490. Pind 2001, 168.

491. *rang gi rgyud* can translate both the Sanskrit *svasantāna* and *svatantra*. See Negi 2005, s.v.

The expression *santānapariṇāmaviśeṣa* is characteristically employed by the Sautrāntikas but can also be found (with a somewhat wider meaning) in Yogāchāra texts.[492] It occurs in the explanation of the karmic consequences of deeds. The idea is that a particular action carried out by an agent and his associated mental stream leaves a certain trace in this stream. As this stream of mental moments develops, that is, as present mental moments (*kṣaṇa*) pass out of existence and are replaced by new ones, a "special transformation" (*pariṇāmaviśeṣa*) changes the trace caused by the action into the experience of the result. The mental moment containing the trace causes an immediately succeeding moment, which in turn causes another moment, until there is finally the mental moment that constitutes the experience of the result of the action.[493]

Unfortunately, it is not very clear how this passage, now understood as referring to the transformation of the mental continuum, is supposed to fit into the context of an argument concerned with pseudo-reasons, and Pind himself admits as much.[494] He nevertheless seems to think that whatever argument is expressed here is fallacious, as he refers to the passage as an "amusing piece of sophistry."[495] He explains:

> [T]he underlying intention seems to be that it is impossible to distinguish between a so-called semblance of a thing (*ābhāsa*) and something real: the perception is just cognition because, no matter how the state of the *svasantānapariṇāmaviśeṣa* is, it can only reproduce what its state at any given time permits.... This would exclude the possibility of determining whether or not something is a semblance of something else.... The author evidently wants to stress the fact that in the final analysis it is the dynamics of the mental series that account for the nature of perception.[496]

492. Schmithausen 1967, 114. See also *Abhidharmakośabhāṣya* 2.36.

493. Schmithausen 1967, 115.

494. Pind 2001, 168: "[I]t is difficult to interpret and contextualize the argument with absolute certainty."

495. Pind 2001, 168.

496. Pind 2001, 169.

Pind's idea seems to be that we would not be able to tell whether we see a real orange (caused by an orange in front of us) or a mere pseudo-orange, an only appearing orange, the appearance of which is caused by the internal dynamics of our mental stream.[497] If this is the case, then what holds for oranges holds for all other kinds of things, and we could also not tell the difference between a real reason and a pseudo-reason. But since the very distinction presupposes (we might argue) that we are able to draw a line between them, at least in some cases, the inability to do so *tout court* makes the notion of a pseudo-reason inconsistent. For this reason, one may conclude, there are no pseudo-reasons.

Which of these two interpretations—that of Tola and Dragonetti, which reads the passage as referring to the transformation of the reason, or that of Pind, which reads it as referring to a transformation of the mental continuum—is preferable?

One advantange of the former is that taking the argument to be about the transformation of the reason lets the development of thought in the commentary on VP 58 appear more coherent, since the text can then be understood as only concerned with the relation between reason and pseudo-reason, without bringing in considerations about the mental continuum, karmic causes and effect, and appearance and reality in general. We might also be tempted to think that, if Nāgārjuna here wants to raise the rather far-reaching idea of the general impossibility of distinguishing a real object from a mere appearance, he would have done so in greater detail and perhaps in a more prominent place.

Secondly, following the Tola/Dragonetti interpretation means we do not have to change the text by regarding the *phyir* as an erroneous addition. We do of course agree with Pind that the phrase *rang gi rgyud yongs su 'gyur ba'i phyir khyad par* is "incomprehensible," but not that it is "evidently incomprehensible in any context,"[498] simply because the Tola/Dragonetti interpretation does not read *rang gi rgyud yongs su 'gyur ba'i phyir khyad par* as one phrase, but rather treats *rang gi rgyud yongs su 'gyur ba'i phyir* as

497. If that is the point being made here, it appears to be much more in line with the Yogāchāra understanding of the term *svasantānapariṇāmaviśeṣa* than with the Sautrāntika understanding, which still regards an external object as the cause of perception (see Schmithausen 1967, 114n20). Pind (2001, 169), however, insists that it must be the Sautrāntika notion that is referred to here.

498. Pind 2001, 169.

containing the reason for *khyad par khams mi mnyam pa nyid las mi nyams pa*.

It might also be useful at this point to add some remarks on Pind's claim that the passage presently discussed establishes the "inevitable" conclusion that the VP "cannot under any circumstances be attributed to Nāgārjuna."[499] This is so, Pind claims, because on his reading the passage contains a reference to the (Sautrāntika) notion of a particular transformation of one's own continuum (*svasantānapariṇāmaviśeṣa*), while Nāgārjuna rejected the (Sautrāntika) notion of a mental continuum[500] in MMK 17:21.[501]

In response, one might point out that, given that the assumption of the Sautrāntika or Yogāchāra notion supposedly referred to here does not fit in with the argument as well and requires an emendation of the text, it would be preferable to conclude that perhaps such a notion is not talked about, thereby avoiding the necessity to account for perceived conflicts with Nāgārjuna's doctrinal commitments.

But even if we hold on to the view that the Tibetan reading is erroneous, contains "a meaningless textual emendation,"[502] and that "a particular transformation of one's own continuum" (*svasantānapariṇāmaviśeṣa*) is referred to here, it is still not clear that this provides "conclusive evidence for rejecting Nāgārjuna's authorship."[503] If we consider the development of the argument in chapter 17 of the MMK, it becomes apparent that Nāgārjuna criticizes a variety of Buddhist theories of how karma works, such as the Sautrāntika view of the transformation of the mental continuum, because they presuppose that there is a mechanism underlying the working of karma at the absolute level.[504] Causes that have passed out of existence, Nāgārjuna argues, are not substantially nonexistent, because they were never substantially existent in the first place. There is, therefore, no worry for the Mādhyamika about how to provide a theory accounting for the ability of a now past, substantially nonexistent cause to bring about a karmic effect.

499. Pind 2001, 170.

500. *cittasantāna*, mentioned in MMK 17:9.

501. Pind 2001, 169.

502. Pind 2001, 152.

503. Pind 2001, 152.

504. Compare Chandrakīrti's rejection of the Yogāchāra notion of a foundational consciousness to explain karma in MĀ 6:39.

But this does not show that Nāgārjuna could not use the notion of a mental continuum in the context of rejecting the Nyāya notion of a pseudo-reason. There is no difficulty with assuming the Sautrāntika analysis of karma in terms of the transformation of a mental continuum at the conventional level, while denying that it expresses a truth at the ultimate level.[505] And, as we argued earlier, it is plausible to assume that the intention of Nāgārjuna's argument here is to reject the validity of the sixteen Nyāya categories at the level of *conventional* truth. It is clear that they cannot exist at the level of ultimate truth, because for the Mādhyamika nothing exists at that level. So, arguing that the notion of a pseudo-reason would be incompatible with the idea of the transformation of the mental continuum would not show that no "Mādhyamika in the original sense of that word"[506] could have written the VP, but is entirely consistent with the fact that Nāgārjuna is here adopting a view of some of his fellow Buddhists as conventionally true in order to reject the Naiyākika notion of a pseudo-reason.

On the whole I believe therefore that the translation by Tola and Dragonetti provides a better reading of the passage, even though I would translate it slightly differently. The point Nāgārjuna makes in this passage seems to be the following: After having argued that a piece of gold is no pseudo-gold, and that a lump of dirt is no pseudo-gold either, he considers the idea that an independently existent substance could be transformed into a pseudo-substance. Yet there are some difficulties with this idea. Once the substance (say, a piece of gold) has been transformed, it presumably differs from the original gold in having different constituents, or in displaying different properties. However, the original piece of gold is still there and has not been destroyed, precisely because we are talking about the transformation of an independent (*svatantra*) thing, and such a thing does not depend on its constituents or properties for being what it is. But this also means that we still have not succeeded in producing a piece of pseudo-gold. On the other hand, if the newly transformed gold does not differ from the original piece regarding its constituents or properties, when we think of this supposed pseudo-gold, we are in fact just referring to the

505. There might be a problem here for the Prāsaṅgika-Mādhyamika, since he would not even accept the postulation of any substantial entities at the conventional level.

506. Pind 2001, 169.

original gold, which is identical with it in all respects. So the notion of a transformation (*yongs su 'gyur ba, pariṇata*) is not able to provide us with a sensible notion of a pseudo-substance either.

If it is fully investigated, a "pseudo-reason" does not exist at all. Since there is no reason and another, third thing other than a reason is not plausible, therefore a pseudo-reason does not exist.

Nāgārjuna here comes back to the opponent's criticism that denying the category of reasons, he has to accept that of pseudo-reasons, since if there are no real reasons, there must at least be apparent reasons. However, Nāgārjuna points out, the two require each other. Without substantially existing reasons, there can be no pseudo-reasons that have some of their properties but lack their essential characteristics. There is no reason (nor any other, third kind of object) such that a pseudo-reason could be understood in contrast to it. The Naiyāyika understanding of pseudo-reasons therefore has to be rejected.

Moreover,

VP 59 **The non-deviating is so because of the absence of deviation.**

If you ask where the non-deviating comes from, whether it is non-deviating by its own self, or whether it becomes not deviating—if it does not become deviating regarding its own self, it does not have the property of deviating. Why is that? Because its own intrinsic nature has not been rejected. Because it exists precisely by that own nature, it will not have the property of deviating.

Well then, the intrinsic nature being rejected, in this way it will also not have the property of deviating. Because of the intrinsic nature having been rejected, that very thing does not exist. Any other position is unreasonable, so that is how it is explained here.

Reason, which has the intrinsic nature of an establisher of what is to be established, is not deviating because of its own nature. That which does not have the intrinsic nature of an establisher of what is to be established does not have the property of deviating, precisely because it is not a reason. There is no third alternative. ⌘ ⌘

VP 59 The nondeviating (ma 'khrul ba, avyabhicārin) is so because of the absence of deviation.

Nāgārjuna now considers the first of the five kinds of pseudo-reason, deviation (*savyabhicāra*).[507] It is so-called because its inferential mark deviates from a unique connection with objects that have the property to be proven, and is also connected with objects that lack this property.[508] In his commentary, Vātsyāyana gives the following example of such a deviating pseudo-reason. Consider the following syllogism:

> Sound is eternal because it is not touchable, like the self, unlike the pot.

While there are concomitant examples (*sādharmya*) like the self, which manifest both the *probandum* (*sādhya*) of eternality, as well as the mark (*liṅga*) of not being touchable, as well as nonconcomitant examples (*vaidharmya*) that lack both (such as an impermanent and touchable pot), there are, unfortunately, also examples of eternal things that are touchable (such as atoms [*aṇu*], according to the Vaisheṣhika system), and noneternal things that are also not touchable.

Since not being touchable is connected with both the eternal and the noneternal, it cannot act as a *probans* in the above inference. Even though "because it is not touchable" looks like a reason (*hetu*), it is in fact only a pseudo-reason (*hetvābhāsa*).

In this *sūtra* Nāgārjuna points out that the justification for a real reason being real and not a pseudo-reason is its lack of the deficiency of deviation.

507. See NS 1.2.5 for a discussion.

508. Its alternative name, *anaikāntika*, literally "not (just) having one end," points at the same property. The object with the property to be proven (*sapakṣa*) and the object lacking this property (*vipakṣa*) are called the two ends (*anta*). In this case of pseudo-reason, the inferential mark is irregularly connected with both "ends," not just with one. See Chattopadhyaya and Gangopadhyaya 1967–76, vol. 1, 140.

> *If you ask where the non-deviating comes from, whether it is nondeviating by its own self, or whether it becomes not deviating*[509]*—if it does not become deviating regarding its own self it does not have the property of deviating. Why is that? Because its own intrinsic nature (bdag nyid rang gi ngo bo) has not been rejected. Because it exists precisely by that own nature it will not have the property of deviating.*

The question investigated here is why a real reason that lacks the deficiency of deviation is the way it is. Is the reason nondeviating due to its intrinsic nature or has it become nondeviating despite its nature, i.e., does it only appear to be a real reason while actually being a pseudo-reason? Nāgārjuna points out that, for something to be a deviating pseudo-reason (*savyabhicāra*), it has to have this property by its intrinsic nature. Anything that is still a real reason by its intrinsic nature is just that, a real reason, and not just a pseudo-reason.

> *Well then, the intrinsic nature being rejected, in this way it will also not have the property of deviating. Because of the intrinsic nature having been rejected, that very thing does not exist. It is not reasonable in another way, so it has been taught.*

Yet, even if we assume that the supposed pseudo-reason lacks the intrinsic nature of a reason, this does not really help. For if the Naiyāyika assumes that everything is what it is by its intrinsic nature, whatever lacks intrinsic nature does not even exist. It is therefore not able to function as a pseudo-reason either.

509. The Tibetan here reads *ma 'khrul ba nyid gang las zhe na | rang gi bdag nyid la 'khrul pa dang bcas pa yin par 'gyur ram ma 'khrul bar 'gyur grang*, which translates as "If you ask where the nondeviating comes from, whether it has the property of deviating regarding its own self, or whether it becomes not deviating." I have changed the *la* in this passage to a *ma*, thereby arriving at the translation given here. The reason for this is that it first of all allows a much more straightforward reading of the passage (compare the rather complex rendering in Tola and Dragonetti 1995a, 87; according to them, Nāgārjuna must be understood as distinguishing two alternatives, of which the second is discussed first, and the first in the following verse [142]); and secondly, misreading *ma* for *la* is not very unlikely given the similarity of the two letters in Tibetan writing, in particular when written in *dbu med* script.

Reason (gtan tshigs, hetu), which has the intrinsic nature (svabhāva, rang bzhin) of an establisher (sādhya, bsgrub bya) of what is to be established (sādhana, sgrub par byed pa), is not deviating because of that own nature (bdag nyid). That which does not have the intrinsic nature of an establisher of what is to be established does not have the property of deviating, precisely because it is not a reason. There is no third alternative.

Nāgārjuna sums up his argument with a dilemma. Either a *savyabhicāra* (and a pseudo-reason in general) is a reason by its intrinsic nature or it is not. If it is, it is a real reason, and therefore no pseudo-reason. But if it lacks the intrinsic feature of a reason, it cannot be a deviating pseudo-reason either, since the entire idea of deviation only makes sense if we presuppose the key qualities of a reason the deviation is a deviation from. These very qualities are of course missing, because it is not a reason (*gtan tshigs ma yin pa*). These qualities may of course be present elsewhere, but that only shows that what makes something a deviating pseudo-reason involves other things and therefore cannot be an intrinsic property. *Ersatz* coffee cannot have the property of being *ersatz* coffee intrinsically, since this property essentially depends on the existence of another one, that of real coffee, which we might expect to find in *ersatz* coffee but do not. But this of course means that *ersatz* coffee cannot have this property in and by itself; it depends on the conceptualizing mind making a link to another property. Therefore, Nāgārjuna concludes, there is a fundamental problem with construing the property of being of a pseudo-reason as anything other than a mind-dependent one.

Objection:

VP 60 **A deviating reason exists.**

It is like this: Space and action indeed do not have a body. For atoms and pots, etc., generality and particularity are similar.

VP 60 A deviating reason (savyabhicāra hetu) exists.

In the discussion of VP 59, Nāgārjuna argued against the existence of deviating reasons. The opponent responds by giving an example of this supposedly problematic category.

It is like this: Space (nam mkha', ākāśa) and action (las, karma) indeed do not have a body. For atoms and pots, etc., generality (spyi, sāmānya) and particularity (khyad par, viśeṣa) are similar.

If we consider the argument "Space is eternal because of bodilessness," it becomes apparent that it is deficient because the inferential mark, "bodilessness," applies both to space (which is eternal) as well as to action (which is not). There is therefore at least one example of a deviating reason where the inferential mark deviates from a unique connection with objects that have the property to be proven (eternality), as is also instantiated by objects that lack this property.

The same holds for the argument "Atoms are eternal because generality and particularity apply to them." The reason "because generality and particularity apply to them" is deficient, since it holds for atoms,[510] which are eternal, but also for pots, which are not. Atoms can be grouped together under generalities, and at the same time differentiated from each other.[511] Yet this is not sufficient as a reason for their eternality, as the same is also true of medium-sized objects such as pots.

510. According to *Vaiśeṣikasūtra* 1.1.8 (*sadānityaṁ dravyavat kāryaṁ kāraṇaṁ sāmānya-viśeṣavaditi dravyaguṇakarmaṇāmaviśeṣaḥ*) and 1.2.5 (*dravyatvaṁ guṇatvaṁ karmatvaṁ ca sāmāyāni viśeṣāśca*), particularities (*viśeṣa*) seem to apply both to atoms and pots, since both are *dravya*. However, Halbfass (1992, 73) notes that *viśeṣa* "reside exclusively in the eternal, non-composite substances, that is, in the individual atoms, souls, and mental organs, and in the unitary substances ether, space, and time." Particularity would thus apply to atoms, but not to pots. Yet how precisely the specific passages in the *Vaiśeṣikasūtra* are to be interpreted is by no means straightforward; Halbfass (1992, 270) himself admits that "the entire complex of *sāṁānya* and *viśeṣa*, as presented by the Sūtra text, left room for variations." For interpretations that accept that particularities can apply to medium-sized objects such as pots, see Bahadur 1979, 36–37; Halbfass 1992, 269–70.

511. "[E]ach atom possesses an ultimate differentiating characteristic called particularity (*viśeṣa*) by means of which it is distinguished from all other atoms. That all atoms are judged as distinct individuals is because each of them has its own particularity." (Bhaduri 1947, 144).

The opponent therefore concludes that there must be something problematic with Nāgārjuna's refutation of the class of deviating reasons, since there are clear examples of members of this class.

VP 61 **If you say this—this is not the case, because of being different from those.**

That does not exist. Why? Because it is indeed different from those. It is not reasonable that the bodilessness of space exists in action and knowledge, since arising and non-arising are contradictory. In this case the bodilessness of action and knowledge, etc., has the property of arising, while that of space precisely has not.

That which is the bodilessness of space does not exist in action, because action has the property of arising—since, if it arises together with bodilessness there is arising, and if it ceases there is cessation. Therefore space and bodilessness are distinct.[512]

It is not reasonable that the bodilessness of space is in action, knowledge, etc. The bodilessness of action does not exist in space.

That which is the establisher, which for some reason exists for establishing and refuting, is not deviating precisely as an establisher. The same should also be said about the refutation. Therefore, there is no deviating reason. Even if it is in fact contradictory, it is not deviating. Therefore, the bodilessness of space is not deviating in establishing eternality. Action, etc., are similar.

VP 61 If you say this—this is not the case, because of being different from those.

512. *nam kha' dang lus can ma yin pa gzhan nyid yin no*. Kajiyama (1974, 398n81) suggests that the Tibetan here should read *nam mkha'i lus can ma yin pa nyid dang las blo la sogs pa'i lus can ma yin pa nyid gzhan nyid yin no*, "The bodilessness of space and the bodilessness of knowledge and action are indeed different from each other."

Nāgārjuna responds by arguing that the alleged examples of pseudo-reasons the opponent has suggested are in fact no pseudo-reasons, since the inferential marks in one set of inferences are different from those in another set.

> *That does not exist. Why? Because it is indeed different from those. It is not reasonable that the bodilessness of space exists in action and knowledge, since arising and non-arising are contradictory. In this case, the bodilessness of action and knowledge, etc., has the property of arising, while that of space precisely has not.*

> *That which is the bodilessness of space does not exist in action, because action has the property of arising—since, if it arises together with bodilessness there is arising, and if it ceases there is cessation. Therefore, space and bodilessness are distinct.*

Nāgārjuna argues that the two inferences—"space is eternal because of bodilessness" and "knowledge is eternal because of bodilessness"—do not share an inferential mark. This is because the specific bodilessness of space differs from that of knowledge. Knowledge is an entity that arises and ceases, and with it, its properties (such as bodilessness) arise and cease as well. Space, on the other hand, does not arise, and so its bodilessness cannot arise either; it has to exist in the same unarisen manner as space. But since arising and non-arising are contradictory properties, nothing can have both properties, and therefore the bodilessness of space cannot be the same thing as the bodilessness of knowledge.

Because of this, there cannot be one reason that proves eternality in the case of space, but not in the case of knowledge; rather, there are two bodilessnesses. The example of bodilessness therefore does not constitute a case of a deviating reason, where a single inferential mark deviates from a unique connection with objects that have the property to be proven, and is also instantiated by objects that lack this property, simply because we are dealing with two inferential marks in this case, not with one. Once we have differentiated the inferential marks in this way, we realize that the inferences should actually be "space is eternal because of non-arising bodilessness" and "knowledge is eternal because of arising bodilessness." One reason is successful in establishing what is to be proven; the other is not, but there is no deviation anymore.

> *It is not reasonable that the bodilessness of space is in action, knowledge, etc. The bodilessness of action does not exist in space.*

The same applies to the bodilessness of other phenomena, such as action. Just because it is called "bodilessness," we cannot assume that we are referring to the same entity in the case of actions, or knowledge, and space, just as the fact that all my shirts have the property of being colored does not imply that there is a color they all share.

> *That which is the establisher, which for some reason exists for establishing and refuting, is not deviating precisely as an establisher. The same should also be said about the refutation. Therefore, there is no deviating reason.*

The function of this passage is not entirely clear. Nāgārjuna appears to be referring here to a higher-order establishment or refutation, something that establishes (or refutes) that there is some reason for establishing or refuting something else. We can, for example, establish an argument, giving a reason for why the reason "because of smoke" can establish the existence of fire. Nāgārjuna points out that this higher-order establisher is itself not deviating "precisely as an establisher" (*sgrub par byed pa nyid du mi 'khrul*). To stay with the example, the inferential mark used in the reason given for "because of smoke," being able to act as a reason, cannot in turn function as an inferential mark to establish that some non-reason is in fact a reason. This is presumably the case because (as in the case of bodilessness) the inferential mark could be "split," giving one mark that successfully establishes that "because of smoke" is a reason, and another that unsuccessfully establishes that the non-reason in question is a reason.

> *Even if it is in fact contradictory, it is not deviating.*[513]

513. This sentence (*'gal ba nyid yin gyi 'khrul pa dang bcas pa ni ma yin no*) looks very similar to VP 63 (*khyod kyi gtan tshigs thams cad 'gal bar brjod pa yin gyi 'khrul pa dang bcas pa ni ma yin no*). Yet it would be difficult to understand them as saying the same thing, given that Nāgārjuna is speaking here, while the opponent is speaking in VP 63.

Consider another kind of pseudo-reason, the contradictory reason (*viruddha*). An example of an inference employing such a contradictory reason is "Sound is eternal, because it is produced." This inference is contradictory, since the inferential mark (being produced) is only connected with impermanent things, so that the reason proves the opposite of the position to be established.

Now one might think that in the case of a contradictory reason, we have a case of a deviating reason, since the inferential mark deviates from connection with the property to be established (eternality in this case) and is instead connected with its opposite (impermanence). This, however, is not sufficient to make it an example of a deviating reason, since in the case of deviating reasons, the inferential mark deviates from a *unique* connection with the property to be proven by also being connected with objects that lack this property. In the case of the contradictory reason, on the other hand, there is *no* connection with the property to be established (in the case of the above example, there is nothing that is both eternal and produced). The category of deviating reasons therefore cannot be understood as being entailed by the category of contradictory reasons.[514]

Therefore, the bodilessness of space is not deviating in establishing eternality. Action, etc., are similar.

Given the fact that we are able to differentiate two different kinds of bodilessness (and would equally have to assume that generality and particularity apply to atoms in one way and to pots in another way), the opponent's examples are not successful in establishing a case of a deviating reason. Nāgārjuna's criticism of this particular form of pseudo-reason from VP 59 therefore still stands.

514. Tola and Dragonetti (1995, 144) read Nāgārjuna here simply as saying that a contradictory reason (*viruddha*) would not be deviating, since contradictory reasons and deviating reasons are two different kinds of pseudo-reasons. This interpretation is not entirely satisfactory, however, since it does not explain why someone should think that a contradictory reason was a deviating reason in the first place.

⁂ Moreover,

VP 62 **Also because of momentariness.**

If, for the thing that is established or refuted, destruction exists, it is not reasonable that it is established or refuted. If both are present, the reason establishes or refutes, but if that is destroyed, it is not reasonable that the reason establishes or refutes. Because both are not present, the deviating reason does not exist. ⁂ ⁂

VP 62 Also because of momentariness.

Nāgārjuna now considers a more general argument against pseudo-reasons, based on the idea of the merely momentary existence of all things (*skad gcig ma nyid, kṣaṇikatva*).

> *If, for the thing that is established or refuted, destruction ('jig pa) exists, it is not reasonable that it is established or refuted. If both are present, the reason establishes or refutes, but if that is destroyed, it is not reasonable that the reason establishes or refutes. Because both are not present, the deviating reason does not exist.*

This is one of several passages in Nāgārjuna's works where he considers the consequences of the idea of momentariness (together with suffering and lack of self, one of the three characteristics of existence according to Buddhist thought) on the process of argumentation.[515] In the present context, Nāgārjuna remarks that if there is some thesis we want to establish or prove, or that we want to refute, neither establishment nor refutation make much sense if once the reason is brought forward, the thesis does not exist anymore.

If we consider the standard Indian example of a syllogism, "there is fire on the hill because of smoke," the thesis to be established is uttered before the reason is pronounced. If we assume that all entities only have momentary existence, the thesis will have passed out of existence once the reason

515. See VV 20, 69, VP 39, 48, 49.

has arrived on the scene, so that there is nothing left for the reason to prove. The relationship of establishment or refutation presupposes that both relata—the thesis established or refuted, and the reason for its establishment or refutation—exist at the same time. But since they are successive entities, with the debater first pronouncing his thesis and then specifying his reason, the assumption of momentariness entails that they cannot exist together.

It is apparent that this argument is not specifically directed against pseudo-reasons, but is of a very general nature, and is applied to this particular case.[516] If there is no possibility of a reason to coexist with a thesis, and therefore no possibility of a reason *being* a reason (since a reason is only a reason in relationship to the thesis it is supposed to establish, and not by itself) there is also no way anything could be a pseudo-reason, a notion that is wholly parasitic on the concept of a real reason.

It is worthwhile to pause at this point to consider the overall aim of Nāgārjuna's rejection of pseudo-reasons in verses 58–62. He points out that his Naiyāyika opponent's assumptions, which carry with them the implications of entities existing by *svabhāva*, lead to problems, once the notion of a pseudo-reason is considered. If we assumed (against Nāgārjuna's arguments concerning the members of a syllogism in verses 33–49) that a reason (*hetu*) existed intrinsically, specified by a characteristic flowing from its own nature, we could not just describe the pseudo-reason as any object that lacked that characteristic, since this would make the set of pseudo-reasons far too broad. Yet if we assumed that pseudo-reasons had their own intrinsic nature, all the difficulties against objects existing by *svabhāva* that Nāgārjuna has already outlined would arise again. Assuming that both reasons and pseudo-reasons exist by *svabhāva* would be necessary in order to argue that both are intrinsically distinct. Taking into account the problems the idea of *svabhāva* entails, we are therefore better off understanding pseudo-reasons relative to the interests and concerns of participants in a debate. Something is not a merely apparent reason in itself but becomes so in dependence upon the expectations and assumptions about what a reason is, a notion that does not exist intrinsically either. The Mādhyamika faces no difficulties in distinguishing pseudo-reasons

516. In fact, this verse can be understood as building on the point Nāgārjuna already made in VP 48.

from real reasons, as long as both are understood in a suitably de-substantialized manner.

⌘ Objection:

VP 63 **Even though for you reason is said to be wholly contradictory, it is not deviating.**

Only what has many ends is deviating. What is an establisher is not deviating with respect to being an establisher. The same should also be said about refutation. Therefore, "because there is no deviating reason" leads to a contradiction. ⌘ ⌘

VP 63 Even though for you reason is said to be wholly contradictory (thams cad 'gal bar, sarvaviruddha), it is not deviating.

This verse connects the discussion of the first kind of pseudo-reasons, deviating reasons (*savyabhicāra*), with that of the second kind (*viruddha*).

The opponent points out that Nāgārjuna will not admit the existence of deviating reasons, though this leads to a contradiction in relation to the category of reason (*hetu*).

Only what has many ends (ma nges pa, anaikāntika) is deviating. What is an establisher is not deviating with respect to being an establisher. The same should also be said about refutation. Therefore, "because there is no deviating reason" leads to a contradiction.

According to the Naiyāyika, there are deviating reasons (*savyabhicāra*), and these are precisely those characterized as "having many ends" (*anaikāntika*).[517] But according to Nāgārjuna's arguments presented in the preceding four verses, anything that actually functions as an establisher or as a refutation (i.e., as a reason) cannot be deviating, because it would then not be able to function in this very way. And as Nāgārjuna argued in his

517. NS 1.2.5. See note 508 above (p. 236).

comments on VP 58 and 59, something that is not able to function in this way cannot be regarded as a pseudo-reason in the Nyāya framework either. This of course leads to a contradiction between the Naiyāyika's and the Mādhyamika's views. For this reason, the opponent argues, Nāgārjuna at least has to accept the existence of the second kind of pseudo-reasons, contradictory reasons (*viruddha*). This argumentative move is frequently employed by the opponent in the VP. When Nāgārjuna sets out to reject a specific Nyāya category, the opponent points out that in the very process of arguing, Nāgārjuna has to employ (and therefore accept the existence of) that very category.[518]

It should be replied:

VP 64 **Because of arising earlier and later, there is no contradiction.**

There is nothing said to be contradictory. First of all, there is no contradiction for the earlier one, because the later one does not exist. There is also no contradiction for what is said later, because the earlier reason does not exist. It is contradictory that the two exist at the same time; there is no occasion for the proponent and opponent giving their replies and counter-replies just at the same time. Because they do not exist together, there is no contradiction.

VP 64 Because of arising earlier and later, there is no contradiction.

After the opponent has attempted to show in the previous verse that Nāgārjuna is committed to the existence of the second kind of pseudo-reasons, contradictory reasons (*viruddha*), Nāgārjuna now sets out to refute the existence of such contradictory reasons. The NS understands contradictory reasons as those that contradict the position one oneself accepts.[519] Yet the notion of a contradictory reason at issue here must be more comprehensive than that, covering not only a debater's self-contradictions but

518. See, e.g., VP 68–70.

519. NS 1.2.6: *siddhāntam abhyupetya tadvirodhī viruddhaḥ.*

also contradictions between two debaters. This is evident from the way the opponent argued for the existence of contradictory reasons in the previous verse. He claimed that because the Naiyāyika and the Mādhyamika hold contradictory opinions on the existence of deviating reason, this entails the existence of the category of *viruddha*. The sense of *viruddha* here therefore must be broader than mere self-contradictions, since the opponent has not accused anyone of self-contradiction in this context.

As we will see in a moment, Nāgārjuna's argument is in fact sufficiently general to apply to *any* type of contradiction, not only those arising in the context of a debate. This might strike us as peculiar, given that there is good evidence otherwise that Nāgārjuna (and his Madhyamaka successors) did accept the law of noncontradiction.[520] How can Nāgārjuna on the one hand rule out entities because they have mutually contradictory properties (*parasparaviruddham*),[521] yet also argue that there are no contradictions? Let us have a look at the details of the argument.

> *There is nothing said to be contradictory. First of all, there is no contradiction for the earlier one, because the later one does not exist.*

In the context of a debate, both contestants take turns to state their positions. When one proposition of a contradictory pair has been stated, there is no contradiction yet, because the opponent did not yet have the opportunity to raise his contradictory position.

> *There is also no contradiction for what is said later, because the earlier reason does not exist.*

At this stage of the argument an appeal to the principle of momentariness is necessary. If we accept this, even after the second contestant has stated his position, there is no contradiction, since the first position, a momentary entity like all things, has already passed out of existence. At

520. See, e.g., MMK 7:30 and 8:7; as well as Ruegg 1969, 384; Westerhoff 2009, 80–81.
521. MMK 8:7.

that moment, just the second member of a contradictory pair exists, and so there is no contradiction either.[522]

> *It is contradictory that the two exist at the same time; there is no occasion for the proponent (vādin) and opponent (prativādin) giving their replies and counter-replies just at the same time. Because they do not exist together, there is no contradiction.*

The only way for both members of the contradictory pair to be simultaneously present (and hence existent) is for both contestants to speak at the same time. Yet in this case there is just a cacophony of overlapping sounds, and without the possibility of discerning any meaning in some utterance, there cannot be a contradiction.

So how are we to understand Nāgārjuna's rejection of contradictions, and the simultaneous appeal to contradictions in his arguments elsewhere? The key point to keep in mind is that Nāgārjuna does not have any qualms about employing the notion of a contradiction at the transactional or relative level.[523] When a debater asserts a contradiction, he has refuted himself, based on the rules of argumentation all participants in the debate accept. Yet in his debate with the Naiyāyika, Nāgārjuna confronts an opponent for whom contradictions, or, more specifically, contradictory reasons are more than concepts employed in transactionally useful rules. As part of the framework of the sixteen Nyāya categories, they are supposed to be instrumental in an individual's obtainment of the highest good of liberation (*niḥśreyasa*). It is this sense of a contradiction as connected with something substantial, as something transcending mere conventional reality and existing *svabhāvatas*, as something that is rejected because it fails to accord with the way things are at the most fundamental level that Nāgārjuna's criticism is directed against, not the existence of contradictions *tout court*.

522. The argument here is similar to the one we find in VP 39 regarding the components of a syllogism, or the sub-syllogistic components such as syllables. All of these are said to be unable to coexist at a single time, and are therefore unable to constitute an aggregate such as a syllogism or a sentence.

523. Ruegg (1969, 384): "Or il ne semble pas que les Mâdhyamika aient en général songé à contester la validité du principe logique de la contradiction dans le domaine qui lui revient en propre, c'est-à-dire en ce qui concerne un *vastu* (hypothétique) dans le domaine discursif du raisonnement...."

Objection:

"A pseudo-reason called '*atītakāla*' exists. Because of the existence of that, a pseudo-reason exists." If you say this, it has to be replied:

VP 65 **The past is past. "*Atīta*" has become past.**

With respect to this, for you the time of the pot itself is the present. The time of the lump of clay is past, and the shards themselves are said to be at a future time. Also for the reason that the shards are future, the times of the lump of clay and of the pot have become past. Because those do not exist at that time, of what will this be the future? If you say that present and past exist—that is not so. Because the past does not exist in the present, and because in the same way the present does also not exist in the past time, it is obtained for all times.

"A pseudo-reason called 'atītakāla' ('das pa'i dus) exists. Because of the existence of that, a pseudo-reason exists."

The opponent continues to argue for the existence of the category of pseudo-reasons by arguing that the third category of pseudo-reasons mentioned in the NS, mistimed reasons (*kālātītaḥ*), exist.[524] The NS defines this kind of pseudo-reason very briefly as a kind of reason "that is put forward having gone past the time."[525] The commentarial tradition disagrees on what exactly this pseudo-reason amounts to. We can distinguish at least three separate ways of understanding the "mistimed reason."

1. The first understands the term along the lines of reason "(brought forward) too late" (*atītakālam*). In the *Carakasaṁhitā* this is characterized as a reason that should have been mentioned earlier in a debate but is

524. Negi (2005, vol. 6, 2548) lists *atītakāla* as the Sanskrit equivalent of the term *'das pa'i dus* used here by Nāgārjuna, not *kālātīta*. Both terms can be found in the ancient Indian debate literature referring to a pseudo-reason that is a reason "gone beyond its time," though there are some differences in interpretations about what precisely "gone beyond" means. As we will see, the interpretation connected with the term *atītakāla* fits best in the interpretation of the present passage.

525. NS 1.2.9: *kālātyayāpadiṣṭaḥ kālātītaḥ*.

not brought forward until it is too late,[526] for example, because the debate has moved on to another topic.

2. The second understanding is defended in Vātsyāyana's commentary.[527] He considers the specific inference "sound is permanent, because it is made manifest by conjunction, as in the case of color." The idea here is that the color of some object, such as a pot, is made manifest by the conjunction of the pot and light, so that it is reasonable to assume that the color is present permanently, although it fails to manifest in certain situations (e.g., in the dark). But we cannot use the same mark "made manifest by conjunction" to construct a reason for the permanence of sound, saying that the sound is always there, but made manifest when the axe hits the tree, for example. This is because somebody standing some distance from the sound-producing woodman will hear the sound some time after the axe hit the tree, since it takes some time for the sound to reach him. In this case, the manifestation of the sound "goes beyond the time of" (happens later than) the conjunction of tree and axe, whereas in the case of pot and light, the two are always coinstantiated. For this reason, Vātsyāyana argues, the reason in the inference discussed is a mere mistimed pseudo-reason.

This explanation of *kālātīta* might not strike us as entirely satisfactory, as the definitions of the other kinds of pseudo-reasons are phrased in quite general terms, and it is unclear how the present example generalizes beyond the specific case at hand. In particular, it appears that the example Vātsyāyana mentions can be best subsumed under the category of deviating pseudo-reasons (*savyabhicāra*; see above), since the inferential mark "manifested by conjunction" is connected both with properties taken to be permanent, such as color, as well as with impermanent ones, such as sound.

3. Vāchaspati Mishra considers *kālātīta* as describing a situation where we attempt to prove the presence of some property, even though its absence has already been convincingly established by a different epistemic instrument. Later Naiyāyikas refer to this pseudo-reason by the term *bādhita*, "contradicted (by a stronger epistemic instrument)." It covers cases like the attempt to prove by reasoning that our colleague next door is in his office after we have already seen that he is not in. The time for establishing it

526. *atītakālāṁ nāma yat pūrvaṁ vācyaṁ tat paścād ucyate tat kālātītatvād agrāhyaṁ bhavatīti* (Sharma 1983–85, vol. 2, 247).

527. Śāstrī 1998, 78–79.

by reasoning is past once its negation has been established by perception; because of this, the reason to prove the *probandum* is considered to be mistimed.[528]

The first understanding of *kālātīta* as *atītakāla* is the most helpful for understanding the opponent's argument. Once again he tries to establish that Nāgārjuna's process of argumentation obliges him to accept the very categories he wants to refute. In his commentary on the previous verse, Nāgārjuna pointed out that, due to the principle of momentariness, whenever a reason is put forward, the subject having the property to be established by the reason has already passed out of existence. The opponent then points out that this implies that for Nāgārjuna all reasons are too late, for a more substantial reason than in the case of the usual understanding of *kālātīta*. The reasons are not too late because the respective debates have already moved on to other topics, but because they are all uttered after the subject of the inference has passed out of existence.

VP 65 The past is past. "Atīta" has become past.

This verse[529] is particulary cryptic, though it does indicate that Nāgārjuna is concerned with the temporal status of different parts of time, as well as with that of notions that make reference to such parts (like *atīta*). Fortunately, matters become clearer in the following commentary.

> *With respect to this, for you the time of the pot itself (bum pa'i bdag nyid) is the present. The time of the lump of clay is past, and the shards themselves are said to be at a future time.*

We can distinguish three different temporal stages in the existence of a material object, such as a pot.[530] If the pot itself is present, the lump of clay, its cause that no longer exists, is past. The shards, which are a result of breaking the pot, do not exist in the present either, but only in the future.

528. Chattopadhyaya and Gangopadhyaya 1967–76, 149. For the connection between 2 and 3, see Oberhammer 1991, vol. 1, 82.

529. *'das pa ni 'das pa'o | 'das pa zhes bya ba 'das par gyur pa'o.*

530. See also the *Śataśāstra* (Tucci 1981, 42).

The following argument essentially relies on the presentist assumption that no existential status can be accorded to past and future entities.

> *Also for the reason that the shards are future, the times of the lump of clay and of the pot have become past.*

The different stages do not have their temporal properties intrinsically.[531] Relative to the shards, i.e., once the shard stage of the pot has become present, both the present pot and the past lump of clay will have become past. The characterizations of the different stages as past, present, or future are subject to change. And once the present has become past, it no longer exists.

> *Because those do not exist at that time, of what will this be the future?*

There are two different ways of understanding this sentence, depending on how "those" (*de dag*), "that time" (*de'i tshed*), and "this" (*'di*) are spelled out:

> *1. Because those (the shards) do not exist at that time (the present), of what will this (the set of shards) be the future?*

The shards are supposed to be the future of the present pot. Yet they do not presently exist, since nothing future exists yet. So how is it that something nonexistent *now* can *now* have the property of being the future stage of the pot? The best we seem to be able to say here is that the shards exist presently as a kind of mental entity, namely as an expectation of what is going to happen to the pot in the future.

531. Compare Nāgārjuna's commentary on *Śūnyatāsaptati* 29: "The very same when examined with respect to the future is called past, the very same when examined with respect to the past is called future. Because they are mixed up in this way they are not established." *de nyid ma 'ongs pa la brtags nas 'das pa yin la | de nyid 'das pa la brtags nas ma 'ongs pa yin te | gang gi phyir de ltar 'chol ba yin pa de'i phyir ma grub pa'o* (D 3831:114b).

> *2. Because those (the lump of clay and the pot) do not exist at that time (the future), of what will this (the set of shards) be the future?*[532]

Once we have an existent set of shards to refer to (that is, once the pot's future is present), the objects required for referring to the shards as their future (the lump of clay and the pot) are no longer there. The property of being future turns out to be explicable, not in relation to really existent times but merely in relation to presently existent memories (in this case, recollections of the lump of clay and the pot).

> *If you say that present and past exist—that is no so. Because the past does not exist in the present, and because in the same way the present does also not exist in the past time, it is obtained for all times.*

Even if the opponent is convinced by Nāgārjuna's critique of the ontological status of the future, the past and present presumably still remain. Yet Nāgārjuna points out that when the opponent claims that present and past exist, he must explain *when* they exist. Obviously the past does not presently exist, because otherwise it would be present, not past. Nor does the present exist in the past, since it did not yet exist at that time.[533] The same difficulty ensues for each pair of two distinct times, if we ask whether the latter exists at the time of the former.

Nāgārjuna's refutation of the mistimed pseudo-reason in this verse is based on the fact that the notion of a mistimed reason depends essentially on the concept of the past. If we want to argue that this kind of pseudo-reason exists in any way substantially as an example of the sixteen categories (as the Naiyāyika wants to claim), we had better be sure that the past (as well as present and future, for we cannot make sense of one without the other two) exists substantially. It is this presupposition that Nāgārjuna's

532. Tola and Dragonetti (1995, 147) adopt this reading, but then understand the argument to show that the future does not exist. I am unsure how this would follow, as all that seems to be involved here is a point about the prerequisites for the shards being *described* as future. The nonexistence of the future is entailed by the argument's underlying presentist assumption in any case.

533. In MMK 19:1 Nāgārjuna uses the fact that the present (and future) do not exist in the past as an argument against their mutual dependence: for one thing to depend on another, they must exist at the same time.

argument attacks. As his preceding remarks show, the substantial existence of time leads to a variety of problems.

Temporal properties such as being present, past, or future are not intrinsic but subject to change, and once something has lost the property of being present, it no longer exists. Past and future objects do not presently exist, so that it is difficult to see how they could enter into any relation with present objects, as such a relation would require two relata. In the same way, the description of any object as belonging to a time made relative to a different time (e.g., if we say that something is future relative to something else that is past) cannot rest on reference to substantially existent times but only on their presently existent mental representations in the form of recollection or anticipation. We cannot say that any two times exist at the same time, yet this seems to be required if we want to assert their mutual dependence. On the other hand, as Buddhapālita points out in his opening commentary on chapter 19 of the MMK, if the three times were independent, we would face the difficulty of accounting for change. If the past were past independent of anything else, it could never have been present, and so nothing could have changed from being present to being past. Given all these difficulties, the idea of substantially existent time should be rejected, together with notions—such as mistimed reasons—that depend on it.

VP 66 **Also, because of the contradictory consequence of the nonexistence of all kinds of expressions.**

In the world there are many kinds of expressions, Sanskrit, non-Sanskrit, and vernacular. The originated is past, the existent is the presently arising, "what will originate" is future. The same should also be applied to non-Sanskrit and vernacular expressions. Do not mention the problem of non-ascertainment by the treatise.

VP 66 Also, because of the contradictory consequence of the nonexistence of all kinds of expressions (rjod byed, jalpa).

This *sūtra* is best understood as a reply to an implicit defense of substantially existent time (and thereby of mistimed reasons) by the opponent. The opponent should be understood as arguing that we have to postulate the existence of time because of linguistic expressions referring to time. Such expressions are meaningful; meaningful expressions need referents; so the different divisions of time have to exist to provide such referents.[534] Nāgārjuna responds by pointing out that the opponent's view would entail the absurd consequence that "all kinds of expressions" (*rjod byed kyi rnam pa thams cad*, here to be understood as a variety of expressions referring to temporal phenomena) could not exist.

> *In the world there are many kinds of expressions, Sanskrit, non-Sanskrit (asaṁskṛta), and vernacular (prākṛtā).*

Nāgārjuna first points out that we can find a variety of such time-related expressions in diverse languages, apart from Sanskrit also in non-Sanskrit and vernacular languages.

> *The originated ('byung bar gyur pa, utpanna) is past ('das pa, atīta), the existent (yod pa, bhava) is the presently arising (da ltar byung ba, vartamāna), "what will originate" ('byung bar 'gyur ba, utpadiṣyati) is future (ma 'ongs pa, anāgata).*

Even in Sanskrit we find a great number of synonymous expressions referring to different times, such as *utpanna* and *atīta*, etc.

534. Compare in this context Ganeri's remarks on the justification of the Vaisheṣhika categories: "The claim is that the Vaiśeṣika categories are in some way the metaphysical correlates of linguistic structures. One way to make this claim more precise would be to note the existence of striking similarities between the Vaiśeṣika system and Sanskrit grammar.... Another way is to observe a distinctive pattern of argument employed, in which the hypothesis that a certain type of substance, quality, etc., exists is supported on the ground that it explains some feature of our linguistic practice (for example, the argument that space exists as it explains our use of directional terms.)" (Ganeri 2012)

> *The same should also be applied to non-Sanskrit and vernacular expressions. Do not mention (ma brjod) the problem of non-ascertainment (ma nges pa'i nyes pa) by the treatise (gzhung, śāstra).*[535]

A similar multiplicity of temporal expressions will be found in the other languages Nāgārjuna has mentioned. The opponent should not disregard these, leaving aside (*ma brjod*) the apparent difficulty (*nyes pa*) that, not being Sanskrit, they are not regulated (*ma nges pa*) by the Sanskrit grammatical treatises (*gzhung, śāstra*). If the aim is to draw ontological conclusions from linguistic usage, it is unclear why we would not want to include all relevant linguistic usage, rather than just a limited part.

We find here just the reason Nāgārjuna appeals to in the refutation of the opponent's argument, though his reply is not spelled out in detail. The idea seems to be something like the following.[536] The opponent wants to argue from the existence of the referring (the meaningful temporal expressions) to the existence of the referent (substantially existent time). This is not an uncommon move in debates between the Naiyāyika and the Buddhist. In VV 9 we find the Naiyāyika opponent objecting to Nāgārjuna's theory of emptiness by claiming that in the absence of *svabhāva* we could not even use the expression "lack of *svabhāva* in things" because "there is

535. *gzhung ma nges pa'i nyes pas ma brjod do.* Tola and Dragonetti translate this sentence very differently: "(Thus) let (the opponent) not speak owing to the defect of (his) *siddhānta* (of the existence of the reason whose time has passed away) not having been ascertained" (1995, 91). Kajiyama (1974, 224) offers yet another reading, understanding it as saying that since the speaker is uncertain regarding authoritative sources (*gzhung*), no examples for the different kinds of expression from the different languages will be given.

536. Our interpretation of the argument differs from that suggested by Tola and Dragonetti (1995, 148). They translate the second sentence of the commentary as "(In *saṁskṛta* it is said): What has (already) arisen is the past (*atīta*); what exists is the present (*vartamāna*), and what will arise is the future (*anāgata*)," and explain this as follows: "In fact languages affirm that what exists is in the present, what actually is before us; what has already arisen and, not being the present, does not exist anymore is the past; and what has not yet arisen and, not being the present, does not exist yet is the future. Thus...the past, according to the testimony of languages, is inexistent...." They therefore interpret the *sūtra* as saying that if the past existed substantially, this would imply that the various expressions in languages referring to the past would be nonexistent (i.e., false). Apart from the fact that this seems to be a somewhat forced reading, it also does not cohere very well with the fact that the commentary also talks about the future and the present, not just about the past. If Nāgārjuna simply wanted to make the point (contentious as it is) that "what has arisen is the past" means that "the past time does not exist," it is unclear why other times are mentioned at all.

no name without a referent."[537] In his commentary on Shāntarakṣhita's *Tattvasaṁgraha* 867–68, Kamalashīla spells out the underlying semantic picture in a bit more detail:

> In everyday life names and notions like "man with a stick" come about based on what is considered as substance (*dravya*), and so on.... In the absence of their substances the notions and expressions such as "man with a stick," etc., would be baseless there.[538]

For the Naiyāyika, all expressions have to link up with the basic furniture of the world (substances, properties, and so on), as determined by the Nyāya-Vaisheṣhika ontology, in order to be meaningful.[539] Yet this entails the difficulty of having to explain why the existence of multiple referring expressions (as Nāgārjuna has just described) does not lead to the existence of multiple referents (different times for each of the different linguistic expressions in the various languages).[540] Of course what the opponent would want to argue is that a single temporal structure is the referent of all the different temporal expressions in the different languages. But the

537. *yadi ca na bhavet svabhāvo dharmāṇāṁ niḥsvabhāva ity evaṁ | nāmāpi bhavet naivaṁ nāmāpi nirvastukan nāsti* (Yonezawa 2008, 238; see also Westerhoff 2010, 104–7).

538. *loke daṇḍītyabhidhānapratyayāḥ pravartante dravyādyupādhinimittāḥ...tatraiṣāṁ dravyādīnāmabhāve daṇḍītyādidhīdhvanī nirviṣayau syātāmiti* (Śāstrī 2006, vol. 1, 238: 16–17, 20–21).

539. See also the discussion in Westerhoff 2010, 105.

540. See also VP 54, where Nāgārjuna points out that things can be given different names in different languages. In this context it is also interesting to compare an argument against the identity of the first and second nature, the conceptual (*paratantra*) and the dependent (*parakalpita*) nature distinguished by Yogāchāra, that is given in Asaṅga's *Mahāyānasaṁgraha*, that a single object would absurdly be many because of the existence of various synonymous names (*ming mang pos bdag mang por 'gal ba* [Lamotte 1973, vol. 1, 36; vol. 2, 119]). Vasubandhu's *Mahāyānasaṁgrahabhāṣya* spells this out in more detail. Thakchoe (2014, 78–79) explains as follows: "The second argument is that dependent nature [corresponding to the referent] and conceptual nature [corresponding to the name] are distinct, because if they were not, then a single person would become many people because a single person can bear multiple epithets.... Take the case of the Buddha himself, who is also referred to as Gautama, Tathāgata, Bhāgavān, Śākyamuni, Arhata, and so on. If the individual is established as the objectively real referent of these names, as the realist opponents assert, then *each* name demands its own uniquely real referent—each name will refer to a unique individual, rather than the same person, in this case the Buddha. And this is absurd, too."

very existence of a multiplicity of expressions may raise doubts for this idea. Assume the different languages would use expressions for time in such different ways that a single temporal structure could not be used to interpret them all.[541] We would have to use one temporal structure as a semantics for modeling temporal statements from language *A*, and a different one in order to model those from language *B*. Interpreting this fact as implying that there are two kinds of time, one for *A*-speakers and one for *B*-speakers, would lead to complex problems.[542] We would rather want to say that the two linguistic communities have different concepts of time that the temporal expressions describe. But in this case, all that is left of the opponent's original argument is the inference from temporal expressions to the existence of the *concept* of time. Nāgārjuna would have no difficulties with the idea of such a mind-dependent time, but it is not the kind of substantial time the Naiyāyika wants to establish in order to support the existence of mistimed pseudo-reasons.

An alternative way of reading the final line of VP 66 (*gzhung ma nges pa'i nyes pas ma brjod do*) was suggested to me by Tom Yarnall. It does not seem to have been considered by any previous commentators on the VP, yet it presents in my view an interesting alternative way of making sense of this fairly cryptic verse. According to this reading the first occurrence of *ma* in the final line is not taken to negate the immediately following *nges pa*, but forms part of the noun *gzhung ma*, meaning "the middle one."[543] The line may then be translated as "Because of the difficulty (*nyes pa*) of ascertaining (*nges pa*) the middle one (*gzhung ma*), it is not asserted (*ma brjod*)."

The "middle one" would here be taken to refer to the second of the three temporal expressions Nāgārjuna has just mentioned, the presently arising (*da ltar byung ba, vartamāna*). The nature of the difficulty ascertaining the presently arising is not described here, but it is evident what sort of problem is likely to result from the kind of theory of momentariness the Mādhyamikas subscribe to. If momentariness is taken to imply

541. The influence of language on the conceptualization of time and space has been well documented by research in psycholinguistics. See, e.g., Boroditsky 2011; Levinson and Wilkins 2006.

542. Even though the existence of distinct times may well be possible, the fact that speakers of the two languages can interact with each other strongly suggests that they both exist in the same time.

543. The *bod rgya tshig mdzod chen mo* glosses *gzhung ma* as *dbus ma* (s.v. *gzhung ma*.).

the lack of temporal extension of any moment, then the present moment, located between the past and future, is also without any temporal thickness.[544] As such, it cannot be identified with any currently occurring process we are familiar with, since such processes are all temporally extended. It is, therefore, difficult to ascertain what a term like "presently arising" could actually refer to. It cannot refer to the extensionless present moment, since this is not an object of our perceptual acquaintance, nor can it refer to any currently occurring process we are familiar with, since these are not wholly present, containing, as temporally extended objects, parts that are past and parts that are future.

What is then "not asserted" (*ma brjod*) is the set of expressions for the three times that we find in Sanskrit, non-Sanskrit, and vernacular. This is because temporal expressions are defined in reference to one another, so that difficulties making sense of any one will spread to the others. This, then, is the reason for the "non-existence of all kinds of expressions" for different periods of time.[545] Understood in this way, VP 66 provides an additional response to the objection that triggered VP 65, namely the claim that a pseudo-reason called '*atītakāla*' exists, and that hence at least one instance of the Nyāya categories of pseudo-reason exists. For if we cannot make sense of temporal expressions for past, present, and future times, we also cannot make sense of terms that essentially involve reference to such times like the mistimed reason (*atītakāla*).

⌘ Moreover,

VP 67 **The past reason or the past time do not exist.**

If you ask "Why?": Because of nonoccurrence.

544. See Westerhoff 2009, 143–44.

545. Note that on this reading of VP 66 the phrase *thal bar 'gyur ba* (*prasaṅga*) in "Also, because of the contradictory consequence of the nonexistence of all kinds of expressions" should be understood simply as a "consequence," and not as a "contradictory consequence," as in our translation above. This is because on this reading we are not dealing with a contradictory consequence arising from a mistaken assumption that the opponent makes (i.e., that time exists substantially), but simply with a consequence from the theory of momentariness that the Mādhyamika himself endorses.

The reason is heard by the auditory faculty, but it is past, because it has passed. The past time is also not reasonable, because the reason is past. The present time is not related to the past reason. What this is related to is the very time of the reason. Therefore, if it is analyzed by arguments like that and others, the past time does not exist and the reason does not exist either.

VP 67 The past reason (atīta-hetu, 'das pa'i gtan tshigs) or the past time do not exist.

In this verse Nāgājuna rejects both the past reason and the past time. We do not have to suppose that by "past reason" (*atīta-hetu, 'das pa'i gtan tshigs*) Nāgārjuna means the same as by "mistimed reason" (*atītakāla, 'das pa'i dus*). Past reason is simply a reason that has been said at a past time, whereas the mistimed reason is one that *ought* to have been said at a past time, but has not, and has now lost its dialectic efficacy as a reason, because it was said too late. In the case of the mistimed reason, it is not the reason itself that is past but the opportunity of its proper utterance. As will become apparent, Nāgārjuna's rejection of the past reason will also apply to the "past opportunity." He rejects the past reason and time together, and gives the following justification:

If you ask "Why?": Because of nonoccurrence (mi srid pa, asambhava).

What is meant here is not immediately obvious but will become clearer in the following commentary. The fundamental idea is that for both to exist, one would occur at the same time as the other—but since this is not the case, both have to be rejected.

The reason is heard by the auditory faculty (rna ba'i dbang po, śrotendriya), but it is past, because it has passed.

This is, once again, a familiar appeal to the principle of momentariness. The reason, when present, is perceived (and, since we are talking here in the context of a debate, it will be perceived as a sequence of sounds). Immediately afterward, however, this momentary phenomenon, the auditory event, has moved from the present moment to the immediate past, and therefore does not exist anymore. To speak of a past reason (or, as a matter of fact, of a past opportunity for giving a reason) is therefore to speak of something nonexistent.[546]

> *The past time is also not reasonable, because the reason is past. The present time is not related to the past reason. What this is related to is the very time of the reason.*

This passage presupposes a rejection of the "container" theory of time, in which time is an independently existent receptacle in which various events have been placed. Instead we have here a relationist understanding of time in which time existentially depends on the various events. The past time, one would assume, therefore depends on the past reason or past opportunity, since these are events or states of affairs occurring at that past time. But the difficulty with this understanding is that the past reason and opportunity have passed out of existence—there is no such thing anymore. However, in order to have a dependence relation between two things, both of them need to exist; one cannot relate an existent to a nonexistent thing. The present time cannot ground its existence in the past reason, since this would presuppose that both, as related by a dependence relation, exist at the same time. But since the past reason is not present, and the present not past, this is not the case. All that the existence of the past reason can be based on is the past time, and this leads to the problems just described.

> *Therefore, if it is analyzed by arguments like that and others, the past time does not exist and the reason does not exist either.*

Nāgārjuna thus concludes that the existence of the reason, both the past reason as well as the past opportunity for a reason, i.e., the mistimed reason, cannot be established substantially, because of the problems that beset both the existence of past entities such as opportunities and reasons as well as the existence of the past time if conceptualized as existing by *svabhāva*.

546. See Lindtner (1986, 277): "Besides, since what is previous is past and gone, a *hetu* localized there cannot form the basis for anything in the present time."

With this, Nāgārjuna concludes his refutation of the *kālātīta* species of pseudo-reasons. It is evident that the Mādhyamika does not question the existence of past entities as part of transactional reality; we do, after all, refer to such entities constantly. Yet, given the theory of momentariness, there is no possibility of ascribing to them any conceptualization-independent existence; they are essentially memories of or thoughts about past (and therefore nonexistent) entities *in the present*. It is in this way that Nāgārjuna's refutation of past entities and, more specifically, of the *kālātīta* species of pseudo-reasons, is to be understood, that is, as directed against an opponent who believes that such entities exist substantially.

⌘ Objection:

VP 68 **For you, all have been said to be equivocations; they are not ultimate.**

If you say that it has to be replied: This is not so. Because the least replies would all become equivocations. Why? All speakers doubtlessly undermine the assertions because of the reason. Therefore, it is reasonable as a reply, but is not an equivocation. Or, if it is not asserted in this manner, there is no equivocation for that reason. ⌘ ⌘

Objection:

VP 68 For you, all have been said to be equivocations (chala, tshig dor);[547] *they are not ultimate.*

Once again the opponent suggests that in the course of his argument Nāgārjuna produces examples of the Nyāya categories, so that his overall rejection of these categories becomes inconsistent. In this verse the opponent considers the category of equivocation (*chala, tshig dor*).

547. The reading *tshig don* (*pada-ārtha*), which Tola and Dragonetti (1995, 92) translate as "logical categories," should be changed to *tshig dor* (*chala*). Sempa Dorje (1974, 43) reconstructs to *tvadvacanam aśeṣaṁ chalamātram na satyam.*

The NS distinguishes different kinds of equivocation,[548] but common to all is that one of the parties in the debate consciously misinterprets a term used by the opponent in a way not intended by him. Vātsyāyana illustrates the first kind, verbal equivocation (*vāk-chala*) by a case of two debaters with different understandings of the term *nava*.[549] One argues that a boy has a new (*nava*) blanket, and his opponent replies: "You have said that he has nine (*nava*) blankets. He has only one blanket. Where do the nine blankets come from?"[550]

Something similar, the Naiyāyika argues, has been going on in Nāgārjuna's argumentation. He has purposefully misunderstood the Nyāya position by assuming that the Naiyāyika wants to establish the existence of the categories in an ultimate (*don dam pa*) sense, while in fact he was only trying to establish them at the conventional level. This has two consequences: First, Nāgārjuna's criticism is unable to refute the Nyāya position in the same way in which criticism of the "nine-blanket-theory" is unable to refute the "new-blanket-theory." Second, by exemplifying the category of equivocation in his own debate, Nāgārjuna demonstrates that at least some of the Nyāya categories exist.

> *If you say that it has to be replied: This is not so. Because the least replies (cung zad lan du brjod pa) would all become equivocations. Why? All speakers doubtlessly undermine (nyams par byed pa) the assertions (tshig) because of the reason ('thad pas).*

Nāgārjuna points out that you cannot claim, simply because an opponent disagrees with a statement the proponent made, that the opponent must have accidentally or deliberately misinterpreted key terms of the proponent's position. If this were the case, any reply whatsoever could be classified as an equivocation, for the reason the Naiyāyika gives. To the opponent finding an inconsistency in our position, we could always say: "You must have intentionally misunderstood my position for something it is

548. NS 1.2.10–17.

549. In his commentary on NS 1.2.12 (Śāstrī 1998, 80–81).

550. *nava kambalā asyeti tāvadabhihitaṁ bhavatā... eko 'sya kambalaḥ kuto nava kambalāḥ* (Śāstrī 1998, 80:4–6).

not (as the nine-blanket-theorist misunderstood the new-blanket-theorist), for in the way *I* understand my position, it is free from inconsistency."

So the opponent needs to say something more on *why* there is an equivocation. He cannot just assume this in order to immunize his position against any criticism. In the case of the nine / new blankets, this would simply consist of pointing out the two different meanings of *nava*. In this context, the opponent gives as a reason the fact that Nāgārjuna considers the Nyāya categories as supposedly ultimately existent, while they are not understood in this way by his opponent.

Yet this is not really satisfactory as a reply. In fact, it is not clear at all that Nāgārjuna and the Naiyāyika regard the categories in different ways. We have to ask ourselves how the Nyāya categories could fail to be understood in an ultimate sense, given their role as an instrument of liberation (*niḥśreyasa*).

Therefore, it is reasonable as a reply, but is not an equivocation.

If there is no equivocation involved, on the other hand, Nāgārjuna's arguments can no longer be considered as failing to have force against the Nyāya position, since they talk about the same kind of entity as the Naiyāyika.

Or, if it is not asserted in this manner (tshul), there is no equivocation for that reason.

If the Naiyāyika then agrees that his own understanding of the categories forces him to consider them as ultimately existent and consequently drops his charge of equivocation against Nāgārjuna, he can no longer assume that Nāgārjuna's own argumentation provides evidence for the existence of the category of equivocations.

Another point that becomes clear from Nāgārjuna's argument is that the category of equivocation cannot just be considered as an objective feature applied to a point in a debate where the opponents interpret a term in different ways. To give a contemporary example, if one disputant claims that mathematics uses the same epistemology as other sciences, since mathematical objects are just properties of spatio-temporal objects, while another claims that it needs a special epistemology, since mathematical objects do not exist in either space or time, this is obviously an example of both having a significantly different understanding of the term "mathematical object." Yet this on its own is not sufficient to give rise to an example of the category of *chala*. What is necessary for this, as the "blanket" example shows, is the intention of one debater to replace the opponent's understanding of the term in question by his own. As such, the arising of an equivocation is not just due to a divergent understanding of a term in a debate but must be connected with specific motives on the part of one of the debaters. It does not arise as an intrinsic feature of a specific debate situation but exists crucially by arising from the presence of human interests and intentions, and therefore cannot be considered as existing by *svabhāva*. Nāgārjuna's argument in this verse can therefore be understood as having a double aim. On the one hand, it rejects the opponent's objection that he himself is equivocating, and thereby both failing as a debater and supporting the Nyāya assumption of the existence of the category of equivocation. On the other hand, he points out that the concept of *chala*, like all of the other Nyāya categories, cannot be regarded as existing with *svabhāva*, but needs to be conceptualized in a way that does not make this problematic substantialist assumption.

⌘ Objection:

"With respect to a pointlessly replying objection that arises due to answering a hundred or a thousand times regarding a definitely ascertained object, the category 'pointless reply' exists." If you say that, it has to be replied:

VP 69 **Because neither the produced, the non-produced, nor both together exist, there is no pointless reply.**

When the question where the expression "pointless reply" comes from is raised—does it arise as produced, or as not produced, or as currently being produced? First of all, it is not produced, because it has already been produced. It also fails to be non-produced, because of not being produced. Because both together do not exist, it is not currently being produced. There is no activity of "currently being produced" apart from the produced and non-produced. ⌘ ⌘

Objection:

> *"With respect to a pointlessly replying objection (ltag chod du thal bar 'gyur ba) that arises due to answering a hundred or a thousand times (brgya 'am stong du lan btab pas) regarding a definitely ascertained object (nges pa'i don), the category (padārtha, tshig gi don) 'pointless reply' (jāti, ltag chod)*[551] *exists."*

It is possible that the opponent claims once more that Nāgārjuna's own argumentative moves commit him to the existence of Nyāya categories—in this case, that Nāgārjuna himself gives pointless replies, so that the corresponding category must exist.[552] Yet, given the diversity of deficient replies subsumed under the category *jāti* by the Naiyāyikas themselves, it is difficult to say which argument of Nāgārjuna's is considered to fall under which of the different kinds of "pointless replies."[553]

Even though the category of *jāti* is introduced in NS 1.2.18, its different kinds (24 altogether) are only enumerated later in the *sūtra*, in NS 5.1.1.[554] Vātsyāyana explains the first kind[555] of *jāti*, through similarity (*sādharmyasamaḥ*), with the example of a hypothetical debate, where one party argues that the self (*ātman*) has activity, because, like a lump of earth,

551. The translation as well as the explication of the term *jāti* is by no means straightforward (Kang [2008, 43]: "[T]he exact meaning of the term *jāti* is still a puzzle, which is more mystified with the time than clarified. Nowhere we can find a reasonable exposition for the exact meaning of the term..."). As translations, we find "falsche Einwände" (Ruben 1928, 129); "sophistical or dialectical refutations" (Randle 1930, 341); "analogue" (Vidyabhusana 1971, 65–66); "futile rejoinder" (Jha 1984, vol. 1, 579); "nicht stichhaltige Entgegung" (Oberhammer 1991, vol. 2, 97); "ausgeklügelte Einwände" (Kang 2006, 161); "fausse analogie," "riposte sophistique" (Angot 2009, 369).

552. As suggested by Tola and Dragonetti 1985, 200n2.

553. The phrase "answering a hundred or a thousand times" presumably refers to the Nyāya claim that there are different kinds of *jāti*s. Vātsyāyana points out in his commentary in NS 1.2.20 that, since the two main varieties of *jāti*, based on similarity or dissimilarity, can be of different kinds, there must be a multiplicity (*bahutva*) of *jāti*s (*tasya sādharmyavaidharmyābhyāṁ pratyavasthānasya vikalpāj jātibahutvam* [Śāstrī 1998, 87:6]).

554. There are considerable difficulties, however, in trying to understand how the different kinds of *jāti* mentioned in NS 5.1.1 could all be subsumed by the understanding of the term in NS 1.2.18. Ruben (1928, 129) considers them as "eine Aufzählung von Einzelfällen ohne eine Theorie." See also Kang 2006, 165–66.

555. In his commentary on NS 5.1.2.

it is a substance endowed with qualities conducive to activity. The opponent then replies that, on the contrary, the self is inactive because it is an all-pervading substance like space (*ākāśa*) that is devoid of activity.[556]

What is deficient about this reply is that there is no decisive reason (*viśeṣahetu*) why the similarity suggested by the proponent should have any more probative force than the similarity mentioned by the opponent.

In explaining the second kind of *jāti*, through dissimilarity (*vaidharmyasamaḥ*), he describes a debate during which the proponent claims that the self has activity because it shares properties with a substance endowed with qualities conducive to activity, such as a lump of earth. But, the opponent objects, the self is also *dissimilar* to the lump of earth, since there are some qualities the two do not share (such as being limited in extent), so we should assume that the self is in fact inactive.[557] Again, the opponent has given us no reason why the failure to share some properties should have greater probative force than the sharing of some (other) properties.[558]

Vātsyāyana's commentary explains the nature of *jāti* by reference to the root √*jan* (to generate, to produce), when he notes in his remarks on NS 1.2.18[559] that "when a reason is put forward, the consequence that is produced (*jayate*) is *jāti*,"[560] and that, "because there is an opposition, *jāti* is 'that which is born' (*jāyamāna*)."[561] The idea seems to be that the pointless reply (*jāti*) is produced when an argument is joined with a counter-

556. *nidarśanam kriyāvān ātmā dravyasya kriyāhetuguṇayogāt | dravyaṁ loṣṭaḥ kriyāhetuguṇayuktaḥ kriyāvān tathā cātmā tasmāt kriyāvān iti | evam upasaṁhṛte paraḥ sādharmyeṇaiva pratyavatiṣṭhate niṣkriya ātmā vibhuno dravyasya niṣkriyatvād vibhu cākāśaṁ niṣkriyaṁ ca tathā cātmā tasmān niṣkriya iti* (Śāstrī 1998, 420:4–7).

557. *kriyāhetuguṇayukto loṣṭaḥ paricchinno dṛṣṭo na ca tathātmā tasmān na loṣṭavat kriyāvān iti* (Śāstrī 1998, 420:10–11).

558. Ruben (1928, 129) concludes that *jāti*s should be regarded either as faulty generalizations of an analogy by means of a distinct example (as in the case of *sādharmyasamaḥ* just explained), or by means of another property of the same example (as in the case of *vaidharmyasamaḥ*).

559. Śāstrī 1998, 86.

560. *prayukte hi hetau yaḥ prasaṅgo jāyate sa jātiḥ*.

561. *pratyanīkabhāvāt jāyamāno 'rtho jātir iti*. Our translation accords with the rendering in Jha (1984), Randle (1930, 342), Chattopadhyaya and Gangopadhyaya (1967–76), and Prets (2001, 548–49). For a somewhat different construal of the meaning, see Angot (2009, 369).

argument similar or dissimilar to it along the lines of the examples described above.[562]

We might be surprised by the generality of this etymological explication. Could we not similarly refer to a contradictory reason (*viruddha*) as *jāti*, since it is produced when a reason is put together with another reason contradicting it? In fact, Vātsyāyana's etymological explanation has been criticized as disingenuous by modern authors,[563] and it has been argued that rather than understanding *jāti* as a kind of production, it should be understood in an alternative sense of the word as a general property.[564]

Be this as it may, the response Nāgārjuna gives is certainly based on the explication of *jāti* in terms of production.[565] It is peculiar that several

562. Ruben (1928, 129): "[D]er Gegner antwortet, um eine Begründung abzulehnen, daß ebensogut (gleicherweise, 'entsprechend') wie die gegegebene Analogie und Begründung die entgegengesetzte gegeben werden kann. Der Name '*jāti*' bedeutet also: 'das, was das Entsprechende erzeugt'; Chattopadhyaya and Gangopadhyaya (1967–76, vol. 1, 158): "Because there is mutual contradiction [between similarity and dissimilarity]. *Jāti* is 'that which is born' (*jāyamāna*), i.e., the resulting refutation"; Jha (1984, vol. 1, 579): "[B]ecause it comes up—*is born*—as an opponent (to the original reasoning)"; Tola and Dragonetti (1995, 151): "[S]ince it arises whenever, against a well ascertained thesis, a *jāti*-objection belonging to its numerous kinds is made under the form of a refutation"; Kajiyama (1984, 22): "これも誤難を，おそらくは 曲解によって，生起と解し."

563. Randle (1930, 342): "[T]here is nothing to recommend the suggestion that this particular sense of *jāti* means 'something generated or produced' from a logical reason"; Kang (2006, 162): "Der Versuch Vātsyāyana's *jāti* im Sinne eines (ausgeklügelten) Einwandes mit *jan* in Verbindung zu bringen, ist nicht überzeugend und nur ein Beleg für sein Unverständnis, warum ein solcher Einwand *jāti* genannt wird"; Kang (2008, 64–65): "It seems highly likely that the term *jāti* is not a derivative from verbal root √*jan*. To my regret, I have not yet come up with any alternative explanation for the term"; Angot (2009, 369n994): "la justification étymologique du nom donnée par Vātsyāyana apparaît spécieuse."

564. Angot (2009, 369n994): "[L]a *jāti* désigne la généralité laquelle est déterminée par la possession des propriétés semblables ou opposées. Il est probable que c'est de là que provient le nom de la *jāti* dans la dialectique *naiyāyika*.... En effet, un des principes de la *jāti* consiste a d'arguer d'une resemblance ou d'une dissemblance extrêmement générale qui est hors sujet (*aviṣayavṛttitva*); or *jāti* a bien le sens de 'généralité: la similitude fondamentale (*sādharmya*) entre le fait et l'exemple est ignoreé au prétexte d'un 'dissimilitude' (*vaidharmya*) pourtant marginale; ou bien l'inverse: on ignore la dissimilitude fondamentale au prétexte d'une similitude superficielle." On the meaning of *jāti* as "general property," see Oberhammer (1991, vol. 2, 97–100), and Preisendanz 1994, 660–65.

565. We can only speculate what Nāgārjuna's reply would have been had he focused on the explication of *jāti* in terms of general property. It is worth noting, however, that a general property is a similarity shared by several objects, so that Nāgārjuna's remarks on similarity from verses 28–31 would be of relevance.

contemporary authors claim that Nāgārjuna is himself here guilty of equivocation (*chala*) by considering *jāti* both in its sense as a debate term and as something "produced."[566] Yet this overlooks that Nāgārjuna's aim is to refute the opponent's understanding, and it is precisely in the Naiyāyika explication of the term that we find the connection between the two senses. Rather than equivocating, Nāgārjuna is pointing out a difficulty resulting from an equivalence suggested by the opponent.

If you say that, it has to be replied:

VP 69 Because neither the produced, the nonproduced, nor both together exist, there is no pointless reply.

Nāgārjuna's reply is based on a familiar Madhyamaka critique of production based on an exhaustive examination of the different alternatives.

When the question of where the expression "pointless reply" comes from is raised—does it arise as produced, or as not produced, or as currently being produced?

If we consider the etymological explication of the category *jāti* in terms of production, we have to ask ourselves how this category is related to the property of being produced. Does it have the property, lack the property, or does it both have it and lack it?

First of all, it is not produced, because it has already been produced. It also fails to be nonproduced, because of not being produced. Because both together do not exist, it is not currently being produced. There is no activity of currently being produced apart from the produced and nonproduced.

566. Lindter (1986, 58n116): "The fact that Nāgārjuna's sophistic reply follows immediately after "*chala*" lends it a particular finesse (which is of course lost in its Tibetan garb)." Kang (2006, 164n74): "Diese Stelle demonstriert eindeutig eine absichtliche Benutzung des Wortes *jāti* in verschiedenen Bedeutungen, nämlich als 'Geborensein' und 'ausgeklügelter Einwand.' ...Wir haben es hier also lediglich mit einem typischen Beispiel für ein *vākchala* (Wortlautverdrehung) zu tun." See also Kang 2007, 205.

Nāgārjuna here uses an argument familiar from MMK 7:20:

> It is not reasonable that the existent, nonexistent, or existent and nonexistent arise; this has been shown earlier.[567]

This is spelled out in a bit more detail in *Śūnyatāsaptati* 4:

> The existent is not produced because it exists. The nonexistent is not produced because it does not exist. There is no existent and nonexistent because that is inconsistent.[568] Because they are not produced, they neither persist nor cease.[569]

This argument can be read with reference to a presentist understanding of the theory of momentariness.[570] A *jāti* is something that has been produced when an argument is joined with a counterargument similar or dissimilar to it (as in the examples described earlier). But by that time the argument has already passed out of existence, due to its momentary nature. Describing a *jāti* as "produced" is misleading, since one of its constituents no longer exists. Referring to a *jāti* as nonproduced is not reasonable either, since we would not want to refer to a category that is supposedly produced when two arguments come together in a specific way as nonproduced. And since the properties "being produced" and "being nonproduced" are contradictory, nothing can have them at the same time. There is little hope in trying to locate a third alternative between the produced and the nonproduced, such as "currently being produced," i.e., something that is presently undergoing the process of production that is not nonproduced

567. *sataś ca tāvad utpattir asataś ca na yujyate | na sataś cāsataś ceti pūrvam evopapāditam.* See also *Lokātītastava* 13: "An existent thing does not arise, nor does a nonexistent, or existent and nonexistent; neither from itself nor from something other nor from both—how is it born?" (*na sann utpadyate bhāvo nāpy asan sadasan na ca | na svato nāpi parato na dvābhyāṁ jayate katham* [Lindtner 1982, 132].)

568. *chos mi mthun, vaidharmya.* Nāgārjuna's commentary in the *Śūnyatāsaptativṛtti* glosses this as "mutually inconsistent" (*phan tshun 'gal ba*; D 3831:110b).

569. *yod phyir yod pa skye min te || med phyir med pa skye ma yin | chos mi mthun phyir yod med min || skye ba med pas gnas 'gag med* (Lindtner 1982, 36). For other instances of this argument, see the discussion in the **Dvādaśadvāraka* (Cheng 1982, 59–69) and the *Śataśāstra* (Tucci 1981, 50–51).

570. Kang (2006, 164n74) considers it as a *traikālyāsiddhi* argument.

(since that process has already started) and not produced either (since it has not been completed). The reason is that such a state would have to be considered temporally extended (lasting for more than one moment) and as such cannot be ultimately real (the moments other than the present that form part of this state have to be supplied by memory or anticipation and are therefore mind-dependent). But the Naiyāyika would want to assume that the categories, including *jāti*, are ultimately real, existing by *svabhāva*, an assumption that Nāgārjuna sets out to refute.

Objection:

"Your explication involves repetition. Because, even though you deny various things by means of existence and nonexistence, it is not in different ways. Therefore, there are the grounds of defeat." If you say that, it is to be replied:

VP 70 **That is not the case. Because earlier and later do not exist as identical and different.**

There is no repetition. If there is a repetition, is it because it is the same or different? Earlier and later words are not identical with the repetition. Why? Because it is uttered, therefore it is not a repetition, because it is that very thing.

Because it is that very thing, even if it were said a hundred times, how could it be a repetition? "Well, it is different from the previous one"—if you say that, it is also not a repetition, because of its difference and because of momentariness. The sound uttered again is different from the previous one, and though similar to the later one, it is also different from it. Therefore, what is repeated is different.

Objection:

"Your explication (rtogs par byed) involves repetition (zlos pa brjod pa, punaruktam). Because, even though you deny various things (sna tshogs pa'i don) by means of existence and nonexistence, it is not in different

ways (rnam pa gzhan du). Therefore, there are the grounds of defeat (tshar gcad pa'i gnas, nigrahastāna)."

The final Nyāya category, the ground of defeat (*nigrahasthāna*), is introduced in NS 1.2.19. In NS 5.2.1, this category is explained as comprising twenty-two different kinds. The thirteenth kind, repetition (*punaruktam, zlos par brjod pa*), the kind Nāgārjuna is concerned with in the present verse, is described in greater detail in 5.2.14–15. The grounds of defeat are constituted by debate moves that result in loss of the debate for the party using them. There is a variety of ways of losing a debate, and the set of grounds of defeat is therefore quite diverse. A debater is considered as losing a debate if he pointlessly repeats either the same words or the same ideas[571] during the debate. One might think that repetition is a fairly mild flaw in a debate (certainly when compared to other grounds of defeat the Naiyāyika lists, such as contradicting oneself [*pratijñāvirodhaḥ*] or giving up the thesis initially proposed [*pratijñāsannyāsaḥ*]). Yet, as Uddyotakara points out in his *Vārttika* on NS 5.2.14, repetition indicates that the debater is not really well acquainted with the mechanics of the debate, since he assumes that repetition has some probative purposes, which it in fact lacks.[572] Repetition therefore constitutes a ground of defeat, as it is indicative of faults in the debater.

The opponent objects by accusing Nāgārjuna of using the same argumentative pattern repeatedly in his refutation of the Nyāya categories. There are various ways in which this pattern of a "denial by means of existence and nonexistence" (*yod pa dang med pa nyid kyis dgag pa byed*) can be understood. We can simply understand it as the argument that if a certain entity exists, a given property would be existent in it or nonexistent in it—but as both alternatives lead to a contradiction, the entity cannot exist. This pattern is frequently employed by Nāgārjuna. In verse 69, he argued that a pointless reply (*jāti*) does not exist as produced or as nonproduced (nor does it exist as both), and for this reason there is no pointless reply. In verse 58, a pseudo-reason (*hetvābhāsa*) is argued to be neither similar nor dissimilar to a real reason. Verse 56 argues that expression and expressed are neither identical nor distinct.

571. *śabdārthayoḥ punar vacanaṁ*, NS 5.2.14.

572. Dvivedin 1986, 565:7–12; Jha 1984, vol. 4, 1761.

Alternatively, "denial by means of existence and nonexistence" could be taken as referring to the first two members of the tetralemma (*catuṣkoṭi*), an argumentative figure characteristic of Madhyamaka argumentation that proceeds by a denial of four alternatives, the existence of an entity, its nonexistence, both, and neither.[573]

Due to the repeated application of the pattern, the opponent argues, Nāgārjuna is guilty, if not of the repetition of words, then at least of the repetition of ideas. This then implies that Nāgārjuna has lost the debate twice over: he has committed a ground of defeat and the falsity of his rejection of the Nyāya categories is established, since at least the category of grounds of defeat must be assumed to have one member.

If you say that, it is to be replied:

VP 70 That is not the case. Because earlier and later do not exist as identical and different.

Nāgārjuna replies that the category of repetition cannot exist, because it faces severe difficulties when analyzed in terms of identity and difference.

There is no repetition. If there is a repetition, is it because it is the same or different? Earlier and later words are not identical with the repetition. Why? Because it is uttered, therefore it is not a repetition, because it is that very thing. Because it is that very thing, even if it were said a hundred times, how could it be a repetition?

If we ask ourselves how a statement and its repetition are related to one another in terms of identity and difference, there are two possibilities: the refutation is either identical with the original statement or different from it.

In the first case, there is no repetition, because there is only one thing. Repetition means repeated production of the same, but this thing already exists, so there is no point in speaking of the statement being repeated.

573. The interpretation of the precise mechanics of the tetralemma is complex. See, e.g., Ruegg 1997, Westerhoff 2006.

> *"Well, it is different from the previous one"—if you say that, it is also not a repetition, because of its difference and because of momentariness. The sound uttered again is different from the previous one, and though similar to the later one, it is also different from it. Therefore, what is repeated is different.*

In the second case there is no repetition either. For if the putative "repetition" is in fact different from the original statement, how could it be a repetition, something that is the repeated occurrence of the *same* statement? If we presuppose momentariness, the idea of a repetition of any entity becomes problematic, since all things pass out of existence as soon as they arise. Their next moment is likely to be very similar to the just-preceding moment, and likely to be similar to the moment following it, but it is nevertheless distinct from both of them.

One might suggest that the difficulty can simply be resolved by reference to the type/token distinction. A repeated proposition is obviously not the same token as the token of the original statement, but even though it is a separate and distinct token, it is still an object of the same type—that is what makes it a repetition of the original statement. Yet the Mādhyamika would hardly be happy with postulating types as abstract, nontemporal objects, since these do not fit in easily with his philosophical outlook—partly because of the theory of momentariness (as nontemporal entities, abstract objects do not decay from moment to moment), and partly because these abstract objects would have to exist independent from causal or conceptualizing relations (and the Mādhyamika claims that nothing could exist in this way).[574] If, on the other hand, types are considered as mind-dependent generalizations abstracted from the properties of the individual instances, this would conflict with the Nyāya idea of the substantial existence of the categories. If the kind of type appealed to here is merely cooked up by the mind by putting together a similarity-class of propositions, it is hard to see how these could have any claim of leading to the highest good (*niḥśreya*) of liberation. The opponent's attempt to introduce repetitions as a category is therefore deficient.

574. Even though the Naiyāyikas do admit non-spatiotemporal entities that are also not mental, they certainly do not embrace the realm of the abstract in an unreserved manner. The distinction between utterance-tokens and the abstract types that these are utterances of would, however, have been acceptable to them. See Matilal and Chakrabarty 1994, 11–12.

Moreover,

VP 71 **The grounds of defeat are similar as well.**

As the pointless reply does not exist, because production, nonproduction and both together do not exist, the grounds of defeat do not exist either.

Does something become a "ground of defeat" because of defeating or because of not defeating? Both together do not exist, therefore that does not exist.

Moreover,

VP 71 The grounds of defeat are similar as well.

After his specific refutation of one ground of defeat, repetition (*punar-uktam, zlos par brjod pa*), Nāgārjuna now offers some more general criticism of the entire category.

> *As the pointless reply (jāti, ltag chod) does not exist, because production, nonproduction, and both together do not exist, the grounds of defeat do not exist either.*

At first he suggests some very general criticism analogous to the refutation of pointless replies in verse 69. The refutation of these *jāti*s was of course connected with their etymological explication as something "produced," but the argument will also work when applied more generally, as Nāgārjuna's usage of it in other places[575] shows.

A "ground of defeat" that has been asserted during a debate cannot be described as "produced," since the previous debate moves relative to which it is a ground of defeat have already passed out of existence. Considering it as "nonproduced" is not helpful either, since a ground of defeat nobody uttered would be no ground of defeat. Since the properties "being produced" and "being nonproduced" are mutually inconsistent, they cannot apply to one object at the same time. The only way we can make sense of

575. Such as MMK 7:20 and *Śūnyatāsaptati* 4.

the existence of a "ground of defeat" is by taking into account that the previous debate, which has now passed out of existence, has to be supplied as a recollection by the mind. An understanding of the category of grounds of defeat as a mind-independent, substantial entity that the Naiyāyika postulates is therefore not available.

Does something become a "ground of defeat" because of defeating (tshar gcad pa, nigraha) or because of not defeating (ma gcad pa, anigraha)?

Nāgārjuna then considers a second, more specific argument against grounds of defeat. We recall that a "ground of defeat" arises when an opponent has made a debate move (such as contradicting himself, repeating himself, or making unintelligible statements) that is deemed to lead to his defeat. Taking the example of self-contradiction, is it the case that a ground of defeat arises because the contradiction means that the contestant has already lost the debate, or is this not the case? If it is, there is not really anything to be produced—as the contestant has already been defeated, because he has contradicted himself, what is the point of postulating the existence of a separate entity, the ground of defeat? But if it is not, what additional ingredient would be needed to constitute a ground of defeat, over and above the fact that the debater has contradicted himself?[576]

Both together do not exist, therefore that does not exist.

It cannot be that a ground of defeat arises because committing some fault (such as a self-contradiction) means that the contestant has already lost the debate, *and* that committing the fault means that he has not lost the debate. Given that these three alternatives are jointly exhaustive (we

576. Tola and Dragonetti (1995, 153–154) interpret the argument as distinguishing the two alternatives that either (1) a ground of defeat arises out of another ground of defeat (in which case we have not really explained anything when introducing grounds of defeat), or (2) a ground of defeat arises from something that is not itself a ground of defeat ("absurd since it would imply that anything can originate from anything" [153]). The difficulty with this way of reading the second alternative is that it could be the case that a ground of defeat arises if some debater first asserts *P*, and later not *P* (or the other way round). Clearly each assertion on its own is not a ground of defeat, though both put together are. So we seem to have an example of a case where a ground of defeat can arise out of two entities that are themselves not grounds of defeat.

can disregard the fourth "neither-nor" possibility in the present context), Nāgārjuna concludes that "that [category of grounds of defeat] does not exist." The point at issue (and the point denied here) is the substantial existence of the Nyāya categories. Nāgārjuna's argument that a ground of defeat cannot really be produced from something that itself already defeats the opponent leaves open the possibility of a mere nominal existence of this category: talking of grounds of defeat is merely a (presumably open-ended) way of summarizing different ways in which one can lose a debate. The category is not an entity over and above the members it subsumes, in the same way in which the category "item on my desk" is just a convenient way of talking about the office supplies presently in my possession but no object in its own right, let alone a substantially existent one.

Moreover,

VP 72 **There is no defeat in the grounds of defeat; it is bound.**

It is also not the case that one becomes defeated at a ground of defeat. For example, at a place of binding, if the place is also indubitably not bound, the ascertainment of this does not exist.

Moreover,

VP 72 There is no defeat in the grounds of defeat; it is bound.

This verse constitutes Nāgārjuna's final argument against the grounds of defeat. The precise nature of the argument is unfortunately not entirely clear.

> *It is also not the case that one becomes defeated at a ground of defeat (tshar gcad pa'i gnas, nigraha-sthāna). For example, at a place of binding (bcings pa'i gnas, bandhana-sthāna), if the place is also indubitably not bound, the ascertainment of this does not exist.*

Nāgārjuna draws a parallel between a ground of defeat (*tshar gcad pa'i gnas, nigraha-sthāna*) and another "point" or "place," *bandhana-sthāna*. This means literally a "place of binding" (*bcings pa'i gnas*) and can denote a stable or stall (a place where animals are bound).[577]

Lindtner[578] reads the argument as continuing the point made in VP 71:

> In any case a *nigrahasthāna* does not exist, either when the charge has been made or when it has not yet been made.[579] As for the third possibility, one is not convicted on any count as long as one is still being prosecuted, any more than one is trussed before the final knot is tied.

This interpretation does not appear to be entirely satisfactory. First of all, it does not seem to be the case that Nāgārjuna is here referring to the proposition leading to a ground of defeat currently being made; secondly, it does not give an account of what argumentative work the reference to the "place of binding" is supposed to accomplish.

A perhaps more satisfactory way of reading this verse is by understanding it as rejecting the intrinsic existence of the category of grounds of defeat. A place like a stable is not a "place of binding" by its intrinsic nature. If there were no cattle and no rope there, it would not be a place of binding, but just another kind of place. It is a "place of binding" only because of the activity that takes place there. When Nāgārjuna says that "the place is also indubitably not bound,"[580] we would thus understand

577. Tola and Dragonetti (1995, 154) translate it as "place of enchainment (a prison for instance)"; Böhtlingk (1879–89, s.v.) gives "in der Gefangenschaft seiend" for *bandhanastha*.

578. Lindtner 1982, 278.

579. It is worthwhile to note the similarity with MMK 16:7–8 here: "If there were binding prior to what is to be bound, then it would assuredly bind [what is to be bound]. But that does not exist; the rest [of the argument is to be understood in terms of] what was said with presently being traversed, the traversed, and the not yet traversed. It is not, on the one hand, the bound that is liberated; nor indeed is the not-yet-bound liberated. If the bound were undergoing liberation, there would be simultaneous binding and liberation." (*bhadnīyād bhandhanaṁ kāmaṁ bandhyāt pūrvaṁ bhaved yadi | na cāsti tac cheṣam uktam gamyamānagatāgataiḥ || baddho na mucyate tāvad abaddho naiva mucyate | syātāṁ baddhe mucyamāne yugapad bandhamokṣaṇe ||* [Siderits and Katsura 2013, 167–68].)

580. *gnas pa yang gdon mi za bar bcings par 'gyur ba ma yin pa.*

him as pointing out that the activity of binding is extrinsic to the nature of the place.

Similarly, the category of grounds of defeat is not intrinsically characterized by defeat. "It is also not the case that one becomes defeated at a ground of defeat"[581] can be understood as meaning that there is no common nature to all of the grounds of defeat, such that a debater would become defeated because his reply has that nature. In the same way that the category of antipyretic drugs has no intrinsic nature, no *svabhāva*, although such categories do function to give a defining characteristic (the category of such drugs all lower fever, but without sharing a common mechanism for doing so), just so the category of grounds of defeat is not indicative of a shared defeating power that is possessed by all its members, but simply collects together different ways in which one can lose a debate.[582] For this reason, there is no ascertainment (*nges pa*) of some argumentative move as a ground of defeat by reference to its intrinsic nature. Once again, Nāgārjuna's aim in his criticism of the sixteen Nyāya categories is not their unconditional rejection, but pointing out that the way in which they are understood by the Naiyāyika makes ontological presuppositions that the Mādhyamika is not prepared to accept.

Objection:

"Negation does not exist either, like the object of negation, epistemic instruments, and so forth." If you say that, it is to be replied:

VP 73 **Because both are not asserted. If that is not established, it amounts to no more than just not being established.**

581. *tshar gcad pa'i gnas la yang tshar gcod par mi 'gyur te.*

582. NS 1.2.20 notes that there are a variety of grounds of defeat (*tadvikalpāj jātinigrahasthānabahutvam*); when considering the way that they are spelled out in NS 5.2.1–24, it becomes clear that their link with their original definition in NS 1.2.19 as based on "misunderstanding or non-understanding" (*vipratipattir apratipattiś ca*) is often somewhat tenuous. (Compare, for example, the case of evasion [*vikṣepa*] defined in NS 5.2.19—this concerns the case of one disputant breaking off the discussion under the pretext of having something else to do.)

If, because epistemic instruments, and so forth, do not exist, negation also does not exist, therefore the two are not established either.

Objection:

"Negation does not exist either, like the object of negation, epistemic instruments, and so forth."

For the Naiyāyika, the sixteen categories constitute not only a list of debating terms but a comprehensive ontology that is a complete system of concepts in which everything that exists finds its place. So, the opponent argues, if Nāgārjuna would have really been successful in his refutation of each one of the Nyāya categories, he would have negated all there is. Since negation is one of the things there is,[583] Nāgārjuna would also have rejected negation, thereby depriving himself of the very possibility of negating the existence of anything his previous arguments presupposed. His position would therefore be inconsistent, since it first presupposes the existence of something it later claims cannot exist.

If you say that, it is to be replied:

VP 73 Because both are not asserted. If that is not established, it amounts to no more than just not being established.

If, because epistemic instruments, and so forth, do not exist, negation also does not exist, therefore the two are not established either.

The "both" here refers to the Nāya categories and the process of negating them. The opponent worries that Nāgārjuna's wholesale rejection of the categories will also imply the nonexistence of negation, and hence the impossibility of negating them. He assumes that Nāgārjuna's rejections will entail a denial of the functional efficacy of the items rejected. However, as

583. Vātsyāyana characterizes negation in his commentary on NS 5.1.33 as the assertion that is joined with the members of the syllogism (the thesis, etc.), is characterized by the counterposition, and removes the original position (*pratijñādyavayavayuktaṁ vākyaṁ pakṣanivartakaṁ pratipakṣalakṣaṇaṁ pratiṣedhaḥ* [Śāstrī 1998, 439:10]).

Nāgārjuna points out at the beginning of VV, the emptiness of an entity (and thereby the rejection of its ultimate ontological status) in no way contradicts its ability to play a functional role at the conventional level. He can therefore reply to the opponent that yes, he is rejecting both the set of Nyāya categories and the possibility of negation at the ultimate level, and argues that "both are not asserted" (*gnyi ga khas ma blangs pa*) at that level, while still maintaining that their functional efficacy is retained and negation can still negate.

If some Nyāya category is not established, this does not entail any more than the absence of its establishment; it does not imply that its negation is now established. Rejecting the substantial existence of some entity does not commit us to accepting the substantial (*svabhāvatas*) nonexistence or negation of that entity. The Mādhyamika intends his negation as non-presuppositional negations (*prasajya-pratiśedha*), where the negation of something having a property by *svabhāva* ("the pot is not red") does not commit us to asserting that it has any of its contraries by *svabhāva* ("the pot is blue or green or yellow…").[584] Nāgārjuna can therefore claim that neither the Nyāya categories nor their negations are established (*gnyi ga yang ma grub bo*).

VP 74 **It is said to be thus; expressions do not exist.**

Because identity, difference, and both together do not exist, all things are said to be nonexistent. Therefore, while things do not exist, referents and expressions do not exist.

Therefore, nirvana and *apavarga* are not distinct.

VP 74 It is said to be thus; expressions do not exist.

584. For more discussion of the different kinds of negations employed by Mādhyamikas, see Ruegg 1977, Westerhoff 2009, 68–70.

The status of this sentence is not entirely clear. As it is included in the VS, it should be counted as an independent *sūtra*, even though Tola and Dragonetti[585] include it as part of the commentary on VP 73.[586] Yet this interpretation is not wholly consistent with the fact that the immediately preceding sentence ends with the words *zhes bya bar 'dod na* ("If one says '…'"), which would suggest that the sentence was said by the opponent. But this sentence effectively says the same as VP 73, and that is definitely Nāgārjuna speaking. This situation is further complicated by the fact that the versions given in VP and VS differ. VP reads *de kho na bzhin du brjod pa yin no*, while VS has *de kho na bzhin du brjod pa* ***ma*** *yin te*, so that one version asserts, and one denies that things are said to be "in this way" (*de kho na bzhin du*).

I consider the sentence to be a separate *sūtra*, and adopt the reading from the VP. My reasons for this are entirely systematic: Nāgārjuna is making a further point here that would in all likelihood be expressed in an additional *sūtra*, and reading it as "it is said to be thus" allows for a more perspicuous interpretation of the argument, since the immediately preceding VP 73 and its short commentary should be understood as Nāgārjuna's own assertions.

> *Because identity, difference and both together do not exist all things are said to be nonexistent. Therefore, while things do not exist referents and expressions do not exist.*

Nāgārjuna now presents us with a reason for the rather startling statement that "expressions do not exist" (*mngon par brjod pa ni med*). In order to do so he makes the even more startling assertion that "all things do not exist" (*dngos po thams cad med pa*), a claim that is backed up by reference to the well-known Madhyamaka argument pattern of identity and difference.[587] This pattern is employed to refute the substantial (*svabhāvatas*) existence of causally produced objects. It points out that if cause and effect

585. Tola and Dragonetti 1995a, 95.

586. Sempa Dorje (1974, 44) reconstructs is as a separate *sūtra*.

587. See MMK 2:21: "If two things are not established as identical or distinct, how will they be established at all?" (*ekībhāvena vā siddhir nānābhāvena vā yayoḥ | na vidyate tayoḥ siddhiḥ kathaṁ nu khalu vidyate*). See also *Śūnyatāsaptati* 7, and Siderits and Katsura (2013, 8), where further examples of this pattern are given.

were identical it would be unclear why cause and effect are not perceived as existing at the same time. If they are substantially distinct, on the other hand, this distinctness entails their existential independence, i.e., the fact that one could exist without the other. Yet cause and effect cannot be taken to be independent in this sense, since the effect cannot exist without the cause having existed first. Combining both positions does not really help, since it entails the difficulties of both.

The argument also applies to expressions and their referents, as one of the causes of an effect such as the expression "pot" is the pot itself. "Pot" and the pot are obviously not identical (otherwise the mere tokening of the term would supply me with something to cook my rice in). But if they were substantially distinct each could go on existing without the other. This seems to be problematic, as expressions are fundamentally relational. If there is nothing they refer to they are no expressions, but just sound events. As substantial identity or distinctness are the only consistent ways in which the substantial existence of expressions and referents can be conceived, Nāgārjuna concludes, neither expressions nor referents can be considered as existing by *svabhāva*.

> *Therefore "nirvana" (mya ngan las 'das pa) and "apavarga" (byang grol) are not distinct.*

Nāgārjuna concludes the commentary on VP 74, and with it the entire text by asserting the nondifference of the Buddhist nirvana and the Nyāya notion of liberation, *apavarga*.[588]

Tola and Dragonetti[589] suggest two different interpretations of this passage. First of all, we could read it as saying that both are identical since they are both (like all things) empty. Secondly, we could regard the passage as stressing not their identity with each other but their nondifference from the main topic of VP 73, namely the equal status of the Nyāya categories and their negations. As neither the categories nor the negations of them exist in any fundamental sense, so neither nirvana nor *apavarga* nor their

588. Vātsyāyana characterizes *apavarga* in his commentary on NS 1.1.9 as "the cessation of the series of birth and death, the removal of all suffering" (*janmaraṇaprabandhocchedaḥ sarvaduḥkhaprahāṇam apavarga iti* [Śāstrī 1998, 29:11–30:1]).

589. Tola and Dragonetti 1995a, 156.

negations exist in any substantial fashion.[590] Connecting this with the immediately preceding sentence, it is evident that nirvana and *apavarga* are not substantially distinct, given that they cannot exhibit any substantial difference at the level of linguistic representation, nor at the level of referents.

As Nāgārjuna has rejected the sixteen Nyāya categories, he has also rejected the result they are supposed to lead to, namely the Naiyāyika conception of liberation. Yet he then also claims that this is not distinct (*don gzhan nyid ni ma yin*) from nirvana, the goal of the Buddhist path. Making this point at the very end of the treatise endows it with special significance, and the point Nāgārjuna appears to be making is the following: We should not conceive of the preceding discussion as a project of rejecting the substantial existence of the Nyāya categories, and the path to *apavarga* they constitute, in order to replace it with a substantially existent Buddhist path, and the substantially existent goal of nirvana this path leads to. It is rather the case that both exist only at the level of conventional reality, the only kind of reality where our conceptual resources can get any traction.[591] This is not to imply any sort of relativism according to which any path to liberation is as good as any other, so that following the Nyāya path or the Buddhist path is very much a matter of preference, not of salvific efficacy. Nāgārjuna believes (and argues in the VP) that the Nyāya system of categories faces difficulties even at the conventional level, since the notion of *svabhāva* it presupposes cannot even be conventionally real. For this reason, this system cannot even be used as a successful account of transactional reality, a difficulty that has consequences for the soteriological efficacy of the Nyāya set of categories conceived at the level of conventional truth.

This is the end of the Vaidalyaprakaraṇa that clears away the sixteen categories, epistemic instruments, and so forth, composed by the noble teacher Nāgārjuna.

590. This second reading of course depends on treating this sentence as part of the commentary on verse 73, and not as part of the commentary on the subsequent verse, 74.

591. Nāgārjuna famously argues that samsara and nirvana are not distinct. See his MMK 16:10 and YṢ 5cd together with Chandrakīrti's commentary, as well as his *Niraupamyastavaḥ* 5–6 (Tola and Dragonetti 1995b, 115, 124).

The Kashmiri scholar Jayānanda and the great Tibetan translator, the Buddhist monk Kudo Dewar, translated it, raised questions about it, and settled them by order of the eminent virtuous friend [Ngar] Yöntan Drakpa.[592]

Kudo Dewar (11th century) was a disciple of Patsap Nyima Drak (1055?–1145?), an influential Tibetan scholar and translator best known for his role in establishing the Prāsaṅgika Madhyamaka teachings in Tibet,[593] who translated key Madhyamaka works such as Nāgārjuna's MMK, Āryadeva's *Catuḥśataka*, and Chandrakīrti's MĀ. Jayānanda, a scholar of Kashmiri origin, was another figure instrumental in establishing the Madhyamaka school in Tibet; he is also the author of the only extant commentary by an Indian scholar on Chandrakīrti's MĀ.[594] Kudo Dewar and Jayānanda translated and revised several Madhyamaka works together, including Nāgārjuna's VV and *Bodhicittavivaraṇa*. Ngar Yöntan Drakpa was another disciple of Patsap's and belonged to a group of his students that is known as the "four sons of Patsap" (*spa tshab bu bzhi*).[595]

592. According to its colophon, the VS was translated by a different team consisting of the Kashmiri scholar Ānanda (whom Ruegg [1981, 114] considers to be identical with Jayānanda) and the monk Drakjor Sherab.

593. See Lang 1989.

594. See Ruegg 1981, 113–14.

595. See Roerich 1979, 343.

Appendix, Bibliography, and Indexes

Appendix
Tibetan Names (Phonetic-Transliterated Equivalents)

Phonetic Rendition	Wylie Transliteration
Butön	Bu ston
Choney	Co ne
Derge	sDe dge
Drakjor Sherab	Grags 'byor shes rab
Könchok Jigme Wangpo	dKon mchog 'jigs med dbang po
Kudo Dewar	Khu mdo sde 'bar
Maja Changchub Tsöndru	rMa bya byang chub brtson 'grus
Narthang	sNar thang
Ngar Yöntan Drakpa	Ngar yon tan grags pa
Patsap Nyima Drak	sPa tshab nyi ma grags
Tsong Khapa	Tsong kha pa

Bibliography

Tibetan Canonical Collections

Choney (C). *Co ne* edition of the Tibetan Buddhist Canon. Microfiches of the Institute for Advanced Studies of World Religions, State University of New York at Stony Brook, 1974.

Derge (D). Bstan 'gyur sde dge'i par ma: Tibetan Buddhist Resource Centre, New York, 2003.

Narthang (N). *sNar thang* edition of the Tibetan Buddhist Canon. Tōyō Bunko, Tokyo.

Peking (P). Daisetz T. Suzuki et al. (eds.). The Tibetan Tripiṭaka, Peking Edition. Reprinted under the supervision of Ōtani University, Tibetan Tripitaka Research Institute, Tokyo-Kyoto, 1955–61.

Taisho (T). Junjirō Takakusu, Kaigyoku Watanabe: Taishō Shinshū Daizōkyō, Taishō Issaikyō Kankōkai, Tokyo, 1962.

Modern Sources (Including Editions and Studies of Sanskrit Texts)

Adams, Ernest W. 1998. *A Primer of Probability Logic.* Stanford, CA: CSLI Publications.

Aikin, Scott. 2011. *Epistemology and the Regress Problem.* New York: Routledge.

Allen, William Sidney. 1953. *Phonetics in Ancient India.* London: Oxford University Press.

Angot, Michel. 2009. *Le Nyāya-sūtra de Gautama Akṣapada, Le Nyāya-Bhāṣya d'Akṣapāda Pakṣilasvāmin.* L'art de conduire la pensée in Inde ancienne. Paris: Les Belles Lettres.

Annacker, Stefan. 2005. *Seven Works of Vasubandhu, the Buddhist Psychological Doctor.* Delhi: Motilal Banarsidass.

Apte, V.S. 1957. *The Practical Sanskrit-English Dictionary*. Revised and enlarged edition. Edited by P.K. Gode, C.G. Karve. Poona: V.G. Joshi.

Arnold, Dan. 2010. "Self-Awareness (*svasaṁvitti*) and Related Doctrines of Buddhists Following Dignāga: Philosophical Characterizations of Some of the Main Issues." *Journal of Indian Philosophy* 38: 323–78.

Bacot, Jacques. 1930. *Dictionnaire Tibétain-Sanscrit*. Paris: P. Geuthner.

Bahadur, K.P. 1979. *The Wisdom of Vaisheshika*. New Delhi: Sterling.

Balcerowicz, Piotr. 2001. *Jaina Epistemology in Historical and Comparative Perspective: Critical Edition and English Translation of Logical-Epistemological Treatises: Nyāyāvatāra, Nyāyāvatāra-vivṛti, and Nyāyāvatâra-ṭippana, with Introduction and Notes*. Stuttgart: Steiner.

Ballantyne, J.R. 1850–53. *The Aphorisms of the Nyāya Philosophy by Gautama With Illustrative Extracts from the Commentary by Viśwanātha*. Allahabad: Presbyterian Mission Press.

Bhadhuri, Sadananda. 1947. *Studies in Nyāya-Vaiśeṣika Metaphysics*. Poona: Bhandarkar Oriental Research Institute.

Bhattacharya, Kamaleswar. 1974. "A Note on the Interpretation of the Term *Sādhyasama* in Madhyamaka Contexts." *Journal of Indian Philosophy* 2: 225–30.

———. 1977. "On the relation between the Vigrahavyāvartanī and the Nyāyasūtra-s." *Journal of Indo-European Studies* 5 (2–3): 265–73.

Bhattacharya, Kamaleswar, Elgin H. Johnston, and Arnold Kunst. 1978. *The Dialectical Method of Nāgārjuna*. Second revised and enlarged edition. Delhi: Motilal Banarsidass.

Bijalwan, C.D. 1977. *Indian Theory of Knowledge Based Upon Jayanta's Nyāyamañjarī*. New Delhi: Heritage Publishers.

Bod rgya tshig mdzod chen mo. 1985. Beijing: Mi rigs dpe skrun khang.

Bodhi, Bikkhu, trans. 2000. *The Connected Discourse of the Buddha: A Translation of the Saṁyutta Nikāya*. Boston: Wisdom.

Boroditsky, Lera. 2011. "How Languages Construct Time." In *Space, Time and Number in the Brain: Searching for the Foundations of Mathematical Thought*, ed. Stanislas Dehaene and Elizabeth M. Brannon, 333–41. London: Academic Press.

Bendall, Cecil, and W.H.D. Rouse. 1992. *Śikṣā Samuccaya: A Compendium of Buddhist Doctrine*. London: J. Murray, for the Govt. of India.

Bernard, Theos. 1981. *Hindu Philosophy*. Delhi: Motilal Banarsidass.

Böhtlingk, Otto. 1879–89. *Sanskrit-Wörterbuch in Kürzerer Fassung*. St. Petersburg: Buchdruckerei der Kaiserlichen Akademie der Wissenschaften.

Bronkhorst, Johannes. 1985. "Nāgārjuna and the Naiyāyikas." *Journal of Indian Philosophy* 13: 107–32.

Brunnhölzl, Karl. 2007. *Straight from the Heart: Buddhist Pith Instructions*. Ithaca, NY: Snow Lion.

Butön Rinchen Drup. 2013. *Butön's History of Buddhism in India and Its Spread to Tibet: A Treasury of Priceless Scripture*. Boston: Snow Lion.

Cardona, George. 1976. *Pāṇini: A Survey of Research*. The Hague: Mouton.

Carroll, Lewis. 1895. "What the Tortoise Said to Achilles." *Mind* 4: 278–80.

Casati, Roberto, and Achille C. Varzi. 1994. *Holes and Other Superficialities*. Cambridge, MA: MIT Press.

Chakrabarti, Arindam. 1990. "On the Supposed Inseparability of Blue and the Awareness of Blue: An Examination of *sahopalambhaniyama*." In *Mind Only School and Buddhist Logic*, ed. Doboom Tulku, 17–36. New Delhi: Tibet House.

———. 2000. "Against Immaculate Perception: Seven Reasons for Eliminating *Nirvikalpaka* Perception from Nyāya." *Philosophy East and West* 50 (1): 1–8.

———. 2001. "Reply to Stephen Phillips." *Philosophy East and West* 51 (1): 114–15.

Chakrabarty, Debasish. 2003. *Vaiśeṣika-Sūtra of Kaṇāda*. New Delhi: D.K. Printworld.

Chandra, Lokesh. 1965–71. *The Collected Works of Bu sTon*. Delhi: International Academy of Indian Culture.

———. 1998. *Tibetan-Sanskrit Dictionary*. Kyoto: Rinsen Book Co.

Chatterjee, Amita. 2011. "Nyāya-Vaiśeṣika Philosophy." In *The Oxford Handbook of World Philosophy*, ed. Jay Garfield and William Edelglass, 112–26. Oxford: Oxford University Press.

Chatterjee, Ashok Kumar. 1975. *The Yogācāra Idealism*. Delhi: Motilal Banarsidass.

Chatterjee, Satischandra. 1978. *The Nyāya Theory of Knowledge: A Critical Study of Some Problems of Logic and Metaphysics*. Calcutta: University of Calcutta.

Chatterjee, S., and D.M. Datta. 1950. *An Introduction to Indian Philosophy*. Calcutta: University of Calcutta.

Chattopadhyaya, Debiprasad, and Mrinalkanti Gangopadhyaya. 1967–76. *Nyāya philosophy: Literal Translation of Gautama's Nyāya-sūtra & Vātsyāyana's Bhāṣya, Along With a Free and Abridged Translation of the Elucidation by Mahāmahopādhyāya Phaṇibhūṣaṇa Tarkavāgīśa*. Calcutta: Indian Studies: Past & Present.

Cheng, Hsueh-li. 1982. *Nāgārjuna's "Twelve Gate Treatise." Translated, with Introductory Essays, Comments, and Notes*. Dordrecht: D. Reidel.

Chimpa, Lama, and Alaka Chattopadhyaya. 1970. *Tāranātha's History of Buddhism in India*. Delhi: Motilal Banarsidass.

Collins, Harry. 2002. "What the Tortoise Said to Achilles. Review of Donald Mackenzie, Mechanizing Proof: Computing, Risk, and Trust." *British Journal for the History of Science* 35 (4): 469–74.

Cozort, Daniel. 1998. *Unique Tenets of the Middle Way Consequence School*. Ithaca, NY: Snow Lion.

D'Almeida, A. 1973. *Nyaya Philosophy: Nature and Validity of Knowledge*. Alwaye, India: Pontifical Institute of Theology and Philosophy.

Daniélou, Alain. 1964. *Hindu Polytheism*. New York: Pantheon Books.

Dasgupta, Surendranath. 1922. *History of Indian Philosopy*. Cambridge: Cambridge University Press.

Davis, Lawrence. 1981. "*Tarka* in the Nyāya Theory of Inference." *Journal of Indian Philosophy* 9: 105–20.

Dhammajoti, Kuala Lumpur. 2007. *Sarvāstivāda Abhidharma*. Hong Kong: University of Hong Kong Centre for Buddhist Studies.

de Jong, Jan Willem. 1962. "La Madhyamakaśāstrastuti de Candrakīrti." *Oriens Extremus* 9: 47–56.

———. 1978. "Textcritical Notes on the Prasannapadā." *Indo-Iranian Journal* 20 (1–2): 25–59.

Della Santina, Peter. 2002. *Causality and Emptiness: The Wisdom of Nāgārjuna*. Singapore: Buddhist Research Society.

Dhruva, A.N., ed. 1930. *The Nyāyapraveśa, Part 1: Sanskrit Text with Commentaries, Critically Edited with Notes and Introduction*. Baroda: Oriental Institute.

Dvivedin, Vindhyeśvarī Prasād, ed. 1986. *Nyāya-Vārttikam: A Gloss on Vātsyāyaṇa's Commentary of the Nyāya-Aphorisms*. Delhi: Eastern Book Linkers.

Feer, Léon. 1884–1904. *Saṁutta-nikāya*. London: Pali Text Society.

Franke, Herbert, Jens-Uwe Hartmann, and Thomas O. Höllmann. 2005–. *Wörterbuch der Tibetischen Schriftsprache*. München: Verlag der Akademie der Wissenschaften.

Frauwallner, Ernst. 1957. "Vasubandhu's Vādavidhiḥ." *Wiener Zeitschrift für die Kunde Süd-und Ostasiens* 1: 104–46.

———. 1973. *History of Indian Philosophy*. Delhi: Motilal Banarsidass.

Ganeri, Jonardon, ed. 2001. *Indian Logic: A Reader*. Richmond, Surrey: Curzon.

———. 2012 (Winter Edition). "Analytic Philosophy in Early Modern India." In *The Stanford Encyclopedia of Philosophy*, ed. Edward N. Zalta. plato.stanford.edu/archives/win2012/entries/early-modern-india/.

Garfield, Jay. 2002. "Vasubandhu's *Treatise on the Three Natures*: A Translation and Commentary." In *Empty Words: Buddhist Philosophy and Cross-Cultural Interpretation*, Jay Garfield, 128–51. Oxford: Oxford University Press.

Garfield, Jay L., and William Edelglass, eds. 2011. *The Oxford Handbook of World Philosophy*. Oxford: Oxford University Press.

Gillon, Brendan, and Shōryū Katsura. 2016. "English Translation of the Upāyahṛdaya (pt. 1)." *Journal of Indian and Tibetan Studies* 20: 195–232.

Gokhale, Vasudev. 1930. *Akṣara-Çatakam. The Hundred Letters: A Madhyamaka Text by Āryadeva, After Chinese and Tibetan Materials*. Heidelberg: Otto Harrassowitz.

Gonda, Jan. 1985. *The Ritual Functions and Significance of Grasses in the Religion of the Veda*. Amsterdam, NY: North Holland.

Goodman, Charles. 2016. *The Training Anthology of Śāntideva: A Translation of the Śikṣā-samuccaya*. New York: Oxford University Press.

Grohma, Otto. 1975. "Theorien zur bunten Farbe im älteren Nyāya und Vaiśeṣika bis Udayana." *Wiener Zeitschrift für die Kunde Südasiens und Archiv für Indische Philosophie* 19: 147–82.

Guha, Nirmalya. 2012. "*Tarka* as Cognitive Validator." *Journal of Indian Philosophy* 40 (1): 47–66.

Hahn, Michael. 1982. *Nāgārjuna's Ratnāvalī. Vol. 1: The Basic Texts (Sanskrit, Tibetan, Chinese)*. Bonn: Indica et Tibetica Verlag.

Halbfass, Wilhelm. 1992. *On Being and What There Is: Classical Vaiśeṣika and the History of Indian Ontology*. Albany: State University of New York Press.

Hiriyanna, M. 1993. *Outlines of Indian Philosophy*. Delhi: Motilal Banarsidass.

Huntington, Clair W. 1986. "The Akutobhayā and Early Indian Madhyamaka." Ph.D. diss., University of Michigan.

———. 2003. "Was Candrakīrti a Prāsaṅgika?" In *The Svātantrika-Prāsaṅgika Distinction*, ed. Georges Dreyfus and Sara McClintock, 67–92. Boston: Wisdom.

Ingalls, Daniel. 1951. *Materials for the Study of Navya-Nyāya Logic*. Cambridge: Harvard University Press.

Iwata, Takashi. 1991. *Sahopalambaniyama: Struktur und Entwicklung des Schlusses von der Tatsache, dass Erkenntnis und Gegenstand ausschliesslich zusammen wahrgenommen werden, auf deren Nichtverschiedenheit*. Stuttgart: Franz Steiner.

Jacob, G.A. 1907–11. *A Handful of Popular Maxims Current in Sanskrit Literature*. 3 vols. 2nd ed. Bombay: Tukārām Jāvajī.

Jäschke, Heinrich August. 1998. *A Tibetan-English Dictionary*. Richmond, Surrey: Curzon.

Jaini, Padmanabh S. 1959. "The Vaibhāṣika Theory of Words and Meanings." *Bulletin of the School of Oriental and African Studies* 22: 95–107.

Jha, Ganganatha. 1939. *Gautama's Nyāyasūtras [with Vātsyāyana-Bhāṣya], Translated Into English With His Own Revised Notes*. Poona: Oriental Book Agency.

———. 1982. *Padārthadharmasaṅgraha of Praśastapāda, With the Nyāyakandalī of Śrīdhara*. Varanasi, Delhi: Chaukhambha Orientalia.

———. 1984. *The Nyāya-Sūtras: With the Bhāṣya of Vātsyāyana and the Vārṭika of Uddyotakara*. Translated into English, with notes from Vāchaspaṭi Mishra's Nyāya-Vārṭika-Ṭāṭparyatīkā, Uḍayana's Parishuḍḍhi, and Raghūṭṭama's Bhāṣyachandra. Delhi: Motilal Banarsidass.

———. 1986. *The Tattvasasaṁgraha of Shāntarakṣita: With the Commentary of Kamalashīla*. Delhi: Motilal Banarsidass.

Jhalakīkar, Mahāmohopādyāya Bhīmācārya. 1996. *Nyāyakośa, or Dictionary of Technical Terms of Indian Philosophy*. 4th ed. Pune: Bhandarkar Oriental Research Institute.

Junankar, N.S. 1978. *Gautama, the Nyāya Philosophy*. Delhi: Motilal Banarsidass.

Kajiyama, Yūichi. 1965. "The Vaidalyaprakaraṇa of Nāgārjuna." *Miscellanea Indologica Kiotiensia* 6–7: 129–55.

———. 1974. ヴァイダルヤ論, 大乗仏典 14 竜樹論集 中央公論社, 183–229, 387–99.

———. 1984. 佛教知識論の形成, in: 講座 大乘佛教 9, 認識論と論理學. 平川彰, 梶山雄一, 高崎直道 ed., 春秋社; 東京, 1–102.

———. 1991. "On the Authorship of the Upāyahṛdaya." In *Studies in the Buddhist Epistemological Tradition*, ed. Ernst Steinkellner, 107–17. Wien: Verlag der Österreichischen Akademie der Wissenschaften.

Kang, Sung Yong. 2006. "Die Carakasaṁhitā in der Geschichte der Indischen Philosophie: I. Nyāya und Carakasaṁhitā." *Wiener Zeitschrift für die Kunde Südasiens* 50: 143–76.

———. 2007. *Pañcāvayava: Die fünfgliedrige Argumentationsform in den frühen Debattentraditionen Indiens mit besonderer Berücksichtigung der Carakasaṁhitā VI, 8, 30–36*. Göttingen: Cuvillier Verlag.

———. 2008. "The New Critical Edition of the Nyāyabhāṣya and Its Meaning for the Research in Early Buddhist Debate Tradition—The Case of Jāti and 相應." *Critical Review for Buddhist Studies* 3: 39–85.

———. 2010. "An Inquiry into the Definition of *Tarka* in Nyāya Tradition and Its Connotation of Negative Speculation." *Journal of Indian Philosophy* 38: 1–23.

Keith, Arthur Berriedale. 1921. *The Karma-Mīmāṁsā*. Calcutta: Association Press.

Kielhorn, Franz. 1962–65. *The Vyākaraṇa-mahābhāsya of Patañjali*. 3rd rev. ed., revised and furnished with additional readings, references, and select critical notes by K.V. Abhyankar. Poona: Bhandarkar Oriental Research Institute.

Klein, Peter. 2011. "Infinitism." In *The Routledge Companion to Epistemology*, ed. Sven Bernecker, 245–56. New York: Routledge.

Kochumuttom, Thomas A. 1982. *A Buddhist Doctrine of Experience: A New Translation and Interpretation of the Works of Vasubandhu the Yogācārin*. Delhi: Motilal Banarsidass.

Lamotte, Étienne. 1970. *Le Traité de la Grande Vertu de Sagesse de Nāgārjuna (Mahāprajñāpāramitāśāstra)*. Louvain: Institut Orientaliste.

———. 1973. *La Somme du Grand Vehicule d'Asaṅga (Mahāyāna-saṁgraha)*. Louvain: Institut Orientaliste.

Lamotte, Étienne, and Sara Boin-Webb. 2003. *Śūraṁgamasamādhisūtra. The Concentration of Heroic Progress: An Early Mahāyāna Buddhist Scripture*. Delhi: Motilal Banarsidass.

Lang, Karen. 1989. "sPa-tshab Nyi-ma-grags and the Introduction of Prāsaṅgika Madhyamaka into Tibet." In *Reflections on Tibetan Culture: Essays in Memory of Turrell V. Wylie*, ed. Lawrence Epstein and Richard F. Sherburne, 127–41. Lewiston, NY: Edwin Mellen.

Levinson, Stephen C., and David Wilkins, eds. 2006. *Grammars of Space: Explorations in Cognitive Diversity*. Cambridge: Cambridge University Press.

Li, Xuezhu. 2015. "Madhyamakāvatāra-kārikā Chapter 6." *Journal of Indian Philosophy* 43 (1): 1–30.

Lindtner, Christian. 1982. *Nagarjuniana: Studies in the Writings and Philosophy of Nāgārjuna*. Copenhagen: Akademisk Forlag.

———. 1986. *Master of Wisdom: Writings of the Buddhist Master Nāgārjuna*. Berkeley, CA: Dharma Publishing.

Loizzo, Joseph. 2007. *Nāgārjuna's Reason Sixty (Yuktiṣaṣṭikā) with Chandrakīrti's Reason Sixty Commentary (Yuktiṣaṣṭikāvṛtti)*. New York: American Institute of Buddhist Studies at Columbia University, co-published with Columbia University's Center for Buddhist Studies and Tibet House US.

rMa bya byang chub brtson 'grus. 1975. *dBu ma rtsa ba shes rab kyi 'grel pa 'thad pa'i rgyan*. Rumtek: Dharma Chakra Centre.

———. 2011. *Ornament of Reason: The Great Commentary to Nāgārjuna's Root of the Middle Way*. Translated by The Dharmachakra Translation Committee. Ithaca, NY: Snow Lion.

MacDonald, Anne. (Forthcoming.) "Seeing Things: The Timira Disorder."

Mani, Vettam. 1979. *Purāṇic Encyclopaedia*. Delhi: Motilal Banarsidass.

Matilal, Bimal Krishna. 1968. *The Navya-Nyāya Doctrine of Negation: The Semantics and Ontology of Negative Statements in Navya-Nyāya Philosophy*. Cambridge: Harvard University Press.

———. 1971. *Epistemology, Logic, and Grammar in Indian Philosophical Analysis*. The Hague, Paris: Mouton.

———. 1974. "Note on the Nyāya Fallacy Sādhyasama and Petitio Principii." *Journal of Indian Philosophy* 2: 211–24.

———. 1977. *Nyāya-Vaiśeṣika, A History of Indian Literature*. Vol. 6, 2: Scientific and Technical Literature. Wiesbaden: Harrassowitz.

———. 1985. *Logic, Language & Reality: Indian Philosophy and Contemporary Issues*. Delhi: Motilal Banarsidass.

———. 1986. *Perception: An Essay on Classical Indian Theories of Knowledge*. Oxford: Oxford University Press.

Matilal, Bimal Krishna, and Arindam Chakrabarty. 1994. *Knowing from Words: Western and Indian Philosophical Analysis of Understanding and Testimony*. Dordrecht: Kluwer.

May, Jacques. 1959. *Prasannapadā Madhyamakavṛtti*. Paris: Adrien-Maisonneuve.

Meuthrath, Annette. 1996. *Untersuchungen zur Kompositionsgeschichte der Nyāyasūtras*. Würzburg: Oros Verlag.

———. 1999. *Die Nāgārjuna zugeschriebene Vigrahavyāvartanī und die Nyāyasūtras: Eine Untersuchung des Verhältnisses beider Texte zueinander*. Reinbek: Dr. Inge Wezler Verlag.

Mukhopadyaya, Sujitkumar. 1939. *The Trisvabhāvanirdeśa of Vasubandhu*. Sanskrit text and Tibetan versions edited with an English translation, introduction, and vocabularies. Calcutta: Visvabharati Sanskrit Series.

Nagano, Yasuhiko. 1997. *A Morphological Index of Classical Tibetan*. Tokyo: Seishido.

Nance, Richard F. 2012. *Speaking for Buddhas: Scriptural Commentary in Indian Buddhism*. New York: Columbia University Press.

Natesan, K. 2003–07. *Collected Works of Vasistha Kavyakantha Ganapati Muni*. Tiruvannamalai: Sri Ramanasramam.

Negi, J.S. 2005. *Tibetan-Sanskrit Dictionary*. Sarnath: Central Institute of Higher Tibetan Studies.

Nyaya-Tarkatirtha, Taranatha, and Amarendramohan Tarkatirtha, eds. 2003. *Nyāyadarśanam: With Vātsyāyana's Bhāṣya, Uddyotakara's Vārttika, Vācaspati Miśra's Tātparyaṭīkā & Viśvanātha's Vṛtti*. Delhi: Munshiram Manoharlal.

Oberhammer, Gerhard. 1963–64. "Ein Beitrag zu den Vāda-Traditionen Indiens." *Wiener Zeitschrift für die Kunde Süd-und Ostasiens* 7–8: 63–103.

———. 1991. *Terminologie der frühen philosophischen Scholastik in Indien: Ein Begriffswörterbuch zur altindischen Dialektik, Erkenntnislehre und Methodologie*. Wien: Verlag der Österreichischen Akademie der Wissenschaften.

Oetke, Claus. 1991. *Zur Methode der Analyse philosophischer Sūtratexte: Die Pramāṇa Passagen der Nyāyasūtren*. Reinbek: Dr. Inge Wezler Verlag für Orientalistische Fachpublikationen.

Oka, K.G. 1913. *The Nāmaliṅgānuśāsana (Amarakośa) of Amarasiṁha with the Commentary (Amarakośodghāṭana) of Kṣīrasvamin*. Poona: Law Printing Press.

Okada, Yukihiro. 1990. *Nāgārjuna's Ratnāvalī*. Vol. 2: Die Ratnāvalīṭīkā des Ajitamitra. Bonn: Indica et Tibetica Verlag.

Palsule, G.B. 1971. "Devānām-priyaḥ." *S.M. Kartre Felicitation Volume* (= Indian Linguistics 29–30), 2: 134–61.

Phillips, Stephen. 2001. "There's Nothing Wrong with Raw Perception: A Response to Chakrabarti's Attack on Nyāya's *Nirvikalpaka Pratyakṣa*." *Philosophy East and West* 51 (1): 104–13.

———. 2012. *Epistemology in Classical India: The Knowledge Sources of the Nyāya School*. New York: Routledge.

Pind, Ole Holten. 2001. "Why the Vaidalyaprakaraṇa Cannot Be an Authentic Work of Nāgārjuna." *Wiener Zeitschrift für die Kunde Süd- und Ostasiens* 25: 149–72.

Potter, Karl. 1995–. *Encyclopedia of Indian Philosophies*. Delhi: Motilal Banarsidass.

Poussin, Louis de la Vallée. 1903–13. *Mūlamadhyamakakārikās (Mādhyamikasūtras) de Nāgārjuna avec la Prasannapadā commentaire de Candrakīrti*. St. Pétersbourg: Académie Imperiale des Sciences.

———. 1912. *Madhyamakāvatāra par Candrakīrti*. St. Pétersbourg: Académie Imperiale des Sciences.

Poussin, Louis de la Vallée, and Gelong Lodrö Sangpo. 2012. *Abhidharmakośa-Bhāṣya of Vasubandhu: The Treasury of the Abhidharma and Its (Auto)commentary*. Delhi: Motilal Banarsidass.

Poussin, Louis de la Vallée, and Leo M. Pruden. 1988–90. *Abhidharmakośabhāṣyam of Vasubandhu*. Berkeley: Asian Humanities Press.

Pradhan, P., ed. 1975. *Abhidharmakośabhāṣyam of Vasubandhu*. Patna: K.P. Jayaswal Research Institute.

Prasoon, Shrikant. 2009. *Rishis and Rishikas: Life, Works and Teaching of the Earliest Exponents of Hinduism*. New Delhi: Param Offsetters.

Preisendanz, Karin. 1994. *Studien zu Nyāyasūtra III.1 mit dem Nyāyatattvāloka Vacaspati Miśras II*. Stuttgart: Franz Steiner Verlag.

Prets, Ernst. 2001. "Futile and False Rejoinders, Sophistical Arguments and Early Indian Logic." *Journal of Indian Philosophy* 29 (5–6): 545–58.

Rahula, Walpola, and Sara Boin-Webb. 2000. *Abhidharmasamuccaya: The Compendium of the Higher Teaching*. Fremont, CA: Asian Humanities Press.

Raja, K. Kunjunni. 1969. *Indian Theories of Meaning*. 2nd ed. London: Adyar Library and Research Centre.

Randle, Herbert Niel. 1930. *Indian Logic in the Early Schools: A Study of the Nyāyadarśana in Its Relation to the Early Logic of Other Schools*. Oxford: Oxford University Press.

Reat, N. Ross. 1993. *The Śālistamba Sūtra: Tibetan Original, Sanskrit Reconstruction, English Translation, Critical Notes (Including Pāli Parallels, Chinese Version and Ancient Tibetan Fragments)*. Delhi: Motilal Banarsidass.

Red Pine. 2012. *The Lankavatara Sutra: A Zen Text*. Berkeley: Counterpoint.

Régamey, Konstanty. 1990. *Philosophy in the Samādhirājasūtra*. Delhi: Motilal Banarsidass.

Robinson, Richard H. 1978. *Early Mādhyamika in India and China*. Delhi: Motilal Banarsidass.

Roerich, George N. 1979. *The Blue Annals*. Delhi: Motilal Banarsidass.

Ruben, Walter. 1928. *Gautama: Die Nyāyasūtras*. Leipzig: Deutsche morgenländische Gesellschaft.

Ruegg, David Seyfort. 1969. *La Théorie du Tathāgatagarbha et du Gotra. Études sur la Sotériologie et la Gnoséologie du Bouddhisme*. Paris: École Française d'Extrême-Orient.

———. 1977. "The Uses of the Four Positions of the Catuṣkoṭi and the Problem of the Description of Reality in Mahāyāna Buddhism." *Journal of Indian Philosophy* 5 (1–2): 1–171.

———. 1981. *The Literature of the Madhyamaka School of Philosophy in India*. Wiesbaden: Harrassowitz.

———. 2002. *Two Prolegomena to Madhyamaka Philosophy*. Vienna: Arbeitskreis für Tibetische und Buddhistische Studien.

Saito, Akira. 1984. "A Study of the Buddhapālita-Mūlamadhyamaka-Vṛtti." Ph.D. diss., Australian National University.

Sakaki, Ryōzaburō. 1916. 梵藏漢和四譯對校飜譯名義大集 (Bon-Zō-Kan-Wa yonyaku taikō honyaku myōgi taishū). Kyōto: Shingonshū Kyōto Daigaku.

Sandal, Mohan Lal. 1923. *The Mīmāṁsā Sūtras of Jaiminī*. Allahabad: The Panini Office.

Sardesai, N.G., and D.G. Padhye. 2009. *Amarakośa of Amarasingh*. Varanasi: Chowkhamba Vidyabhawan.

Sarmah, Thaneswar. 1991. *The Bharadvajas in Ancient India*. Delhi: Motilal Banarsidass.

Sastry, R. Ananthakrishna. 1927. *The Vishnu Sahasranama with the Bhashya of Sri Sankaracharya*. Madras: Theosophical Publishing House.

Śāstrī, Swāmī Dwārikādās, ed. 1998. *Mahāmuni Vātsyāyan's Nyāya-Bhāṣya on Gautama-Nyāya-Sutras with Prasannapadā Commentary of Pt. Sudarśanācārya Śāstrī*. Varanasi: Bauddha Bharati.

———, ed. 2006. *The Tattvasaṅgraha of Ācārya Śāntarakṣita with the 'Pañjikā' Commentary of Ācārya Kamalaśīla*. Varanasi: Bauddha Bharati.

Schayer, Stanisław. 1931. *Ausgewählte Kapitel aus der Prasannapadā*. Cracow: Polska Akademja Umiejętności.

Searle, John. 1995. *The Construction of Social Reality*. New York: The Free Press.

Sempa Dorje. 1974. *Vaidalyasūtram*. Vārāṇasī: Tibbatī-Hindī Kendra.

Sen, Prabal Kumar. 1996. "The Nyāya-Vaiśeṣika Theory of Variegated Colour (*Citrarūpa*): Some Vexed Problems." *Studies in Humanities and Social Sciences* 3 (2): 151–72.

Sharma, Chandradhar. 1991. *A Critical Survey of Indian Philosophy*. Delhi: Motilal Banarsidass.

Sharma, Ram Karan, and Vaidya Bhagwan Dash. 1983–85. *Agniveśa's Caraka Saṁhitā. Text with English Translation & Critical Exposition Based on Cakrapāṇi Datta's Āyurveda Dīpika*. Varanasi: Chaukhambha Sanskrit Series.

Siderits, Mark. 1988. "Nāgārjuna as Anti-realist." *Journal of Indian Philosophy* 16: 311–25.

———. 2004. "Causation and Emptiness in Early Madhyamaka." *Journal of Indian Philosophy* 32: 393–419.

———. 2007. *Buddhism as Philosophy: An Introduction*. Indianapolis, IN: Hackett; Aldershot: Ashgate.

Siderits, Mark, and Shōryū Katsura. 2009. "Mūlamadhyamakakārikā I–X." *Journal of Indian and Tibetan Studies* 9: 129–85.

———. 2013. *Nāgārjuna's Middle Way: Mūlamadhyamakakārikā*. Boston: Wisdom Publications.

Siderits, Mark, Tom Tillemans, and Arindam Chakrabarti. 2011. *Apoha: Buddhist Nominalism and Human Cognition*. New York: Columbia University Press.

Sinha, Jadhunath. 1969. *Indian Epistemology of Perception*. Calcutta: Sinha Publishing House.

Skilling, Peter. 2013. "Vaidalya, Mahāyāna, and Bodhisattva in India: An Essay towards Historical Understanding." In *Bhikkhu Nyanatusita: The Bodhisattva Ideal: Essays on the Emergence of Mahāyāna*, 69–162. Kandy, Sri Lanka: Buddhist Publication Society.

Sorensen, Roy. 2008. *Seeing Dark Things: The Philosophy of Shadows*. Oxford: Oxford University Press.

Sprung, Mervyn. 1979. *Lucid Exposition of the Middle Way: The Essential Chapters from the Prasannapadā of Candrakīrti*. London: Routledge & K. Paul.

Srinivasan, Liny. 2011. *Desi Words Speak of the Past: Indo-Aryans in the Ancient Near East*. Bloomington, IN: AuthorHouse.

Stcherbatsky, Theodore. 1936. *Madhyānta-Vibhanga: Discourse on Discrimination Between Middle and Extremes, Ascribed to Bodhisattva Maitreya and Commented on by Vasubandhu and Sthiramati*. Moscow: Academy of Sciences of USSR Press.

Strawson, Galen. 1997. "The Self." *Journal of Consciousness Studies* 4 (5–6): 405–28.

Stutley, Margaret, and James Stutley. 1977. *Harper's Dictionary of Hinduism: Its Mythology, Folklore, Philosophy, Literature, and History*. New York: Harper & Row.

Suzuki, Daisetz Teitaro. 1932. *The Laṅkāvatāra Sūtra: A Mahāyāna Text*. London: Routledge.

Taber, John. 2010. "Kumārila's Buddhist." *Journal of Indian Philosophy* 38: 279–96.

Tatia, Nathmal. 1976. *Abhidharmasamuccaya-bhāṣyam*. Pāṭaliputra: Kāśīprasāda Jāyasavāla-Anuśīlana-Saṁsthā.

Thakchoe, Sonam. 2014. "Reification and Nihilism: The Three-Nature Theory and Its Implications." In *Madhyamaka and Yogācāra: Rivals or Allies*, ed. Jay Garfield and Jan Westerhoff, 72–115. Oxford: Oxford University Press.

Tillemans, Tom J.F. 2011. "How Far Can a Mādhyamika Buddhist Reform Conventional Truth? Dismal Relativism, Fictionalism, Easy-Easy Truth, and the Alternatives." In *The Cowherds: Moonshadows: Conventional Truth in Buddhist Philosophy*, 151–64. Oxford: Oxford University Press.

Tola, Fernando, and Carmen Dragonetti. 1981. "Nāgārjuna's Conception of 'Voidness' (Śūnyatā)." *Journal of Indian Philosophy* 9: 273–82.

———. 1982. "Dignāga's Ālambanaparīkṣāvṛtti." *Journal of Indian Philosophy* 10: 105–34.

———. 1990. "Some Remarks on Bhartṛhari's Concept of *Pratibhā*." *Journal of Indian Philosophy* 18: 95–112.

———. 1995a. *Nāgārjuna's Refutation of Logic (Nyāya): Vaidalyaprakaraṇa / Źib mo rnam par ḥthag pa źes bya baḥi rab tu byed pa*. Delhi: Motilal Banarsidass.

———. 1995b. *On Voidness: A Study on Buddhist Nihilism*. Delhi: Motilal Banarsidass.

———. 2004. *Being as Consciousness: Yogācāra Philosophy of Buddhism*. Delhi: Motilal Banarsidass.

Tsong kha-pa. 1975. *The Collected Works (gsung 'bum) of rJe Tsong-kha-pa blo-bzang-grags-pa reproduced from an example of the old Bkra-sis-lhun po redaction from the library of Klu 'khyil monastery of Ladhakh*. New Delhi: Ngawang Gelek Demo.

Tucci, Giuseppe. 1947. "Minor Sanskrit Texts on the Prajñāpāramitā: 1. The Prajñāpāramitāpiṇḍārtha of Diṅnāga." *Journal of the Royal Asiatic Society* 79 (12): 53–75.

———. 1981. *Pre-Diṅnāga Buddhist Texts on Logic from Chinese Sources*. Madras: Vesta.

Tversky, Amos. 1977. "Features of Similarity." *Psychological Review* 84: 327–52.

Vaidya, P.L. 1963. *Saddharmalaṅkāvatārasūtram*. Darbhanga: Mithila Institute of Post-Graduate Studies and Research in Sanskrit Learning.

Venkata, Ramanan Krishniah. 1966. *Nāgārjuna's Philosophy as Presented in the Mahā-Prajñāpāramitā-śāstra*. Published for the Harvard-Yenching Institute by Charles E. Tuttle. Rutland, Vermont.

Vidyabhusana, Satis Chandra. 1971. *A History of Indian Logic: Ancient, Mediaeval, and Modern Schools*. Delhi: Motilal Banarsidass.

Westerhoff, Jan. 2006. "Nāgārjuna's Catuṣkoṭi." *Journal of Indian Philosophy* 34 (4): 367–95.

———. 2009. *Nāgārjuna's Madhyamaka: A Philosophical Introduction*. Oxford: Oxford University Press.

———. 2010. *The Dispeller of Disputes: Nāgārjuna's Vigrahavyāvartanī*. Oxford: Oxford University Press.

Williams, Paul. 1978. Review of *Indian Metaphysics and Epistemology: The Tradition of Nyāya-Vaiśeṣika up to Gaṅgeśa*, by Karl H. Potter. *Journal of Indian Philosophy* 6: 211–91.

Yamaguchi, Susumu. 1944. 正理學派に對する竜樹の論書　ヴアーイダルヤ (Vaidalya) について, 中観佛教論攷, 山喜房佛書林, 113–66.

Ye Shaoyong, ed. 2011. *Mūlamadhyamakakārikā*. Beijing: Research Institute of Sanskrit Manuscripts & Buddhist Literature.

Yonezawa, Yoshiasu. 2008. "Vigrahavyāvartanī: Sanskrit Transliteration and Tibetan Translation." *Journal of Naritasan Institute of Buddhist Studies* 31: 209–333.

Indexes

Index of Canonical Texts Cited

Index of Canonical Authors Cited

General Index